For the Land They Loved

RICHARD FALLIS, *Series Editor*

For the Land They Loved

Irish Political Melodramas, 1890–1925

Edited and with a Critical and Historical Essay by

CHERYL HERR

SYRACUSE UNIVERSITY PRESS

First Edition 1991

91 92 93 94 95 96 97 98 99 6 5 4 3 2 1

The paper used in this publication meets the minimum requirements of American National Standard for Information Sciences—Permanence of Paper for Printed Library Materials, ANSI Z39.48–1984. ♾™

Library of Congress Cataloging-in-Publication Data

For the land they loved : Irish political melodramas, 1890–1925 / edited and with a critical and historical essay by Cheryl Herr.-- 1st ed.
p. cm.—(Irish studies)
Includes bibliographical references.
ISBN 0-8156-2481-6
1. Political plays, English—Irish authors. 2. Political plays, English—Irish authors—History and criticism. 3. English drama—20th century. 4. English drama—19th century. 5. Ireland in literature. 6. Ireland—Drama. 7. Melodrama. I. Herr, Cheryl, 1949– . II. Series: Irish studies (Syracuse, N.Y.)
PR8795.P64F67 1990
822'.912080358—dc20 90-31070
CIP

Manufactured in the United States of America

For SÉAMUS DE BÚRCA
and all who dared to speak of '98

CHERYL HERR is an Associate Professor of English at the University of Iowa. She has contributed articles to many scholarly journals and is the author of *Joyce's Anatomy of Culture* (1986).

CONTENTS

ILLUSTRATIONS

PLATES

DIAGRAMS

ACKNOWLEDGMENTS

MY PRINCIPAL DEBT during the preparation of this edition is to Séamus de Búrca, who generously shared with me his manuscripts, his collection of Irish plays, his invaluable memories of performances, his ready wit, and his unflagging confidence in this project. Jimmy is an Irish national resource of the highest order. I am also grateful to Dr. Cyril Cusack, who allowed me to interview him about his experiences with melodrama from 1916 to the present. In addition, my thanks are happily owed to Stephen Watt of Indiana University for encouragement in pursuing this project and for sharing with me his soon to be published research into Irish melodrama. Professor William Murray helped me to gloss colloquialisms in the plays. Carrie Beth Foresman carefully transcribed from microfilm and manuscript to disk the initial working versions of these plays. Chrys Mitchell and Geetha Varadarajan, graduate research assistants at the University of Iowa, provided much help with bibliographical matters, research details, and conversational support. Mr. Mitchell brought considerable order to the nightmare of history by investigating the recording of theatrical events in the *Irish Times* in the 1890s as well as by exploring Whitbread's use of W. J. Fitzpatrick's *Secret Service under Pitt*. The undergraduate students in "Irish Literature and Culture," who read the plays in manuscript, showed me the value of these works for classroom use; it was with these students in mind that I wrote the introduction to this edition. My editors at Syracuse University Press—Richard Fallis, Cynthia Maude-Gembler, and Joyce Atwood—oversaw the production of this book with skill and good humor. My thanks to all.

At the outset of my work on this project, when I was still engaged in Joycean explorations, I received funding for travel and time to work from both the National Endowment for the Humanities and the Center for Programs in the Humanities at Virginia Tech. Later, when the melodrama edition proper became a reality, I received an NEH Travel to Collections Grant and a University of Iowa Old Gold Fellowship. These agencies have my profound gratitude, as has the University of Iowa's University House (directed by Jay Semel with help from Lorna Olson), where I was the happy recipient of quiet work space and morning coffee during the final stages of work on this edition. The staff at the National Library of Ireland was, as always, professional and helpful; the library at Virginia Tech graciously purchased for me some of the microfilms from the British Library used in early stages of this project; the British Library consented to the publication of J. W. Whitbread's works; Colin Mabberley, the curator of the Raymond Mander and Joe Mitchenson Theatre Collection in London, provided expert guidance to the Whitbread materials in his care, and I shall long remember with delight the Collection's providing afternoon tea for me.

Finally, my thanks, as always, to my son John, a thoroughly enlightened adolescent who took a real interest in the plays and also reminded me when to take a break.

ABOUT THE TEXTS

WHILE CONDUCTING RESEARCH into Irish popular culture for a study of James Joyce (*Joyce's Anatomy of Culture*, Urbana: University of Illinois Press, 1986), I was fortunate to make contact with the playwright Séamus de Búrca, whose father, P. J. Bourke, wrote two of the plays in this edition. De Búrca kindly allowed me to borrow the manuscripts of *When Wexford Rose* and *For the Land She Loved* and provided invaluable help as I worked toward understanding the historical significance of Irish political melodrama. Although I was familiar with the writings of Dion Boucicault, I knew that few if any later and more politically potent melodramas were available in print. In fact, I could not locate manuscripts for many of the plays that I believed to be important, works by J. W. Whitbread and Hubert O'Grady, for instance. Hence I was enormously gratified to discover, almost simultaneously, that Stephen Watt had used some of the plays I was seeking in his University of Illinois dissertation and that manuscripts of many Irish melodramas were housed in the Lord Chamberlain's plays in the British Library, Manuscript Collection. *Lord Edward, Or '98* and *Wolfe Tone* are both part of that collection in typescript form, having been submitted to the British censor by Whitbread for production in England. I am grateful to the British Library for permitting reproduction of these out-of-copyright plays and for the pleasure of working in the Manuscript Room with so many of the dramas I had been seeking.

Both writers posed special problems in transcription and editing. Although the Whitbread plays were prepared for this edition from the British Library's typed copy (apparently the only original copies extant of these dramas), both the writer and the typist introduced various kinds of editorial challenges into the texts. In some cases, an "error" is obvious and the "correct" word as unmistakable as such things may be said to be. These obvious matters, such as typos and misspellings not designed to suggest an "Irish" pronunciation, have been silently emended in this edition. Some abbreviations have been replaced by the words they represent. Where there is a question about a word or phrase, where I have introduced substantive material, or where the typescript is unclear, I have indicated editorial uncertainty or changes by bracketing the words or letters involved. If a reading is unrecoverable, I have indicated the missing words or letters with multiple asterisks. On the rare occasions when Whitbread deleted something from the typescript that is legible and seems of possible interest, I have indicated the deleted material as follows: ⟨xxx⟩. Whitbread, perhaps because he wrote earlier than Bourke, uses more idiomatic Irishisms; such terms in each of the four plays have been marked with a single asterisk and glossed at the end of the edition. As far as spelling, capitalizations, and punctuation are concerned, neither Whitbread nor his typist appears to have worried overmuch about standard forms or standardizing practice. For example, Whitbread generally places a comma before rather than after parenthetical stage directions occurring within a speech; I have deleted most of these commas because they interfere with clarity without adding anything to meaning. I have also added apostrophes to contractions, supplied a number of commas, added some periods (especially where a comma was in place and appeared to be a typo) and capitals, and regularized an occasional agreement error. In contrast to such cosmetic issues, Whitbread from time to time allows dialectal spelling to infiltrate his stage directions; I found this mannerism charming rather than distracting and did not disturb these spellings.

A note must be added about characters' names. Whitbread and Bourke handle names like "McNally" variably; sometimes a space is introduced after "Mc" and sometimes not; Whitbread occasionally replaces the "c" with an apostrophe ("M'Cabe"). Overall design considerations for this edition prompted a compromise solution. When such a name appears capitalized—as in the cast list or in stage directions—either the apostrophe is retained (a relatively rare situation) or a space is introduced (MC NALLY). When such a name is included in the speech of another character, the more frequent and more historical usage prevails, and the character appears as "McNally." To scholars who quote from or otherwise refer to these plays in print, I would suggest that one form be followed throughout—McNally.

One question that my copy editor asked that helped me to clarify my own editorial practice was whether it would not be wise aggressively to "Americanize" and "modernize" the playtexts for ease in reading. The changes involved would be relatively simple ones; what appear to be eccentric and inconsistent capitalizations would be standardized; unruleful punctuation would be corrected, while implied punctuation would be liberally added; spellings of dialectal words would be made consistent across the plays. My copy editor further queried whether any information would be lost to the scholar if these changes were made to accommodate the modern reader, particularly the reader who happens to be an undergraduate student in an Irish literature class. Having considered this question at length and altered portions of manuscript on disk to see what the effect of modernization would be, I determined that wholesale changes, particularly those involving capitalization and spelling, would seriously undermine the historical force and ideological content of the scripts. Apart from the cultural imperialism implied by the whole notion of "Americanizing" a text, we would distort our sense of how the plays were written and how they were received in their own time. Consider that for many of Whitbread's characters, involved as they were in revolution against the state, the English government is truly "the Government." In this context, a so-called traitor faces the "Scaffold," capitalized to indicate its fearful presence in that historical field. Capitalizations make many words into abstractions, thereby pointing to differences of scale in the consciousness of the period—political radicals inhabiting a world of concrete immediacies over which loomed a realm of monumental forms of oppression. That oppression infiltrated material reality at all social levels, even down to the practical mechanics of writing—or so Whitbread's scripts suggest. And yet, against the grain of anything like monolithic ideological determinations, we find portions of text in which theatrical considerations outweigh political ones. For example, the Redcoat soldiers appear at times as "red coats," a formulation that I find evocative and attendant to the drama of costume, something that was very important not just to actors but also to Lord Edward Fitzgerald and to Theobald Wolfe Tone as they prepared for battle or for trial. Turning to spelling issues, for certain characters a dispatch is a "despatch" and carries its own edge of desperation. And even when we consider the presence or absence of commas, we realize that a villain like Francis Higgins speaks with minimal punctuation because the resulting rhythms precisely indicate his maniacal drivenness. Further, there is a compelling uniformity to a minimally punctuated text (as James Joyce knew when he wrote the "Penelope" episode of *Ulysses*), and it would be distorting to introduce massive amounts of modernizing punctuation. By allowing various idiosyncrasies to stand, I hope to have provided each reader with the opportunity to consider whether such textual problems require interpretation or merely tolerance. Although in minor presentational matters I have silently moved toward some degree of uniformity across the dramas, especially in matters of punctuation and largely to accommodate student readers, I have remained faithful to the spirit of the texts—documents from a working theater, tidied up a bit to satisfy the censor.

The British Library microfilmed their copies of the Whitbread plays for my use; after producing computer copy, I returned to London in order to compare fuzzy portions with the original manuscripts. The accuracy of the texts has thus been verified and preserved to the extent of my ability to do so while bearing in mind my editorial goal of enabling the contemporary reader's entry to the plays. For scholars who want to consult the originals, I should note that microfilms of the Whitbread plays are easily available from the British Library; similarly, I will be happy to facilitate scholarly access to photocopies of the Bourke plays. One further note: the typescript to *Wolfe Tone* includes partly typed but mostly hand-drawn and lettered set diagrams; Cheryl Jacobsen rendered these drawings using eighteenth-century calligraphy for this edition.

To turn from Whitbread to Bourke, *For the Land She Loved* exists in only one version, a typescript that speaks to the perhaps hasty initial production of the play and to the fact that the first production was closed down by the English military. *When Wexford Rose* exists in three units. Manuscript A, on which this edition bases its text, is clearly a fair copy. According to de Búrca, the hand is that of his uncle, Peadar Kearney, and the date is ca. 1907. Manuscript A is clearly written and carefully punctuated; the speech rhythms appear to have been tried and honed in performance; the play has few rough edges. But there are several pages missing from this copy as well as occasional portions that are, owing to the poor condition of the manuscript and age of the paper, unreadable. Inserted into Manuscript A were eight short typed pages—here designated Manuscript C—that run from the beginning of the drama into Act I, scene 2. Omissions in these pages, when compared with Manuscript A, indicate their less authoritative status; perhaps they were produced by a trial-typist. Manuscript C, though brief and corrupt, does have more detailed stage directions, as if prepared in transcription of an actual production. These directions have been introduced into this edition with the notation [MS. C: . . .]. Manuscript B, which is partly typed and partly in script and which is also incomplete, is an early version of the play, showing handwritten corrections, additions, and deletions. Because the emendations have the feel of rehearsal revisions, I have selectively included material from Manuscript B into Manuscript A, either to clarify passages made puzzling by omissions (perhaps oversights on the part of the copyist) or to sustain performance rhythms. These additions, when substantive and not merely cosmetic, are bracketed in the text as follows: [MS. B: . . .]. Otherwise unidentified bracketed words are unclear in all of the manuscripts. I speculate that Peadar Kearney, in addition to copying the manuscript, drew on his own writing talents to standardize spelling, punctuation, and other graphic presentational details. Hence the typescript of *For the Land She Loved* is rougher, less literary, than the manuscript of *When Wexford Rose*. Where simple cosmetic changes in the texts improved clarity and readability, I have made those changes silently. Throughout Bourke's plays, I have left unchanged most of the nonstandard capitalizations, which, as in the Whitbread plays, have their own emphatic quality in describing sets and attitudes. A final note here on Bourke's manuscripts involves an aspect of melodrama not addressed in the volume—the musical accompaniment to the plays. A twelve-part score for *When Wexford Rose* is housed in the Irish Theatre Archive, Dublin.

For help in glossing colloquial expressions in all of the plays, I am indebted to William Murray, a member of the English Department at the University of Iowa. I have also consulted glosses in modern editions of various Irish plays as well as P. W. Joyce's classic study, *English as We Speak It in Ireland* (1910); where a specific source has supplied a meaning, I have parenthetically indicated that source by the author's last name in the glossary. Some of the more familiar or self-evident Irishisms have been left unglossed; most readers are aware that terms like *bedad* are variations on "By God" but carry their own ethnic flavor and generalized significance. The lengthier glosses present synopses of Professor Murray's responses to these phrases. Talking with him about performances by touring companies in small towns throughout Ireland and about Irish speech patterns has helped enormously to bring the plays alive for me and has enhanced my conviction that Irish political melodrama generically aims to promote social change.

For the
Land They Loved

Part One

THE ESSAY

IRISH POLITICAL MELODRAMA

Form and Functions

In words that each day take on more resonant urgency, Frantz Fanon has asserted that the "colonised man who writes for his people ought to use the past with the intention of opening the future, as an invitation to action and a basis for hope."[1] Fanon speaks prescriptively, but he does so echoing the practice of writers in occupied countries; the facts are that not only might politically committed writers work creatively to impel their worlds' emancipation, but that many artists have done so without having their task defined for them by non-native observers. Taking hold of existing and usually imposed literary genres, often of the most conservative line, such authors have forged links between foreign aesthetic conventions and living, radical historical imperatives. Doing so, they have turned received forms toward the complicated ends of the temporal extrications we call freedom. Certainly this is the case in late nineteenth-century and early twentieth-century Ireland (before the partition), when the fervently sought reality of a whole, independent, and in every way united nation often seemed to be just over the horizon.

It is not merely hindsight that makes so much of the literature composed during this period shimmer with possibilities for social change. But hindsight of a kind does play a role in my analysis, for often the works that glow the most for us now are the ones that looked backward, that gestured toward revolutionary activities embarked upon in pasts that were made to seem unusually immediate. The plays reproduced in this volume, representative of an important but neglected aspect of Dublin's early modern theatrical repertoire and never before printed, fall into this category. These dramas were written between 1894 and around 1912. In terms of cultural values and direct influence, their era extends from around 1890 through at least 1925 (a fact signaled by the subtitle of this volume). All four turn nostalgically and with extraordinary familiarity on the complex events of a century before their composition, when various uprisings took place in Ireland. The plays therefore convey the nationalist and utopian ideologies of what we now sum up under the tag of "1798," and they do so with the intense hope of "opening the future"—orienting it toward challenge and change. One of the premises of this introduction is that these plays materially succeeded in their forward-looking aims.[2]

Additionally, one of the questions explored here is what made these writers, both of them entrepreneurs of modest social status and addressing a popular audience, take upon themselves the task of promoting Irish nationalism from the stage. To move toward some understanding of the cultural conditioning, conception, execution, and impact of these plays requires attention to the venues in which they were produced, to the historical situation of 1798, to the political tensions that flared into the Easter Rising of 1916, and finally to the subsequent creation of that myth-ridden political Janus, an Ireland that is both Free State and postimperial domain.

THE QUEEN'S ROYAL THEATRE
Missing Manuscripts and Conditions of Production

Dublin has been lucky in its theaters and unlucky in its modern urban development. In place of the historic Abbey Theatre (designed by Joseph Holloway), which is sought each summer by countless busloads of tourists but which burned to the ground in the 1950s, we have the boxlike brick building that insists architecturally on its discontinuity with the contexts of the past. In place of the Queen's Royal Theatre, which was torn down in 1969, we have, unfortunately, no architectural reminder at all. To make matters worse, many of the plays that are most strongly associated with the flourishing of the Queen's had been, until a few years ago, presumed lost; occasionally scholars mentioned that patriotic melodramas had been popular in Ireland—plays such as Hubert O'Grady's *Famine* (1886), J. W. Whitbread's *Wolfe Tone* (1898), P. J. Bourke's *When Wexford Rose* (1910), Ira Allen's *Father Murphy* (1909)—but the researcher had to dig hard to discover that not only were these pieces unpublished but also difficult if not impossible to track down in manuscript form. The lack of a union library catalog in Ireland makes research into popular culture a hit-or-miss affair.[3] Interestingly, until about ten years ago researchers had not looked into the Lord Chamberlain's records for such Irish productions because of the logical reasoning that the Lord Chamberlain had never wielded authority in Ireland. But entrepreneurs like Whitbread did submit their work to his scrutiny so that they could market their plays in England. The erroneous assumption by scholars that these plays would have little or no audience outside of Ireland highlights our collective misconceptions about the functions of these dramas and about the nature of English dramatic censorship, which was not monolithic but shifting in purpose and impact. Happily, these works, along with theater documents and memorabilia, have begun to surface, released for publication both from private collections and from the British Library's manuscript division.

The Queen's itself has an admirable advocate in its principal historian, Séamus de Búrca. The son of P. J. Bourke, de Búrca has written a memoir of the Queen's that lovingly brings to life the ethos of that theatrical institution. It should be emphasized that the Queen's was an institution in Dublin; the plays that it produced did not, as was sometimes the case at the Abbey and the Gaiety, occasion popular controversy. They were consensus dramas, propagated in villages, towns, and cities throughout the nation and in other countries as well. As for the theater itself, stories abound in memoirs about the atmosphere there—produced by audiences that sang with the actors, remonstrated over inadequate performances, knew the older plays by heart and corrected the errant actor, howled at the villains, and covered the floor with orange peels (see plate 1). De Búrca's *Queen's Royal Theatre Dublin* (1983) presents the history of this local legacy, from its beginning in 1829 until its demolition in 1969, targeting the period 1882–1907 as the golden age. These prime years coincided with the management of James W. Whitbread, an Englishman born in 1848, who developed strong sympathies for Ireland and died in a year of revolution, 1916.[4]

Whitbread oversaw the shift at the Queen's from the stock company system to the accommodation of touring companies. An 1893 newspaper interview with Whitbread, reprinted by de Búrca, presents the manager's position on the stock company, which had been the staple of Queen's drama. Whitbread points out that better travel facilities, especially by rail, had enabled the touring system to take hold in the eighties.[5] Periodicals like *The Era* advertised companies and plays to let, which would be booked throughout the English-speaking world. Sometimes Whitbread's own company played at the Queen's; at other times, it toured. Alternatively, his plays were sometimes put on by other touring companies ("fit-ups") such as P. J. Bourke's or Kennedy Miller's; advertisements for his *Wolfe Tone* in *The Era* eventually proclaimed that the drama had toured Australia, England, Scotland, and the United States, running a total of 2,000 nights for the initial production troupe. In short, after having been an actor himself, Whitbread ran a theater in Dublin and also wrote plays, some of which were widely produced: *Shoulder to Shoulder* (1886), *The Nationalist* (1891), *The Irishman* (1892), *The Spectre of the Past, Or Homeless in the Streets of Dublin* (1893), *The Victoria Cross* (1896), *Lord Edward, Or '98* (1894), *Theobald Wolfe Tone* (1898—the use of "Theobald" in the title was variable, and I have dropped it in this edition), *Shadowed* (1899), *Rory O'More* (1900), *The Ulster Hero* (1902), *The Insurgent Chief* (1902), *The Sham Squire* (1902), *Sarsfield* (1905), *The Irish Dragoon* (1905), and *The French Huzzar* (1906).[6]

That Whitbread composed so many plays on such a regular schedule suggests that they were based on conventional structures, but it does not convey Whitbread's concern with history as it was lived, with knowing the "facts" that had shaped life in his adopted country. Under his management the theater made Irish melodrama one of its staples, which occupied, around the turn of the century, approximately one-third of a year's offerings; hence in a theater that rarely closed except during Easter week or occasionally during the entire Lenten season, perhaps fifteen weeks or more annually would be devoted to Irish history, melodrama, comedy, and music. This native base was complemented by imported English companies doing melodrama and comedy, or by a troupe like Mr. F. S. Gilbert's Grand Opera Company, which would present over the course of a twelve-day run such favorites as *Maritana, Il Trovatore, The Daughter of the Regiment, Faust, The Bohemian Girl,* and *Fra Diavolo.* These operatic offerings aligned, in terms of overt conventionality and wide emotional appeal, with the popular dramatic forms presented at the Queen's.

The Whitbread Era (or, *Arrah! No Brogue*[7])

Reviews of plays produced in Dublin constitute a compelling subtext to the story of Irish culture during the late nineteenth century, and the firsthand reports that we have of Whitbread's plays take a prominent place in that subtext, for they convey decorously

Plate 1. "An Old Playgoer," sketched by Joseph Holloway at the Queen's Theatre, 2 March 1912. From Holloway's "Diary of a Dublin Playgoer." Courtesy of the National Library of Ireland.

the surprisingly direct responses that audiences had to political dramas. For example, on 27 March 1894 Dublin's *Evening Herald* reported on the new play, *Lord Edward*, which had opened at the Queen's the previous evening to "a crowded house." The paper found this play one of the most successful that Whitbread had produced, a historically accurate portrayal of the 1798 Rising well-packaged in terms of theatrically effective dialogue, "picturesque" sets, and "excellent" staging. The Kennedy Miller Company was immensely popular in and of itself, and its villain, Frank Breen, one of the legends of melodrama tradition in Ireland. The tale still circulates about Breen's being hissed by street children as he left the stage door after performances. Inside the theater, vocal responses to villains were more pronounced; as the *Evening Herald* had it, a "treacherous advocate" in *Lord Edward* raised "the ire of the gods [upper balcony] to an alarming extent." By 28 March, when Joseph Holloway visited the Queen's, pandemonium had taken over. In his "Impressions of a Dublin Playgoer," he says, "The place was packed when I reached there & I had to stand most of the time. The piece proved effective and was well played. . . . The audience were most enthusiastic & hissed & shouted to their hearts [*sic*] content."[8]

No doubt such testimonials helped Whitbread to book his drama on the road; *The Era* for 12 May 1894 includes an ad for *Lord Edward* asserting that bookings had already been made at the Pavilion in London for the August Bank Holiday, at the Royal in Belfast, the Gaiety in Brighton, the Princess's in Glasgow (a return booking), in Cork (also a return), at the Prince of Wales's in Grimsby, at the Royal in Preston, and at "many other First-class Theatres." Three years later (20 April 1897), the *Irish Times* reported of Whitbread's "well-known" *Lord Edward* that "In the popular portions of the house it was impossible to get even standing room at the rise of the curtain, and the other sections were likewise well filled. This work of Mr. Whitbread's never fails to prove a strong attraction to patrons of the theater . . . and the place which it holds among latter-day contributions to Irish drama is accurately attested by the large measure of patronage invariably extended to it." Even after the end of Whitbread's management of the Queen's, this highly effective, stirring work continued to hold its own.

The year 1898 was the centenary of the earlier rising, and celebrations in Dublin organized by, among others, W. B. Yeats, memorialized Wolfe Tone's contributions to the revolution. Whitbread's gift to Dublin was his drama *Wolfe Tone*, which debuted on 26 December. The *Evening Herald* not only praised the work but celebrated its style. It was, the reviewer asserted, "a realistic presentment of a series of episodes the most interesting in the romantic history of our land." Whitbread's accuracy and ability to overcome his Englishness were praised. "He is thoroughly in sympathy with Ireland. He has caught the vernacular. He draws his characters naturally and puts on his colour with a broad, bold brush. Of Irish characters he is a master. . . . The dialogue is witty; it is natural, it is convincing. There is action, there is energy, there is deep human interest in the play . . . and the audience follows it with the deepest interest." The villainous Frank Breen "is beyond praise," and the play's informers received a "storm of hisses."

Never one to miss a significant opening, Holloway has supplied us with his own version of the play's reception:

> I have been present in many noisy audiences, but never in such a noisy one as that assembled in the Queen's Theatre on the afternoon of December 26th, 1898, to witness the first performance on any stage of J. W. Whitbread's romantic Irish Drama, in four acts, entitled "Theobald Wolfe Tone." . . . I think all the small-boy population of Dublin tried to scrooge itself into the limited space of the gallery, so that they were fairly on top of one another, and those under had to assert themselves by shouting at those over them not to squash the life out of them.
>
> Such a pandemonium of discordant sound I have seldom heard, and at times one could scarcely hear ones ears, especially when the villains held the stage.
>
> As far as I could judge by the scraps of dialogue I heard here and there from those on the stage, I should say that the quality of the writing was much above the average, while in dramatic construction and stage effects it far surpassed anything yet attempted in its way by the popular manager of this theatre—Mr. J. W. Whitbread—and I noticed, with extreme pleasure, the entire absence of buffoonery in the comic interludes. . . . It is a step in the right direction to try to create a new type of true Irish play without too much of the "arrah-begorra" element in it, so inseparable from the old form of Irish drama, where everybody, from the highest to the lowest, spoke with the vulgarest brogue (often mingled with a Cockney accent).
>
> Why not have educated Irishmen and women speak, as in everyday life, as Mr. Whitbread has endeavoured in this play to make them do? We have had enough and plenty of Irish caricatures on the stage, God knows, in the past; let us have a little of the genuine article now by way of a change.
>
> "Wolfe Tone" (though cast on melodramatic mould) is a distinct cut above the usual sensational play.

Holloway printed the above as part of an article in a 1900 issue of *The Irish Playgoer*, but the sentiments occur almost verbatim in his diary, there followed by a telling line that he cut from the published text: "This is the sort of a play that will ultimately put a new spirit into Ireland."[9]

So it was that by the second performance on 26 December the newspapers reported that "hundreds of people who thronged the doors, were obliged to go away, disappointed at obtaining even standing room." When the street filled with people, the police had to ask Whitbread to open the doors so that traffic could pass.[10] Certainly, this agreement between mass enthusiasm and the generally elitist Holloway signals Whitbread's success in representing Irish nationalism and identity in ways that a cross section of Dubliners powerfully validated as well as in ways that mediated Irishness for audiences in England and Scotland.

The Next Generation: Bourke and World War I

After Whitbread left the Queen's in 1907, the theater was closed from 19 March 1907 through 13 September 1909, with only a briefly abortive reopening in 1908.[11] The new patentee, F. W. Marriott-Watson, a minor playwright, emphasized sensational English melodrama, pantomime, and occasional film-vaudeville-variety shows. He and his manager, however, put on "seasons" of Irish plays like J. B. Buckstone's *Green Bushes*, the Irish-American *Kathleen Mavourneen*, and Dion Boucicault's *Colleen Bawn*. By the 1910s, the mood reshifted, owing in part to the professional debut of Patrick J. Bourke. This actor-manager-playwright, with his "No. 1 Company," became a strong force in Dublin's dramatic life. Born in Dublin in 1883, Bourke was orphaned by age twelve and quite early began to earn his living by driving a department store van. But around age ten, while Whitbread was still the controlling figure at the Queen's, he had begun to haunt that theater. By the time he was twenty, he initiated his theatrical life in local halls—producing, acting, managing, touring, and finally writing plays himself. Along the way, Bourke performed key roles in Whitbread's plays (*Sarsfield, Lord Edward, Wolfe Tone,* and *Michael Dwyer*) at the Queen's and saw his own work put on there as well as throughout the countryside.[12] Bourke's was a talent for the times—politically passionate, thoroughly theatrical, socially aware. He brought patriotic Irish melodrama to its most pertinent form in *When Wexford Rose* (produced in the Father Mathew Hall in 1910 and in the Queen's in 1912 and following), *For the Land She Loved* (produced in 1915), *The Northern Insurgents* (1912), *For Ireland's Liberty* (1914), and *In Dark and Evil Days* (1914). He died in 1932, having written and produced the first full-length film made in Ireland (*Ireland a Nation*) and thus having initiated the transition from melodrama on stage to melodrama in film.

When Whitbread's heir began to appear on the Queen's stage, he was joined by Ira Allen, another person of many talents, whose plays (*Father Murphy* [1909], *The Bailiff of Ballyfoyle* [1911]) appeared regularly in that theater. At this time, as sociopolitical agitation of various kinds built up in Dublin, Irish drama reasserted its presence, and the Queen's produced works not only by Allen but also by the always popular O'Grady, the beloved Boucicault, and lesser writers like Fred Cooke (who wrote *'98, Or Faugh-a-Ballagh* [1874], *The Diver's Luck* [1888], and *On Shannon's Shore* [1895]).

By 1915 the Defense of the Realm Act, which extended from English soil onto Irish, had begun to exert pressure on local managers. The Queen's list for that year attends much more to the plight of women (*A Woman's Honour, Her Luck in London, Only a Woman, The Shop Girl and Her Master, The Old Wife and the New, The Queen of the Redskins, The Mother's Heart*) than to that of the country. About the "surprising preponderance of romantic and pathetic women's plays" in 1916, Robert Hogan and Richard Burnham comment, "There were no plays at all about the War, and perhaps the theatre's offerings reflected a desire for escapism as well as the fact that much of the male audience was now in the army."[13] It is also true that suffragism had begun to be a public force before the war. In addition, managerial fears of governmental suppression induced a strong self-censorship,[14] which in the Queen's shifted the emphasis from the problems of Cathleen Ni Houlihan in search of autonomy to more generic but equally embattled female figures. Through the discourse of English women's plays, issues of power and domination continued to be popularly mediated in forms that masked the national question but that highlighted the socioeconomic underpinnings of any approach to "home rule." Many of these plays, following the lead of the perennial favorite *East Lynne*, objectify issues of contested identity and forced disguise that also marked debates over national self-determination.

By late 1916 and early 1917, the wartime inability of dramatic troupes to cross the Irish Sea from England ironically produced a return to Irish drama at the Queen's. Hogan and Burnham speak at length about the "semi-professional" theater of that era, indigenous and often local actors forming companies to cover the portions of the calendar not filled by English groups.[15] Thus at the Queen's from 1917 through 1920, we find Irish companies like Delany and Condron's, P. J. Bourke's, Lena and Dermont's, Ira Allen's, P. P. Nayr's, J. F. Mackey's, and J. B. Carrickford's. Hogan and Burnham state that had the war not transformed booking conditions, many Irish companies would have played only in local halls throughout the countryside. I take this assessment to be important from the standpoint of consensus culture; what played well across the country now had to make it in Dublin; a closer dialogue about national self-representation was established between city and country.

Some comments by the distinguished actor Cyril Cusack support this analysis. In a tribute to the Queen's, Cusack writes, "I follow your actor sons and daughters sent out to the four quarters of Ireland—let us remember—Roberto Lena, Ira Allen, O'Brien and Ireland, Dobell, Lilian Carrickford . . . Breffni O'Rorke . . . Chalmers Mackey, the McEntee's, Bourke himself—all those magnificent touring companies hailed from door and half-door as the actors strode down the main street of—Cloughjordan, Collooney, Athy, Monastrevin, Ballycastle . . . all those lovely, innumerable dates!"[16]

And one could add to that list Belfast, Cork, Limerick, Galway, and Tipperary. Cusack speaks from experience, as his stepfather and mother ran their own company, and for about ten years after the 1916 arrival of his family in Ireland, he performed child roles in melodramas. So it is that on a one-week-per-town basis (playing a different piece every night), Cusack witnessed the effectiveness of such works and became, by his own frequent public admission, a champion of Boucicault. "The melodrama most emphatically has a place in the theatre, and Boucicault in the Irish theatre. Melodrama had been ridiculed and put out of court by intellectual and literary coteries. But it found its way back into the popular theatre. It is good theatre; theatre theatrical, not theatre of the intellect. . . . The plays of Synge and O'Casey are overtired; but Boucicault's plays, with their strong sense of theatricality, will not tire."[17]

Anyone who saw the National Theatre's production during the 1988 London summer season of Boucicault's *Shaughraun*—with Stephen Rea in the starring role—knows how effectively Irish melodrama can still be staged, how delighted a modern audience can be with such a play's wonderfully paced ironies and inevitabilities.

The Genre of Irish Political Melodrama

Boucicault, Whitbread, and Bourke moved in the same direction but followed somewhat different paths in their writing of melodrama. The usual gesture made by theater scholars is to embrace Boucicault as a sort of lively diamond in the rough and to exclude his heirs, but that maneuver dismisses much that is important in understanding the constitution of Irish cultural life from the 1860s through the partition of the nation. The movement from Boucicault to Bourke maps out significant transformations in the genre of Irish melodrama, and following those changes allows us to recognize a particular moment that is properly construed as Irish *political* melodrama.

Some background to this thesis must be presented here. When we look back to a classic study like Peter Kavanagh's *Irish Theatre* (1946), we find his treatment of the nineteenth century focusing with pleasure only on the Theatre Royal. The Queen's remains an aside to the major action, and the vogue of O'Grady, whom Kavanagh erroneously calls the "most popular dramatic author in Ireland during the last decade of the century," is dismissed as irrelevant, for his plays "appealed to that section of the public for whom the wolfhound and the round tower were the highest and purest symbols of Ireland." Kavanagh's very brief chapter on Boucicault calls him "hardly a good third rate dramatist" and determines that his plays "are only of historical interest, for they are completely detached from that vital dramatic movement that reached its zenith in the plays of Synge, Robinson, MacNamara and O'Casey."[18] Obviously, such an assessment conflicts strongly with that of Cusack and other contemporary theater specialists who have the benefit of temporal distance from Boucicault and O'Grady. In fact, it is clear that Kavanagh's rejection of melodrama's comic Irishmen, stock characters, elaborate gestures, ready emotions, and predictable plots was not so much a critical evaluation as it was a marker. What it marked, among other things, was a phase in the ongoing struggle of people in a partially occupied country to come to terms with their national identity in all of its variety. In contrast to that moment of rejection, writers like Synge were and are valued precisely because they did not attempt to displace their cultural past with all of its schismatic self-portraits; they embraced native tradition, theatrical and otherwise, while transforming rather than neutralizing it. An excellent exhibit on "Dion Boucicault and the Irish Melodrama Tradition," put on in 1983 by Dublin's Irish Theatre Archive, emphasizes the perception of continuity on the part of many Irish playwrights, their full comprehension of debts to the past. In *Prompts*, the archive's bulletin, we find bridges being identified between Boucicault's wily shaughrauns and O'Casey's "paycocks," between Boucicault and Wilde, Shaw, Synge, Lady Gregory, Behan, M. J. Molloy, J. B. Keane, A. J. Potter, and Brian Friel.[19]

In large measure, the grounds for negative evaluations of Irish melodrama amounted to two things: a denunciation of the "stage Irishman" and a celebration of the Abbey Theatre movement and its stylized *haut*-folk. The literature on the first issue is now quite extensive; here it may be sufficient to note the current critical agreement that Boucicault's stage Irishman had considerably more nuanced vitality than the imported versions so long marketed in English stock companies, each of which had its "Irish" comic actor. Enabling effective agency to replace inebriated passivity, Boucicault at least partly freed the stereotype from within. And as Stephen Watt demonstrates in an article rich with insights, Boucicault's move away from the portrayal of simpleminded comic characters found echo and fruition in Whitbread's historical dramas, which focused on serious political issues. Watt defends the historical value of these works, arguing, "Historical drama such as Boucicault's *Robert Emmet* and J. W. Whitbread's *The Ulster Hero* constituted . . . a major stream that fed into the creation of the modern Irish history play." He points to the minimization of the traditional stage Irishman in Whitbread's work, and he finds Boucicault's shaughrauns to be primary vehicles through which contemporary political issues achieved the symbolic "resolutions" that Whitbread later eschewed, despite the steady increase of political content in Boucicault's Irish plays. *Robert Emmet*, a "heroical tragedy," stands as a transition from melodrama in the Boucicault mode to Whitbread's style and purpose. Watt points to the politicization in the later plays of villains, English soldiers, central conflicts, and dramatic endings (often "grossly sensationalistic executions" of heroes).[20] So it is that when we consider the transformations of Irish self-representation from early Boucicault through late Bourke, we find a progression, a political enrichment so historically logical as to make dismissive comments about these writers (or their simple exclusion from the Irish theatrical canon) shortsighted in the extreme.[21]

Of course, Boucicault's most popular play and the one most typical of nonpolitical melodrama, *The Colleen Bawn* (first produced in 1860 in New York), mitigates much of its historical content. Even *The Shaughraun* rescues from possible censure Captain Molineux, the English officer with a surname as soothingly French as his author's; the story turns less on the Fenian movement represented by the hero Ffolliett (another Francophile name that emphasizes essential links between English officer and Irish rebel) than it does on the extrication of love from mortgage payments. Boucicault's work sustains a troubling rapprochement between competing political factions. In contrast, Bourke occupies a radically different historical moment from either Boucicault or Whitbread. The fractures that ran throughout Irish culture could no longer be healed or smoothed over by rhetoric or by a more vigorous foreign policy on the part of the English government. Whitbread celebrated Irish patriotism; Bourke wrote against the tide of events that could well have crushed nationalism—and that, given the imminence of partition and the Irish Civil War, impelled its redefinition and regrouping on several levels. Whereas Boucicault opened the melodramatic terrain to new formulations,[22] it remained for Whitbread and Bourke to enact the implications of those developments. To some extent, of course, Whitbread wanted to produce an audience, but Bourke, whose republican sentiments were well known, wanted to produce a revolution. Both writers thus occupy key places within the Boucicauldian conventions that they embraced and reshaped.

The Role of the Censor

So it is that Bourke's work, overshadowed by war's alarms and the general confusion in Dublin, limited to production within Ireland, did not receive testimony of its importance in the format open to Whitbread. In fact, some principal marks of its success come to us negatively, by the fact that Dublin Castle determined Bourke's work to be seditious. De Búrca narrates the first occurrence of such censorship, when in 1914 the Castle ordered pictorial posters advertising Bourke's *In Dark and Evil Days* to be expunged all over Dublin. (Subsequently, this work was played several times in the city, the final time being in 1925.) The year following this suppression saw Bourke's production of *For the Land She Loved*, this time not in the usual venue but at the Abbey. De Búrca states that the Castle "remonstrated with the manager St. John Ervine, for permitting 'this piece of sedition to be performed.'" Ervine responded by barring Bourke from the Abbey from 1915 forward. Finally, Bourke's film *Ireland a Nation*, in which he played the role of Michael Dwyer, was shown in Dublin at the Rotunda—to this day a major downtown Dublin film theater—on 8 January 1917 "and banned by the British on the following day."[23] Among other things, the censorship suffered by Bourke kept his later work from undergoing the in-production editing and refinement that earlier plays demonstrate; perhaps for this reason a piece like *For the Land She Loved* occasionally betrays a raw urgency that spoke to the contemporary oppressions of an occupied country.

It is instructive to compare the reviews of the 1912 *When Wexford Rose* with the reception of *For the Land She Loved* in 1915. In a handsome notice, the *Evening Herald* found *Wexford* "powerful," scenic, and compelling. The hand of Whitbread hovers over the play in the sense that the reviewer perceives the portrayal as showing "wonderful accuracy" of setting.[24] Bourke's attention to musical and variety formats, evident in his version of *Kathleen Mavourneen*, here led him to include songs and Irish dancing, which proved popular; his actors performed "Clare's Dragoons" and "The Wearing of the Green," the latter of which had, according to infamous theatrical legend, been banned by the English when Boucicault had attempted to use the song on stage. Although Bourke was, this early in his career, relying on amateurs to stage his plays, the work received a warm welcome, and the play continued to be produced until 1925. Holloway rendered his opinion, too. Although he would have liked the production to have more "finish," he noted the "frequent and hearty" applause of the audience, "the novelty of a female, instead of a male informer," the "keenly relished" musical portions, and the acting of Marian Culler, who played a heroine and "conveyed bravery in a marvellous way in her presence & bearing & played with a breeziness that was refreshing to behold."[25]

By the time that Bourke produced *For the Land She Loved*, the repressive atmosphere in Dublin had intensified, and the play was certainly not calculated to calm anyone's nerves. Nor was it addressed to the usual Abbey patrons; Holloway noted of the play, "The audiences have been a strange lot who insist on smoking & tell the assistant to go to Hell! when informed that No Smoking is allowed. They are a law unto themselves."[26] Holloway's final sentence nails the distinction between audiences; not only were Bourke's patrons working class in the main, but they also constituted precisely the group whose radicalization was at stake in his plays and in the pressure cooker that was Dublin in 1915. Holloway, having had a considerable change of heart with the prominence of the Abbey players after the turn of the century, and having decided that the Queen's represented only a decadent form of theater, found himself out of sympathy with much in the production, but even he found the climax "effectively managed, & well interpreted." Further, his words provide a wonderful glimpse of the production. "The drama is studded with patriotic sentiments all of which the audience swallowed whole, & often became quite enthusiastic & when Jack Sullivan . . . sang 'The Clare Dragoons'—almost all the audience joined in harmoniously in the chorus.—& the song was encored. While he sang he was bathed in a strong ray of limelight that shone forth to hear him sing!"[27] Melodramatic cliché, yes, but obviously one that sustained rather than threatened the text of patriotism being refurbished in this play.

By September of 1916, when the General Post Office had been gutted and Irish patriots martyred by the English, Bourke's *Insurgent Chief* drew high praise from the *Evening Herald* and from the Queen's Theatre audience.[28] And an *Evening Telegraph* review for 27 April 1920 tells us that Bourke's company "had a rousing reception last night in the Queen's Theatre in the stirring '98 drama, 'For the Land She Loved.' "[29]

The Impact of Irish Political Melodrama

Above, I cited two issues that determined some tepid evaluations of Irish melodrama—the vexed status of the stage Irishman and the twentieth-century celebration of the Abbey Theatre movement. The second matter, that of the relationship between the Abbey and melodrama, cannot be settled quickly or in this introduction. But it is worth noting again that most of the major dramatists who wrote for the Irish Theatre Company and the National Theatre Society had substantial debts to melodrama—and that writers like O'Casey and Synge made no secret of having attended the Queen's. Hence the radicalization of audience and playwright that took place in the site of melodrama had its reverberations in that 1798 drama of Yeats's, *Cathleen Ni Houlihan,* for without the theatrical conventions and resolutions that Yeats evokes, the power of the Old Woman's request for aid would be incomprehensible.

Yeats and Lady Gregory had, in fact, felt the need to enrich their own Ascendancy ambiance by retrieving and stylizing Irish folk materials. Owing to the relative scarcity of such material in written format as well as to its antiquity, the folklore explored by the Abbey ("fetishized" is not too strong a word) became reasonably safe baggage for the privileged classes to assimilate, to promote, to propagandize. This is not to argue that there was no popular political content to the Abbey's act of restoration; the spasmodic audience responses to Synge's *Playboy of the Western World* and to Yeats's *Countess Cathleen* provide incontrovertible evidence of real engagement on the popular level between a sanitized "folk" and the troubles of early modern Ireland. What is not often factored into these equations of cultural life, however, is the notion that theaters such as the Gaiety and the Queen's, by producing mass-oriented pantomimes and emotionally charged melodramas, had primed Dublin's theatergoing audience at all levels to an interactive and subliminally politicized response.[30] Ideological material that was missing from classic Abbey productions was supplied by a theatrically literate audience that knew what "should" be part of such presentations; similarly, material that was there in embryonic form gestated in the collective mind to emerge as political commitment or, more simply, as varieties of outrage and solidarity. Because some fundamental conflicts were endlessly replayed at the Queen's, because the many voices of Ireland continued to converse through popular dramatic formats, Abbey productions were read partly in the terms already established by the theatergoing community. More than we have acknowledged, our concept of the Abbey requires attention to the drama of the Queen's. An analysis of the relations between these two theaters can begin to clear the way for a less programmatically linear and more open-textured view of theatrical development in Ireland and in other third-world countries. This analysis also promises to enrich our understanding of Irish class conflicts and conformities as these were mediated in dramatic taste.

It is useful to reemphasize here the extent to which the Queen's traditions worked through issues of self-image for the Irish populace. The stage representations of historical and imaginary characters changed in value and force because Irish society en masse was changing in ways that the stage both attended to and impelled. The Queen's was, as de Búrca claims, a people's theater, as valuable for the solidarities of class-specific and national vision reinforced there as for the plays it produced. On the other hand, it took considerable effort for many Irish people to see themselves in the Abbey style, with its radically different pace, presentation of character, and structural effects. Holloway tells a wonderful story about attending Lady Gregory's *Kincara*, in what seems to have been a tenuous production by the Abbey Players. He discussed the play with William Boyle, author of *The Building Fund*, who said that "he was not moved by the acting as it was lacking in life & movement & failed to impress him as being natural. . . . [A]ll the actors, only lit up when they were actually having their 'say.' This I explained was the method adopted by the company with pure malice aforethought, & whether rightly or wrongly *that* was their system of interpreting the plays submitted to them. . . . Mr Boyle is evidently not a believer & when Yeats shook hands with him he made a joke about the interval choral noises with reference to the play which drove Yeats away without saying a word."[31]

Boyle, unused to the Abbey's conventions but apparently

schooled in those of the Queen's, failed to perceive "nature" where he was supposed to. Compare the sentiments of a columnist in "The Irish Playgoer" for 1900, who notes that "Nearly every year sees some addition to the lengthy list of Irish dramas truly racy of the soil, and more entitled to be enrolled as pillars of an Irish Literary Theatre than the curious group of plays produced the last two years, and claiming to be representative of the country."[32]

'98 IN HISTORY
Self-Consciousness and History

Séamus de Búrca says that his father spoke of the '98 patriot Michael Dwyer as if he knew him. That deep personal knowledge of folk-lore-history characterized the highly traditional countryside of Ireland, where local legends of oppression and insurrection maintained their own power through generations of storytellers. In Dublin, a theatergoer was as likely as not to know very little of such events except through theatrical representations. So in a sense the absence of English influence during the great war opened a space for an enriching exchange, for melodramatic tradition to blend with rural lore, historical research, current events, and economic demands to create a new generic formation—the Irish political melodrama—which had an initial incarnation in the urbane Whitbread and a second enriching avatar in the works of Bourke and Allen. And certainly the performance by their companies of earlier plays took on, through improvisation and reaction to context, new shades of political meaning. For most purposes, this political meaning came to a focus in the endless melodramatic replaying, from various angles, of the events of 1798. Even in their own time, the major events of 1798 were treated by diarists and historians with a high degree of self-consciousness that often can only be called theatrical.

This self-consciousness was also almost religious. From the first, the insurrections in Ireland were framed in what we might call a figural or typological fashion. In the same way that Moses' life was taken by patristic scholars as a prefiguring or type of Christ's, so the effort to free Ireland, with French aid, from English rule was regarded as figurally related to the American and French revolutions. Insofar as the Irish did not wrest their country out of the English grasp, their revolutionary activities have been read by many historians as failures. These scholars, whether advocates for freedom or justifiers of British supremacy, have been greatly exercised by the effort to target precisely the reasons for failure. And the underlying sorrow among "Irish-Ireland" proponents carries a tone of outrage and near-incredulity; for Ireland to have failed in 1798 is almost like having Jesus depart from the patristically sanctified Mosaic pattern in order to introduce, at the last moment, antichristic events. There is a degree of disorientation and of disappointment here that begs for interpretation.

Although it may seem to border on blasphemy, this biblical parallel works for us as we attempt to understand the continued cultural significance of 1798. For one thing, the Enlightenment sentiments of liberty, equality, and fraternity that motivated the fight for freedom in Ireland during the late eighteenth century had the air of a gospel. The French-styled good news was propagated by disciples organized into groups that were small, secret, and doomed for betrayal. Indeed, by 1795 the United Irishmen had organized themselves into clusters of twelve, each group bound together by an "oath of secrecy and fidelity."[33] For another thing, like the late nineteenth century's fallen chief, Charles Stewart Parnell, the heroes of Ireland's 1798 revolution were almost immediately assimilated into the cultural standard of the martyred savior. Lord Edward Fitzgerald and Theobald Wolfe Tone figure prominently in the Irish pantheon of patriotic demigods that includes Robert Emmet, Napper Tandy, James Connolly, and Patrick Pearse. With great alacrity, Irish culture shaped into a quasi-scriptural mythos the multitudinous, contradictory, violent, and exhilarating events of 1798. But one consequence of this elevation from history to myth, from in some sense autonomous enterprise to prefigured reality, is that we have kept in our collective foremind the belief that 1798 marks a departure from the expected and the normative, that conditions actually supported a different ending to the story, but an outcome that remained maddeningly and mysteriously elusive. The endless damning coincidences, the infinite penetration of patriotic enclaves by Castle spies, make us wonder, still, why history remained so recalcitrantly against Ireland's liberation. Again and again analysts educe parallels among the American, French, and Irish revolutions only to falter on Irish economic backwardness, factionalism, lack of an adequate communications network in Ireland, the superiority of the English spy and information system in a colony closer to home turf than the American colonies, and even the peculiarly intractable but seemingly somehow deeply intrinsic problems of bad weather (which thwarted the landing of French troops in Bantry Bay) and Irish informers (which appear sometimes to be regarded, ludicrously, as a sign of some fundamental moral problem in the Irish personality). In the same way, in the American South there are folk historians who replay Robert E. Lee's battle maneuvers in an incredulous effort to come to terms with the fact that the Confederacy did not win the war of secession. I have the same feeling when I attend to histories and memoirs of 1798; the mind rebels against things having gone so persistently wrong.

The fact is that Irish politics resisted assimilation to the Enlightenment model of revolutionary cultural change. A reading of late eighteenth-century Irish history as one of failure—a reading that includes a subtext of guilt, self-hatred, and cosmically mandated dependency—does the Rising and the cause of Irish republicanism a great injustice. And for this reason it is extremely important that not everyone has accepted this assessment of the rebellion. Along with the dominant interpretation of 1798 in Irish culture, there has persisted well into the twentieth century an alternative take on this historical period. Primary vehicles for this alternative tradition were the plays created by Whitbread and Bourke at the Queen's Royal Theatre.

This is not to say that their work appeared ex nihilo, without attention to the complex dramatic traditions that preceded them. Not at all. But Whitbread and the generation of patriotic dramatists who responded to his work used the stage to recast selectively the military defeats of 1798. Their work asserts a typological patterning in order to resuscitate the triumphs of the highly varied political undertakings often too indiscriminately gathered together as the 1798 Rising. Attending to political activities in France and Ireland, in the north and in the south, in the city and throughout the countryside, these melodramas display the diversity of the rebellion/civil war/revolution that contributed to a splintered historical moment; they emphasize the coexistence of success and defeat.[34] Ultimately, Whitbread and company entered into the dialogue that produced the Easter Rising of 1916, the Anglo-Irish Treaty, the civil war of the early twenties, and the partition that coincided with the formation of the Free State. Given the rhetoric of blood sacrifice that supported the twentieth-century freedom movement, it is easy to see that the religious metaphor cited above retained its potency. In fact, a reader might observe that by emphasizing the positive achievements of 1798, the Queen's Theatre writers asserted against historical fracture the stronger typological coherence that the society demanded of it- itself.

Self-consciousness vis-à-vis history found expression not only in the cultural myth described above but also in small-scale formats such as memoirs and historical studies. When we look at memoirs, for instance the famous narrative produced by Bishop Stock and made currently prominent by its use in Thomas Flanagan's enormously successful novel *The Year of the French,* we discover that the Rising as viewed from Stock's class position and geographical location is very different from the Rising as seen in Wexford by, say, a local farm girl. In fact, it is clear that we are dealing with struggles that may very well be profoundly different social constructions.

Alternatively, when we read histories produced during the nineteenth century, we immediately notice the difficulties faced by their authors in organizing such disparate materials. Take, for instance, the famous work by Richard Musgrave (self-described in the 1801 second edition as a "member in the late Irish Parliament")—*Memoirs of the Different Rebellions in Ireland, from the Arrival of the English: Also, A Particular Detail of That Which Broke Out the XXIIId of May, MDCCXCVIII; with the History of the Conspiracy which Preceded It and the Characters of the Principal Actors in It.*[35] Musgrave immediately communicates his loyalist sentiments, which are presented with so little reflection that even the unaligned contemporary reader may feel put off. More compelling are the look and feel of this volume, which carry their own messages of diversity and interpretive play. My copy, unfortunately redone in modern binding, still cannot hold all of the material that the author crammed into it. It is strewn with bunchy, fold-out maps of considerable detail, from a full design of Ireland to a "Plan of the Town of Arklow with part of the circumjacent Country to illustrate the account of the Attack of the Rebels on that Town June 9th, 1798"—this dotted with trees and hedgerows. In fact, the volume delineates forty-some battles that took place as part of the 1798 Rising. And it is these battles that Musgrave really means us to see as the "different rebellions" of his title. Although he spends forty-six pages on early Irish history and the conflicts thereof from the fifth century through the 1780s, Musgrave's real topic, '98 proper, occupies him in the remaining 590 large pages of text and over 200 closely printed pages of appendix. Despite his rigid political stance, Musgrave revels in the multiplicities, the differences, that constituted the Irish "rebellion." The documentary style of his presentation allows him to introduce material that brings many of the conflicts to a kind of three-dimensional life, however biased in political viewpoint.

Holding in mind this vision of the Rising as in actuality several risings prepares the way for understanding both the fact that a great many plays on 1798 were produced and the lively debates that continue to animate historical discussion of this period in Ireland. I have tracked varying perspectives, both older and more recent, to produce the following narrative of 1798. Not losing sight of diversity, I try to tell a composite story that brings into relation the protagonists and sites of the four plays in this edition. As the reader will notice, Whitbread and Bourke took some liberties with facts when they composed their plays, but it is also true that the authors accurately reproduced a great deal of accepted folklore about 1798 and a substantial amount of documented research about the period. What formed within the melodramatic tradition was a complicated alignment of often contradictory sociohistorical material. And the thrust of that alignment was to assert the rebels' successes, both material and ideological.

Irish Civilization and Its Discontents

The uprisings grew out of several sources of and reasons for discontent. On the Irish side of the water native traditions of resistance cohered in, on the one hand, the secret societies of the Catholic Defenders and, on the other, the rhetorically egalitarian United Irishmen.[36] These groups organized opposition to internal oppression both socioreligious and political; the Defenders hoped to reclaim lands originally held by Catholics but denied them owing to English occupation of the country, and the United Irishmen sought universal suffrage. Although mostly Protestant in their leadership,[37] the United Irishmen supported Catholic emancipation from the oppressions formalized in the earlier Penal Laws. Eventually, this society also proposed ethical and philosophic reorganization of Ireland. Their having been influenced by Enlightenment principles of liberty, equality, and fraternity assumed, at some level, cooperation across religious barriers and within Ireland to assure the greater good of all, irrespective of Ireland's continued connection to or dissociation from England.

Given this pressure-cooker situation, in which agitation for social change took place both in the lower, primarily Catholic, class stratum and in the highest, the war between the French Republic and England was perfectly timed. The late eighteenth-century military conflict quite naturally disposed Ireland to seek alliance with Paris, a choice enhanced by the Catholicism of the French—although the practice of that faith differed considerably between France and Ireland. In addition, the French Revolution, reinforcing as it did the extraordinary accomplishments of the American colonial war, provided both role modeling and rhetorical priming for Irish autonomy. Add to this mixture a sufficiency of English misrule, and there was every reason to strike against the British in the 1790s. Not that this reasoning was seamless, across-the-board, or even all that rational at times. In her fine study of the period, Marianne Elliott notes that the events of the 1790s produced an "uneven response" in Ireland, with most adherence to political causes taking place in the "more prosperous areas in the north, the east and the midlands."[38] These locales had the most to lose to English control of industrial or agrarian pursuits and had the liveliest sense of their right to universal suffrage. But Ireland had also been networked by the Irish Volunteers. Founded in 1778 in Ulster to defend an island whose men had been requisitioned for wartime service in America, the Volunteers were a kind of native standing army. In fact, they loomed behind the Society of United Irishmen, for the Volunteers invited Dublin's Wolfe Tone to visit Belfast and collaborate on social planning—an action that produced the national organization.

The United Irishmen, formed within a countrywide communications network, included persons not only of influence but also of political courage and Romantic enthusiasm. The names that melodramatists and patriots came either to conjure by or to deplore as traitors can be found on the society's roll, from Wolfe Tone and Lord Edward Fitzgerald to Napper Tandy, Samuel Neilson, Thomas Russell, James Reynolds, Samuel Turner, Francis Magan, Archibald Hamilton Rowan, Leonard McNally, Henry Sheares, and Thomas Addis Emmet. Although their formally agreed upon agenda was modest (not the displacement of monarchy but merely "the abolition of tithes and hearth-tax, the establishment of a national system of education by a reformed parliament, and a reduction of taxation indirectly through cheaper government and the abolition of sinecures"[39]), the society's ultimately mythic cultural presence can still be sensed in Irish republican discourse. Seeking greater prosperity for their country and their class, they imbued a spirit of, in Tone's word, "regeneration."

Lord Edward Fitzgerald, Revolutionary

Much of this regeneration took place symbolically and, in line with Irish tradition, from a position of exile. From the early 1790s on, Irish patriots migrated to Paris and envisioned radical social change for their country; it helped tremendously that they were in a place where such transformation was, in fact, happening.[40] One United Irishman whose career as such properly began in France was Lord Edward Fitzgerald, a member of the historically important governing family known as the Geraldines. The Duke of Leinster's younger brother and a British officer with an affectionate and openhearted temperament, Lord Edward was "a man singularly amiable, estimable, and lovable";[41] these are unusual adjectives to be applied to a patriot, but all well-disposed historians speak of him in similar language, even while quietly regretting his lack of decisiveness and intellectual depth.

Certainly one of the important events of his life was a trip to America during the revolution; he returned to Ireland with a new vision of social possibility and with a black servant named Tony (who becomes a seemingly gratuitous character in Whitbread's play). By 1792 he resided in Paris, along with other Irish "radicals"; as Elliott tells it, he joined the Jacobin Club and "had become so enamoured of French principles that when he returned from Paris at the end of 1792 even the United Irishmen thought him a secret French agent and feared the ill-repute he might bring to a Society still seeking to establish its constitutionalism."[42] W. H. Lecky gives us a livelier picture of Lord Edward in France, one that emphasizes the pleasing internationalism of radical thought in this era: "In the autumn of 1792 he was staying at Paris with [Thomas] Paine, and he took part in a banquet to celebrate the victory of the Republic over the invaders, at which toasts were drunk to the universal triumph of the principles of the Revolution and the abolition of all hereditary titles and feudal distinctions." On this occasion, Lord Edward actually renounced his title.[43] Relieved of his commission as a result of such behavior,[44] a matter dramatized by Whitbread, Lord Edward served in the Irish Parliament and waited for the revolution in Ireland.

Later, he did so as military leader of the Provincial Directory of Leinster, which was the organization ultimately empowering the many local cells of the United Irishmen throughout Leinster. Lecky's comments about Lord Edward's leadership, directed toward accentuating his good intentions but intellectual limitations, also point archly to a central issue of the Rising, the matter of class relations. "The cooperation of a member of the first family of the Protestant aristocracy was of no small advantage to the conspiracy in a country where the genuine popular feeling, amid all its aberrations, has always shown itself curiously aristocratic, and where the first instinct of the people when embarking in democratic and revolutionary movements has usually been to find some one of good family and position to place at their head."[45] Although Lecky's tone may be attributed to his Ascendancy bias, it is worth noting that inequities of class both undermined the Rising and actuated rebellion in Ireland as a series of partly parallel, partly askew movements.

While in France, Lord Edward had married a foundling named Pamela who had become part of the family of Philippe Egalité, duc d'Orleans, "one of the French revolutionary leaders." Pamela provided an entree to "Madame de Genlis and her cousin Madame de Sillery, prominent French *émigrés* in Hamburg"[46]—hence Whitbread's *Lord Edward* opens in Madame de Sillery's garden (Whitbread conflates the two cousins into one character). By 1796 Lord Edward was trying to convince the French Directory that an invasion of Ireland would be to their mutual advantage. Even without the highly romantic ending to his story (his death on the eve of the Rising in Leinster), Lord Edward contributed many elements of drama and panache to the events of 1798. At one point, days before he was discovered by the military, he and Samuel Neilson, another United Irishman, traveled by horse to scout the Dublin area. To evade the patrol's questioning, Lord Edward pretended to be a doctor; Neilson pretended to be drunk (an incident that Whitbread makes use of). Stories about his conduct all convey this same air of boyish confidence. With his lighthearted geniality, his loyalty, courage, and socialite spouse, he lived elements of melodrama long before he was represented in one.

Wolfe Tone: Melodrama and Tragedy

Another prominent figure in the French negotiations was Wolfe Tone. Born in 1763, Tone had little wealth but was nonetheless educated at Trinity College in Dublin, an Ascendancy stronghold. Neither at Trinity nor later in law school in London did Tone distinguish himself as a student. At the age of twenty, he flirted with a career in the theater, acting with Richard Martin's troupe and falling desperately in love with his employer's wife. A playbill exists from 1783 in which "Mr. Tone" plays roles in both "the celebrated Tragedy of DOUGLAS" and a farce entitled "ALL THE WORLD'S A STAGE."[47] Like Lord Edward, Tone was soon to become a character in a drama so complex that it demanded his life. But Tone left the stage proper and Mrs. Martin with it, and two years later he fell in love with Matilda Witherington, who was seven years younger than he. In his biography of Tone, Henry Boylan notes that Matilda "lived in Grafton Street with her maternal grandfather, a rich old clergyman named Richard Fanning." In July of 1785 they eloped. Tone entered law school in 1787, but as his wife was not with him in England, he engaged in numerous infidelities. By 1788 he was back in Ireland at his father's home in Bodenstown; his wife had "grown delicate, principally from the anxiety about the uncertainty of her position."[48] Throughout the remaining decade of his life, Tone's political commitment precipitated similar illnesses and strains in Mrs. Tone, but he became a devoted husband and father all the same.

Living in Ireland and having decided to pursue the law in some fashion, Tone became involved in pamphlet writing and in other proto-insurrectionary activities. To read Tone's autobiographical accounts of those heady days in Ireland, when self-styled Enlightened males philosophized and drank until dawn, when Church of England Protestants, Dissenters, and Catholics sat down together to enjoy such intellectual and literal feasts, is to be impressed by the extravagant optimism of the time. An exhilaration born of empowering transgressions moved participants to actions whose outcome they might try to anticipate but could not control. By 1795 Tone was in Philadelphia, gathering support for the United Irish cause and establishing contacts that would serve him well in France, where he later represented the society.

In France, Tone was lonely, poor, and unable to communicate efficiently owing to his initially almost nonexistent French skills. Nonetheless, his enthusiasm and persistence, his downright resilience against great odds, won him attention by the French Directory. Unfortunately, Tone's understanding of the social situation in Ireland became increasingly stylized and inaccurate over time. His vision of an inevitable mass rising, his rhetorical diminishing of the problems that existed between Catholics and Protestants, and his notion that the British navy included sufficient numbers of Irishmen for it to be overwhelmed from within, all created problems when put to the test.[49] His enthusiasm paid off in the short term when, in December of 1796, under the command of General Hoche and with Tone in the company, a naval invasion of Ireland was attempted.

Hoche's fleet included "forty-five vessels and a total military force of 14,750 men." In every way, this expedition was ill-fated; arriving in Bantry Bay, the fleet, which had lost some of its vessels, encountered storms and winds that prevented its effective landing in Ireland. Hence, the ships turned around and made their way back to the port of Brest in France. The arrival of Tone's wife in Hamburg restored his spirits after this fiasco[50]—perhaps the biggest disappointment, from a tactical standpoint, of the whole rebellion. But 1797 brought not only Mrs. Tone but also the death of Hoche and some puzzling meetings between Tone and Napoleon Bonaparte. Tone's wonderfully detailed journal, written while he was in France, describes Bonaparte and comments as follows under the heading of 23 December 1797: "His manner is cold, and he speaks very little; it is not, however, so dry as that of Hoche, but seems rather to proceed from languor than anything else. He is perfectly civil, however, to us; but, from anything we have yet seen or heard from him, it is impossible to augur anything good or bad. We have now seen the greatest man in Europe three times, and I am astonished to think how little I have to record about him. . . . Yet, after all, it is a droll thing that I should become acquainted with Buonaparte.[51]

A few weeks afterward, Tone discussed with Napoleon his commission in the *Armée Angleterre*, explaining that while he was not a soldier, he could nonetheless hope to "be serviceable to him on the other side of the water. . . . *'Mais vous êtes brave,'* said he, interrupting me. I replied that, when the occasion presented itself, that would appear. *'Eh bien,'* said he, *'celà suffit.'* " Whitbread's play captures something of the tone of those meetings—Napoleon's brusque self-containment and grudging acknowledgment of the needs of the Irish patriots.

In 1798, although he was significantly out of touch with Irish reality, Tone did receive news that most of the Leinster Directory had been arrested and that rebellion was under way in Wexford.[52] By October, Tone was back in Ireland, after having been part of another unsuccessful French invasion, one that Tone knew in advance would fail.[53] Captured immediately, he stood trial in Dublin the following month and was sentenced to hang. Elliott describes Tone's poignant position. "The man who had played such an important part in giving the United Irish movement its French dimension seemed strangely unimportant in the Dublin of November 1798. The carriage which brought him prisoner to the city on 8 November passed through the haunts of his former celebrity without raising more than an antiquarian interest. Most of the state prisoners in the city would not have known him, and little effort was made to save him in comparison to the fuss which had been occasioned by the plights of Lord Edward, Bond or Byrne, whose contribution to Irish republicanism had been minute in comparison."[54] In contrast and in a style that evokes the apocryphal, Henry Boylan assures us that

Tone's trial "aroused great public excitement," and certainly Tone's return to Dublin in the "brilliant uniform of a French colonel, a large cocked hat with broad gold lace, blue uniform coat with gold and embroidered collar and gold epaulettes, blue pantaloons and short boots bound with gold lace"[55] emphasized the theatrical quality of even this penultimate scene in Tone's short life.

By this time, Lord Cornwallis, who had already had his own difficulties with colonials in America, was Lord Lieutenant of Ireland, and it was he who denied Tone's request to be shot instead of hanged. For this reason, Tone slit his throat, although he did not actually die for another week. Boylan comments, "There were rumours that he was murdered by his captors to avoid surrendering him to the court. But surely they would have found more efficient means to dispatch him and avoided the risk of denunciation by a victim who was only wounded, however grievously."[56] On the other hand, Tone's legal adviser had opened the issue of whether civil law or martial law had priority in Dublin at the time and thus whether Tone's trial was legal,[57] and it is this dispute that generated rumors and contradictory stories about Tone's final days.

One highly interesting shape in which such rumors congealed can be found in a play called *Wolfe Tone*, which, though never produced, was written in 1907 by Peadar Kearney, patriot and author of the Irish national anthem.[58] Delightfully, Kearney portrays much of the Tone legend that Whitbread excluded or simply never imagined. He includes conversations with Hoche; Lord Edward praising Tone as "Ireland's greatest man . . . the heart and soul of our movement," whose "position by right is President not representative of our Republic"; Tone on board ship, along with Bonaparte himself (a highly unhistorical moment); and the infamous trial. Major Sirr, the town major of Dublin and an actual enemy of the Republic who became almost a generic melodramatic villain in these plays, makes his entrance after the trial to set up the putative suicide.

> SIRR *(pacing to & fro)* On the success of today's business depends my chances of future ease and comfort. Government is already in my debt, and if I succeed in bringing Tone to the scaffold my pension is assured. That rascally lawyer Curran has been a sore thorn in our sides. Had he compromised himself I could have had him under lock and key but with consummate cleverness he has kept clear of all treasonable plans, but conscious of his innocence he defies us with impunity and confounds us with our own laws.

Sirr refers here to Tone's defense, stated when General Lavau had placed him under military arrest, that he was not a traitor but rather a prisoner of war, a soldier of France; and in fact Tone never was an English soldier subject to English courtmartial.[59]

Kearney's play follows closely the trial as described by Tone's son in his *Life of Theobald Wolfe Tone*. Kearney's Major Sirr admits that Tone's attorney had proved the verdict invalid and had "received an order to postpone the execution." When the Provost, who is in charge of the execution, questions Sirr's resolve to proceed in advance of the stop order, Sirr whispers his plan to wound Tone mortally. In the final scene of his play, Kearney wonderfully takes us into a local forge, where the disappointed revolutionaries are planning to rescue their hero from prison. Receiving news of Tone's death, the blacksmith immediately rejects the story of suicide: "Ah God wither the tongue that started that foul lie, an' may his curse shrivel an' blight the murderers of Tone. Oh God in heaven to think we should be so powerless an' our best bein' murdered like rats in a trap."[60] Rather than fall utterly into despair, the gathered men head out to join forces with the historical patriot Michael Dwyer as he continues to fight in the Wicklow mountains.

Given Tone's well-known resolve to end his own life rather than be publicly hanged—the decision of, among other things, a gentleman of the period—debate over the means of his death does seem unnecessary. But Kearney's handling of the elements of legend—rumor, dramatic decorum, and the primal desire that things be other than they were—demonstrates the rhetorical possibilities inherent in these seemingly unpromising narratives. There is just enough leeway in these stories, just enough interaction between lived romance and intransigent fact, to allow optimistic or at least stirring renditions of the gratefully unrecorded bits of history.

Lord Edward: The Drama of Betrayal

Wolfe Tone died on 19 November 1798. Even before he left France, the Leinster Directory had been decimated by arrests on 12 March, arrests that had, however, left Lord Edward Fitzgerald still unaccounted for. With the leadership of the Geraldine, there could still be a Rising, and plans went forward even without a large central committee. Although, ironically, none of the four expeditions ultimately sent by the French coincided with a mass rebellion, the activity in Ireland was intense and significant. Given the constant surveillance of United Irishmen and the ever-present necessity to outmaneuver the Castle's secret service, the prospective rebels accomplished a great deal toward their liberation. What role did Lord Edward play in these preparations? Most commentators agree that in this genial aristocrat's status lay his principal force; he symbolized a united Ireland that, for all of its autonomy, might retain something of its heritage of social organization and cohesion. Elliott comments that despite Lord Edward's symbolic value, he "lacked the ability to take an overall lead at the decisive moment"; rather, he waited with his fellow conspirators for a French invasion to support indigenous military action.[61] Nonetheless, like his French and English military counterparts, Lord Edward was to have led the uprising in a splendid uniform. Froude notes—and this detail expresses many of the contradictions of the Rising as well as its inherent sense of drama—that in the Geraldine's room "were found a green uniform and the official seal of the Irish Union. In a pocketbook was the sketch of the plan for the surprise of Dublin, in which he was to have taken the command."[62] Nicholas Murphy, in whose house the arrest occurred, wrote a narrative of that event, and he describes receiving the uniform:

> I knew not what it contained, but to my surprise, when I opened it, I found it to be an uniform, of a very beautiful green colour, gimpt or braided down the front, with crimson or rose-colour cuffs and cape: there were two dresses—one a long-shirted coat, vest, and pantaloons; the other, a short jacket, that came round quite close, and was braided in front; there was also a pair of overalls, that buttoned from the hip to the ankle, with, I think, black Spanish leather on the sides. I suppose they were intended for riding. The bundle contained a cap of a very fanciful description, extremely attractive, formed exactly like a sugar-loaf—that part that went round the forehead green, the upper part crimson, with a large tassel, which inclined on one side or other occasionally when on the head.[63]

The stage was set, the costumes and props readied, but as with the winds in Bantry Bay, the security of Lord Edward's hiding place proved beyond control.

Despite his violent bias against Lord Edward, James Anthony Froude mostly adheres to the factual story of his discovery and death, and the narrative as classically told always involves a blow-by-blow delineation of this encounter. The nature of the blows, whether inflicted by knife or by pistol, the number of stabbings and shootings vary remarkably according to the narrator,[64] but this discrepancy seems far less important than the writers' shared obsession with detail for its own sake. After all, those who recite this story are condensing into the events of a few moments patriotic emotions suitable to a far more epic conflict. With the fetishizing of details reserved for descriptions of accidents, sympathetic writers about the last days of Lord Edward play out in slow motion the agonizing betrayal of their hopes. I quote Froude's version both to demonstrate that even the unsympathetic adopt that obsessive narrative style and to set up a contrast with the story told by W. J. Fitzpatrick, whose volume *Secret Service under Pitt* (1892) provided the basis of Whitbread's drama.

> On the 18th of May Major Sirr received communications from a quarter unhinted at in the most secret letters of the Viceroy, telling him where Lord Edward could be found; and on Saturday, the 19th, between five and six in the evening, Swan, Sirr, and Ryan, with eight soldiers, in plain clothes went quietly and without attracting attention to the house of a featherman in Thomas Street, named Murphy. As they approached the door a woman, who had observed them, was seen to rush in and up the stairs, to give the alarm. Major Swan was too quick for her, and running close behind her, entered a room at the stair-head, when he discovered Lord Edward, lying on a bed, in a dressing-jacket. . . . Major Swan told him quietly that he had a warrant for his arrest; resistance would be useless, but he would be treated with the respect due to his rank. Lord Edward cared nothing for his rank. He had abjured his title six years before in Paris, and in Dublin among the initiated he was called Citizen Fitzgerald. But below his citizenship ran the fierce wild blood of the Geraldines. Springing from the bed, he levelled a pistol at Major Swan's head. The pistol missed fire, and he leapt on him with a dagger, and stabbed him through and through. It was the work of a moment. Captain Ryan had followed at his best speed, and when he came in he found Swan bleeding on the ground, and Lord Edward striking at him. Ryan, too, snapped a pistol. The flint-lock failed him. He had a sword-cane, and made a lunge with the blade, which bent on Lord Edward's side, and forced him back upon the bed. In an instant he was up again. Ryal closed with him. Lord Edward . . . hurled him to the ground, rolled upon him, plunged his dagger into him again and again and again with such fury that in a few seconds he had given him fourteen wounds.
>
> He then sprang to his feet and attempted flight. Major Sirr, now entering, met Lord Edward struggling towards the

> door, endeavoring to extricate himself from the grasp of the two officers, who, though lying on the floor, with the blood streaming from them, still clung to his legs.
>
> Major Sirr's pistols were in better condition than his comrades'. He fired. Lord Edward fell struck heavily in the shoulder, and surrendered. A guard of cavalry was sent for, and he was conveyed to Newgate through a silent, sullen crowd. Major Swan recovered. Captain Ryan died of his wounds in a few days.[65]

On 4 June, the Geraldine died also, having been betrayed by an inner-circle spy. Froude presents Lord Edward as if he were a wild animal; he also indicates that no one knows who betrayed the Irish patriot. When Fitzpatrick published his book only four years after Froude, he had solved this perplexing mystery and identified as the perpetrator one of the three members remaining, at the time of Lord Edward's capture, in the Leinster Directory—Francis Magan. As Fitzpatrick demonstrates, many names had been put forward over the intervening century for this traitor. Using documents previously kept secret by Dublin Castle, Fitzpatrick pieces together the fascinating story in which Francis Higgins, the owner of the *Freeman's Journal* at the time, worked with Magan, a highly placed attorney, to bring down the revolution.

Many details from Fitzpatrick's historical sleuthing and retelling of the story find a place, however transformed, in Whitbread's *Lord Edward, Or '98*. For instance, Fitzpatrick tells us of Higgins's spying on Pamela, Lady Edward Fitzgerald; he portrays a search of Leinster House by Major Swan, who "said to Lady Edward: 'This is an unpleasant duty for any gentleman to perform.'—'It is a task which no gentleman *would* perform,' was the reply." Fitzpatrick adds, "It was during this anxious period that Lord Edward, venturing out at night, had an interview with Pamela in Denzille Street, when their little child was taken from its cot to see its father, and a servant suddenly entering the room found the parents in tears."[66] Such poignant moments begged to shape an aesthetic portrayal into what we might call a realistic melodrama. Whitbread also makes use of the fact that a "carpenter named Tuite—who worked in Dublin Castle, and knew Moore [a patriot who at one point sheltered Lord Edward]—having overheard . . . that Moore's house should be searched, gave a timely hint to Moore, who therefore fled to Meath, previously telling his daughter to provide for Lord Edward's safety." Not suspecting her friend Magan to be an informer, she took counsel with him about how to ensure that safety. So it was that when

Lord Edward was to be moved by his friends from Moore's on Thomas Street to Magan's own house, Major Sirr showed up with a party of soldiers and would have captured his prey had the major not slipped and fallen, allowing time for Lord Edward to be whisked away.[67] In fact, Whitbread's play risks a certain amount of incoherence or inconsequence by trying to dramatize the many incidents uncovered and pieced together in Fitzpatrick's wonderfully detailed book. If a contemporary reader feels puzzled by a seemingly irrelevant character or encounter in one of Whitbread's plays, there is almost always a specific source whose findings were too exciting for him to ignore.

Fitzpatrick, as Whitbread's major and cited informant, certainly influenced the dramatist's presentation of the capture. "Lord Edward was lying on his bed in Murphy's attic, after having drunk some whey to relieve a bad cold, when Major Swan and Captain Ryan peeped in at the door, exclaiming that resistance would be vain. At once Fitzgerald started up like a lion from his lair and rushed at Swan. Revolvers were as yet unknown and his pistol missed fire; he then drew a dagger."[68] As Froude notes, after stabbing Swan, Lord Edward was in turn shot in the shoulder by his victim. A misfire then occurred for Ryan, but he and Swan were able to constrain the prisoner until Sirr arrived and shot him again in the right arm.[69] With 200 soldiers present, Lord Edward still attempted another escape and was stabbed in the neck.[70] A fortnight later Lord Edward was dead, and the Rising had splintered into a number of local and quickly extinguished struggles.

Violence and Propaganda

To understand the complex aftermath of this assassination, it is necessary to recall the extent to which the British worked explicitly to keep the country in a state of religious division. Had those divisions not been fostered, had the various native public and parliamentary gestures toward universal emancipation been allowed to mature without imposed external restraint, Ireland would certainly have followed the American colonies in securing independence. But, as Elliott points out, when desire for Irish Catholic emancipation heated up in 1795, and when the English government under Sir William Pitt refused to allow any significant reform, political discontent rose and fused with coincidental widespread economic distress. Thus when circumstances produced the Protestant-militant Orange

Order, the Catholic Defenders were increasingly assimilated into the United Irishmen, whose agenda had become distinctly republican rather than reformist.[71] Commentators are agreed that English insensitivity to Irish social necessities fed into structural shifts to generate the antithetical pressures that made 1798 mythic and that, sadly, inscribed militancy and internal division rather than emancipation as the historical inevitabilities.

A loyalist but also an Anglo-Irishman, Lecky provides powerful insights about the Irish position, being much exercised by the intransigencies, shortsightedness, and cruelties inflicted by British rule. Specifically, he counters the story of Irish history offered by Froude; as Lecky's contemporary editor L. P. Curtis states, "Froude's stereotype of the unstable Irish Celt made his history read like a Tory brief on how to solve the Irish question, and his conclusion in *The English in Ireland* that Irishmen and 'Asiatics' required equally firm, authoritative government left little to the imagination."[72] He was an apologist for the Ascendancy in Ireland, certainly, but Lecky also brought to his analysis a lively sympathy for Irish affairs. Thus he argued that England brought the Rising upon itself, stating, "It had been one of the great misfortunes of the English government that, during a considerable period of its history, it had been either compelled or persuaded to adopt as its method of managing Ireland, the worst of all expedients, that of endeavouring to inflame the animosities and deepen the divisions between the Protestants and Catholics." In fact, he asserted, the story of Ireland might have been very different had "all religious disqualifications . . . been removed in 1793 or 1795," before "the relations of classes and creeds . . . were hopelessly convulsed by the rebellion of 1798."[73] When threatened by the egalitarian movement, the English government monitored and suppressed its critics and stirred up fears among wealthy Protestants that their land was targeted, in the name of liberty, for Catholic confiscation.[74]

But it was the military activity allowed by the British during the 1790s that horribly detonated the uneasy rapport between England and Ireland. After blocking Catholic emancipation in parliament and outlawing the Society of United Irishmen, the English executive encouraged military reprisals against potential insurrectionaries. Throughout the countryside, "armed Yeomanry were allowed to plunder," fanning intense hostilities between Catholic and Protestant populations, hopelessly muddling issues of religion with those of economics and politics. Like the dreaded "Auxies" of 1916 and following, the British militia and their auxiliary "yeos" destroyed property, murdered citizens, and institutionalized varieties of hatred. Although the constitutional situation in Ireland demanded reform, it was the level of atrocity that radicalized the ordinary laborer and encouraged support of republican activities. Froude disagrees with this analysis. He paints a picture of an England overeager to accept blame and argues that seven years of Irish preparation for uprising created the actual revolt, not temporary and relatively insignificant "cruelties."[75] But J. J. O'Meara counters, "We have it upon the authority of English statesmen, soldiers and historians, whose authority cannot be called in question, that the people were goaded into open resistance. . . . The oceans of Irish blood that were shed in the rebellion of 1798—a rebellion designedly fomented by Pitt and his confederates—the gigantic bribery employed to purchase votes in favour of the Union—these things remain in imperishable record as showing the animus of the authors. Pitt knew that he could not carry the Union unless the strength of Ireland should first be broken by civil war."[76]

In the north from 1797 on, especially around the United Irishmen territory of Belfast, the militia and the yeomanry "acted almost without restraint: in the search for arms, houses were burnt down, suspected persons were flogged or tortured to make them reveal what they might know, and hundreds were sent off to the fleet." Such actions deterred potential rebels and turned up great quantities of arms. From Ulster, this military abuse spread to Leinster and the rest of the country.[77] It was, in fact, the government's finally having realized the extent of the United Irishmen's power that resulted not only in the March 1798 arrests and the hunt for Lord Edward but also in the "repression" of the south.[78]

Most historians, however exercised by the atrocities committed with governmental assent, treat these actions succinctly. Robert Kee is nothing if not concise, but his television history of Ireland does usefully bring to life this grotesque side of the Irish experience. He details the "savage ritual" of flogging to extract, along with chunks of flesh from the victim's back, information about the United Irishmen's activity in the neighborhood. He goes on: "There was also pitch-capping, in which a brown paper cap filled with pitch was jammed on to a man's head and then, after it had begun to set a little, was set fire to." (Commentators agree that the pitch-cap was created by the dreaded North Cork Militia.) Finally, various forms of hanging, from gradual to abrupt, were used to produce informers and to punish those supposed to be guilty.[79] Whole towns were reduced to the status of state prisoners undergoing torture; not only were people maimed and murdered, but houses were invaded at will and burned with or without cause, activities noted in Bourke's *When Wexford Rose*. Civil rights were utterly in abeyance. The almost millennialist fears and hopes of the insurrectionaries were revealed in the practice that developed in Wicklow and Wexford of putting red tape on the necks of Catholic children; the anti-Irish Richard Musgrave states, "The pretext was, to protect them from the effects of a contagious disorder which would soon appear in the country, and be fatal to many of its inhabitants; but experience has since taught us that it was to enable the rebels to discriminate protestant from popish children in the massacre which was intended of the former."[80] Obviously, a propaganda of violence activated both sides in this dispute, and dire fears shaped the behavior of the Catholic population in southeast Ireland.

For generations after these events, Irish schoolchildren knew intimately these stories of patriotism, terror, and betrayal. Enacting these narratives in political melodramas reinforced that learning, fundamental to a sense of Irish nationhood as it actually evolved, in peculiarly vivid and stirring ways. It is significant, too, that none of the melodramatists in this genre whose work I have encountered, either in print or in manuscript, radically exploited the simply horrific in portraying English torture and its victims.[81] Certainly, stage decorum of the time demanded a higher degree of physical propriety than we are accustomed to, but the more compelling observation is that these plays are relentlessly patriotic; rather than abuse the oppressors, the dramas linger on heroism, challenge, and opportunity.

The results of troop quartering and generalized oppression were the scattered risings chronicled in song and story. At one point, the United Irishmen had approximated the number who would rise at 279,894, but far fewer actually took up arms. Officially, Carlow county rose first, on 26 May, and in fear of even worse reprisal than they had already experienced, the townspeople of Carlow mostly just kept off the streets.[82] But according to Musgrave (whose reports are always deeply suspect but highly interesting as folk history), the first real activity took place in Rathfarnham, three miles outside of Dublin city. A loyalist civilian, one Samuel Bennet, reported seeing "a great concourse of rebels armed with muskets, pikes and pistols. . . . They had two carts laden with pikes and ammunition. . . . [T]he rebels in great numbers were risen, and were in the road and in the adjacent fields as he went to Dublin. In the city, particularly in the suburbs, he saw a great number of rebels with pikes, in the gate-ways, alleys and stable-lanes, waiting the beat of their drums, and the approach of rebel columns from the country, which they expected; and as he passed, they frequently cried out, animating each other, 'Come, on boys! who's afraid?'" And "a lady, resident at Rathfarnham," reported that passing rebels were heavily armed and "cried out frequently, 'Liberty, and no king!'"[83] In similar detail, Musgrave catalogs all that he could find about each movement of the United Irish sympathizers.

Such local rumblings did not come to much, but about twenty thousand rebels were able to gather in Wexford, and they temporarily won the towns of Enniscorthy and Arklow. This is the territory targeted by P. J. Bourke in *When Wexford Rose,* which is set in late May of 1798. Bourke's narrative invokes a well-known chronology to describe events in Wexford proper. But he deviates from historical accuracy, however, when he has news arrive of General Humbert's landing of French troops in Killala Bay and their march to take Castlebar; those events did not take place until late August, well after the stirrings in Wexford had been laid to rest. But it served Bourke's purposes to introduce Humbert before his time, the well-known and ultimately disastrous losses in Wexford being more suitable to a tragedy than to his patriotic melodrama.

The Wexford rising was led by Father John Murphy (plate 2), and Musgrave finds this Seville-educated priest so formidable a fighter that he exaggeratedly calls Murphy's "career . . . as destructive as that of Attila, Gengis Kan, or Tamerlane."[84] It is true that Father Murphy appears to have had considerable strategic skill, but popular wisdom has it that his motivation was neither to flout the church's prohibitions against civil insurrections nor to establish a military reputation—rather to extricate his parishioners from the tortures they had been forced to undergo.[85] The priest's initial victory, on 27 May, was against some North Cork militiamen temporarily on duty in the region.[86] Because it was Whitsunday, Father Murphy said mass and then led his men into battle on Oulart Hill[87] where "the difficulty of finding any easy nationalist pattern in the rebellion is shown by the fact that the Catholic militia were refused mercy by their fellow Catholic captors though they pleaded for it in Irish, a language which Wexfordmen no longer understood."[88] The next day, a "military centre" called Enniscorthy had been carried. Lecky suggests the extreme uncertainty of that conflict: "For some time a disorderly fight continued, with so fluctuating a fortune, that orange and green ribbons are said to have been alternately displayed by many in the town."[89]

Plate 2. Father John Murphy. Below the portrait, the stanza reads, "God grant you glory, brave Father Murphy / And open heaven to all your men; / The cause that called you may call tomorrow / In another fight for the Green again." Courtesy of the Wexford Museum.

When I went to Wexford and Enniscorthy in 1983, hoping to be able to imagine better what the terrain looked like in upheaval, an official of the Wexford Museum gave me a memoir of the Enniscorthy campaign. Written by Jane Barber, a Protestant whose father owned a farm two miles outside of the town, this memoir of 1798 reflectively presents the disorderly nature of the conflict.[90] On Sunday, 27 May, after they saw eleven fires burning near their home, Barber and her family drove, first stopping to milk their cows, into Enniscorthy, where her sixteen-year-old brother, a novice yeoman, had already preceded them. At first, the town was reasonably quiet on that Whitsunday, and around six o'clock in the evening Jane returned to the farm with a servant to milk the cows again. She claims, "We found all as we had left it, with the poor cows standing lowing to be milked. We each brought away a large pitcher and, on the road home met several Roman Catholic neighbours with whom we had been on the most friendly terms; we spoke to them as usual, but, they looked in our faces as though they had never seen us before and passed on. I have since thought that they either looked on us with abhorrence, as those devoted to destruction in this World and in the next, or, knowing our doom and pitying us, were afraid to trust themselves to speak to us."

As the fighting began on 28 May and spread through the town, Barber and her family were burned out of the relative's house in which they had been given shelter, and they moved into streets covered with dead bodies. She tells of violence that has become almost generic to this type of battle—a four-year-old piked to death, a former friend who kills Jane's father and mutilates his face with a leather-cutter's knife; her mother's emotional retreat into numbed shock; a man running naked with open wounds down his sides; the wholesale destruction of their farm; her brother's mental disorientation; the family's retaining only the clothes on their backs and some yards of blue cloth to sleep under. She tells also of some lighter, puzzling moments: the mother of a former laborer on their farm is spotted "dressed completely in new and excellent clothes and, in particular, a remarkably handsome beaver-hat." Barber remarks, "I was so much astonished at this, for she was very poor, that forgetting for the moment all my anxiety and fear, I asked her who had given her the hat."

Barber closes her narrative with a thesis about the wider social ramifications of the rising:

> Before I conclude, I must mention one evil, not generally known, that arose from the rebellion, but, the ill effects of which

> may be said still to continue. The yeomanry was composed mostly of fine boys, the sons of farmers, some of whom had scarcely attained the age of sixteen. These, removed from the eyes of their parents, with weapons placed in their hands, raised to the rank of men before they had discretion to behave as such, and exposed to all the temptations of idleness, intoxication, and bad companions, when peaceful times returned were totally unable to settle to their farms—too often, by their father's death, left to them alone—but, continued the same careless, disorderly life, 'till they became quite unable to pay their rents. They then were ejected, and emigrated to America and, on the very ground which, thirty years ago, were in possession of old Protestant families, there now live the descendants of those very rebels, who may be said to have been the origin of all this evil.

Considering her strong feelings, Barber shows restraint here, but fails to add the further observation that the Penal Laws' dispossession of Catholic owners had established claims to property that superseded those of the more recent Protestant proprietors. In any event, her analysis suggests one of the many ways in which the Rising echoed throughout the years and influenced remote matters of economics and demographics. Barber ends the story in that far-reaching spirit—both sides in Wexford remain fearful and suspicious, she says, and two generations will have to die before these memories will fade. It is into this complicated legacy of recollection and desire that Bourke introduced his plays. Unlike Whitbread's and like Barber's narrative, Bourke concentrates in *When Wexford Rose* on common people and their response to war.

After the battle at Enniscorthy, Father Murphy, who quickly assumed mythic and semidivine status in the eyes of his followers, received support from another priest, Father Michael Murphy, a native of Wexford who had attended seminary in Bordeaux.[91] Encounters between the rebels and their rivals (soldiers, militia, yeomanry) also took place in the towns of Arklow, Gorey, Wexford, and New Ross as well as at numerous other locations. The conflicts extended from May into June, becoming more desperate and "almost suicidal."[92] Father Michael Murphy died on the ninth of June, and the revolutionaries experienced many losses and much confusion. One famous point of reference in this county is Vinegar Hill (plates 3–5), a high green mound outside of Enniscorthy, on which Father John Murphy and his followers camped and from which surveillance of the entire countryside is readily had. An estimated ten thousand people joined the priest there.[93] In a ruined windmill, prisoners of war were housed. The Irish victories were, of course, all temporary.

Plate 3. Vinegar Hill. Engraving from Richard Musgrave's *Memoirs of the Different Rebellions in Ireland* (1801), showing locations of the "Light Infantry with Howitzer"; of "Gen. Lake where his Horse was Killed"; of the brigades of Generals Wilford, Dundas, Loftus, and Duff; of the "Rebels Fort of Vinegar Hill"; of "Rebel Lines and forest of Pikes" (dipping down the hillside); and of the "Enniscorthy side of the Slaney."

Poor organization, lack of supplies, and lack of field experience all took their toll against a movement activated alternately by nationalism, mortal fear, occasional opportunism, and accumulated outrage. Under orders from General Lake, General Needham routed the revolutionaries from Vinegar Hill, while General Johnson disputed territory around Enniscorthy with soldiers of the Irish republic.[94] The Hill was "captured" on 21 June.[95] Father John Murphy, who himself became the hero of a melodrama by Ira Allen (a play for which, although apparently no manuscript is extant, we do have the playbill, see plate 6), died at Tullow; he was reportedly courtmartialed, flogged 500 times, and beheaded. His body was placed in a pitch barrel and burned on 26 June.[96]

Plate 4. Vinegar Hill today.

The Northern Insurgents

Overlapping the southern uprising were various battles in Ulster. Henry Joy McCracken, a founder of the United Irishmen in Belfast, took up arms on 7 June to tackle the town of Antrim in a brief and unsuccessful confrontation. County Down's rising was led by Henry Munro (also spelled Munroe and Monro), who saw encounters in Saintfield and Ballynahinch. By 13 June his troops were defeated in the latter town.[97] Elliott comments:

> On the 11th the Down insurgents took Ballynahinch with the full support of its inhabitants, and the following day an army of 5,000 rebels prepared to face the troops sent against them. But Nugent's soldiers had already completely suppressed the Antrim rising, and military strength was concentrated against the Down rebels with similar results. . . . Most of the carnage at Ballynahinch occurred after victory had been gained by the military. The fleeing rebels were pursued by mounted troops and cut down in the neighbouring woods, and reprisals continued for many days after the defeat.[98]

Plate 5. "Brits Out" and "Ireland Free" are still the slogans on Vinegar Hill.

Ballynahinch, which was burned,[99] is the setting for Bourke's *For the Land She Loved*. Most histories, following the sexist norms prevalent until recently, mention women in the Rising only peripherally. Women are the picturesquely dutiful wives of heroes; they are terrified aristocrats who flee to London; they are Catholic peasants who cluster on Vinegar Hill to cook, gape, and tremble; they are, at their most vigorous, auxiliary fighters, fierce but unnamed. But *For the Land She Loved* provides a bracing alternative. It tells the story of Munro on an angle, for it is really the tale of Betsy Gray's love for Munro and her death on his behalf. Betsy Gray is, however, above and beyond her role as sacrificial sweetheart, a hero. Unlike Lord Edward and Wolfe Tone, who never saw open battle in Ireland, Gray (who according to folk history was "dressed from head to foot in green silk"[100]) joins the revolutionaries in field conflict at Ballynahinch. Of course, Bourke has revised her story, as did Whitbread the tales of his heroes. It seems factually demonstrable that she was twenty years old in 1798, a well-educated only daughter of a widowed, financially secure farmer.[101] In the play, Gray is engaged to Munro; in real life, her lover was not Munro at all but William

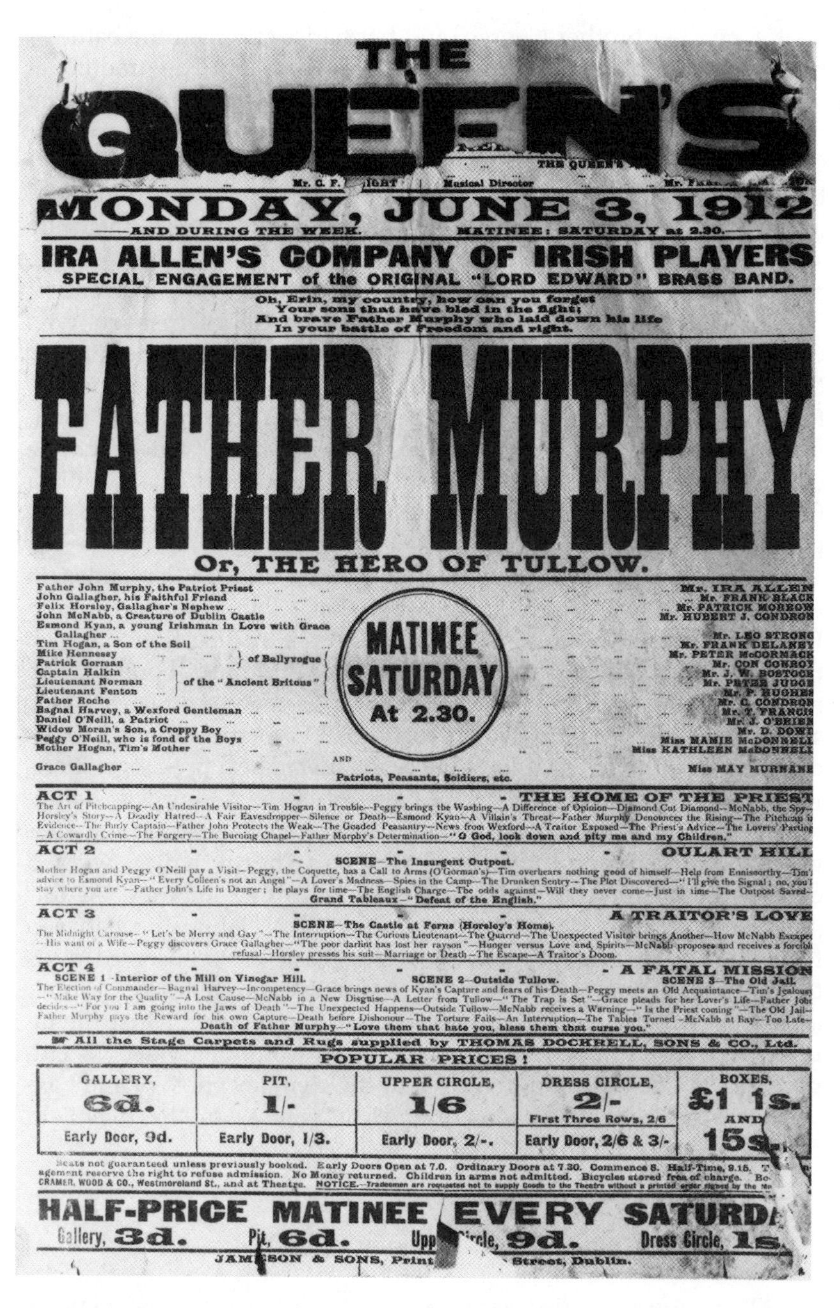

Plate 6. Playbill for Ira Allen's *Father Murphy,* originally staged 1909. Courtesy of Séamus de Búrca.

Boal. Gray, her brother George, and her fiancé survived the battle of Ballynahinch only to be murdered by yeomen.[102] The traditional story has it that when her lover and brother were wounded by the paramilitaries, Gray closed with them in a vain attempt to save George, who was not yet mortally wounded. But the yeomen cut off her hand, blew out her brains, and stripped her of clothing and jewelry. W. G. Lyttle claims that her murderers were universally shunned after this event. So it is that although her nemesis in the play, Major General Nugent, did indeed force Down to surrender, he also elevated several more patriots to the roll of Irish martyrs; Gray's grave and her sword have been identified and honored.[103] Munro himself was courtmartialed, hanged, and beheaded; just before the hanging, one version of his end states that he took a moment to repay, "with all the coolness of deliberation," a debt that he owed a neighbor.[104] Another says that he spoke privately with a friend before propelling himself into the air to preempt the executioner.[105]

The final throes of the Rising continued until 23 September in Connaught. It was not until October that Wolfe Tone arrived in Donegal,[106] when the curtain had fallen on the insurrection in which he had hoped to play a leading role. Ironies of timing abound in the narratives of 1798. They support an analysis that sees in place of a single rebellion a number of revolutions. Each movement had its own adherents; each shared only certain ideological presuppositions with others; each thought that its version of the Rising was definitive. What historians are rediscovering about 1798—its startling multiplicity of design and motive—the Queen's Theatre writers worked out on the stage and in their dialogue with one another. At this juncture, two points must be made about the relationship between their work and history: first, the Rising itself was conceived *in its time* in dramatic terms[107] as a series of scenes and tableaux; second, although political melodrama forms a distinct genre in Irish literature, within that category the portrayal of revolutionary actions emphasized not historical uniformity but the complex etiology and consequences of civil discontent in 1798 as well as in the twentieth century. Both of these points are developed below.

Theater as Historical Context

To support the first assertion, consider the theatrical contexts in which the principal actors themselves were involved. For example, Lord Edward's wife, Pamela, had been courted during a stay in England by the playwright R. B. Sheridan. Sheridan's wife had recently died, and when he proposed to Pamela he was accepted. It is said that Mrs. Sheridan looked remarkably like Pamela. Lord Edward, who had formed a friendship with Mrs. Sheridan, seems to have fallen in love with Pamela instantly when, after Mrs. Sheridan's death, he saw her French counterpart at a play in Paris. Madame de Genlis, who looked after Pamela, had no difficulty in extricating her from Sheridan's offer, after which she accepted Lord Edward's proposal of marriage.[108] Even allowing for exaggeration of coincidence, a reader must be intrigued by the interweaving of love relationships, by the convention of love at first sight, and by the initial encounter of Lord Edward and Pamela's being almost on stage. Like Wolfe Tone, who adored the theater and once fell in love with an actress, Lord Edward was also an actor of sorts, on a national platform. Similarly, Leonard McNally, a leader of the United Irishmen and an informer, was a playwright. Richard Madden lists twelve plays authored by McNally between 1779 and 1796, and the night that Lord Edward was captured, Castle officials were attending one of McNally's comic operas at the Theatre Royal.[109]

Froude's history of this period in fact adopts as a leading trope that of the "yet uncompleted drama." He is capable of saying, to describe activities in the Irish Parliament, that "the plot was now rapidly thickened."[110] And he invests an important transaction, in which a major informer contacts Lord Downshire to offer his services, with all the cloaked mystery of Drury Lane. Responding to Froude and identifying the previously unknown informant, Fitzpatrick reveals rhetorically to what extent the Rising had always been conceived within a theatrical matrix. He says that Froude's "striking scenes, his dramatic situations, his fine painting and accessories, remind me of a stage where the movements of a few men convey the idea of an advancing 'army.'" He tells of the "Romance of Rebellion" and makes clear that Lord Edward was in many ways a performer in Parliament, "undistinguished by talent, but conspicuous for the violence of his language."[111] On at least one occasion, Lord Edward ventured into the streets of Dublin in disguise. According to Fitzpatrick, little did the aristocrat know that his steps would be dogged by the disguised visitor of Lord Downshire, who came to Downshire with his evidence in the dark of night. Further, he tells us that the informer Magan "acted his part so plausibly that on the very night Lord Edward lay a bleeding captive in Newgate, he was raised by the votes of United Irishmen to a still higher post in the organisation." Fitzpatrick informs the reader of his original intention to call his work "A Lanthorn through some Dark Passages, with a Key to Secret Chambers,"[112] and his sometimes overexcited rhetoric strengthens this connection to the melodramatic as a model for the scenes in the revolution. By the time that Dion Boucicault, Ireland's greatest writer in this genre, wrote *The Fireside Story of Ireland* (1881), it was perhaps unsurprising to readers of history that Boucicault divided the story into four sections—four acts, really—each with its own high conflicts and stylized denouements. What we find here are tableaux from Irish history, moments in themselves so hortatory that they need little or no language, merely histrionic gesture, to communicate the depth of injustices committed against the beleaguered heroine, Cathleen Ni Houlihan.

Such formal and literal allusions to the theater emphasize how natural it must have seemed to Whitbread to represent serious revolutionary activity in melodramatic terms.[113] The dialectic between limelight reality and daylight history produced changes in the dramatic forms themselves, but those forms also exercised power; they became the vehicles through which history made itself available to a mass audience. I am interested here in the issues foregrounded by the melodramatic, by the topical differences exhibited by the four representative plays in this volume because quite apart from treating the Rising in France and in Ireland, in the South and in the North, these works also targeted different issues of social importance during Whitbread's and Bourke's own time. This emphasis on historical symmetries makes the plays valuable as documents of their period, with specific messages to be read by an audience that was also caught up in revolutionary undertows, powerful forces that would result in both independence and national partition.

'98 IN POLITICAL MELODRAMA
Whitbread's *Lord Edward, Or '98*

In *Lord Edward*, for instance, the central question becomes not whether the hero will succeed or fail—a foregone conclusion—but the relationship between espionage and civil order. Whitbread signals this fact by noting on the typescript submitted to the Lord Chamberlain that the play is "Founded on the Revelations in W. J. Fitzpatrick's work 'Secret Service under Pitt.'" This play has not one but six villains, three of them soldiers doing their duty (Major Sirr,

Major Swan, and Captain Ryan), the other three informers whose motivation remains as unconvincing as Iago's (Francis Higgins, Francis Magan, and Samuel Turner). Appearing to have read Fitzpatrick's lengthy, detailed exposé in a state of high excitement, Whitbread sees himself, I think, as righting popular history. Specifically, he exonerates the long-suspected Neilson of wrongdoing against Lord Edward and makes evident Magan's and Turner's complicity with the governmental secret service.

Whitbread does so on the basis of Fitzpatrick's considerable research into the British secret service, and it seems likely that he wants his audience to take to heart in their own patriotic fashion the author's admonition about the lesson to be learned in his book: "The organisers of illegal societies will see that, in spite of the apparent secrecy and ingenuity of their system, informers sit with them at the same council-board and dinner-table, ready at any moment to sell their blood."[114] Although the English manager of the Queen's Theatre was certainly more concerned with revenues than with revolution, the message of *Lord Edward* could not fail to register with its Irish audience, especially when reinforced by countless details and ironies taken from real life. Fitzpatrick had taught Whitbread that Turner, who was in exile from Belfast because of his republican conspiring, went to Hamburg, where he lived in Lady Edward's home and acted as a political go-between in the communications between Paris and Ireland. Turner was a "barrister-at-law,"[115] who, like his colleague Magan, gave the legal profession a tenuous reputation among Irish patriots after the fiascos of 1798. It was Turner who visited Lord Downshire in London on a dark night in 1797 and offered his services as a spy. Because he was terrified of discovery by his United Irish colleagues, Turner's identity was protected by the English more lavishly than that of any other informer.[116]

Fittingly, Turner was spied upon by Francis Higgins, whom Fitzpatrick found an unusually able informer. It was Higgins, the owner of the *Freeman's Journal*, to whom the Castle paid £1,000 (plus an annual sum of £300) for betraying Lord Edward's hiding place in May 1798. Satirically nicknamed the "Shamado" by the journalist John Magee, Higgins acted as the conduit into Dublin Castle for information received from the lawyer Magan. In Whitbread's play, Magan, who lived near Moira House, where Lady Edward stayed when her husband was a fugitive,[117] emerges forcefully as a character and to some extent takes on the venomous traits of his fellow spies. He cites his love for Pamela as the reason for his extreme hatred of her husband. In real life, Magan did not conform to the melodramatic convention of loving the hero's wife,[118] but turned over his information to Higgins (who passed it on to Under-Secretary Edward Cooke and thence to Major Sirr) for reasons that remain unclear but were probably financial. The historical Magan, complexly introverted, also held the highest positions in the United Irishmen and served as legal counsel for members of that organization.[119]

Discussing the ins and outs of the Rising, some commentators have emphasized that owing to their detailed knowledge of United Irish activities, the English could readily have quelled the rebellion before blood was shed, but the English allowed these proceedings in order to secure their own eventual dominance in the 1800 union between the two countries; in addition, the government had good reason to desire indigenous uprising before French troops arrived. Hence espionage served the ends of state in more than one way as the English manipulated Irish actions. In Whitbread's play, spying prevails as the most popular pastime for nonrevolutionaries. From the first scene, we find rebels and counterrevolutionaries conversing, and we discover the difficulties of identifying the opposition, of penetrating their act. Banter, courtesy, outrage—all may hide evil designs. And rapid shifts in tone enhance this phenomenon. For example, in the initial scene, Lord Edward, who is courting Pamela, finds himself chastised by the French General Lemoines for wearing an English officer's uniform. When Lord Edward, in some distress, acknowledges that Lemoines is right, the infamous Turner is at his elbow to say, "Then why not act upon it." No sooner does Turner exit with an aside to the effect that Lord Edward is a "prize" waiting to be "plucked," than Magan enters. His dialogues with Neilson and Turner deftly demonstrate how the conversation of these United Irishmen operated on several levels and concealed multiple ironies—one spy recognizing another, another passing unknown. France emerges in Act I as an alien ground in which spies and patriots, English, French, and Irish, all interact while pursuing private agenda. But Act II, which takes place in Leinster House, Lord Edward's Dublin home, poses equal risks to heroism and sanity. Ironically, Magan reminds the candid and enthusiastic Lord Edward that "walls have ears." Throughout, Pamela is far more sensitive to the atmospheric duplicity than anyone else is; she tells her husband, "The horrible uncertainty of not knowing friend from foe, that is sapping my life away."

Whatever the motivations of these men—ambition, fear, love, or money—the narrative of their machinations creates an atmosphere of intense anxiety; the world that they sustained reeled with dangers. And Whitbread admirably reproduces that threatening intensity in his play, in a melodrama that reads like what we know of the life endured by Irish patriots in 1798. So it is that when playgoers familiar with Whitbread's play saw it advertised in the streets of Dublin by way of David Allen's full-color painting (plate 7), the pictorial alone signified a social experience and worldview still highly relevant in the days of labor union organization, of women's suffrage, of Home Rule agitation, and of political networking before the Easter Rising.

Whitbread's *Wolfe Tone*

Whitbread capitalized on the popularity of his celebrated *Lord Edward* when, a few years later, he composed *Wolfe Tone*. There, too, Whitbread's principal vision of Irish society—as baroquely spy-ridden and inwardly undermined—surfaced. The problem with that vision, however, is that it requires a good deal more in the way of evil machinations—of historically verifiable melodramatic complications—than Tone's story offers. It was Tone's distance from that scene of anxiogenic, rapid change and uncertainty that created many of his problems in negotiations with the French. As noted above, Tone unknowingly misconstrued events in Ireland once he went into exile. In counterpoint to the totalizing rhetoric of the United Irish cause stood an Irish class structure tormented by religious conflict, the fragmentation and utter inadequacy of the radicals' communications system within and outside of Ireland, the relative poverty of the country, and the superior strength of both the English military and the English intelligence network. Various empowering myths transcended these discordant realities at pivotal moments, but messy actuality constantly intervened to make affiliation, negotiation, and invasion incredibly complex undertakings. In Ireland itself, the multiplicity of parallel risings provided more than the usual opportunities for espionage; there were many hallways for spies to sleuth in. The continent was also infested with informers like Turner, but their actions did not cause events to pendulum dramatically in a nation coming increasingly under the stern control of Bonaparte. For these reasons, Whitbread modeled Tone's story on *Lord Edward* but had to introduce extraneous elements that would communicate the same feelings of urgency and excitement on alien soil.

Wolfe Tone opens with the prelude to the Tones' elopement. Still a student at Trinity, the impoverished Tone is courting Miss

Plate 7. Pictorial advertisement for J. W. Whitbread's *Lord Edward, or '98* (1894). The *Saturday Herald* for 17 March 1894 reported in its review of the play, "The wall advertisements of the new play—13½ by 8 feet—shows [*sic*] that in Ireland as good work of this class can be performed as in any part of the United Kingdom. The figures and accessories have been splendidly drawn by Walter Mills, and the poster, full of life, colour, and action, has been lithographed beautifully by Allen, of Belfast. Nothing better or more artistic has ever been posted in the city of Dublin" (p. 5). This drawing was prepared in the theater from a scene in the Whitbread play. Although these ads appeared all over town, the only known copy of this picture hangs in the Lord Edward Restaurant opposite Christ Church Cathedral in Dublin. Print courtesy of Pat Johnston, Curator, Dublin Civic Museum.

Witherington, whose name has been changed from the historical Matilda to the more mellifluous Susan. Charmingly, when considered in terms of melodramatic conventions, Turner has become a rejected suitor for Susan's hand. With a presumably fictitious and equally unethical cohort, Joey Rafferty, Turner the spy attempts from this point on to thwart all of Tone's actions; he and Rafferty absurdly invade the grandparental garden during the Tones' nuptial celebration; later, Turner continues his gratuitous plotting against her happiness. By Act II, some years after the marriage, Turner has been reinstated as a respected friend and a United Irishman, and he appears at the Tones' home with McNally, the notorious informer.

Turner and Rafferty follow Tone to France, where they interact with Bonaparte much as does the United Irishmen's legitimate ambassador. Apocryphal as it is, this paralleling of action admirably communicates the fact that Tone's mission did not insulate him from the suspicions of the French Directory; he had to demonstrate his patriotism before receiving their approval. The ending to *Wolfe Tone,* which draws together these various strands, is pure fantasy shaped by melodramatic expectations. In fact, the play demands a climax, and Tone's demise could hardly be seen as that, nor was his death a direct result of espionage and betrayal. To maintain his dramatic vision of Ireland in 1798, then, Whitbread assigns an appropriate end to his fabricated informer, Rafferty, preserving the historical Turner for further evil endeavors in the real world. Tone's final words, which condemn traitors, fall in line with Whitbread's coherent focus on the perils of information flow.

While blockage, leakage, and betrayal characterize much of the historical interpretation offered by Whitbread, P. J. Bourke portrays a world in which the stakes are just as high but in which the principal players are neither aristocrats nor barrister-statesmen but folk more humbly placed in the social hierarchy. Whitbread does give us glimpses of working-class life; in each of the plays printed in this edition, his "high" couple is balanced, Shakespeareanly, by a "low" couple. For instance, in *Wolfe Tone,* the stage Irishman Shane McMahon exists, like his theatrical forebears Conn the Shaughraun and Danny Mann (in *The Colleen Bawn*), to be of service to the hero. When Tone the Trinity student lacks money to marry his Susan, Shane comes up with the required amount, telling his own Peggy, "There's a dale ov pleasure in lendin' muney to a gintleman." Throughout the work, Shane, the real hero of the piece, stands ever ready to bail the Tones out of awkward fiscal situations. Especially in exile, Shane represents the idealized people of Ireland; funding the exploits of the "genteels," rich in generosity and, surprisingly, possessed of more than a sufficiency, they redress the wrongs committed by informers like Turner, who are motivated by varieties of lust, greed, and envy.

Bourke's *When Wexford Rose*

This positioning of class relations has a great deal more to do with melodramatic tradition than with Ireland in the era of the Queen's Theatre, and by Bourke's time, such sentimentalizing of the

For THE DEFENCE of IRELAND FUND

ABBEY THEATRE,

Monday Next, November 15th, at 8 p.m.,

And during the Week. Matinee Saturday, 2.30.

Mr. P. J. Bourke's No. 1 Company of Irish Players, presents for the first time on any stage the entirely new Irish Historical Drama of Antrim and Down in '98.

"FOR THE LAND SHE LOVED."

By P. J. Bourke.

Early doors at 7 o'clock. Late doors 7.30.

Stalls 3/- ; Balcony 1/6 ; Pit 1/- and 6d.

Plate 8. Advertisement for Bourke's *For the Land She Loved*, placed in *The Workers' Republic* (1915). Courtesy of Séamus de Búrca.

class system was highly anachronistic. Coincident with the social valuing of the fashionable and the rich was the emerging visibility of appalling poverty, especially in Dublin. By 1913 the overcrowded tenements, the inadequate clothing and nutrition, and the unemployment and despair that marked the lives of one out of four Dublin residents produced, with the aid of labor leaders like James Larkin and James Connolly, a strike and lockout involving the Irish Transport and General Workers Union (ITGWU). From this dispute with employers and the resultant threats to laborers in Ireland grew the Irish Citizen Army.[120] By 1911 the *Irish Worker*, "the first successful Labour publication" and the Larkin-edited voice of the ITGWU,[121] had appeared to add its accents to the increasingly audible labor agitation. *When Wexford Rose*, Bourke's fourth play, debuted in 1910, in the midst of this enhanced attention to the labor movement, and *For the Land She Loved* was advertised in 1915 in another labor organ, *The Workers' Republic*, edited by James Connolly (plate 8). In focusing on local instead of national heroes, Bourke achieved a shift in emphasis from the truly or metaphorically aristocratic to the position normally occupied by the stage Irishman. But in Bourke's hands that position was opened up to more realistic treatment, and the ordinary worker-as-hero found her or his place on the Queen's stage. Recall, too, that the prelude to 1798 included economic distress throughout Ireland, a situation echoed in early modern Dublin and undoubtedly seen by Bourke as a prerevolutionary sign being repeated.

On the local scene, not only is the informer in *When Wexford Rose* not a barrister but a crone called Croppy Biddy, but also the nongenteel characters emerge in strong outline and are capable of independent thought and action. In particular, Mary Doyle and Kitty Cassidy, designated by the English Colonel Needham as the "Rebel hussies," take their part in the Rising and refuse to be intimidated by the soldiers. Father John Murphy, a relatively inconspicuous hero in this play, gathers his flock, advises them to take up arms, and unceremoniously begins to defeat the North Cork Militia. No great stir is made when Kitty goes to war; the Widow Gallagher comments, "It's a quare idea she has now goin round fightin like a man." (Later, she admits, "I'm sorry I'm not a bit younger meself.") And as Donal Byrne[122] recites the story of Ross, it becomes clear that the "mass of men" rather than individual heroes had carried the day before the trained soldiers defeated them. Mary Doyle proves herself a good warrior, but no single character bears, like Lord Edward or Wolfe Tone, the ethos of the Rising. Despite acts of bravery, we can see the justice, when a French officer arrives in Wexford, of his observation, "And there you have the weak spot in your movement. The mob is willing, but organising ability is wofully lacking." In Bourke's plays, the conventions appear in lowercase, approximating a realism in the treatment of 1798 that was to develop later in, for instance, Christine Longford's *United Brothers* (1942).

But it must be emphasized that while political melodramas modulated toward realism, real life once again veered toward the theatrically heroic. Amid the alarms of the Great War, we find Dublin Castle's secret service network monitoring the sermons of local clerics and discovering that some viewed England's difficulty as Ireland's opportunity for freedom. For example, in Wexford in 1915 the Reverend Albert Lennon, C.C., told his flock "not to leave their places if the Germans came, that the Germans were not as bad as they were painted." Several priests told their congregations to join the Irish volunteers and to arm themselves instead of accepting conscription; one told his parishioners to do so "even if the only arms they could get was a two-pronged fork."[123]

So it is that, just as the United Irishmen waited for French ships to arrive in Ireland, so some Irish eyes were turned, in 1914, out to sea in the hopes that German submarines might arrive with arms and men. The famous incidents surrounding Sir Roger Casement's gunrunning efforts highlight this parallel with 1798 in eerie ways. In April 1916, Casement, a difficult man but also a patriot who had secured from the German government "a statement of German support and friendship for the cause of Irish independence"[124] along with more tangible aid, was arrested in the west of Ireland near Tralee Bay after having been put ashore by a German submarine. As Dorothy Macardle tells it, those arresting Casement "seemed to have no suspicion as to who their prisoner was";[125] like Tone a century earlier, he went unrecognized at first. Like Tone, Casement was accompanying a foreign invader's gift of arms; a German vessel called the *Aud* had on board "arms for a rising" but was self-defensively sunk by its crew after being captured near Kerry by the English.[126] The parallels with 1798 continue, right up to the expectation among Irish revolutionaries that Casement was to be in Dublin for the Rising. As with the ill-fated events in Killala Bay, the abortive Casement invasion might have mobilized the west and promoted the chances for a widespread revolt. Internal organization for the Easter Rising was too complex to be addressed here, but it is important to note that republican actions both mirrored 1798 behavior and conformed to melodramatic priming.

Bourke's *For the Land She Loved*

In modern Irish history, not only do such symmetries and repetitions abound, but some figures take on central importance because of their participation in the various causes loosely aligned around the time of Bourke's writing and acting. One thinks of the Countess Markiewicz,[127] who not only acted in plays at the Abbey but also joined the Irish Citizen Army, supported the labor movement, epitomized one style of Irish feminism, and took part in the

Easter Rising. Another such figure is Peadar Kearney, who worked with both the Abbey and Queen's, who wrote the Irish national anthem, who stood his ground in an embattled factory on Easter of 1916, and who was the brother-in-law of P. J. Bourke. These complex interrelations support the assertion that in Ireland art always influences life and help to explain the fact that Bourke produced plays ideologically in tune with both labor interests and feminism. In *For the Land She Loved* (a play that, in addition to being advertised in Connolly's paper, was also a benefit for "The Defence of Ireland Fund"), the playwright introduces all three radical agenda—nationalism, labor power, and feminism.

Bourke begins the play with a scene that echoes parts of Kearney's 1907 *Wolfe Tone*. Gathered at Matt McGrath's forge in Ballynahinch, blacksmiths chorus their pleasure that "now is our time to make the blades / That sets [*sic*] Ould Ireland free." Apart from the initial focus on actual work, this opening emphasizes the material production that sustained the several risings. Every writer on 1798 finds reason to mention the Irish pike, pounded out and hoarded in great quantities all over Ireland before the events in question (plate 3 pictures some pikes). This instrument has a ferocious reputation among its makers; Lecky, writing mostly to a non-Irish audience, feels compelled to emphasize that although Father John Murphy had untrained troops, he could rely on the fact that "even the most unpractised found the pike a weapon of terrible effect. No other weapon, indeed, employed by the rebels, was so dreaded by the soldiers, especially by the cavalry; no other weapon inflicted such terrible wounds, or proved at close quarters so formidable."[128] Kilmainham Prison, now a nationalist museum in Dublin, includes in its collection several pike heads, which merge the features of a bayonet and an axe. Lord Edward's written plans for taking Dublin stated precisely the length of pike to be placed at the front line, and blacksmiths were prime targets for military questioning, a fact emphasized in plays and narratives of 1798. Bourke's blacksmith, Matt, is proud of his work, knows his value to the movement, and constructs the immediate future optimistically. His companion, Shamus, although a patriot, stands cynically apart from Matt's enthusiasm, asserting that speech making serves the ends of parliamentary orators but not the rank and file: "we still have to work. We are still the blacksmiths makin' pikes an' horseshoes, an' anthin' else that comes along. It's hard enough for poor men to live without goin' out to fight with the French that has no soul or no God; think o' that now."

Most of the play deals with circumstances surrounding the battle at Ballynahinch, from which even Shamus returns elated. He and Matt praise Betsy Gray for her soldiering and bravery, and indeed, Gray provides one of the most interesting female portraits in the genre of political melodrama. To provide balance in the play, her strength finds an appropriate archenmity in Lady Nugent. The daughter of the infamous Colonel Nugent, Lady Nugent is presented as beloved of George Gray until she fell in love with Munro. Traditionally in melodrama, the woman is the pawn, the cipher for an estate to be "married" or the price to be paid for extrication from bankruptcy. Here, the women decide to go into battle or to work out their own amorous destinies, a movement that neatly intertwines courtship and country.

Certainly, in this play, as in *When Wexford Rose*, the women get the best parts and bear most of the ideological burden. In *Wexford*, for example, even the repulsive Biddy's role is altogether more engaging than those filled by the British officers. Biddy's unexpected force has a dramatic consequence, too, in calling forth a convincing portrait of the fighting clergy. Balancing the evil committed by the informer and her merely tolerant employers in the British army is the figure of Father John Murphy, whose martyrdom is reported by Bourke. This balance is enhanced by the fact that the priest specifically discusses his abnegation of a peaceful message for the active pursuit of freedom. His unconventional, although not singular, behavior, which made him the hero of Allen's melodrama, is in Bourke's hands a version of the role reversal played out by the heroic women of the play. It comes as no surprise, then, when the final scene of *When Wexford Rose* is turned over to Biddy and Grace Doyle. Grace speaks words of comfort and courage and rejects the nefarious Needham's plea for mercy, much as Donal refuses Biddy's request to be spared. Like male informers, she is punished by death.

To return to *For the Land She Loved*, it is likely that to appreciate Betsy Gray's strengths, we must compare her posture with that of Boucicault's "colleen bawn," for like all political melodramas of the period, Bourke's work recodes its precursors for some of its burden of meaning. Almost everyone familiar with English drama knows in some form the story of Boucicault's play. Like its American and English counterparts, it has at core a dispute over a mortgage. Both Hardress Cregan and his mother find themselves in maritally awkward situations because one of them has to marry for money. By the end of the generic English melodrama, such things are sorted out by the defeat of the villain and the hero or heroine's coincidental discovery of a source of financial security that does not demand the loss of romantic bliss. *The Colleen Bawn* follows this pattern, and everyone marries the mate revealed by the drama as socially appropriate. Eily's fondest wish, that she be accepted by Hardress's mother and aristocratic friends, is fulfilled. Any political subtext set up by the dispute over who owns the Cregan estate is either put to rest by the ending or shunted into discussion over whether or not it is all right to speak with a brogue.

It is worth noting here that the British Library manuscript collection includes a version by Henry Young of the Boucicault play, a takeoff first produced in 1861, the year after *The Colleen Bawn* hit the boards. This pirated version emphasizes the perception of this Irish context by a presumably English or Anglophile (or markedly inattentive) author. Young's *Bride of Garyowen,* which first played in Staffordshire (according to the Lord Chamberlain's stamp of approval), has the same cast of characters as does Boucicault's drama, but they are curiously sea-changed, to the extent that the language issue has been left out. In the final scene, Eily says nothing more than the name "Hardress." Given that Young represents himself on the manuscript as the author of *Uncle Tom's Cabin,* perhaps it would be too much to hope for more than a hack rendition of the main action line. But I think that this pirated version highlights what melodrama legitimately involved for an English audience and signals differences from the Irish plays that writers after Boucicault made more emphatic.

Another play worth adducing here is Yeats's *Cathleen Ni Houlihan* (1902), in many ways a bizarre work, which begins with the marital preparations that typically marked closure in English melodramas. Like *The Colleen Bawn, Cathleen* takes place in the late 1790s as preparations for battle were in process. The Old Woman, whose transformation depends on the *non*-marriage of men like Michael, becomes a queenly Colleen Bawn who explicitly directs attention to her identity with the land. I think that for an audience fed from childhood on imported plays and partially weaned from English pap on Boucicault, Yeats's gestures of disavowal and commitment must have taken on a heightened theatrical meaning beyond what we can imagine. The melodrama is there, only fractured; Yeats's colleen is stridently not Boucicault's. Bourke's *For the Land She Loved,* although clearly able to stand on its own, shimmers when we attend to this dramatic lineage.

Even without this theatrical ancestry, however, Bourke would have had ample materials for the development of his strong female characters. The social history and cultural traditions he had at his disposal find summary statement in Bonnie Kime Scott's *Joyce and Feminism*. Scott sketches the history of Irish feminism and brings her synopsis into alignment with the varying status of Irish women over time from early mythic representations through twentieth-century realities. She writes, "In the Celtic [era] . . . of Ireland, women enjoyed considerable power,"[129] and she implies a continuity among the strong women of *The Táin*, the stone-carved Sheela-na-gig figures that occur throughout the Irish countryside, and the power exerted by modern women such as Maud Gonne, Constance Markiewicz, and Hanna Sheehy-Skeffington. These aesthetic and historical precedents help to position the stylized women of Irish political melodrama. Of course, Boucicault, less radical and much earlier than Bourke, sometimes assigned women more than passive roles,[130] and Bourke may be viewed as following and extending Boucicault in allowing many of his women heroic status. But we would be mistaken in looking only to an immediate theatrical influence as the model for Bourke's fighting females; we need instead to recognize the sense in which Irish melodrama adumbrated both contemporary feminist politics and roles comfortably native to Celtic aesthetic tradition.

We can be quite specific about the feminist politics during the period in which Bourke was writing. As Dermot Keogh represents the era, Maud Gonne founded the women's social work organization Inghinidhe na hEireann in 1903; Hanna Sheehy-Skeffington headed the suffragette movement in Dublin during this time; and James Larkin's sister Delia joined him in Dublin in 1911 to set up the Irish Women's Workers' Union.[131] Margaret MacCurtain's discussion of the suffrage movement in Ireland provides more detail and a broader sense of the radical movements dovetailing with Irish feminism. She notes the militance of the Irish Women's Franchise League (IWFL), which Sheehy-Skeffington and Margaret Cousins founded in 1908, a group that "from its inception harried the Irish Parliamentary Party on the injustice of excluding women from the Home Rule Bill." In 1912 and continuing until 1920, the newspaper called *The Irish Citizen* brought together suffragist sympathies and "the growing awareness of war, strikes and eventually revolution."[132] And 1910 brought to Dublin the speaker Christabel Pankhurst and the first arrests of suffragists. The movement even invaded the theater; in addition to topical references to suffragism in the 1912 Queen's Theatre pantomime, we find that the feminist Francis Sheehy-Skeffington, "who had been banned from entry to the Theatre Royal," nonetheless put on a clerical costume, became part of the crowd gathered there to hear the English prime minister, and was "heckling" him about universal suffrage before being thrown out. Throughout 1912 increasingly militant agitation continued, with arrested individuals going on hunger strike for the vote. By 1913 the lockout had enhanced the importance of James Connolly's recent appearance on an IWFL platform, a moment marvelously bringing into one constellation the efforts for emancipation at the level of gender, class, and nationality.

So it is that Betsy Gray's stage story echoes the context for women outside the theater and more aggressively than the English women's plays produced in wartime Ireland. Like the militant Old Woman of Yeats's play, Betsy is a serious nationalist. Her patriotic fervor is complicated by the obligatory love triangle of non-Irish melodrama, but this aspect of the play is far less important than the political energy of her actions. Gray's much-contested union with Munro represents in two-dimensional fashion the efforts of Irish patriots to achieve the unity required for successful historical intervention. Colonel Johnston's desire to acquire her must be read not only on the personal level but also as the wished-for difficulty of England to contain its Celtic colony. Gray herself quickly takes on emblematic status. She becomes a force akin to Delacroix's *Liberty Leading the People,* rifle and flag in hand as she vanguards for the insurrectionaries. She is an icon for the contested space of Ireland, to the extent that the final scene ends with her death by sword—by two swords, really. When she tries to save her lover during a duel, she is literally skewered from the one side by an English colonel and from the other by her United Irish fiancé. She falls dead, a victim not of romance but of international discord. It is against the grain of such dramatic conflations of love and patriotism that we must measure stage deaths like that of Minnie in O'Casey's canonical play *The Shadow of a Gunman*. In the case of Bourke's offering, as noted above, the chief secretary of Ireland was troubled enough about Gray's dramatic fate to label the play a "piece of sedition."[133]

Whereas the message of *When Wexford Rose*—in contrast to the received romantic ideology of English melodrama—is that even a woman can defeat a British soldier, Gray's story suggests the more complex vision that all worthwhile love is a version of patriotism, that within the purview of history, psychological and emotional states like desire and hatred are surrogates for social forces like insurrection and oppression. Bourke's implicit demand of his contemporary audience at the Queen's or in the "smalls" through which he toured was that if the appropriate situation presented itself, they should perform the heroisms depicted. But even more important was his affirming the power of the ordinary person to change history and of the ordinary melodramatic heroine to align with Celtic myth and Irish culture. The plays were less propaganda than they were arguments that political change was possible and that this change could be initiated and sustained by the masses. That female characters are the principal vehicles for this argument suggests that the manipulation of cultural (and especially theatrical) stereotypes, what Umberto Eco might label the breaking of codes, in itself can generate some of the energy that refigures cultural attitudes and fuels sociopolitical change. In this Irish shaping of melodrama, the generic determinants are the resistance to closure within the play and the production of real-world energies. If 1798 proved not to be the moment, then the moment waited somewhere in the future.

Many critics would agree that one defining characteristic of melodrama in general is that it "deals with an action that is [only] temporarily serious."[134] The plays represented in this volume break with this characteristic and thus produce a remapping of the melodramatic ground in terms that are situational, significant, colonial, and long-term. In this regard Irish political melodrama as a genre deserves comparison less with English productions than with plays produced under colonial rule in India and Africa. Although a comparative analysis is well beyond the scope of this essay, Homi Babha's "The Other Question—the Stereotype and Colonial Discourse" points toward a key issue. Babha argues that within imperialistic governments, colonial discourse is "an apparatus of power . . . an apparatus that turns on the recognition and disavowal of racial/cultural/historical differences. Its predominant strategic function is the creation of a space for a 'subject peoples' through the production of knowledges in terms of which surveillance is exercised and a complex form of pleasure/unpleasure is incited. It seeks authorization for its strategies by the production of knowledges by coloniser and colonised which are stereotypical but antithetically evaluated."[135] Localizing Babha's global observation, I would say that Irish playwrights made use of a theatrical discourse that was, for all intents and purposes, imposed, alien, a colonializing of popular consciousness. A writer like Bourke placed within his world a heroine who had all of the stereotypical virtues of an English melodramatic woman but whose added differences made her into another kind of icon, one whose ideological force was to resist the colonization of consciousness. *For the Land She Loved*, like its companion plays *Wolfe*

Tone and *Lord Edward*, uses the 1798 theme of putatively failed revolution to reinvent the melodrama as resistance to the apparatus Babha describes. Specific historical defeats were turned into a complex form of theatrical and ideological pleasure that short-circuited the connection between fact and possibility. The dialectic between linear history, in which the risings were at some level unsuccessful, and theatrical space, in which the 1798 setting signifies the energies of revolution, charts an effort to neutralize historical fact. And this reformulation is a primary defining feature of Irish political melodrama. The genre showcases the revolutionary moment as the one that counts.

From these plays to a major contemporary Irish work like Brian Friel's *Translations* is a logical transition;[136] like Whitbread and Bourke, Friel also explores the reinvention of what historians have labeled "failure." Seamus Deane looks in the direction of this comparison when he says of Friel's drama, "Paradoxically, although his theme is failure . . . the fact that the play has been written is itself an indication of the success of the imagination in dealing with everything that seems opposed to its survival." Deane concludes, "No Irish writer since the early days of this century has so sternly and courageously asserted the role of art in the public world without either yielding to that world's pressures or retreating into art's narcissistic alternatives."[137] I agree, but I question language like "the success of the imagination," which threatens to move Friel's achievement into the never-never land of the so-called universal values that the study of English culture has traditionally been reputed to acquaint us with and that my graduate students from India and Africa so strenuously object to as neither universal nor especially specific to the experience of colonial writers. Such artists are more likely to aim for refiguring the historical past and, as Fanon indicates, for reenvisioning the material future than to be content with successes limited to the imagination.

Given the tortured context of Northern Ireland today, I find it useful to consider the links between Hugh's wonderful speech about the rising in *Translations* and the plays that in their own way produced the recodings that characterize Friel's work on the stage and in the politicized field of his society. Hugh insists that his son Owen recognize that "it is not the literal past, the 'facts' of history, that shape us, but images of the past embodied in language." He goes on to note that "we must never cease renewing those images"; and then he says to the sleeping Jimmy, "The road to Sligo. A spring morning. 1798, Going into battle. Do you remember, James? Two young gallants with pikes across their shoulders and the *Aeneid* in their pockets. . . . We were gods that morning, James. . . . By God, sir, we were magnificent. We marched as far as—where was it?—Glenties! All of twenty-three miles in one day. And it was there, in Phelan's pub, that we got homesick for Athens, just like Ulysses. The *desiderium nostrorum*—the need for our own. Our *pietas*, James, was for older, quieter things."[138] What Hugh describes is the situation of Irish political melodrama, a genre that altered its foreign sources to renew itself in terms of local settings, a genre that resisted the inscribed facts of history and thus not only produced some powerful theatrical offspring but also stirred up national feeling throughout Ireland, creating a different kind of revolutionary activity in 1916 and for many years after.

NOTES TO PART ONE

1. Frantz Fanon, *The Wretched of the Earth* (New York: Grove Press, 1966), 187.

2. In *The Heart Grown Brutal* Peter Costello argues "that the cultural revival made possible the political revolution by creating a new ideal of Ireland, and that the literature of the revival provides what might almost be called 'the secret history' of the Irish revolution" (Dublin: Gill and Macmillan, 1977), xi. I would add that the plays represented in this edition must be acknowledged as powerful components in the ideological reorientations Costello charts.

3. This problem posed itself forcefully while I was conducting research for my study, *Joyce's Anatomy of Culture* (Urbana: Univ. of Illinois, 1986), which includes a bibliography for the study of popular culture in Ireland. In searching for Irish melodramas, I went through several channels. I talked with people associated with principal theaters in Dublin; I placed a classified ad in the *Irish Times* in which I requested information on Irish melodramas produced between 1880 and 1930; I checked pertinent library collections in Ireland, the United States, and England. Allardyce Nicoll's *History of English Drama* catalogs manuscripts submitted to the Lord Chamberlain; Nicoll lists plays by writers such as Whitbread, O'Grady, and Fred Cooke. O'Grady, in particular, has received some much needed attention recently; Stephen Watt has edited O'Grady's *Emigration* (1880) and *The Famine* for the *Journal of Irish Literature* 14 (January 1985).

4. The obituary for Whitbread printed in *The Era* cites his death date as 9 June 1916. Stephen Watt pointed out to me that Whitbread retired to Scarborough, England, the place of his wife's birth. Watt maintains that Whitbread began his management of the Queen's in 1884 ("Boucicault and Whitbread: The Dublin Stage at the End of the Nineteenth Century," *Éire-Ireland* 18 [Fall 1983]: 24). For my purposes, the Queen's Royal Theatre began operation in 1844 rather than in 1829; see John McCormick, "Origins of Melodrama," *Prompts* 6 (September 1983): 5.

5. Séamus de Búrca, *The Queen's Royal Theatre Dublin, 1829–1969* (Dublin: de Búrca, 1983), 18, 3.

6. This list of Whitbread's plays derives from de Búrca (*Queen's Royal Theatre*) and was checked against the list prepared by Joseph Holloway for Stephen J. M. Brown's *Guide to Books on Ireland* (1912; New York: Lemma, 1970). The only addition is *Shadowed*, cited in an 1899 advertisement in *The Era*. Watt has also located a Whitbread play called *The Soldier Priest* (1915). Of these plays, only *Sarsfield* has been pub-

lished in a modern edition (Dublin: Séamus de Búrca, 1987). *The Nationalist* and *Shoulder to Shoulder* appeared in contemporary printings. The Raymond Mander and Joe Mitchenson Theatre Collection in London owns some of the Whitbread papers. These include a printed pantomime (*Dick Whittington*) produced at the Queen's by Joseph Eldred assisted by Whitbread and Augustus Wheatman (1882–83); an "operatic burlesque" called *Miss Maritana; or, 'Not for Jo!—See?'* (1890) by George Nugent and Whitbread; a printed version of *The Nationalist* (1892); a printed version of *Shoulder to Shoulder* (1888); and manuscripts of some stories and of a play called *Pat*. There is also a story by Frank Fairfield, which Colin Mabberley suggested to me may be a pseudonym for Whitbread. The cover of *Shoulder to Shoulder* identifies Whitbread as the author of "Race of Life," "The Foster Brothers," "Staunch and True," and other works. This denomination suggests that Whitbread had an alternate career as a writer of fiction or non-Irish plays and that we have not yet pinpointed the pen names under which he pursued this career. Whitbread did submit the printed *Nationalist* to the Lord Chamberlain, and if we were to assume that he would have done so whenever a work had been published, we could conclude that plays occurring in the British Library in typescript, such as *Wolfe Tone* and *Lord Edward*, probably were withheld from publication to guard against pirating and illegal production.

7. In the memoir of English theater called *Fifty Years of a Londoner's Life* (New York: Dodd, Mead, 1916), H. G. Hibbert speaks of a burlesque of melodrama called *Arrah! No Brogue*, a titular response to Boucicault's famous *Arrah-na-Pogue*. A manuscript of the burlesque is in the Lord Chamberlain's collection in the British Museum. Whitbread did cut down significantly on the "begorra" aspect of Irish melodrama.

8. Joseph Holloway, "Impressions of a Dublin Playgoer," National Library of Ireland MS. 4452 (ii), 18. Quotations above from the *Evening Herald*, 27 March 1894, are from p. 2.

9. Joseph Holloway, *The Irish Playgoer*, 19 April 1900. Originally, this article was an entry in Holloway's diary, National Library of Ireland MS. 1796 (ii), 674–75, 678. Quotations above from the *Irish Times*, 20 April 1897, are found on p. 2 and from the *Evening Herald*, 26 December 1898, on p. 3.

10. *Evening Herald*, 27 December 1898, pp. 2, 3.

11. Joseph Holloway, "Queen's Theatre Dublin, List of Plays, 1898–1928," National Library of Ireland MS. 12074.

12. Séamus de Búrca, interview in *Journal of Irish Literature* 13 (January-May 1984): 3.

13. Robert Hogan and Richard Burnham, *The Art of the Amateur 1916–1920* (Dublin: Dolmen, 1984), 53.

14. For discussion of the mechanisms of self-censorship in Irish popular journalism, theater, and theology, see Herr, *Joyce's Anatomy of Culture*, 33–66.

15. Hogan and Burnham, 69–70.

16. Quoted in de Búrca, *Queen's Royal Theatre*, viii.

17. Quoted in Des Hickey and Gus Smith, *A Paler Shade of Green* (London: Leslie Frewin, 1972), 22–25, 28.

18. Peter Kavanagh, *The Irish Theatre* (Tralee: Kerryman, 1946), 401, 406.

19. See *Prompts* 6 (September 1983): 3, 17, 21, 38, 40–47. Richard Pine's comments bear quoting: "This has been a cursory look at some figures, principally Friel and Potter, whose contribution to the modern Irish stage has highlighted the contri-

bution of melodrama to the modern world, and, perhaps, to the solution of some of its problems. I have not attended to the works of Manning, Colum, Shiels, Robinson, the Longfords, O'Kelly, Flann O'Brien, Conor Cruise O'Brien, Behan, Bryan MacMahon, all of whom have used melodrama to some extent. I have not asked whether the works of Hugh Leonard, Thomas Murphy, or Heno Magee, Bernard Farrell or J. Graham Reid, have melodramatic content, awareness or relevance. . . . I should perhaps have discussed *The Shewing Up of Blanco Posnet* and *Heartbreak House, Sharon's Grave, Living Quarters, The Bishop's Bonfire, The Star Turns Red* . . . but perhaps what I have said has been disturbing and intensive enough" ("After Boucicault: Melodrama and the Modern Irish Stage," *Prompts* 6 [September 1983]: 48). To Pine's evocative list, I would add the fiction of James Joyce and would emphasize the poetry of W. B. Yeats (whom Pine mentions), both of which are permeated by the postures, attitudes, and demands of native melodrama. Compare Watt, "Boucicault and Whitbread," 23–24, especially n.2; like Watt's dissertation, this article argues for the role of Irish popular tradition in producing the work of Yeats, Shaw, Synge, and O'Casey.

20. Watt, "Boucicault and Whitbread," 23–24, 27, 32, 36–38, 44–45, 50–52.

21. Even Pine, who eloquently defends Boucicault, undervalues Boucicault's heirs. When he discusses the Abbey Theatre companies, he contrasts their work with "the more vulgar manifestations of melodrama. In 1909 the Queen's was staging *The 10.30 Down Express*, and Ira Allen's and P. J. Bourke's companies continued to maintain the melodrama 'tradition' both on tour and in the capital, e.g. *In Dark '98* presented by Bourke at the Queen's in 1913" ("After Boucicault," 40). Given that the Bourke play mentioned has to my knowledge been lost and that until 1984 none of Bourke's original work was in print, Pine's implied assessment of Bourke appears to lack support. In any case, Bourke's plays are ideologically very different from *The 10.30 Down Express*, a sensationally popular English melodrama.

22. Watt (in "Boucicault and Whitbread") charts the fact that Boucicault's early work conforms to a typical melodramatic pattern, with only the later material taking on the tones of despair and political outrage that mark Boucicault's *Fireside Story of Ireland* (1881).

23. De Búrca, *Queen's Royal Theatre*, 4–5.

24. *Evening Herald*, 5 March 1912, p. 5.

25. Joseph Holloway, National Library of Ireland MS. 1813 (i), 281–843.

26. Joseph Holloway, National Library of Ireland MS. 1823 (18 November 1915), 961.

27. Holloway, National Library of Ireland MS. 1823 (19 November 1915), 920–21.

28. *Evening Herald*, 12 September 1916, p. 4.

29. *Evening Telegraph*, 27 April 1920, p. 3.

30. For a useful discussion of the ritual value of rehearsing violence and sacrifice onstage, see Mary K. Dahl, *Political Violence in Drama: Classical Models, Contemporary Variations* (Ann Arbor: UMI Research Press, 1986). Obviously, because the stories in these plays were known by heart, often line-by-line, these plays extended a different social and epistemological function than, say, a mystery novel would. They enacted ritual reinforcement of the social structure and enhanced cultural cohesion in Ireland.

31. Joseph Holloway, National Library of Ireland MS. 1803 (i; 24 April 1905), 214.

32. "W. MacA.," *Irish Playgoer* (19 April 1900): 6.

33. W. E. H. Lecky, *A History of Ireland in the Eighteenth Century*, abr. and ed. L. P. Curtis, Jr. (Chicago: Univ. of Chicago Press, 1972), 295.

34. Compare Richard Pine's comment in "After Boucicault," 45. Discussing Brian Friel's *Translations* and its debt to melodrama, Pine says, "Perhaps the greatest difference between this drama and the melodrama of the nineteenth century is that there is no happy ending, no resolution of the threat to Baile Beag's existence except the release of tension through the new tongue." Here and elsewhere, I believe that Pine undervalues the genre typical of Ireland, Irish political melodrama, in which historically accurate resolution is ipso facto impossible.

35. Musgrave's title goes on: *"To this Edition is Added, A Concise History of the Reformation in Ireland; and Considerations on the Means of Extending Its Advantages Therein."*

36. Marianne Elliott, *Partners in Revolution: The United Irishmen and France* (New Haven: Yale Univ. Press, 1982), xvi. (I have found Elliott's work enormously stimulating and useful throughout this project.) The Public Record Office of Northern Ireland's Education Facsimile No. 66, on the United Irishmen, defines Defenderism as "a popular movement, swelled by the religious fanaticism and the agrarian grievances of the ignorant catholic peasantry. It was therefore very different from the United Irish movement, which was purely political and drew its support from men who were comparatively well-educated and were most of them either protestants or people of no religion at all. Indeed, the two movements were contradictory, in that Defenderism was based on the old religious hatreds, and the United Irish movement on the new ideal of the brotherhood of man which the French Revolution had inspired. In spite of these fundamental differences, however, the two began to fuse from 1796 onwards—especially in Ulster—and it is a safe guess that the majority of the catholics who rose to arms in 1798 had formerly been Defenders."

37. One especially interesting feature of the United Irishmen's leadership is that precisely those persons empowered by English rule—aristocrats and educated professionals, Anglo-Irishmen, and Protestants—banded together to foster Irish self-determination.

38. Elliott, *Partners in Revolution*, 16.

39. Ibid., 27.

40. Ibid., 54.

41. Richard Robert Madden, *The United Irishmen: Their Lives and Times*, ed. Vincent Fleming O'Reilly (New York: Catholic Publication Society of America, 1916), 4: 172.

42. Elliott, *Partners in Revolution*, 54.

43. Lecky, *History of Ireland*, 259–60.

44. Madden, *United Irishmen*, 4: 210.

45. Lecky, *History of Ireland*, 350–51.

46. Elliott, *Partners in Revolution*, 25, 101.

47. William Smith Clark, *The Irish Stage in the County Towns 1720 to 1800* (London: Oxford Univ. Press, 1965), 11–13. Tone remained interested in the theater; during his long negotiations in France, he attended performances frequently, seeing both legitimate drama and various "revolutionary shows" (Pierre Joannon, "Wolfe Tone in Paris [1796–1797]," *Cahiers Irlandais* 2–3 [1973–74]: 87–88). These plays evoke the patriotic gestures of the plays in this edition.

48. Henry Boylan, *Theobald Wolfe Tone* (Dublin: Gill and Macmillan, 1981), 8, 11.

49. Ibid., 72–75.

50. Ibid., 87–88, 107.

51. Quoted in Madden, *United Irishmen*, 3: 156. Madden quotes the political portions of the journals. In the next paragraph is another quotation taken from Madden, *United Irishmen*.

52. Boylan, *Theobald Wolfe Tone*, 107–25.

53. Madden, *United Irishmen*, 3: 186.

54. Elliott, *Partners in Revolution*, 236.

55. Boylan, *Theobald Wolfe Tone*, 129.

56. Ibid., 128–33.

57. Elliott, *Partners in Revolution*, 236.

58. The manuscript for this play is owned by Séamus de Búrca, who supplied the history of the piece: "Now WOLFE TONE by Peadar Kearney was written when he lived with my parents at 10 Lr Dominick Street, Dublin. . . . I remember reading it carefully and discussing it with Peadar in 1932/33 when I was collecting material for the book I eventually would write about him. . . . He did say, 'At that time all we had about Tone was the small paperback Cameron, Ferguson (Glasgow) edition of the Journals.' It owes nothing to the Whitbread play, but I have no doubt that Peadar would have seen that in the Queen's—and indeed all the other Whitbread Irish Historical plays" (Letter to the author from Séamus de Búrca, 14 May 1983). Quotations from the play are made with the permission of Séamus de Búrca from the manuscript in his possession.

59. Madden, *United Irishmen*, 3: 190, 209.

60. The imagery of withering and shriveling, although generic to the discourse of curses, may have a closer etiology for Kearney; Fitzpatrick notes that when Lord Edward's betrayer could not be identified, "A Dublin ballad expressed the fierce anxiety felt to discover and destroy the veiled betrayer—*May Heaven scorch and parch the tongue by which his life was sold, / And shrivel up the hand that clutched the proffered meed of gold*" (W. J. Fitzpatrick, *Secret Service under Pitt* [London: Longmans, Green, 1892], 116).

61. Elliott, *Partners in Revolution*, 199.

62. James Anthony Froude, *The English in Ireland in the Eighteenth Century* (New York: Scribner's, 1888), 3: 350.

63. Quoted in Madden, *United Irishmen*, 4: 267. The *Freeman's Journal* for Tuesday, 22 May 1798 reported the arrest of Lord Edward. The article represents Swan as very concerned not to kill "His Lordship" and entreating him to surrender; this piece includes a long, blow-by-blow account of the struggles of the various agents in this event. The *Journal* also noted, "A Rebel uniform was found in the house of Murphy, where Lord Edward Fitzgerald was arrested—and another, we hear, at the Counsellors Sheares. It is a bottle-green faced with crimson velvet" (p. 3).

64. Madden, *United Irishmen*, 4: 290.

65. Froude, *English in Ireland*, 348–50. Froude's three-volume work, *The English in Ireland in the Eighteenth Century*, has become famous for its aggressive persistence in denouncing the Irish, so much so that Froude was answered by many critics, whether they were full-time historians or public speakers. One of the latter, Father

Nicholas Burke, lectured contra Froude when he toured Irish-American sites in the late nineteenth century with his own flamboyant mixture of "old sod" rhetoric, patriotic Catholicism, and showmanship.

66. Fitzpatrick, *Secret Service under Pitt*, 121.

67. Ibid., 121–22.

68. Ibid., 132.

69. Madden claims that Lord Edward never used a pistol in this encounter, that Ryan was not shot but only stabbed, and that Swan had only minor cuts (*United Irishmen*, 4: 291).

70. Fitzpatrick, *Secret Service under Pitt*, 132–33.

71. Elliott, *Partners in Revolution*, 68–70, 72.

72. L. P. Curtis, "Introduction," in Lecky, *History of Ireland*, xxv.

73. Lecky, *History of Ireland*, 292, 294. Compare Edith Mary Johnston, *Ireland in the Eighteenth Century* (Dublin: Gill and Macmillan, 1974): "The Penal Laws had a further purpose, to divide the Irish nation . . . so that the two might never again unite." Johnston points out that the Ascendancy class further discriminated against other Protestant groups, principally the Presbyterians (pp. 33–34).

74. Johnston, *Ireland in the Eighteenth Century*, 38–39. In the next paragraph, I quote again from page 38.

75. Froude, *English in Ireland*, 339–44.

76. J. J. O'Meara, *Lecture on Father John Murphy and '98* (Dublin: Sealy, Bryers and Walker, [1898]), 5.

77. J. C. Beckett, *The Making of Modern Ireland: 1603–1923* (New York: Knopf, 1966), 260–61. Compare statement in Public Record Office of Northern Ireland Educational Facsimile No. 67: *United Irishmen* (Her Majesty's Stationery Office, 1974, n.p.): "In the early winter of 1796 Co. Down was in a disturbed and threatening condition. This was to some extent the result of the attempts of local landowners to put into effect an act passed in October for raising yeomanry corps. Yeomanry were quite different from militia. They were not raised by ballot or on a county basis. They were part-time soldiers, who drilled and trained for not more than two days in the week except when on active service, while the militia were full-time soldiers who were kept permanently under arms. Moreover, yeomanry corps were used only for the defence and policing of the neighbourhood where they had been raised. Militia, on the other hand, could be called upon to serve in any part of Ireland and were almost never stationed in their county of origin."

78. Robert Kee, *Ireland: A History* (London: Sphere, 1982), 61.

79. Ibid., 63.

80. Musgrave, *Memoirs of the Different Rebellions in Ireland*, 317.

81. Ira Allen's *Father Murphy* does include one scene involving pitch-capping, but because we know this fact only from the extant playbills and not from any extant script, I do not know whether the representation was discursive or enacted.

82. Elliott, *Partners in Revolution*, 190, 201.

83. Musgrave, *Memoirs of the Different Rebellions in Ireland*, 211–12. The *Freeman's Journal*, a loyalist paper at the time, totally aligns with this popular rhetoric. Compare the report of 2 June 1798 (p. 3): "Every day brings to our knowledge new acts of atrocity committed by the Rebels. In the co. of Wexford, among many instances of massacre, the following excites particular detestation and horror:—The

Rev. Mr. Haydon, a Protestant Clergyman much-esteemed, having had some of his neighbours to spend the evening with him, a Miss Clifford, residing in his house, whose beauty and whose virtues, made her the admiration of the country, was requested to sing "Croppies lie down;"—she did so, little thinking that her compliance would have been the cause of her death! The next morning, the house was attacked by a party of Insurgents, and the whole family massacred with circumstances of the most horrible cruelty.—The servant who attended the family at supper the preceding night, snatched a pike from one of his brother Demons, and plunged it into the beautiful bosom of Miss Clifford, exclaiming, at the same time, "There, you d—d w—e, take that for your Croppy lie down!!!" / Four infants were not spared, but tossed, in Hellish sport, on the points of the pikes!—who that ever felt or acknowledged the ties of a father, an husband, a son, or a brother, that would not move Heaven and Earth to the destruction of those Monsters?"

84. Musgrave, *Memoirs of the Different Rebellions in Ireland*, 327.

85. Barry O'Brien, *Portraits in Leadership* (Fermoy: Eigse Na Mainistreach, 1980), 83.

86. Beckett, *Making of Modern Ireland*, 263.

87. O'Meara, *Father John Murphy and '98*, 13.

88. Kee, *Ireland*, 64.

89. Lecky, *History of Ireland*, 375, 376.

90. Jane Barber, "Recollections of the Summer of 1798," typescript. A copy of Barber's memoirs is housed in the National Library of Ireland. The quotations from this memoir are from the typescript.

91. Musgrave, *Memoirs of the Different Rebellions in Ireland*, 338.

92. Elliott, *Partners in Revolution*, 202.

93. Musgrave, *Memoirs of the Different Rebellions in Ireland*, 347, 357.

94. Ibid., 479.

95. Beckett, *Making of Modern Ireland*, 263.

96. O'Meara, *Father John Murphy and '98*, 24–25.

97. Beckett, *Making of Modern Ireland*, 264–65.

98. Elliott, *Partners in Revolution*, 206.

99. Musgrave, *Memoirs of the Different Rebellions in Ireland*, 557.

100. W. G. Lyttle, *Betsy Gray or, Hearts of Down: A Tale of Ninety-Eight* (Belfast: Carswell, n.d.), 128. Thomas Pakenham reports that after the battle of Ballinahinch, "They also found the bodies of two beautiful women fantastically dressed in green silk, who had carried the rebel standards. They had been known as the Goddess of Liberty and the Goddess of Reason, and were apparently the town prostitutes" (*The Year of Liberty: The Story of the Great Irish Rebellion of 1798* [New Jersey: Prentice-Hall, 1969], 231).

101. Lyttle, *Betsy Gray*, 15.

102. Johnston, *Ireland in the Eighteenth Century*, 40.

103. Lyttle, *Betsy Gray*, 149–50.

104. Musgrave, *Memoirs of the Different Rebellions in Ireland*, 557.

105. Lyttle, *Betsy Gray*, 142.

106. Beckett, *Making of Modern Ireland*, 266.

107. Watt usefully traces symmetries between nineteenth-century Dublin

newspaper rhetoric, which presents history melodramatically, and Whitbread's myth of history ("Boucicault and Whitbread," 28–31). I agree with his analysis and would emphasize that Whitbread unerringly chose as principal sources works that underscored their vision of history-as-melodrama. The additional situation that in its own day the Rising was conceived in dramatic terms allows us to press quite far the significance of the dialectic between historical representations and melodramatic conventions as embodied in all kinds of cultural materials. And I find it especially intriguing that Elliott, a skilled and energetic historian, states, "My first debt is to my parents, for the original interest in this topic arose from their early tutelage in Irish history and from the vivid repertory of United Irish plays staged by my father's amateur dramatic company, the Rosemary Theatre Group in Belfast. If I have succeeded in infusing my characters with the same life as such dramatic representations, I will be well satisfied" (*Partners in Revolution*, ix).

108. Madden, *United Irishmen*, 5: 100–110.

109. Ibid., 8: 112–14. Compare Fitzpatrick, *Secret Service under Pitt*, 179, 183–84. As men of culture, the United Irishmen discovered and then created many instances in which history and art could not be separated. Pakenham states of the evening Lord Edward was captured that "Lord Camden and his party left the Castle and took their seats in the Theatre Royal for a gala performance of *Robin Hood* (a comic opera written, oddly enough, by McNally, the Government spy)" (*Year of Liberty*, 93).

110. Froude, *English in Ireland*, 5, 27.

111. Fitzpatrick, *Secret Service under Pitt*, 58, 1.

112. Ibid., 134, 9.

113. Here I agree wholeheartedly with Watt's assessment. In "Boucicault and Whitbread," he argues compellingly that "Whitbread's and other similar history plays advance a myth of Irish history which is both melodramatic and heroic"; he adds that "to many people, as I have tried to demonstrate through popular newspaper biographies and news accounts of the Boer War, history *was* melodrama—and melodrama was often the vehicle for a historically 'precise' account" (pp. 25, 47).

114. Fitzpatrick, *Secret Service under Pitt*, v–vi.

115. Ibid., 3–4, 8.

116. Ibid., 96.

117. Ibid., 13, 118, 124, 137.

118. The source of this love interest in Whitbread's play is not difficult to discern; it was conventional for the villain to be moved by love of the hero's female friend or spouse. But another source of inspiration occurs in Fitzpatrick, who mentions that one of Turner's pseudonyms was Richardson: "Richardson, the popular author of 'Pamela,' was then a specially familiar name, and one which would readily occur to a well-read man who divulged the secrets of a real Pamela" (ibid., 47). In Whitbread's play, when Magan confesses his love to the disgusted Lady Edward, she threatens to stab him if he comes close to her. The motif of preserving one's honor is at the heart of Richardson's epistolary novels, and Fitzpatrick's notes probably contributed to this imaginative side of Whitbread's writing. Whitbread's eclectic style drew as readily from Richardson as from Shakespeare and Dickens, probably the major non-Boucicauldian influences on his work.

119. Ibid., 146–48.

120. O'Brien, *Portraits in Leadership*, 40, 98–99.

121. Mitchell, *Labour in Irish Politics*, 34.

122. Both Donal Byrne and Mary Doyle were historical figures. In the pamphlet "The Women of 'Ninety-Eight," we are told the story of Mary Doyle's heroism; in fact, she is called "the heroine of Ross," and William Rooney's poem about her is cited. Doyle is said to have done "sentry duty at the Insurgent Camps. The success of the Irish forces at Ross was due in an especial measure to her, who in one of the turns of the fight, when hesitation might have resulted in a rout, leaped out in front of the Insurgents, brandishing a scythe, with which she cut the cartouche belts of the fallen enemy, and threw their contents, among the Wexfordmen, to replenish their stock, calling on them to be resolute and follow." Later, she sat on a cannon and "refused to move unless the gun was taken" with the departing troops. "It is said she perished amid the flames, that consumed so much of the heroic town of New Ross." (*Who Fears to Speak of '98?* [London: Joseph Fowler, n.d.], n.p.). Like many of the characters in Irish political melodramas, Donal Byrne is also represented in other plays (e.g., E. J. Foley's *Croppy Boy* [see the playbill in de Búrca, *Queen's Royal Theater*, where a Donal Dun O'Byrne, "A United Irishman," appears]) and in fiction (e.g., Denis Holland's *Donal Dun O'Byrne: A Tale of the Rising in Wexford in 1798* [Glasgow: Cameron and Ferguson, (1869)]. Holland's novel includes Grace Bassett, Myles Cassidy, and Ned Traynor, much of the cast of Bourke's *When Wexford Rose*.).

123. Breandán Mac Giolla Choille, *Chief Secretary's Office, Dublin Castle. Intelligence Notes 1913–16—Preserved in the State Paper Office* (Dublin: Oifig an tSoláthair, 1966), 173, 170.

124. Dorothy Macardle, *The Irish Republic: A Documented Chronicle of the Anglo-Irish Conflict and the Partitioning of Ireland, with a Detailed Account of the Period 1916–1923*, 4th ed. (Dublin: Irish Press, 1951), 128.

125. Ibid., 161.

126. Leon Ó Broin, *Dublin Castle and the 1916 Rising* (New York: New York Univ. Press, 1971), 81. Below, I refer to information on pages 114 and 133.

127. Her husband Casimir Markiewicz's play about 1798, *The Memory of the Dead*, appeared first at the Abbey in 1910 and the following year, after some revisions, at the Queen's.

128. Lecky, *History of Ireland*, 375.

129. Bonnie Kime Scott, *Joyce and Feminism* (Bloomington: Indiana Univ. Press, 1984), p. 9. Below, I refer to pages 11–13, 17, and 29–53.

130. For commentary on Boucicault's aggressive, complex women characters, see Watt, "Boucicault and Whitbread," 36–37, 46. Compare Musgrave's claim that on Vinegar Hill the "female rebels" were "more vehement than the male" and that "Great numbers of women were in the camp" (quoted in D. E. S. Maxwell, *A Critical History of Modern Irish Drama 1891–1980* [Cambridge: Cambridge Univ. Press, 1984], 99n). Musgrave cites his source as "Rossiter's Affidavit."

131. Dermot Keogh, *The Rise of the Irish Working Class: The Dublin Trade Union Movement and Labour Leadership 1890–1914* (Belfast: Appletree Press, 1982), 180.

132. Margaret MacCurtain, "Women, the Vote and Revolution," in *Women in Irish Society: The Historical Dimension*, ed. Margaret MacCurtain and Donncha ÓCorráin (Dublin: Arlen House, 1978), 48–49. Below in this paragraph, I refer to pages 50 and 51. In the same issue of the *Evening Herald* in which *When Wexford Rose* was cited as having its first performance (4 March 1912), an article called "SUFFRAGETTES AGAIN" reports, "A Suffragette window-smashing raid took place to-day in Knightsbridge. A

number of Suffragettes smashed the windows of various firms, and several arrests were made." The women even broke "a heavy glass panel of the porch of the Lord Chancellor's residence in Eaton place"! About thirty women are reported as involved in the disturbances, which included an attempt to burn down the General Post Office.

133. Letter to the author from Séamus de Búrca, 14 February 1987.

134. William Paul Steele, *The Character of Melodrama* (Orono: Univ. of Maine Press, 1968), 6.

135. Homi Babha, "The Other Question—the Stereotype and Colonial Discourse," *Screen* 24 (1983), 23.

136. See Pine, "After Boucicault," 43–46, where Pine traces Friel's debt to melodrama.

137. Seamus Deane, Introduction, *Selected Plays*, Brian Friel (Washington, D.C.: Catholic Univ. of America Press, 1984), 22.

138. Quoted from *Translations*, Friel, *Selected Plays*, pp. 445–56.

BIBLIOGRAPHY

THIS LIST excludes newspaper articles cited and most of the Irish plays researched for the edition and introduction (plays both published and unpublished, from the period 1860 to 1950). The division of works by categories (Theory of Culture and Dramaturgy, Theater History, and Irish Political and Social History) reflects the uses made by this text of the writings in question; the boundaries between categories are neither fixed nor airtight.

THEORY OF CULTURE AND DRAMATURGY

Babha, Homi. "The Other Question—the Stereotype and Colonial Discourse." *Screen* 24 (1983): 18–33.

Brooks, Peter. *The Melodramatic Imagination: Balzac, Henry James, Melodrama, and the Mode of Excess*. New York: Columbia Univ. Press, 1985.

Cawelti, John G. "Myths of Violence in American Popular Culture." *Critical Inquiry* 1 (1975): 521–41.

Chaim, Daphna Ben. *Distance in the Theatre: The Aesthetics of Audience Response*. Theater and Dramatic Studies, no. 17. Ann Arbor, Mich.: UMI Research Press, 1984.

Cudjoe, Selwyn R. *Resistance and Caribbean Literature*. Athens: Ohio Univ. Press, 1980.

Dahl, Mary Karen. *Political Violence in Drama: Classical Models, Contemporary Variations*. Ann Arbor, Mich.: UMI Research Press, 1986.

Fanon, Frantz. *The Wretched of the Earth*. New York: Grove Press, 1966.

Heilman, Robert B. *Tragedy and Melodrama: Versions of Experience*. Seattle: Univ. of Washington Press, 1968.

Hermassi, Karen. *Polity and Theater in Historical Perspective*. Berkeley: Univ. of California Press, 1977.

Herr, Cheryl. *Joyce's Anatomy of Culture*. Urbana: Univ. of Illinois Press, 1986.

Jameson, Fredric. "Reification and Utopia in Mass Culture." *Social Text* 1 (1979): 130–48.

Lindenberger, Herbert. *Historical Drama: The Relation of Literature and Reality*. Chicago: Univ. of Chicago Press, 1975.

Rahill, Frank. *The World of Melodrama*. Philadelphia: Univ. of Pennsylvania Press, 1967.

Silverman, Kaja. *The Subject of Semiotics*. New York: Oxford Univ. Press, 1983.

Steele, William Paul. *The Character of Melodrama: An Examination through Dion Boucicault's* The Poor of New York, *Including the Text of the Play*. University of Maine Studies, 2d ser., no. 87. Orono: Univ. of Maine Press, 1968.

THEATER HISTORY

Booth, Michael R. *English Melodrama*. London: Herbert Jenkins, 1965.

______. *Hiss the Villain*. New York: Benjamin Blom, 1964.

Brown, Stephen J. M. *A Guide to Books on Ireland*. Part 1. 1912; New York: Lemma, 1970.

Clark, William Smith. *The Irish Stage in the County Towns 1720 to 1800*. London: Oxford Univ. Press, 1965.

de Búrca, Séamus. *The Queen's Royal Theatre Dublin, 1829–1969*. Dublin: Séamus de Búrca, 1983.

Disher, Maurice Willson. *Melodrama: Plots That Thrilled*. New York: Macmillan, 1954.

Duggan, G. C. *The Stage Irishman: A History of the Irish Play and Stage Characters from the Earliest Times*. 1937; New York: Benjamin Blom, 1969.

Friel, Brian. *Selected Plays*, intro. Seamus Deane. Irish Drama Selections, no. 6. Washington, D.C.: Catholic Univ. of America Press, 1984.

Hibbert, H. G. *Fifty Years of a Londoner's Life*. New York: Dodd, Mead, 1916.

Hickey, Des, and Gus Smith. *A Paler Shade of Green*. London: Leslie Frewin, 1972.

Hogan, Robert, ed. *Towards a National Theatre: The Dramatic Criticism of Frank J. Fay*. Dublin: Dolmen, 1970.

______, and Richard Burnham. *The Art of the Amateur 1916–1920*. The Modern Irish Drama: A Documentary History, vol. 5. Dublin: Dolmen, 1984.

______, and James Kilroy. *The Irish Literary Theatre 1899–1901*. The Modern Irish Drama: A Documentary History, vol. 1. Dublin: Dolmen, 1975.

———, and Michael J. O'Neill, eds. *Joseph Holloway's Abbey Theatre: A Selection from His Unpublished Journal* Impressions of a Dublin Playgoer. Carbondale: Southern Illinois Univ. Press, 1967.

Holloway, Joseph. Impressions of a Dublin Playgoer. Unpublished manuscripts. National Library of Ireland, Dublin.

Hunt, Hugh. *The Abbey: Ireland's National Theatre*. Dublin: Gill and Macmillan, 1979.

Irish Theatre Archive. "Dion Boucicault and the Irish Melodrama Tradition." *Prompts* 6 (September 1983).

Journal of Irish Literature 13 (January-May 1984): Bourke–de Búrca double number.

Journal of Irish Literature 14 (January 1985): Hubert O'Grady number.

Kavanagh, Peter. *The Irish Theatre*. Tralee: Kerryman, 1946.

Kiberd, Declan. "The Fall of the Stage Irishman." In *The Genres of the Irish Literary Revival*, ed. Ronald Schliefer, 39–60. Norman, Okla.: Pilgrim Books; Dublin: Wolfhound Press, 1980.

Krause, David, ed. *The Dolmen Boucicault*. Dublin: Dolmen, 1964.

McCormick, John. "Origins of Melodrama." *Prompts* 6 (September 1983): 5–12.

Malone, Andrew E. *The Irish Drama*. London: Constable, 1929.

Maxwell, D. E. S. *A Critical History of Modern Irish Drama 1891–1980*. Cambridge: Cambridge Univ. Press, 1984.

Molin, Sven Eric, and Robin Goodefellowe. "Nationalism on the Dublin Stage." *Éire-Ireland* 20 (March 1986): 135–38.

Nicoll, Allardyce. *A History of English Drama*. Vol. 5. Cambridge: Cambridge Univ. Press, 1962.

O'Connor, Frank, and Hugh Hunt. *Moses' Rock*, ed. Ruth Sherry. Washington, D.C.: Catholic Univ. of America Press, 1983.

O'Driscoll, Robert, ed. *Theatre and Nationalism in Twentieth-Century Ireland*. London: Oxford Univ. Press, 1971.

Ó hAodha, Michéal. *Theatre in Ireland*. Oxford: Basil Blackwell, 1974.

Parkin, Andrew, ed. *Selected Plays of Dion Boucicault*. Irish Drama Selections, vol. 4. Washington, D.C.: Catholic Univ. of America Press, 1987.

Pine, Richard. "After Boucicault: Melodrama and the Modern Irish Stage." *Prompts* 6 (September 1983): 39–50.

Watt, Stephen M. "Boucicault and Whitbread: The Dublin Stage at the End of the Nineteenth Century." *Éire-Ireland* 18 (Fall 1983): 23–53.

———. The Making of the Modern History Play. Ph.D. diss., University of Illinois at Urbana-Champaign, 1982.

———. "Nationalism on the Dublin Stage." *Éire-Ireland* 21 (1986): 137–41.

Wolfe, Francis R. *Theatres in Ireland*. (Dublin): Amateur Dramatic Defence Association, 1898.

IRISH POLITICAL AND SOCIAL HISTORY

Beckett, J. C. *The Making of Modern Ireland: 1603–1923*. New York: Knopf, 1966.

Boucicault, Dion. *The Fireside Story of Ireland*. London: George Routledge, 1881.

Boylan, Henry. *Theobald Wolfe Tone*. Dublin: Gill and Macmillan, 1981.

Butler, Hubert. *Wolfe Tone and the Common Name of Irishman*. Mullingar: Lilliput Press, 1985.

Choille, Breandán Mac Giolla. *Chief Secretary's Office, Dublin Castle. Intelligence Notes 1913–16—Preserved in the State Paper Office* (Dublin: Oifig an tSoláthair, 1966).

Costello, Peter. *The Heart Grown Brutal: The Irish Revolution in Literature, from Parnell to the Death of Yeats, 1891–1939*. Dublin: Gill and Macmillan; Totowa, N.J.: Rowman and Littlefield, 1977.

Cowell, John. *Where They Lived in Dublin*. Dublin: O'Brien, 1980.

Cronin, Sean, and Richard Roche. *Freedom the Wolfe Tone Way*. Tralee: Anvil Books, 1973.

de Búrca, Séamus. *The Soldier's Song: The Story of Peadar O Cearnaigh*. Dublin: P. J. Bourke, 1957.

Dixon, R., ed. *Ireland and the Irish Question: A Collection of Writings by Karl Marx and Frederick Engels*. New York: International Publishers, 1972.

Edwards, Ruth Dudley. *An Atlas of Irish History*. 2d ed. New York: Methuen, 1981.

Elliott, Marianne. *Partners in Revolution: The United Irishmen and France*. New Haven, Conn.: Yale Univ. Press, 1982.

Fitzpatrick, W. J. *Secret Service under Pitt*. London: Longmans, Green, 1892.

Flanagan, Thomas. *The Year of the French*. New York: Holt, Rinehart and Winston, 1979

Fox, R. M. *Rebel Irishwomen*. 1935; Dublin: Progress House, 1967.

Freyer, Grattan, ed. *Bishop Stock's 'Narrative' of the Year of the French: 1798*. Ballina: Irish Humanities Centre, 1982.

Froude, James Anthony. *The English in Ireland in the Eighteenth Century*. Vol. 3. New York: Scribner's, 1888.

Gallagher, Frank. *The Indivisible Land: The History of the Partition of Ireland*. 1957; Westport, Conn.: Greenwood Press, 1974.

Granville, Gary, ed. *Dublin 1913: A Divided City*. Dublin: O'Brien Press, 1982.

Joannon, Pierre. "Wolfe Tone in Paris (1796–1797)." *Cahiers Irlandais* ["France-Ireland, Literary Relations"] 2–3 (1973– 74): 83–103.

Johnston, Edith Mary. *Ireland in the Eighteenth Century*. Dublin: Gill and Macmillan, 1974.

Joyce, P. W. *English as We Speak It in Ireland*. 1910; Dublin: Wolfhound Press, 1979.

Kee, Robert. *Ireland: A History*. London: Sphere, 1982.

Keogh, Dermot. *The Rise of the Irish Working Class: The Dublin Trade Union Movement and Labour Leadership 1890–1914*. Belfast: Appletree Press, 1982.

Lecky, W. E. H. *A History of Ireland in the Eighteenth Century*, abridged and ed. L. P. Curtis, Jr. Classics of British Historical Literature. Chicago: Univ. of Chicago Press, 1972.

Lyttle, W. G. *Betsy Gray or, Hearts of Down: A Tale of Ninety-Eight*. 9th ed. Belfast: Carswell, n.d.

Macardle, Dorothy. *The Irish Republic: A Documented Chronicle of the Anglo-Irish Conflict and the Partitioning of Ireland, with a Detailed Account of the Period 1916–1923*. 4th ed. Dublin: Irish Press, 1951.

MacCurtain, Margaret, and Donncha Ó Corráin, eds. *Women in Irish Society: The Historical Dimension*. Dublin: Arlen House, 1978.

Madden, Richard Robert. *The United Irishmen: Their Lives and Times*, ed. Vincent Fleming O'Reilly, vols. 1–12. New York: Catholic Publication Society of America, 1916.

The Mercenary Informers of '98: Containing the History of Edward Newell, Major Sirr, Jemmy O'Brien, and Thomas Reynolds with the Secret List of the Blood Money Paid by the English Government, From 1797 to 1801. Dublin: James M'Cormick; London: Strange, n.d.

Mitchell, Arthur. *Labour in Irish Politics 1890–1930: The Irish Labour Movement in an Age of Revolution*. Dublin: Irish Univ. Press, 1974.

Musgrave, Richard. *Memoirs of the Different Rebellions in Ireland, from the Arrival of the English: Also, A Particular Detail of That Which Broke Out the XXIIId of May, MDCCXCVIII; with the History of the Conspiracy which Preceded It and the Characters of the Principal Actors in It; To this Edition is Added, a Concise History of the Reformation in Ireland; and Considerations on the Means of Extending Its Advantages Therein*. 2d ed. Dublin: Milliken, 1801.

O'Brien, Barry. *Portraits in Leadership*. Fermoy: Eigse Na Mainistreach, 1980.

Ó Broin, Leon. *Dublin Castle and the 1916 Rising*. New York: New York Univ. Press, 1971

O'Meara, J. J. *Lecture on Father John Murphy and '98*. Dublin: Sealy, Bryers and Walker, [1898].

Pakenham, Thomas. *The Year of Liberty: The Story of the Great Irish Rebellion of 1798*. Englewood Cliffs, N.J.: Prentice-Hall, 1969.

Public Record Office of Northern Ireland. *The United Irishmen*. Education Facsimiles 61–80. Her Majesty's Stationery Office: 1974.

Scott, Bonnie Kime. *Joyce and Feminism*. Bloomington: Indiana Univ. Press, 1984.

Shaw, Bernard. *The Matter with Ireland,* ed. David H. Greene and Dan H. Laurence. London: Rupert Hart-Davis, 1962.

Wall, Richard. *An Anglo-Irish Dialect Glossary for Joyce's Works*. Syracuse: Syracuse Univ. Press, 1987.

Ward, Margaret, *Unmanageable Revolutionaries: Women and Irish Nationalism.* London: Pluto Press, 1983.

Who Fears to Speak of '98? 11 leaflets. London: Joseph Fowler, n.d.

Part Two

THE PLAYS

Plate 9. Lord Edward Fitzgerald. Reproduced by kind permission of the National Library of Ireland.

LORD EDWARD, OR '98

(Founded on the Revelations in W. J. Fitzpatrick's work
"Secret Service under Pitt")

[Transcribed with minor silent emendations from MS. 113,
Lord Chamberlain's Plays, British Library Manuscript Collection]

J. W. WHITBREAD
[1894]

CAST

LORD EDWARD FITZGERALD	one of the noblest figures of Irish history [also called "the Geraldine"]
MAJOR SIRR	The Fouché of Dublin
MAJOR SWAN	Assistant Town Major
CAPTAIN RYAN	
FRANCIS HIGGINS	an Attorney-at-Law, nicknamed the "Shamado"
FRANCIS MAGAN	a Barrister-at-Law, an Informer
[SAMUEL] NEILSON	a faithful adherent of Lord Edward's
TONY	a Negro servant to Lord Edward
THADY M'GRATH	a boy of the right sort, true to the core
MR. JAMES [O']MOORE	Merchant, 119 Thomas Street
MR. MURPHY	Feather Merchant, 151 Thomas Street
PALMER, GALLAGHER	Clerks in [O']Moore's employ
M'CABE	[unidentified]

Plate 10. Lady Pamela Fitzgerald and her children. Reproduced from Richard R. Madden's *United Irishmen*, V (1916), cited there as being "From an Engraving by Scriven, after the Celebrated Painting by George Romney."

NAPPER TANDY	a General in the Irish Army of Rebellion
GENERAL HOCHE	of the French Army
SAM TURNER	an Informer
LORD HENRY FITZGERALD	[brother of Lord Edward]
MADAME DE SELLIRY	the Comtesse de Genlis
LADY LOUISA CONNELLY	[aunt to Lord Edward]
PAMELA	[married to Lord Edward]
EDWARD, LUCY	Children of Lord and Lady Fitzgerald
MRS. [O']MOORE	
MISS [O']MOORE	
KATEY [KITTY] MALONE	[a servant]
SOLDIERS, PEASANTS, ETC.	

ACT I

MADAME DE SELLIRY (THE COMTESSE DE GENLIS) SALON, PARIS

Enter MADAME DE SELLIRY *and* GENERAL HOCHE, *L.C. They come down.*

MADAME (*with French accent*) Ah my dear General, I am so very pleased to see you, and so vill his Lordship be, ze Lord Edward Fitzgerald, who is here once more from Ireland, wiz a Mr. Samuel Turner zey arrived zis morning.

HOCHE I am of ze opinion I know ze attraction zat brings him so quickly back to Paris, ze fair Pamela.

MADAME (*laughing*) No! No! It is ze unhappy state of his unfortunate country.

HOCHE But my dear Madame, he is a British officer.

MADAME But not for long. He vill throw off his allegiance.

(*Enter* TURNER *L.C. and* NAPPER TANDY.)

TURNER Will become in fact what he is in sentiment, an Irish Patriot.

MADAME (MADAME *R.,* TURNER *C.,* GENERAL *L.*) Ah, my dear Monsieur Turnair, and ze brave Napper Tandy. (*To* TURNER) So you have completely recovered from ze fatigues. Permit

Plate 11. Major Henry Charles Sirr. Reproduced from Madden's *United Irishmen*, XII (1916). In Madden, Sirr is called "The Fouché of the Irish Rebellion," and the picture is identified as being "From the Only Known Portrait in Existence, in the Possession of Dr. Thomas Addis Emmet."

me (*indicates* GENERAL) ze brave General Hoche. (*Talks to* NAPPER TANDY.)

TURNER Whom I have had the honour of meeting before. Glad to see you General. (*Shakes hand.*)

HOCHE You are straight from Ireland?

TURNER Almost as the crow flies, General.

MADAME (*to* TURNER) I compliment you, you are ze first down. Ze Lord Edward—

NAPPER TANDY Is, and has been for the past hour most pleasantly engaged.

GENERAL Wiz Pamela?

TURNER (*bows*) Precisely.

MADAME No, No! It is impossible! Ze fair child is not out of her room.

TURNER At the present moment she is giving Lord Edward a lesson in Horticulture.

NAPPER TANDY They are devoting much attention to your magnificent lilies.

MADAME Ah, ze dear child is so fond of ze flowers.

GENERAL And Lord Edward of ze lady.

MADAME No! No!

GENERAL Oui! Oui!

TURNER You are right General. But his country, his ill-starred country must have first place in his heart for years. When her wrongs are righted, time enough to yield to the tender passion.

MADAME Oh you shocking man to talk of ze grande passion in zat way.

GENERAL Monsieur Turnair has been too long married, or he would not so speak. Too much beauty has spoiled him.

(*Enter* LORD EDWARD *and* PAMELA, *L.C.*)

MADAME Ah, zere they are! (TURNER *goes R.*) (TURNER *R.*, MADAME *R.C.*, LORD E. *C.*, PAMELA *C.L.*, GENERAL *L.*)

LORD E (*kissing* MADAME*'s hand*) Your servant Madame! (*To* GENERAL) Delighted to see you again, General. (PAMELA *bows to* TURNER *and to* NAPPER TANDY.) Who is that whom too much beauty has spoiled?

MADAME Ze Monsieur Turnair. He is one most wicked man. He condemns ze love, ze grand passion.

Plate 12. Monica Kelly, who played Kitty Malone in Kennedy Miller's production of *Lord Edward* during Whitbread's reign at the Queen's. *The Irish Playgoer* for 11 January 1900 reports, "Her style is very natural, and she can be pathetic or humorous as occasion demands; while her love-making is always racially droll and mirth-provoking to watch. Need I add she is a 'thundering' great favourite with her audiences!" (p. 13). Courtesy of the National Library of Ireland.

NAPPER TANDY Not for his country.

MADAME No, but for us ladies!

PAMELA Impossible!

LORD E Oh, that is rank rebellion.

GENERAL Twenty years of married life has disgusted him; he wants no more.

MADAME (*to* TURNER) Are you an Irishman?

LORD E One of the best and truest.

NAPPER TANDY Yes, Ireland has no more faithful adherent to her cause. (*Goes up and then to table L.* TURNER *goes up and then he,* GENERAL, *and* LORD EDWARD *at Table L.*)

MADAME (*aside to* PAMELA) Which I very much doubt. (*Aloud to gentlemen*) If a man do not love ze ladies he cannot truly love his country. (TURNER *bows, then sits.*)

GENERAL No, No. (*Sits.* LORD EDWARD *smiles and sits.*)

PAMELA (*R. to* MADAME) You are prejudiced.

MADAME (*aside to* PAMELA) Bah! He is one big bag of deceit. Trust him no farther my shild than you can see him. (*They walk up then back and sit on couch R.* GENERAL, TURNER *and* LORD E. *are in earnest conversation during the foregoing, the latter constantly eyeing* PAMELA.)

TURNER (*in earnest tones*) Matters, General, I am pleased to say are progressing most satisfactorily. And if you could but extract a promise from the Minister for Foreign Affairs to send us aid, I'd guarantee that not an English Flag would be flying from a flag staff in the country by the end of the year.

LORD E My dear Turner, I am a British Officer.

TURNER In name only my Lord. (LORD E. *looks at* PAMELA.)

GENERAL Five thousand! Diable! It is impossible. (*They talk.*)

MADAME (*L. of* PAMELA) Has ze leetle word been spoken my dear?

PAMELA Spoken? What Little word?

MADAME Ah, as if you did not know, oh leetle Miss Innocence, and ze poor boy dying for love of you zis minute. Zee, zee, how he keeps looking at you, and zey talking of war, and rebellion all ze time. Oh, zeese Irish shentlemen, how zey do love to fight and fight for love. (*They talk.*)

GENERAL Has England any suspicion?

TURNER None, whatever.

GENERAL 'Tis good, she is von big sleepy nation.

NAPPER TANDY And before she wakes the mischief will be done.

MADAME Ze Shentlemen seem much absorb. (*They talk.*) I zink we are de trop. (*They rise.*)

LORD E (*rising hurriedly—to them*) You are not going?

MADAME (*with affected vexation*) You do not want us. You are too much engrossed in pusiness. Ze attraction (*indicating herself and* PAMELA) is gone, [O]of! [Off?] Fly away! (*She goes up.*)

LORD E (*to* PAMELA) You do not think so?

PAMELA I could not disagree with Madame. (*Smiling.*)

LORD E (*softly*) But your heart does?

PAMELA (*laughing softly*) But my heart cannot speak.

LORD E (*earnestly*) Let me teach it—

PAMELA To speak. How?

LORD E Through your eyes.

PAMELA Of what?

LORD E Love.

PAMELA Ah, I'm afraid you are like our own French gallants.

LORD E Only in the depth and capacity of my admiration for you.

PAMELA Flatterer! (*Enter* SERVANT *R.C.*)

MADAME Vell, what is it?

KITTY Ze English Captain, Madame. [*Then exits.*]

MADAME Goot. Ve vill shoin him in ze garden. (*To* PAMELA) Come my shild; ze brave English officer is here; ve vill go to him.

LORD E (*to* PAMELA, *in vexed surprise*) Who is he?

MADAME (*laughing*) Ze most handsome man I have ever seen.

LORD E (*to* PAMELA) Not a lover?

MADAME Ze most devoted. (*Comes down R.*)

PAMELA (*laughingly*) No, No.

MADAME Oui, Oui. His passion is like ze color of his hair. Rosy, no, no. What you call Fiery. Zat is it. Fiery in ze extreme.

LORD E (*greatly annoyed*) Red Headed! He must answer to me for this. (*Is about to draw sword when he observes them laughing*) Ah, you are jesting. (PAMELA *turns to go.*) Allow me to escort you.

PAMELA No, No. You must stay; must transact your business with your friends. (*She goes up.* LORD E. *crosses to* MADAME.)

MADAME Zat is so, you will conspire here, and ve vill conspire outside vith ze brave English officer. (*Laughs, goes up.*)

NAPPER TANDY (*calling*) Lord Edward—

MADAME Zat is right. Messieurs (*to* TURNER *and* NAPPER TANDY, GENERAL HOCHE, LORD EDWARD) Adieu. (*They bow.* GENTLEMEN *do the same.* LADIES *exeunt.*)

LORD E (*goes up*) How beautiful she is.

TURNER (*calls*) Lord Edward. (LORD EDWARD *goes to table.*)

LORD E (*impatiently*) Well, what is it? (*They sit.*)

TURNER The General guarantees—

GENERAL HOCHE (*with decision*) I repeat, I object to the disclosure. He must not know.

TURNER (*with surprise yet with dignity*) But he is to be relied on.

GENERAL HOCHE (*shrugging his shoulders*) That may be so.

NAPPER TANDY And is one of us.

GENERAL HOCHE (*with a sarcastic laugh*) And one of the enemy too.

LORD E (*with asperity*) What mean you, General?

GENERAL HOCHE Nozzin. I only say, no man can with honour serve two masters.

LORD E Permit me to inform you that I am the best judge of my own honour.

GENERAL HOCHE (*coolly*) I zink not.

LORD E (*with suppressed anger*) Ah.

GENERAL Or you would act differently.

LORD E (*going R.*) My sword can solve that problem.

GENERAL HOCHE My young friend, you are like ze rest of your countrymen—too hot-blooded, too hot-headed.

LORD E But we always know when and how to repel an insult. I demand an explanation.

GENERAL HOCHE Of what?

LORD E Your reflection on my honour.

GENERAL HOCHE Which was true. (*Rising.*)

LORD E (*with heat*) You must meet me.

GENERAL HOCHE I shall not.

LORD E No?

GENERAL HOCHE No. My courage is known ze vourld ovare. If I meet you we do not fight on equal terms.

LORD E (*proudly*) I am an Irish gentleman, sir.

GENERAL HOCHE (*coolly*) And I a French General. You kill me, France sustains one great irreparable loss. I kill you, vell, vat does your country lose?

LORD E A Patriot.

GENERAL HOCHE Who vears King Shorge's uniform. Bah! my young friend, you must be either one zing or anoder. Sitting between two stools you vill fall to ze ground, where you vill not only hurt yourself, but Ireland too. (*Goes up*) I must know you to be a man, one in whom I can trust, before I can place my confidence and that of La Belle France in your keeping. I go to shoin ze ladies. Adieu! (*Exit L.*)

LORD E (*going up*) Confound him.

NAPPER TANDY My Lord, no violence, I will follow the General.

TURNER Calm yourself, take no notice of his remarks.

LORD E But I must. (*Going R.*)

TURNER He spoke unthinkingly.

LORD E He spoke the truth.

TURNER (*in surprise*) Eh?

LORD E (*crosses to L.*) The plain unvarnished truth.

TURNER Then why not act upon it.

LORD E (*crosses to R.*) Because of my family. Because such a step would break my mother's heart.

TURNER (*bitterly*) What of the heart of your country? That heart that has been slowly breaking for centuries, that at this very moment lies bleeding, almost pulseless in its dire distress and anguish.

LORD E (*with agitation*) Leave me, man. Leave me or I shall go distracted. (*He sits at table, head in hands in grief.*)

TURNER Very well. (*Aside, coolly sarcastic.*) Family and country are at war in his breast, but country will conquer. When it does, and my plans are ripe, what a prize I shall have plucked. (*Laughing softly.*)

(*[To]* MAGAN *and* NEILSON, *who enter L.C., in different tones.*) Ah, my dear friends pleased to see you. Let us retire, Lord Edward has expressed a wish to be alone.

NEILSON }
MAGAN } Has he joined?

TURNER Not yet. The hour, though long delayed, is near at hand, observe—(*indicating* LORD E.) He is fighting out the battle now.

MAGAN (*R.*) The cause must go ahead if he joins.

NEILSON (*L.*) His name alone will be worth 10,000 men.

TURNER (*C. taking their hands in his*) More, my friends, more. (*Aside—going L.*) and more than £10,000 to me. (*Exit.*)

MAGAN (*aside*) He and I must become better acquainted. With his assistance it will be my own fault if I do not build myself up a fortune. On his ruin, I will rise. His downfall, my elevation. (*Exit.*)

NEILSON (*who is down whilst* MAGAN *is speaking, looks pityingly at* LORD EDWARD *quietly struggling with his feelings, then returns to C.*) Shall I speak to him? No, let him fight out the battle alone. I will not be the one to influence him in ⟨such a⟩ [this] supreme moment. Once he has decided, if for us, he will be one of the firmest friends ould Ireland has ever had. I wish I could say the same of others of her sons. (*Exit.*)

LORD E (*raising his face to audience*) How shall I act? How shall I act? How noble the General's words, how despicable my own. I must decide. Oh mother, if I go against you, forgive me. It is not that I love you less, but that I love my country, poor bleeding Ireland, more. But Pamela, ah, will she leave home, Paris—the gaieties surrounding her on every side, to share the uncertainties the dangers, the misery, that must be mine if I take this step. A step once taken irrevocable and final. If I can read aright the language of her eyes, those bright windows of her soul, she will. I will end this indecision, throw open the portals of the mystic future, and learn once and for all what fate has in store for me. (*Goes up, looks off.*) There she is. How beautiful, how incomparable, an Empress among a gala[x]y of Queens. She separates from them. Is alone with an officer. It is the English man. He stoops; she blushes and droops her head. Ah, what do I see. He kisses her hand. Enough! I have my answer. Pamela and love are not for me. (*Comes down.*) Henceforth, Ireland, I am thine, and thine only. (THADY *sings outside.*) 'Tis Thady, his honest eyes must not see the pain in mine. I must crush out my sorrow alone, alone. (*Exit R.*) (*Enter* THADY, *singing; sees* LORD E *and calls.*)

THADY Hi, Masther! Lord Edward! Sir! He doesn't hear me; come back and cheer up me heart wid the music ov a bit of rale ould Irish, I'm bothered entirely wid these French foreigners, and their jabber; begorra* it's all jabber. (*Enter* KITTY.) By the mud on my brogues who have we here? (*She doesn't see him, does business with table or couch.*) Tare an' ages,* but she's a rale beauty. I wondher if she's from County Wicklow? I'll ax her. Top ov the mornin to yez, miss!

KITTY (*gives a slight scream*) [Par Dieu]! Un homme.

THADY Home. I wish I was.

KITTY Qu' avez vous dit? (What did you say?)

THADY She's anodher ov thim. Theres as thick as bees here. I see yere a Frenchman.

KITTY Pardonnez moi!

THADY Did you spake?

KITTY Oui.

THADY Tare an ages* but there's a lot ov whey in this country.

KITTY Non comprennez vous.

THADY Arrah* me girl, for the love ov Heaven, don't be afther botherin' a poor bhoy that way.

KITTY Oui, Oui. You no understand. You (*poking him in the ribs*) English.

THADY Bedad I'm not, I'm true Irish.

KITTY Oui.

THADY No, me.

KITTY Bah, you no comprennez, you parlez, talk, speak English.

THADY Bad luck to me soul that's thrue. It's a curse on the ould country to have to say so.

KITTY Non.

THADY I wondher if she'd understand a bit ov the rale article. I'll tip her a pace on it. (*Does so.*)

KITTY Non, non.

THADY (*scratching his head*) The divil's in it entoirely an' no mistake. That's worse than the other, what am I to do at all, at all. When Ireland's free I'll get the masther to compil ivery other nation in the world to spake Irish. (*To her*) My [Weeskey] Girsha,* for the love ov Heaven give us a taste of somethin', me tongue's dhry wid the turst it's got thryin to make ye understand.

KITTY Votre servante.

THADY Eh?

KITTY Oui.

THADY Are yez a Christian at all, at all?

KITTY (*arms akimbo—change of tone altogether*) As much a Christian as you are Mr Thady McGrath.

THADY Light ov glory to me sowl, is that yerself or ye ghost that's spaken?

KITTY Mesilf.

THADY An' ye understand Irish?

KITTY No, but I understand English, and I'm exceedingly obliged to yez for all the good things ye've been sayin' about me.

THADY Ah, don't be hard on a poor bhoy. Sure how was I to know ye was English.

KITTY I'm not, I'm Irish, and as good Wicklow born an' bred as yersilf, me bhoy.

THADY Listen to that now. An' ye're no Frenchman?

KITTY Sorra a bit.*

THADY Then give us a kiss for the sake ov the ould counthry. (*He tries to kiss her but she eludes him.*)

KITTY Ye're an impudent bosthoon.*

THADY An' ye're a swate little colleen.

KITTY Am I? (*Sits on R. on couch.*)

THADY Wid as nate a pair ov brogues undher yez petticoats as iver danced the heart out of a man. (*She draws her feet up.*) Ah ye nadn't be afther thryin' to roost them like a bantam hen wid her first clutch of eggs. (*She jumps up.*) That's the way to fetch me, me girl.

KITTY Bon soir! (*At back as if leaving.*)

THADY She's swearin' now. (*Aloud.*) All right, don't mind me, swear away as long as ye do it in French.

KITTY (*comes down*) I'm not swearing. You are rough.

THADY And ready.

KITTY Not polite like to [the?] French.

THADY No, an' I don't jabber like them ayther.

KITTY What! (*Goes up to him fiercely.*)

THADY Arrah,* come here, (*he takes her in his arms*) an' don't let us be blatherin' nonsense any longer; ye're as swate as a new nut in Autumn; yez eyes sparkle like dewdrops defyin' the mornin' sun; an' ye breath is like a whiff ov air from off the top ov the Wicklow Mountains, it's so fresh and pure.

KITTY (*sliding out of his arms*) Ye're thryin' to put the comether* on me now.

THADY How long have ye been in Parrhee?

KITTY Me father brought me over when I was a child.

THADY Did he? Might I ax his name?

KITTY Ye may, Michael Moriarty.

THADY Ye don't say so; ov where?

KITTY Ov Woodenbridge, County Wicklow.

THADY Glory to me sowl! He was my own cousin on me mother's side.

KITTY Then we are related.

THADY We are, darlint, as thick as blood can make us; ah give us a kiss for the sake of ould times. (*They embrace.*) Bedad it all comes back to me as plain as ould Biddy's sow that used to have the staggers. Sure it's meself that used to nurse ye whin ye mother was diggin' up the praties.* Do ye remember now?

KITTY I do, every bit ov it.

THADY An' the polthogues* ye used to trate me to on this snout?

KITTY I do.

THADY An' the way ye used to twig me hair wid the shovel if I didn't plaze you.

KITTY I do, it was fine fun.

THADY It was, grand. Ah come an' let me nurse ye agin. (*They embrace. Enter* LORD E., MADAME, PAMELA. THADY *with his arm round* KITTY*'s neck; they don't notice the others.*) Ah darlint, this is a taste ov the ould times over agin, only it's a dale swater for the kapin'.

LORD E Thady, what are you doing here? (*Slight exclamation.*)

THADY Coortin' yer honor. What do you think?

KITTY (*struggling*) Oh, let me go, let me go.

THADY Not at all, just stop where ye are. (*To* MADAME.) How do ye do ma'am—Fine day Miss? (*To* PAMELA. *Both ladies look surprised, then laugh.*)

LORD E (*annoyed*) You're forgetting yourself, sir.

THADY Not at all, I'm just remimberin' all about it, so is Kitty here; aren't ye?

MADAME Did you say you were courting here?

THADY Ov coorse Ma'am, an' it's not at all a bad place for the job. If it's good enough for his lordship, sure it's good enough for the likes ov me. (*Both ladies laugh.* PAMELA *goes up,* LORD E *joins her.*)

KITTY Let me go, let me go, I say.

THADY If ye must, I suppose ye must. (*He lets her go.*)

MADAME Zat is rich. Magnifique! What you say His Lordship was here for?

THADY Ah, as if yer Ladyship's grace didn't know; sure isn't it swate heartin' he is? an' its fine runnin' he's makin' ov it. (MADAME *laughs and joins* PAMELA.) I'm thinkin'.

LORD E (*coming down R. in a rage*) How dare you?

THADY It's all right, yer honor, she's a fine sthrappin' Colleen—a rale beauty, an' as nate about the pasterns as the two year old filly at home, God bless her.

MADAME He is grand, un bon comedian. (*To* LORD E.) You must have ze patience.

LORD E But—

MADAME (*putting up her hand*) No, no. He is too funny. (*To* THADY.) And what are you doing?

THADY Just followin' his lordship's example by way ov variety. (MADAME *laughs heartily.*)

LORD E (*to* KITTY) Take him away at once, before I lay my hands on him.

KITTY Come in out ov that, sure ye've done enough mischief for one day. (LORD E *joins* PAMELA.)

THADY Arrah, woman, what mischief have I done?

KITTY Ye've vexed his Lordship there, an' ye've disgraced me, that's what ye've done; ah, ye're a gom* altogether.

THADY Her Ladyship didn't say I was.

KITTY She did.

THADY I'll ax her. (*Is going towards her but is pulled back by* KITTY.)

KITTY Ye'll do no such thing. (*Pulls him round to R.*) That's your road, me man. (*Exeunt, talking etc.*)

[THADY (*Exiting*)] Am I a gom* me lady?

MADAME (*laughing*) Ah, I laugh so much zat I veep at ze funny man. (*Rising.*)

LORD E (*coming down*) Then I am honoured at having him at my poor service to amuse, entertain you. (*She bows, etc.*)

MADAME (*aside*) I will leave zem alone. (*Aloud.*) I vill go and make ze brave General laugh at ze story.

LORD E You are cruel, Madame.

MADAME (*laughing and shaking fan*) Not so, I am most kind, ze most shenerous of ladies. (*Laughs.*) Adieu! Adieu! Adieu! (*Exits,* LORD E *bows.*)

LORD E (*To* PAMELA, *who has been looking at book or picture and is now following.*) Will you not stay?

PAMELA But the gardens, though it is so late in the year, are lovely, heavenly.

LORD E My Heaven is here.

PAMELA Indeed!

LORD E And the loveliest flower therein—Yourself.

PAMELA (*coyly*) Oh, I must really go.

LORD E No, stay, I implore you.

PAMELA To what purpose?

LORD E That I may tell you how much I love you.

PAMELA (*in apparent surprise*) My Lord!

LORD E How much I idolize you (*she is moving*), oh, stay, I beseech you; stay till I lay bare my heart before you, and by its very love beatings for you, draw your own into its keeping.

PAMELA Impossible! I have known you but one little month.

LORD E (*passionately*) A whole life time to me. Ah Mamzelle Pamela, here at your feet let me beg, implore you, (*kneels*).

(*Enter* HIGGINS *L.U.E.*)

HIGGINS I hope I don't intrude—

LORD E (*hands handkerchief to* PAMELA, *rises*) Not in the least sir. (*Goes L.—aside.*) Confound him.

HIGGINS (*coming down, sotto voce*) Very nately done, indade. I couldn't have done it bether mesilf. The Gentleman evidently has been at the game before. (*Aloud to* PAMELA) I have not the honour of your acquaintance Mamzelle. (*To* LORD E) Nor ov yours, sir.

LORD E For which we are both devoutly thankful. (*PAMELA turns up R., LORD E, L.*)

HIGGINS As Shakespeare says, The cut direct.

PAMELA (*from back*) Whom may you require, Monsieur?

HIGGINS (*turning back to audience and facing them*) Captain [Major] Swan, of His Britannia Majesty's forces, at present here on special juty.

PAMELA You will find him in the grounds.

HIGGINS Much obliged. (*Turns, aside*) She wants me out ov the way, but I'm not goin' (*Sits R.*) Oh dear no!

LORD E This is right down insolence. Your name, sir?

HIGGINS Higgins, (*LORD E starts.*) Francis Higgins, Attorney-at-law, an' confidential legal adviser to His Excellency the Lord Lifftenant ov Ireland.

LORD E Ah,—

(*Enter MADAME, CAPTAIN [MAJOR] SWAN, HOCHE, MAGAN, NEILSON, and others L. and R.U. entrances. THADY and KITTY R. E.*)

LORD E And your business?

HIGGINS Concerns yerself. (*Rising*) An' which this Gentleman (*indicates SWAN*) will now proceed to explain. There are the papers. (*Hands them, all are greatly surprised.*)

THADY What's the matther at all, at all?

KITTY Hush.

SWAN (*to LORD E*) Lord Edward Fitzgerald, I have a most unpleasant duty to perform.

LORD E Then the more brief you are in the performance, the sooner will it be accomplished.

SWAN I am here, my Lord, by command of His Royal Highness, The Duke of York, to inform you that, owing to seditious language uttered by you in Dublin, in London, and more recently here in Paris, your name has been erased from His Majesty's Army list, and to demand from you the commission which you hold as a British Officer.

LORD E There it is. (*Throws paper on floor.*) And it affords me the greatest possible pleasure to return it.

(*HIGGINS picks up the paper.*)

THADY One w'd think he was a rag picker, he's so used to the job.

SWAN I regret to hear it. (*To LORD E*) The Irish Government's always just.

LORD E Just! I call it by a very different name.

SWAN (*sternly, and with emphasis*) It is a Government sir, sworn to do its duty, and to crush out a vile conspiracy.

LORD E Conspiracy. It is the upheaval of a whole nation, the just determination of a race no longer to submit to tyranny and crimes that have dyed our country a crimson red.

SWAN Why you are a rebel, steeped to the very lips in treason.

LORD E (*with dignity*) I am a member of the Irish House of Parliament, sir.

HIGGINS Yes, worse luck.

LORD E And an Irish Gentleman to boot. And I tell you, as I shall tell the Government from my place in the House, that treason lies within your own hateful rule, and not with us, that the fiend you have called into being, is your own offspring, and henceforth I set myself to the task of regenerating my beloved country.

SWAN (*with a sneer*) And to that end I assume, you are here to seek French—foreign aid—

HOCHE And what if he is?

LORD E And what if I am? England sought it in 1688. If she had the right to invoke it then, Ireland has a right to invoke it now.

SWAN With that I have nothing whatever to do. I am here to carry out the orders of His Majesty's Government. I demand your sword.

LORD E Which I refuse to yield. The sword is mine, sir, not the King's. It has been used in his service on many a distant field, and it rests with his Government if it is ever used against him.

SWAN (*L.*) I will not further listen to such treasonable speeches. Such melodramatic displays may suit your constituents, but they are out of place here.

THADY It's not the only thing that's out ov place, I'm thinkin'.

SWAN Who are you fellow? (*To THADY.*)

THADY As good a man as yersilf, me bouchal,* though you are an officer in full jerrimentals. (*SWAN turns away in disgust.*)

KITTY Hush!

SWAN (*to PAMELA*) I am sure you will agree with me.

PAMELA No, sir, but I agree with every word this gentleman has spoken. (*PAMELA turns to LORD E.*)

LORD E (*to SWAN*) You have your answer, sir. (*They walk up.*)

SWAN (*hits LORD E. on shoulder with sword*) And you have yours.

LORD E (*turns and draws sword, is R. of PAMELA*) Ah! (*TURNER, NEILSON and MAGAN half draw theirs. THADY is kept back by KITTY. HOCHE tries to restrain TURNER, NEILSON and MAGAN. MADAME half alarmed. PAMELA half indignant and others surprised.*)

PAMELA No, no. (*Stops LORD E.*)

MADAME (*turning to SWAN*) Sare, you forget yourself; this is my Salon—not an English barrack-room. (*Goes to PAMELA, then up.*)

PAMELA (*to SWAN*) Not half an hour ago, you asked me to become your wife.

SWAN (*with a bow*) I did Mademoiselle, but this is not the place to speak on such a subject.

PAMELA Permit me, after what has occurred, it is of all places the best. You wanted my answer, well here, before all my friends, I give it to you.

SWAN I am much honored. (*Bows.*)

LORD E Ah, she loves him.

PAMELA This gentleman (*indicating LORD E*) also did me the honour to say he loved me and to ask me to be his wife.

SWAN Did he dare? He, a rebel, false to his country and his King.

PAMELA He did dare. You want your answer. It is—that I love him and hate you. (*To LORD E offers hand.*) There is my hand, and I shall esteem it an honour worthy of a throned queen to call myself your wife.

LORD E To you, and my country, henceforth, then, I devote my life. (*With sword upraised.*)

TABLEAU

Music

End of Act I

ACT II

Scene 1

ROOM IN LEINSTER HOUSE, KILDARE STREET

(*Discovered at door R.,* MAGAN *standing C.,* [O']MOORE *L.C.*)

MAGAN Tell his Lordship we await his pleasure.

KITTY Yis, sir. (*Exits door R.*)

MAGAN (*crossing to chair L. of Table R.*) I understand, he has this morning received most important despatches from France.

[O']MOORE By whom?

MAGAN Neilson. (*Sits.*)

[O']MOORE Then they are safe from discovery.

MAGAN (*with meaning*) I believe so.

[O']MOORE (*quickly rising*) Believe? Are you not sure?

MAGAN We can be sure of no one in these troublous times. And I have noticed that whenever Neilson is the Envoy, the purport of his despatches is quickly in the possession of the Castle.

[O']MOORE (*in alarm*) You think him a—

MAGAN I trust no one, too much or too far. (*Spoken with meaning.*)

[O']MOORE Perhaps you distrust me?

MAGAN At times I have. ([O']MOORE *rises,* MAGAN *crosses to* [O']MOORE.) And old, reliable friend that you are, I tell you, if I had but the smallest particle of evidence of your infidelity, I would not hesitate to put an ounce of lead in your heart.

[O']MOORE (*sitting down*) Which I should unquestionably deserve. Ah, if every man in the cause had been as firm and staunch as you, how different the results would have been to Ireland.

MAGAN How different indeed. (*Aside crossing to seat.*) He will never suspect me after that.

(*Enter* LORD E *with* CHILD, *followed by* PAMELA *and* NEILSON.)

LORD E (*joyously*) Ah, my dear friends, news, glorious news! the French Cabinet—

MAGAN (*putting up his hand warningly*) Hush, my Lord, walls have ears.

LORD E (*to* CHILD) There, run away to Kitty, or Mr. Magan will say that these little pitchers (*pulling his ears*) will be carrying mischief. (*Exits* CHILD *R.C.*)

MAGAN It is better to be on the safe side.

LORD E (*laughing*) What a careful mortal you are to be sure, Magan. Why there's not a soul in this house would exhale even a breath of treason let alone turn informer. (*Slaps him affectionately on the shoulder.*)

[O']MOORE (*laughing*) Why, my lord, he has even doubts of my good faith.

LORD E (*shaking [O']MOORE by the hand*) Of you, my good old friend, and mentor; why, if that's the case he will even look askance at me.

PAMELA (*with meaning and curtseying*) And me.

MAGAN (*bowing profoundly*) I trust your ladyship in all things.

PAMELA (*another curtsey*) I am greatly honoured. (*Turns to LORD E.*)

NEILSON (*crossing to MAGAN*) Perhaps then you suspect me?

MAGAN I did not say so.

NEILSON (*sternly*) But you inferred it.

MAGAN Inference is not evidence.

NEILSON (*more sternly*) But it is an insult, and as such must be met. Let the fifteen acres in the Phoenix Park tomorrow morning at 6 o'clock decide the question.

LORD E Gentlemen, gentlemen, This must not be. Neilson (*with arm round his shoulder*), you fire eater, are you forgetting a lady is present.

NEILSON No, my lord. (*Crossing to PAMELA.*) And so well have I the honour of knowing her ladyship, that I am confident she will not refuse extending her approval to a man who has had the audacious temerity in her own drawing room to defend his reputation.

PAMELA I should have thought ill of you indeed, had you hesitated one moment in dealing as you did with the aspersion, and vindicating your character. Those who are themselves inclined to roguery are ever the most suspicious of others. (*To MAGAN.*) You remember the axiom Mr. Magan?

MAGAN (*with deference*) Perfectly, my lady, but logic and analysis can always upset obsolete proverbs.

LORD E (*laughing*) A truce, a truce. (*To NEILSON*) There shake hands. Forget and forgive. (*They do so.*) Her ladyship smiles on you again. (*MAGAN bows, she acknowledges it.*) Now (*cheeringly*), no more logic, no more doubts; we are friends once more.

PAMELA My husband's friends are always mine.

MAGAN An honour, my lady, I have ever striven to retain.

[O']MOORE Well, what news does our Ambassador bring this time?

LORD E The best. The Directory has promised to send immediately the long promised aid. Five thousand men are already equipped, and will, by sunset to-night, be on transports, and under convoy of three French Frigates well on their way to Ireland. The wind is favorable, and we may hope that they will land within the next forty-eight hours.

MAGAN And Napper Tandy?

LORD E Is with them.

MAGAN Then no time is to be lost.

LORD E Not a moment. Reliable and speedy messengers are already on the road, North, South, and West, to concentrate our scattered contingents. Those of County Dublin, Wicklow and Kildare assemble at Finglas tomorrow night.

MAGAN And you think it practicable that it can be done?

LORD E (*exultingly*) Why man! it's virtually done already. Every detail has been so carefully arranged, every danger weighed and prepared against, that we cannot possibly fail.

MAGAN Unless by betrayal.

LORD E Unless by betrayal. And even that contingency is too remote to give us one moment's uneasiness or trouble.

[O']MOORE It is a crucial moment for Ireland.

LORD E It is. (*Rising, all do the same.* PAMELA *has stood behind him during the foregoing.*) And now friends, as my eyes once we commence operations will not know sleep for forty-eight hours, I claim your indulgence to take what rest I can in the little time left. (*Shakes hands and exits L.*)

NEILSON (*to* PAMELA) Adieu, my lady. (*Kisses her hand and goes up.*)

[O']MOORE (*also kissing her hand*) And may success crown your gallant husband's efforts.

PAMELA I have no fear gentlemen, if friends remain true.

NEILSON (*at door C.*) Nor I.

[O']MOORE (*at door C.*) Nor I.

MAGAN (*at table R. deliberately*) Nor I.

PAMELA (*to* MAGAN) Are you not following our friends?

MAGAN In one moment, my lady. (*To* NEILSON *and [*O'*]*MOORE) I will join you at the corner of the street. (*They bow and exeunt. To* PAMELA) I have remained to impress on you the desirability of watching over his lordship's safety.

PAMELA (*with dignity*) He is always safe sir, with his wife.

MAGAN That goes without saying, my lady. I referred to the servants. Are they faithful?

PAMELA (*with even more dignity*) They love him, sir, as I do, and where love is, security follows. If that is all you have to say to me, I will bid you adieu, and retire.

MAGAN I humbly ask your pardon, and with all humility take my leave. (*He bows profoundly and goes up.* PAMELA *crosses to door R. They bow, she exits. He returns stealthily to door R. then to C., speaks in subdued but concentrated tones.*) She dislikes me, and I, the cold blooded lawyer, love her. He (*pointing to door L.*) is there, and safe enough for my purpose (*looks off* C.L.). Ah, those fools have gone, and now to Higgins to give him the word. (*Looks at door R.*) In ten minutes he (*pointing to door L.*), your husband, will be a prisoner in the hands of the Military. Then my lady, you will turn to me, and find what a friend I am—and can be.

(*Exit L.C.*)

(*Re-enter* PAMELA *door R.*)

PAMELA Thank Heaven, that man has gone. My very heart sinks when his cold, cruel eyes look into mine. (*Calls.*) Tony! (BLACK SERVANT *appears. Calls.*) Thady! (THADY *appears out of Pedestal.*) At your posts, I see.

THADY Arrah,* my lady, d'ye think we could desert so fair a commander as yer purty self. An' by the same token when danger forninst* ye an' the masther, isn't it our place to be there as well.

TONY It is our duty; we are his servants, my lady.

PAMELA (*with feeling*) And friends, too; you are in his Lordship's confidence.

THADY An' may the tongues wither in our mouths whin we lose it.

PAMELA We are on the eve of terrible events.

THADY That's good news anyways. That manes fightin', and I'm gettin' paralytic for the want of somethin' to bate.

PAMELA You know his lordship is resting, sleeping in that room.

THADY May the angels sit heavily on his eyelids till we wake him.

PAMELA It may be the last sleep he may ever enjoy here, in the home of his ancestors.

THADY An' a fine brave lot they are, too, all in glory this blessed minute, long life to them.

PAMELA I go to watch over him, there, and you must watch and guard him here.

THADY The first man who steps over the saddle of that door I'll convert into a corpse.

TONY Have no fear, my lady, we will defend him with our lives.

PAMELA I know you will, and I trust you both. (*Exits into room L.*)

THADY Swate bad luck to me, but she is in terrible disthress. (*SERVANT moves chairs in front of door L.*) What are yez doin' at all?

TONY I watch here.

THADY (*taking another [chair] to C.*) That's an asey way ov doin' it. I'm thinkin, I'll do the same on the balcony. (*Sits and hides in chair.*)

(*Enter KITTY door R.*).

THADY (*looking over chair*) Who's that? Ah, it's only Kitty. (*TONY takes no notice except just to glance round once.*)

KITTY Sure I don't know what's comin' to the house at all, at all. There's the masther, his lordship, bless him, worried out ov his life. There's her ladyship, an' her ladyship's mother, the Duchess, that was, half the day and the whole ov the night cryin' their eyes out. And there's Thady as full ov importance an' consate as an ould gander stuffed wid parsley and praties on show in a poulterer's shop. (*Sees TONY's wig.*) Ah, bad luck to it, there's the masther's wig left out again. Thim men sarvants are not worth a pinch ov salt. (*Seizes wig, TONY rises with it, she gives a slight scream. THADY looks over back of chair.*)

TONY Hush, you'll wake his lordship. (*Points door L.*)

KITTY Oh, it's my own wake I thought I was at, ye were afther frightenin' me so, whatever did they make black min at all for?

TONY To admire pretty Irish girls.

KITTY None ov yez blather now, ye're no betther than that blackguard Thady McGrath, only he's a bit dale pleasanter to look at; that's the only differ I see between yez.

TONY Ah, you love him.

KITTY (*tossing her head in disdain*) Love him, that spalpeen,* a man that's born to die wid a hempen rope round his neck; such riff raff as that is not good enough to be my husband.

THADY [*aside*] Is that so? I'll take the starch out of ye tongue for that me girl.

KITTY (*snapping her fingers*) That for Thady McGrath and his love.

THADY (*snapping his over chair*) An' that for Kitty the nurse girl an' her impudence.

KITTY (*R.*) Oh ye're there are yez, ruinin' the furniture wid yez dirthy stable clothes; listeners never hear any good ov themselves.

THADY No, nor ov the spakers ayther. There's a quid pro quo for yez; swallow it if yer can.

KITTY I'm thinkin' there's a pig in the room.

THADY Lave it then, and it'll be gone.

KITTY Ye're very polite.

THADY I am—to ladies—when I see them.

KITTY Is that so? one step more an' ye'll be nearer the divil.

THADY Then kape yer distance, I'm near enough to be comfortable.

KITTY Oh, ye villain ye (*threatening him*).

THADY Aisy now, or ye'll be squintin'.

KITTY (*in a rage*) Squintin'.

THADY Aye, looking crooked.

KITTY Oh!

THADY Aye, cross at me.

KITTY (*sarcastically*) How sharp we are—Where did you slape last night?

THADY In ould Mother Rafferty's hen-house. An' I heard so much cacklin' this mornin' that I'm afther catchin' the complaint.

KITTY An' did I give up Paris, an' the fine brave lookin' men over there for the likes ov yez?

THADY Aye, an' glad enough ye were at the chance, ye jumped at me.

KITTY Well, it's sorry I am now, at any rate.

THADY So am I.

KITTY Oh!

THADY (*with assumed dignity*) Go back! go back, to yer frog-eatin' onion growin', dirthy wine drinkin' Parlez-vooers; ye're not good enough for a dacent Irishman.

KITTY Oh!

SWAN (*outside, in loud tones, L.C.*) Halt! watch every window. Guard every door. (*Clash of arms,* THADY, TONY *and* KITTY *greatly alarmed.*)

THADY Poison to my soul, it's the sogers. (*To* TONY.) Wake him, and bid him fly at wanst. (TONY *exits door L.*)

VOICE (*outside L.*) Halt! Surrender! (*Pistol shot fired L.*)

LORD E Never. (PAMELA *screams outside.* KITTY *screams and falls in chair.*)

KITTY Oh, I will be kilt.

THADY No such luck.

KITTY (*jumping up*) Ye Gallows bird, ye.

THADY Arrah* whisht* when there's so much danger astir.

RYAN (*outside door R.*) Guard the door.

(*Enter* LORD E *and* PAMELA *hurriedly from door L.* TONY *follows.*)

THADY For the love ov Heaven fly, the back way.

LORD E Impossible, the stairs and doors are doubly guarded.

PAMELA (*rushes to Pedestal*) In here!

THADY Sure that's the first place they'll search.

PAMELA Then you are lost.

THADY Sorra the bit* ov it. (*Rushes to fireplace.*)

SWAN (*outside R.C.*) Follow me, and shoot down any one who attempts to escape.

PAMELA (*clinging to him*) Oh husband, what's to be done?

LORD E Surrender or die.

THADY Nayther one nor the odher. In here quick; what have I been workin' for all these months, if not preparin' for such times as these. It leads to the stables and from there ye can escape to O'Moore's house in Thomas Street. We'll join you there to-night.

VOICE (*outside*) Halt!

THADY Quick away wid yer. (*LORD E exits, fire-place is replaced. PAMELA leans on armchair L.C., TONY L., KITTY R., THADY C.*)

(*Enter MAJOR SWAN followed by SOLDIERS C. Others enter door R. and L.*)

THADY Good-day Major, plased to see yer; ye're becomin' quite at home visitin' her ladyship so often.

SWAN (*to PAMELA*) I regret Lady Fitzgerald that I should so soon have to annoy you with my presence, and that of my men, but a soldier knows only his duty.

PAMELA (*with apparent ease but dignified*) And that is?

SWAN To institute another and a more rigid search for your husband, Lord Edward.

PAMELA He is not in the house.

SWAN Pardon me, my instructions are, that he is, and not only in the house, but that he has in his possession despatches which arrived by special envoy from Paris this morning.

TONY (*PAMELA, THADY, and others surprised.*) Ah.

THADY (*aside*) Anodher informer.

PAMELA (*aside*) Betrayed again. (*Aloud*) Since you are so well instructed and elect to believe an informer's word in preference to a lady's I have no alternative but to quietly submit to your will. (*Curtsey.*)

SWAN My commands are imperative, my lady, and though they may prove, in the carrying out offensive in the extreme to you, as they undoubtedly will be to my sense of honour, still, like you, I have no alternative left open to me but to obey.

PAMELA (*pointing to room L. proudly*) There is my husband's—our bedroom. I assume that is the only place remaining to be searched.

SWAN The only one, with the exception of this.

PAMELA Had you not better examine it then, even to the furniture, in case he might be hidden in some portion of it, and escape while you are prosecuting your detestable work there.

SWAN I do not consider such a proceeding necessary.

PAMELA That is for you to decide.

THADY Search the clock, Major, an' dont forget Sambo there.

KITTY Maybe he would like to search me.

THADY I'd like to catch him at it. (*During this* MAJOR *walks round the room as if searching for* LORD E.)

SWAN (*at door of room L., to* PAMELA) I ask your pardon humbly for the intrusion.

TONY (*makes a movement as if to prevent him,* PAMELA *raises her hand,* TONY *pauses.*)

PAMELA No gentleman should suffer himself to be degraded by asking it for such a purpose. (SWAN *bows and exits into room L.*)

THADY It's a grand growin' mornin' for the scarlet runners.

PAMELA Thank Heaven, he is safe. (SWAN *re-enters.*) Are you satisfied?

SWAN Perfectly. Believe me this police work is a most unpleasant duty to perform.

PAMELA It is a task *no* gentleman *would* perform.

SWAN I bow meekly to your Ladyship's severe censure, and will, without further delay, relieve you of our presence.

PAMELA The more expeditious your leave-taking the greater the compliment. (SWAN *bows to* PAMELA, *signals to his men, they exeunt.*)

THADY Oh, stay a little longer, we'll ordher dinner for yez.

SWAN (*outside*) Forward! March!

PAMELA (*going up*) Thank Heaven! they're gone. (LORD E *pushes back fireplace and re-enters.*)

LORD E Pamela! Wife!

PAMELA Husband! (*They embrace,* THADY *and* KITTY *do the same.* TONY *closes fire place, then goes up and watches.*) Oh, Edward what brings you back?

LORD E The impossibility of escaping from the stables, they were too well guarded; and where am I so happy but with my brave little wife. (THADY *looks round as if to watch them.*)

KITTY (*pulling his face back again*) Arrah, kape yer eyes this way, and lave thim alone.

THADY Sure I was only lookin'.

KITTY Well look at me, I'm good lookin' enough for you.

THADY Bedad ye are (*They go up and talk and exeunt R.C.*)

PAMELA (*clinging to* LORD E) My heart fails me now that danger so closely dogs your steps, oh would it not be better, wiser, to take your mother's advice and quit the country, every port is open to you yet.

LORD E That is only a decoy to lure me into their clutches.

PAMELA No, No. Lord Clare himself has said it, has written to that effect. See, see! there is the letter. Your mother only gave it to me an hour ago, before she left for Carton.

LORD E (*reads*) "Let Lord Edward fly. I pledge myself that every port in the Kingdom shall be left open to him." (*Regretfully*) And would my wife desire, wish, I sh'd do so? Leave friends, hopes, country, steal away like a coward, and a thief, at the first sign of danger?

PAMELA It is my love, my anxiety, my fears.

LORD E (*with great earnestness*) I have put my hand to the plough and I cannot lift it till my work is done.

PAMELA But it never will, it never will. Treachery and betrayal fatten too much in our midst for you ever to succeed.

LORD E Then I must die.

PAMELA (*clinging close to him*) Die!

LORD E Yes darling, with my face to the foe, fighting for liberty and Ireland. (*She sobs.*) Have you forgotten our compact in dear old Paris, when our lives were young; where with your heart beating against my own as it beats now; eyes, and lips, speaking tender devotion, you swore my life sh'd be dedicated to my country? It has grown with our lives, and now that the hour approaches for the blow to be struck, I must be there to give it.

PAMELA (*sobbing*) No, no.

LORD E What more glorious ending to a soldier's life than to fall on the field of battle.

PAMELA Oh it is not that I dread, not that I dread. It is the fear of the assassins' knife. The horrible uncertainty of not knowing friend from foe, that is sapping my life away.

(*Several cries of "Halt!" given simultaneously R.C. and L., also crash of arms, shouts and screams. Enter* THADY, TONY *and* KITTY.)

THADY Fly yer honor, fly, the red coats are here. (PAMELA *and* LORD E *alarmed, to* TONY.) Quick, open! (TONY *tries to open fireplace and fails.*)

TONY It's fast! (THADY *rushes to assist* TONY.)

PAMELA Then you're lost. (LORD E *rushes to door R.* TWO SOLDIERS *appear and hold bayonets at the charge; with an exclamation he rushes to door L.* SWAN *appears and presents pistol,* LORD E *seizes him and throws him well down C. Pistol falls,* PAMELA *picks it up.* LORD E *rushes again to door L. but is confronted by two soldiers who bring their guns to the charge. He then turns to C., when* SIRR *with* FOUR SOLDIERS *[including* RYAN*] appear[s].)*

SIRR Surrender!

LORD E Never. (SWAN *snaps pistol,* LORD E *seizes him and throws him round to R. By this time* THADY *and* TONY *have succeeded in opening fireplace.)*

THADY Here ye are, fly.

HIGGINS (*appears at the fireplace*) No, ye don't.

THADY Yes, we do. (*Pulls him out and throws him C.* LORD E *springs over him and exits.* THADY *and* TONY *close door rapidly.)*

SWAN (*in a rage down C. with* RYAN) Seize him!

(SOLDIERS *all make a movement.)*

PAMELA (*standing between* THADY *and* TONY *points pistol at* SWAN.)

TABLEAU

THADY The Shamrock for ever.

End of Scene 1

Scene 2

DAME STREET OR ST. THOMAS STREET

(*Enter* LORD EDWARD *R. disguised in long cloak and beard.)*

LORD E That was a narrow escape. The Government evidently prefer my society to my absence. My disposition is a very obliging one, but I must positively decline accepting their exceedingly pressing invitation to Dublin Castle. Some day in the near future I may be able to return the compliment and invite a few of the prominent members to meet me there. (*Laughs, looks R.*) Ah, whom have we here? As I live it is Higgins and Magan. What business can possibly bring those two together. (Hides L.)

(*Enter* HIGGINS *and* MAGAN *R.)*

HIGGINS I tell ye I had hould ov him—absolutely hould ov him—an' if it hadn't been for the military, I'd have captured the rebel single-handed.

LORD E (*appearing*) Ah!

MAGAN And the money would have been—(*sees* LORD E, *changes tone at once*) and the money—the cursed blood money would have been yours.

HIGGINS (*in surprise*) Eh!

MAGAN (*aside to him*) Hush! (*Aloud*) Yes.

HIGGINS (*understanding*) Oh!

MAGAN (*sternly*) And had Lord Edward been arrested, friends, though you and I have been for years, so dearly do I appreciate and reverence his noble character, I would have called you out and run you through with as little compunction as I would a rat.

LORD E Honest fellow, and true, aye, true as steel.

HIGGINS (*with assumed warmth*) Would ye? Take care me fine possessor of a barrister's wig and gown, yer don't get yer neck in a noose for upholding such a fanatical Patriot an' the rest of the disthurbing fraternity. They're corruptin' ye already.

MAGAN (*with equal warmth*) Let them, I care not how quickly, how soon. To-morrow perhaps I may throw off all disguise and proclaim myself.

HIGGINS (*ironically*) Lave that to the Government, my bhoy; they'll proclaim ye fast enough, an' so well, too, that there won't be a hole or corner in Ireland small enough for yer to hide in.

MAGAN (*sarcastically*) Ah, I suppose even you, if you found it worth your while, would betray me?

HIGGINS I would, an' glory in the action for I may just as well enrich mesilf at your expense, as let anodher man do it. I don't fancy though ye'd be worth so very much afther all, a palthry hundred or two. Now me bould Lord Edward—

MAGAN (*fiercely*) Is safe from your clutches. Interfere with him at your peril.

HIGGINS Bah, if the young scoundrel who has turned the country upside down and made it unfit for dacent people to live in were to show his face this minute I'd arrest him widout a moment's hesitation.

(LORD EDWARD *steps between them, they start apart.*)

LORD E Then the opportunity is yours, Lord Edward stands before you.

MAGAN (*in apparent alarm*) My lord, this exposure is terrible, dangerous to foolhardiness.

LORD E (*laughing*) Do you call this worm, this ingrate, this trafficker in blood money, this seller of men's lives, dangerous? Why with him I am perfectly safe.

HIGGINS Are yez?

LORD E Why don't ye arrest me? (*Crosses to R.*)

HIGGINS An' so I will. (*Lays his R. hand on LORD E's L. shoulder.*)

LORD E (*exposing pistol, HIGGINS starts*) Exactly, rather a surprise, eh? Now if you raise your hand from my shoulder, or move the other till I give you permission, the contents of this pistol will place you face to face with your master. (*Men heard marching in the distance R.*)

MAGAN Great Heavens, it is the Military. Escape, my lord, escape.

HIGGINS If yer don't ye're lost.

LORD E (*Jauntily*) That is where you make the mistake, Mr. Higgins. I am safer with you at this moment than anywhere else in Dublin. Major Sirr will never think of looking for the redoubtable Geraldine in the company of Mr. Higgins, the Castle Attorney. Do not imagine my pistol is removed, it is under my cloak with muzzle pointing at your head, and my finger on the trigger. One treacherous move, one hint at betrayal, and you precede me into the land of Shadows.

(*During this, men's footsteps have increased in sound, and as he finishes speaking they enter; LORD E resumes beard.*)

SIRR Halt! (*SOLDIERS halt.*)

MAGAN, HIGGINS } Good-night Major.

SIRR (*gruffly*) Good-night. (*Indicating LORD E*) Who is this?

HIGGINS (*aside*) Who the divil are yez?

LORD E (*aside*) A cousin.

HIGGINS Oh, just a cousin of mine.

SIRR A Dublin man?

HIGGINS Sorra the haporth* ov Dublin's about him except the mud on his brogues. He's from Bally-Slattery, d'ye know where that is, Major?

SIRR No, nor don't want.

HIGGINS (*aside*) Neither do mesilf. (*Aloud*) Shall I introjooce ye?

SIRR I'd rather be excused.

HIGGINS Ye're very polite.

SIRR What's he doin' here?

HIGGINS Oh, he's up for an operation on his throat.

SIRR Not a hempen one I hope.

HIGGINS Bedad I hope—(*LORD E touches him with pistol*) not.

SIRR Then take my advice and make a lawyer of him.

HIGGINS An' why may I ask?

SIRR It's the only way to keep him from turning Patriot or Rebel.

HIGGINS Ye will have ye little joke, Major.

SIRR Well come with me, I hate your company, but as I have something important to impart, I must for once in way endure the infliction.

HIGGINS Wid pleasure. (*Is going.*)

LORD E (*aside*) Stay.

HIGGINS I'm awfully sorry Major, but a very pressing engagement with a nobleman precludes the possibility of accompanying you at this exact moment; I'll folly. (*Aside*) When I'm let.

SIRR Very well, Good night. (*To men*) Forward! Quick march!

MAGAN Saved. (*Crosses to R. MAJOR, SOLDIERS exeunt L.*)

LORD E There, what did I tell you, who w'd think of looking for a Patriot in the company of the Shamado.

HIGGINS Am I at liberty to relave mesilf ov your presence?

LORD E You are, but permit me first to thank you for your disreputable society and the protection it afforded.

HIGGINS I'll have me revenge for this. (*Is going L.*)

LORD E Not that way, this (*points R. He crosses to R.*) Thanks, it will better enable me to effect a retreat.

MAGAN (*aloud to HIGGINS*) Breathe a word of this encounter and you have to reckon with me. (*Aside to him*) I will see you later. (*Aloud*) Good-night, and remember, betrayal means death.

LORD E Good-night.

HIGGINS Good-night, an' may the grass soon grow above ye.

LORD E If it does it will at all events grow above what has been an honest man.

HIGGINS The divil fly away wid ye and yer honesty. (*Exits R.*)

MAGAN Thank Heaven that blackguard's gone. Let's hurry. Where are you staying?

LORD E At Portobello; but to-night I dine and sleep at Moore's.

MAGAN Ah, you are secure there.

LORD E No place more so. Come, I have much to say to you.

MAGAN (*aside*) I must give the word. (*Aloud*) It will be safer if we go different ways.

LORD E Why, we are close to the house; no friend, you and I must not part again till Dublin is ours.

MAGAN As you will, as you will. (*Exeunt L.*)

End of Scene 2

Scene 3

MOUNTAIN PASS, NEAR FINGLAS

(*Tents L. Raking pieces R. to L., and L. to R. Bridge at top. Men grouped about in picturesque positions. Stand of guns. Pikes etc. [Ruin nearby].*)

(NEILSON, GALLAGHER, *and* PALMER *discovered.*)

NEILSON Well boys, we're to have grand doin's at last. We're all to meet at Finglas to-night, and when Dublin's fast aslape we're to march straight into the city.

GALLAGHER By whose orders?

NEILSON Lord Edward's.

GALLAGHER He means work then.

NEILSON He does.

GALLAGHER Bedad, the red coats'll get a fine wakenin'.

PALMER What if they sh'd be ready to receive us?

NEILSON They won't. The secret has been too well kept. The very boldness of the step will insure success.

GALLAGHER There'll be wigs on the green afore mornin'.

NEILSON And broken skulls in Dame Street.

GALLAGHER And more blood in the gutters than watther.

PALMER It'll be a sad day for Ireland, I'm thinkin' when the sun rises to-morrow.

NEILSON A glorious one you mean.

PALMER No, I mean what I say. I don't like this war makin'.

GALLAGHER (*sneeringly*) Then ye'd betther make yerself small while yez skin whole on yer back.

NEILSON And yer neck safe from the rope.

PALMER I'm nayther afeard ov me skin nor me neck.

NEILSON (*sternly*) Are yez faithful?

PALMER (*warmly*) As any man here, but it's the road we're goin' I deslike. Mark me, Ireland will never gain freedom by force, only by peace.

GALLAGHER It's in pace you'll soon be if the bhoys hear ye blatherin' that way. (*Drum sounds in the distance.*)

NEILSON (*all alert*) Whisht!* what's that?

(*A PEASANT rushes on.*)

PEASANT Hide boys, the red coats are out. (*The tent is struck.*)

NEILSON (*to GALLAGHER*) It's the Patrol. (*They all hide.*)

(*Enter SOLDIERS from L. come down raking pieces and exeunt R.I.E. SIRR and HIGGINS last. Drum is kept playing till well off. NEILSON and all appear.*)

PALMER There they go, and Higgins wid them.

NEILSON And Sirr in command.

GALLAGHER The curse ov the crows in the two ov thim.

PEASANT May the divil, whin he gets them, scorch their bones to nothin'.

(*Enter THADY in full dress.*)

THADY Amin to that swate prayer.

GALLAGHER Is that yersilf?

THADY Yis, I'm all here together.

GALLAGHER You're lookin' fit.

THADY Aye for business, like a Xmas turkey.

GALLAGHER Ye look fine, grand, man.

THADY Like a pay-cock on church parade. How the divil's a poor bhoy to fight like this?

GALLAGHER Ye'll want no tachin' whin ye once see the red coats.

THADY Bedad, I've just seen them.

PALMER An' what did ye do?

THADY Got out ov their way.

GALLAGHER (*all laugh*) Ye're a brave bhoy so ye are.

THADY Aye, I'm like the rest ov yez. (*Aside*) I had thim that time. (*Aloud*) Ye see I wanted to live so that I might have the pleasure ov seein' thim die. (*They all laugh.*) Will one ov yez ase me ov this picklin' machine? (*One takes gun.*) That's a grand relafe.

GALLAGHER Is the Captain comin'?

THADY Is it the Geraldine?

OMNES Yes, yes.

THADY Isn't he here?

OMNES No—

THADY Then he's comin'.

GALLAGHER When?

THADY When he's on the road. (*Shrill whistle L.*) What's that? (*All listen.*)

NEILSON It's Lord Edward.

(LORD EDWARD *[masked] and* MAGAN *appear C. on rake.*)

THADY A cheer for the Geraldine.

LORD E No, boys, no.

THADY There isn't a red coat in sight, yer honor.

LORD E I know that.

THADY An' if there was isn't this the night we're to show them the straight road out ov Ireland. (*To all*) Hurroo boys.

OMNES (*Cheer.*)

LORD E Thanks, boys, thanks. It stirs the blood within me to hear your manly voices raised in such hearty welcome. Your brave hearts give courage to my own. And your honest faces flushed with the dawn of hope lend strength to my arm, and firmness to my resolution to bring freedom to our country.

OMNES (*Cheer.*)

LORD E Boys, to-night fight, fight with eye, brain and heart. Remember glorious liberty is on our side, rope and an ignominious death on the other. Let hope nerve your arm, hate steel your heart, and with eye and brain clear to see and to act. Victory—Glorious heaven-sent Victory will be, must be ours.

OMNES (*Cheer*) Long life to the Geraldines. Hurroo! (*A whistle heard R.; all on the alert.*) What's that? (NEILSON *hurries off R.*)

LORD E Don't be alarmed boys. Only friends can be out at this hour. (*To* NEILSON *who re-enters R.*) Who is it?

NEILSON A stranger in charge of one of the boys.

(*Enter* PEASANT *with* HIGGINS.)

LORD E Whom have we here?

THADY Why it's the dirthy little Shamado, ould Higgins. (*Making an advance movement.*) The spy, Shamado.

LORD E Back boys. (*To HIGGINS.*) They know you.

HIGGINS So it seems.

LORD E And your character—a spy.

HIGGINS I'm no spy, but a paceable law abidin' citizen of His Majesty King George.

[OMNES] (*Groans.*)

HIGGINS An' it would be betther for yez all, if ye gave up this fool's business an' wint yez ways like senseable dacent men.

LORD E That's our affair. What are you doing here?

HIGGINS (*fiercely*) That's mine.

LORD E Where's your pass?

HIGGINS Where it's goin' to remain, in my pocket.

LORD E What if I deprive you of it?

HIGGINS Ye dare not.

LORD E Dare not?

HIGGINS Aye, dare not, an' that's plain English.

THADY Ye lie, ye spalpeen,* its d—d impudence.

HIGGINS Lay a finger on me, an' I'll hang the lot ov ye.

THADY Ye wag a long tongue for so small a man.

LORD E What if we take the initiative and hang you first?

THADY Here's the rope. (*Showing it.*)

GALLAGHER An' here's a tree.

THADY It's a fine dance ye give us on nothin'.

PEASANT An' I'll play the tune.

THADY Seize him bhoys. (*Some do.*)

HIGGINS (*falling on his knees in terror*) Oh don't kill me, boys.

MAGAN (*to LORD E*) You will not resort to such extreme measures?

HIGGINS 'Tis Magan, then I'm safe.

LORD E (*feelingly*) My dear Magan, unprincipled as I know this fellow is, spy as I have every reason to believe him to be, I would not harm a hair of his head. I love Ireland's sons too well even to do one of them—base though he may be—willingly an injury. (*Aloud to BOYS*) Let him go. (*They do so. LORD E goes up.*)

HIGGINS (*to* MAGAN *who has crossed to R.*) Am I safe?

MAGAN Yes.

[OMNES] (*threateningly advancing*) Hang the divil.

LORD E (*coming down*) No boys no. (*They give way. To* HIGGINS) After you have answered a question I must put to you, you are free to go.

HIGGINS (*audaciously*) Stop me at your peril.

THADY How brave ye are when yez know yez neck's safe.

LORD E What's the pass word to-night?

HIGGINS I refuse to give it.

LORD E Then I'm afraid we must make necessity a virtue and compel you.

MAGAN (*to* HIGGINS) Be civil man, your life has been spared, do something in exchange. (*Aside*) Don't rouse the devil in them again, or I will not answer for the consequences. (*Aloud*) Reply.

LORD E I am waiting.

HIGGINS Cornwallis, thin, if ye will have it. (*Aside*) That's a lie but it doesn't matther.

LORD E (*bows*) Now you are at liberty to depart.

THADY (*in alarm*) Sure ye wouldn't take his word, yer honour? The lie was on his lips, like the hate in his eye. Search him an see for yersilf. (HIGGINS *starts and is going.*) Stop him boys. (*They stop him.*)

LORD E (*sternly*) Show me your pass.

HIGGINS I will on one condition.

LORD E You'll do it without, man, I command here.

HIGGINS A fine commandeher. A thafe ov a white boy.*

OMNES (*Groan.* LORD E *puts up his hand to restrain them.*)

HIGGINS Or a horse staler. (*Groans.*) Why don't ye take off the rag that hides yer face?

LORD E Because I don't choose.

HIGGINS (*with venom*) Because ye're afraid.

LORD E Indeed. Of whom?

HIGGINS Of an honest man seeing you.

LORD E But you're not an honest man.

HIGGINS No?

LORD E No, but as great a rogue as ever the Castle employed to the destruction of Ireland.

HIGGINS Thin why don't ye kill me?

LORD E Because we don't murder in cold blood. We leave that to you and your masters. We live to work to fight, and if necessary, to die for the regeneration of our country.

HIGGINS Bosh, bosh. Wid all your fine speeches ye're a coward. (*LORD E starts.*) Aye, a coward. I dare ye to show yer face.

OMNES Don't do it, yer honour. (*NEILSON and others talk to him.*)

MAGAN (*aside*) You're going too far.

HIGGINS (*fiercely*) Divil a bit. I'll see his face if I die for it. It'll be fine evidence when he's on his trial. I'll hang him.

LORD E He is right, it is rank utter cowardice. (*Turns to HIGGINS.*)

HIGGINS (*to LORD E*) Have ye done arguing wid ye conscience?

LORD E I have. (*Tears off mask.*) There is my face.

HIGGINS I thought so. Lord Edward Fitzgerald. (*Advances threateningly.*)

LORD E (*with drawn sword*) A step more forward and it is your last.

THADY (*twists HIGGINS round to R. to LORD E*) Ah, don't be afther soilin' yer clane sword wid his thick dirthy blood. (*To the BOYS*) Hang the Shamado.

OMNES Hang him! hang him!

MAGAN (*aloud*) Away with him to the nearest tree.

HIGGINS (*startled*) What! (*To MAGAN*) Is it you w'd hang me?

THADY Aye would he, an' it's a fine puddin' for the crows ye'll make.

MAGAN (*aside to HIGGINS*) Quiet fool. If I appear to show you mercy now, both our fates are sealed. Submit and I'll save you yet. (*Aloud*) Away with him.

OMNES Away wid the Shamado. (*Exeunt with HIGGINS who struggles fiercely.*)

LORD E Stop them, Magan, and let the wretch go.

MAGAN Let him hang, my lord, he deserves no better death.

LORD E No, no.

THADY (*outside*) Where's the rope bhoys?

OMNES (*Groans outside.*)

LORD E Let him go, I say, let him go.

MAGAN Your leniency will cost you dear.

THADY (*outside*) Now then, ready, bhoys.

LORD E (*passionately*) I care not if it cost me my life.

MAGAN (*aside*) Which it will. (*Aloud*) You wish him to live?

LORD E Yes, yes.

THADY (*outside*) Up with him, bhoys. (*Cheers.*)

LORD E Quick, quick. Bid them let him go ere it's too late.

MAGAN As you will. (*Exits L. shouting.*) Stop, stop I say. (*Groans outside.*)

LORD E Some terrible curse must be on our land, that it sh'd yield existence to such wretches as that—beings born only to become informers, and traitors. (*Re-enter* MAGAN.) Is he safe?

MAGAN Yes. (*Groans outside very loud.*) That is their expressions of dissatisfaction at his life being spared.

LORD E Ah, Magan, trusted, valued friend, tell me, how it is that we let the insidious canker-worm of mistrust and treachery thrive in our bosoms?

MAGAN (*startled*) It's a mystery, my lord.

LORD E It is indeed, one insolvable to this poor mind of mine. (*A shrill whistle heard L.U.E.*) What's that?

(*Enter* GALLAGHER *hurriedly L.E.*)

GALLAGHER Her ladyship, my lord.

LORD E (*to* MAGAN) What, what can bring her here?

MAGAN Something of importance you may be sure.

(*Enter* PAMELA *in riding-habit and cloaked, followed by* BLACK SERVANT.)

LORD E (*Goes to meet her.* MAGAN *goes L.C. Enter* THADY *followed by* BOYS.) Pamela, wife, what portends this sudden unlooked for visit of your sweet self?

PAMELA (*in agitated tones*) Oh husband, the Castle is aware of your plans.

LORD E (*startled*) Ah!

PAMELA You are betrayed.

LORD E Again! (*Looks at* MAGAN.)

[TABLEAU]

PAMELA LORD E MAGAN THADY

PAMELA The troops were assembling when we left and in an hour will be marching in this direction.

LORD E Boys, to your posts, and a guinea to the man who first sights a red coat.

THADY Begorra,* I'm that man. (*All exit at separate points.*)

LORD E (*to* THADY) Stay.

THADY But I want the guinea, General.

LORD E And I want you here.

THADY Ah let me go.

LORD E And leave us defenceless?

THADY Sorra a bit* ov me'll stir a fut afther that.

LORD E (*to* PAMELA) Come, with me, here you can tell me all, and while I listen to your sweet voice and watch the love shining out of your eyes, I can arrange what's to be done.

PAMELA (*tenderly*) Oh, let me stay with you to share your perils, be by your side to cheer you, in your struggles, let, oh let me stay. These cruel separations are breaking my heart.

LORD E And mine dear, but God will give us strength to endure and to suffer, and we shall yet live to hear our country bless us for all that we have gone through in her cause. Come, time hurries on apace, and I would know all you have to impart. (*Exeunt R.*)

(*MAGAN is following when THADY touches him on the shoulder, servant goes and stands before entrance [of the ruin].*)

MAGAN (*sternly*) What is it?

THADY Has Trinity College taught ye no betther manners than that?

MAGAN Than what, fool?

THADY Than to shadow thim wid your presence at this moment.

(*MAGAN turns to enter ruin but is stopped by SERVANT who opposes him.*)

MAGAN (*in a rage*) Let me pass.

TONY Massa Fitzgerald say, no.

MAGAN And I say, yes. (*Moves forward.*)

TONY (*brings bayonet down to the charge*) Back, or I'll run you through.

MAGAN Ah!

THADY Hurroo, Tony. Skiver* him up; he's only a lawyer an' won't be missed.

MAGAN Would you dare, sir; let me pass. (*Pushes bayonet on one side.*)

TONY (*bringing bayonet back again*) I'll see you damned first till Massa Fitzgerald gives you leave.

(LORD E *appears at door.*)

LORD E What's this disturbance about?

MAGAN Your servant has refused to let me enter, has threatened me with cold steel if I persist.

LORD E (*advancing to him*) That Magan is the outward sign of the faithful heart within, and you should be the very last to condemn him, for such an exhibition of love and fidelity.

THADY Thrue for yez Lordship. (*To* MAGAN) Swallow that if ye can.

LORD E (*patting* SERVANT *on shoulder*) This Gentleman, Tony, is my friend; let him pass.

TONY Yes, my Lord. (*They exeunt into ruin.*) I don't like that man.

THADY I believe he's the blackest divil in the county this minute, no offense me bhoy to yerself; ye own face is black enough, but it's white, so it is, to his heart.

TONY He's no true.

THADY Sorra's the day that Ireland ever bred him.

TONY Sit down.

THADY I'm thinkin' I will, I'm mortal tired. (*They sit. Places his gun where* KITTY *can get at it.*)

TONY Missy Kitty here!

THADY Man alive, is that so? Bad scran* to me. Butthered toast foreninst* me and niver to taste it.

KITTY [*aside*] I'll give ye butthered toast me man, if that's all ye can say ov me. (*She takes up hat, places it on her head, then picks up his gun and throws cloak over her shoulder man's fashion.*)

THADY (*to* TONY, *they having been talking during the foregoing piece of business*) Ye don't say so (*laughs*).

TONY Yes. (KITTY *comes down, slaps* THADY *on the shoulder.* THADY *jumps up in alarm.* TONY *falls to the ground.*)

THADY Tundher and turf,* what's that? (*Sees her.*) Ah!

KITTY (*in disguised voice*) Stand and deliver.

(*Presents gun.*)

THADY (*looking round for it*) Where's my cannon?

KITTY Here. (*He moves.*) Move a slip, an' ye're a live corpse.

THADY Blow me away cock-sparrow, it's not loaded, but this is. (*Pointing big pistol.*) Down on ye benders an' say a morsel ov prayers, if ye can think ov any, while ye've time.

KITTY (*She gives a slight scream, drops gun, falls on her knees, and holding out her hands, says in natural tones*) Oh, don't murdher me.

THADY The divil's cure to me, if it isn't Kitty.

KITTY Oh, don't shoot me, sure I'm only a woman.

THADY How do I know that, me girl?

KITTY Sure I'm yez own Kitty.

THADY Are yez?

KITTY Yes, sure I only wanted to give ye a bit ov a fright.

THADY An' got a mighty big one instead, me girl. Don't play with dangerous weapons that way.

(*Enter* LORD E, PAMELA, *and* MAGAN.)

LORD E What's the matter here?

THADY Only Kitty playin' at sodgerin' yer honour.

(*Shrill whistle heard R., repeated L. Business can be introduced here.*)

LORD E Ah, an alarm! (*Rushes to* THADY. TWO [THREE] MEN *appear R. and L.*)

1ST PEASANT (*hands letter*) The Kildare men are on the road.

2D PEASANT (*hands letter*) So also are the Maynooth men.

LORD E Well, what is it?

[3RD] PEASANT A body ov men are approaching, my lord.

LORD E Friends or foes? (*Enter* NEILSON *L.*)

NEILSON Friends, my lord. (*Enter* GALLAGHER *L.*)

GALLAGHER 'Tis the Tallaght boys, yer honour. (*Enter* PALMER *L.*)

LORD E Well?

PALMER The Carlow men are roundin' the hill below.

LORD E What news bring they?

PALMER That the Dublin troops are marching South.

LORD E Not on Finglas?

PALMER No, my lord.

LORD E This corresponds with your news. (*To* PAMELA.)

MAGAN (*aside*) Both wrong.

THADY (*aside to* MAGAN) Ye've a lot to say to yersilf to-night.

LORD E (*music heard in the distance*) Hark, what's that?

PALMER The Carlow boys with their band.

LORD E Then the news is true, and though we have been once more betrayed, this time the betrayer has overreached his mark.

LORD E They come, boys. (*To* PAMELA.) You shall have a brave escort back to town. The strains rouse the blood to fever heat in our veins. (*Raises sword.*) For Dublin. Tonight boys, we write a glorious page in Ireland's History.

(*Band increases in ⟨violence⟩ volume, marches on followed by* MEN, *till* TABLEAU.)

End of Act II

ACT III

Scene 1

CHAMBER IN HOUSE IN DENZILLE STREET

(MAGAN *discovered seated at table R. reading Proclamation.*)

MAGAN "£1000 Reward for the arrest, or any secret information that may lead to the same, of Lord Edward Fitzgerald, May 11th, 1798." Well, I have nothing to do but to hold out my hand and grasp it. Shall I? Only I were sure of her, of the beautiful Pamela, I'[d] have him arrested at once; death would soon follow; and to whom would she turn for solace and affection, but the man who has done so much for his safety. Ha! Ha! (*Crosses to R.*) Safety! Yes, in keeping them apart and harassing his life, till existence must, by this, be a positive torture. (*Sitting.*) Once the sod is over him, she will turn to me to dry her tears.

(*Enter* TONY *door L.*)

MAGAN Well?

TONY A Gentleman to see you, sir.

MAGAN What does he want?

(*Enter* HIGGINS.)

HIGGINS You, me bhoy (MAGAN *rises suddenly and lifts left hand warningly.* HIGGINS *turns to servant*). Lave us. (TONY *does not move.*) D'ye hear, lave us, ye black divil.

MAGAN (*crossing to* TONY) You did wrong to admit him, Tony. Go now, but do not be far away. (*Crosses to table,* HIGGINS *goes to sideboard.*)

TONY (*aside*) I won't, but Missy shall know he's here.

(*Exits.*)

MAGAN (*angrily*) What brought you here?

HIGGINS Yersilf, ye wouldn't come to the mountain, so the mountain's come to you. (*Fills glass with wine from decanter.*)

MAGAN Do you want to endanger my life?

HIGGINS No, I want to fill yer pockets; yer health Magan. (*Drinks, spits it out again, goes L.*) Arrah,* man, why don't yer kape a drop ov dacent dhrink in the house? That stuff is not fit for a gentleman at all, at all.

MAGAN It's good enough for me.

HIGGINS Aye, but you are not a gentleman. (*Opens door.*) Gone, I see.

MAGAN Yes, he's not an eavesdropper like yourself. (*Goes up to sideboard.*)

HIGGINS Is that so, tit for tat; well, I forgive ye. (*Crosses to table.*) Still a student, eh?

MAGAN (*comes down R. of table*) Student of what?

HIGGINS (*points to bill*) The Newgate Calendar. (*Holds it up.*) An important page out ov the book me bhoy.

MAGAN How I regret the work cruel necessity compels me to do.

HIGGINS Aye, (*sits*) an' the Government's also regretting the money they're payin' ye.

MAGAN (*sits*) I'd willingly give them back every penny I've had from them.

HIGGINS Yes, over the left, arrah* man, don't be thryin' the penitent dodge wid me. It won't wash.

MAGAN Indeed.

HIGGINS That's so, I have to dale wid too many of yer kidney to be taken in wid crocidile lamentations and twidde[nme] twaddenm[e] bosh. The Government want Lord Edward Fitzgerald.

MAGAN Well?

HIGGINS An' they do you the honour, being the big scoundrel ye are, an' knowin' his exact domiciliary residence at the present moment.

MAGAN I am much flattered.

HIGGINS They want him immajitly or—

MAGAN Or what?

HIGGINS They withdraw on Monday next the £1000 reward.

MAGAN (*surprised*) Ah!

HIGGINS I thought that would surprise ye. Have a glass of vinegar to steady yer nerves. (*Indicating wine on sideboard.*) Where is he?

MAGAN (*surely*) I don't know.

HIGGINS That's a lie, now let's have a bit ov thruth to vary the monotony. Where is he?

MAGAN I tell you I don't know, and if I did—

HIGGINS Ye wouldn't split. Another lie. Look here, Magan, I've £500 in my pocket for the information an' the balance is to be had when he's safe in Newgate. For the third and last time, Where is he?

MAGAN (*fiercely*) Curse you, I don't know.

HIGGINS (*jumping up*) Then I'm off. (*Goes rapidly across the room.*)

MAGAN Stay.

HIGGINS (*turns sharp around*) Thin ye know?

MAGAN Yes.

HIGGINS It's a small word, but bedad it's taken a dale ov exthraction. (*Crosses to table.*) Where is he?

MAGAN Give me the money.

HIGGINS Give me the information.

MAGAN My poverty, and not my will, consents.

HIGGINS That's the biggest lie ov all. (*Counts out notes.*)

MAGAN (*furiously*) Enough. The money.

HIGGINS Right, ye are. Ten ov them each one worth £50. Where is he?

MAGAN He will be in this house to-night.

HIGGINS (*jumping up*) Tare an' ouns.* Ye don't say so.

MAGAN Curse you, speak low.

HIGGINS (*sitting down*) Bedad, that's glorious.

MAGAN Two hours hence, if all your arrangements are complete, he can be in your possession.

HIGGINS Right. Sirr an' his men shall be on the job at once. (*Suspiciously.*) But if he sh'd fail to nab him?

MAGAN He won't, but if he should, I guarantee he shall be your prisoner within forty-eight hours. Will that suffice?

HIGGINS It will. (*Rising.*) I'm off.

MAGAN Won't you have another glass?

HIGGINS I won't, one ov that brand's enough for a lifetime. (*Turns, and sees* LADY FITZGERALD *entering.*) Ah, ten thousand apologies me lady. (*Bows profoundly.*)

PAMELA Who are you sir?

HIGGINS No one ov any importance, me lady. Good day. (*Crosses behind her to door. She crosses to C.*) That settles the job entoirely to my satisfaction. Where the hen is the cock-bird won't be far off. (*Exit door L.* MAGAN *has gone up to wave him out of room. She crosses to table.*)

PAMELA Who is that man?

MAGAN (*crossing to L.C. and closing door*) A friend, and— —

PAMELA (*interrupting and facing him*) What, the Castle bloodhound (MAGAN *starts*) and leach your friend.

MAGAN (*bowing*) Both friend and enemy.

PAMELA (*sarcastically*) A strange mixture.

MAGAN (*another bow*) But necessary in these times. You know him?

PAMELA I never forget a face or a voice once seen or heard. (*With emphasis.*)

MAGAN (*apologetically*) My duty to the cause brings me in contact with strange characters.

PAMELA Evidently, when I find Higgins, the Castle Attorney, closeted with you in this house. (*Sees money on table.*)

MAGAN It appears he had followed me. He came as a special emissary of the Government. (*She looks at him.*) I admit it, to persuade me to be false to my oath.

PAMELA (*with cutting sarcasm*) And succeeded.

MAGAN No, signally failed.

PAMELA (*with contempt*) And I say, succeeded, for here, (*taking up the notes*) is the blood money. (MAGAN *starts.*) The price of your treachery. What have you to say now?

MAGAN (*in injured tones*) Only this, if such is your opinion, burn them at once in the flames of that candle. That done, bury this dagger (*producing one*) in my heart. Better, far better, their destruction and my death, tha[n] you sh'd believe me capable of such sordid baseness, such heartless villainy. You hesitate, learn then, how deeply you have wronged me. Double that amount (*pointing to it*) of money was borrowed at ruinous interest for your husband (*she starts*) and for the cause. It was lying there (*pointing to table*) when that man entered, so far from his giving or adding to the sum, I had to reduce it by one-half to purchase information from the mercenary scoundrel. (*She looks at him doubtfully.*) Yes, information, but for which Lord Edward would be a prisoner within the next twelve hours.

PAMELA (*with an effort*) Is this true?

MAGAN Let my actions be my only answer.

PAMELA (*advancing towards him*) If I have—nay I must have wronged you (*holds out her hand—he takes it*). I ask your pardon and forgiveness.

MAGAN (*with feeling*) This moment repays me for all.

(*Kisses her hand, she shudders.*)

PAMELA (*crossing to R. aside*) Why, oh why, can't I trust him. His words are good, his acts self-sacrificing, yet his presence only irritates and annoys me, whilst his touch is like ice round my heart. (*Sits.*)

MAGAN (*aside*) I am progressing. A little more seemingly disinterested attention will open the safety valves of emotion, gratitude, will soften sorrow, and love shall follow both.

(*Enter child* EDWARD *crying, Mama?*)

EDWARD Mama! Màma! (*Goes to* PAMELA, *she embraces him.*)

PAMELA What is it darling?

EDWARD I want to see Papa.

PAMELA Ah my darling, and so does Mama.

MAGAN (*advancing*) Shall I bring him to you?

EDWARD (*facing him*) Go away, I don't like you.

PAMELA Hush, dear. (*Embraces him closely.*)

MAGAN Why don't you like me?

EDWARD Because you always make my Mama cry; and you keep Papa away from us.

MAGAN Not willingly, my boy, not willingly.

EDWARD (*stamping his foot*) You do, you know you do, for Kitty says so.

PAMELA Hush dear, Kitty mustn't say such things.

EDWARD But she does, and she will. (*To* MAGAN.) I like Kitty, and I hate you.

PAMELA But you must try to like him, for Papa loves and trusts him.

EDWARD Does he?

PAMELA Yes, and Mama likes and trusts him too. (MAGAN *gives a smile of satisfaction.*)

EDWARD Will it please you if I try?

PAMELA So much.

EDWARD Then I will. (*To* MAGAN, *holds out his hand.*) If Papa loves and trusts you, I will do so, too.

PAMELA That's my own brave boy. (*Embraces him affectionately. Noise heard outside—[*PAMELA*] in alarm*) What's that?

MAGAN What sh'd it be, but that which will bring gladness to your heart, the presence of your husband. (*She starts.*) I promised you sh'd see Lord Edward here. (*She rises.*) And I have kept my word.

PAMELA My husband! Edward, and here.

(*Enter* LORD EDWARD *followed by* THADY, TONY, *and* KITTY.)

LORD E Yes, love, here. (*They embrace. Crossing to* MAGAN.) How can I thank you for this glimpse of happiness?

MAGAN By allowing me to retire. Seeing the light of love in her eyes is reward enough for me.

LORD E Noble and generous as ever. (*To* PAMELA.) Have you no word of thanks for our best friend?

PAMELA (*with gladness in her tones*) Oh, a thousand (*taking his hand*). A thousand, whatever doubts, whatever fears I have allowed to take root in my heart, let this (*kisses his hand*) eradicate once and for ever.

LORD E (*to* CHILD) And you Teddy. (*Lifts him up.*) And have you nothing to say?

EDWARD Oh yes, (*to* MAGAN) God bless you for bringing Papa to Mama and me.

LORD E (*slaps* MAGAN *on the shoulder*) He deserves a kiss for that sweet prayer.

MAGAN And he shall have it. (*Kisses him,* CHILD *runs R.*)

TONY The kiss of Judas. (*Exits door L.*)

THADY (*to* CHILD) Don't ye like the taste ov it?

EDWARD No Thady, I don't.

THADY (*gives sugarstick*) There, tickle yer gums wid that; that'll soon take it away. (*LORD E and PAMELA laugh. MAGAN goes to door L.*)

MAGAN (*aside*) If he is arrested here, her belief in me will again waver, so when Sirr arrives I must aid his escape, and earn still another installment of gratitude.

THADY (*to him*) What a divil ye are, sir, for colloquing wid yersilf?

MAGAN Am I? It's a habit of mine.

THADY Thin get rid ov it at once afore yer let out any saycrets.

MAGAN I'm not afraid. I have nothing to conceal. (*Turns.*)

THADY I'm not so sure of that, I don't altogether like the look in that off eye of his.

MAGAN I go to watch below, so that no harm may come to your Master. (*Exit door L.*)

THADY An' I'm thinkin' it'll be no loss if I watch you. (*Exit door L.*)

KITTY An' I'm thinkin' I'll watch the both ov yez. (*Exit door L.*)

LORD E (*sitting in chair R.C. PAMELA at his feet, CHILD leaning over top of chair*) Four long weeks darling since I looked into your bright eyes, heard your dear voice uttering sweet words of love and sympathy.

PAMELA Would I could speak words of hope as well.

LORD E But you will, for they, our hopes, were never brighter than at this moment.

PAMELA So you said on that night in March, before Finglas. But the dark shadows of treachery that ever dog your steps, destroyed then in an hour your labour of months—cast dismay amidst your followers, drove them panic stricken back to their homes, and made you a fugitive and an outlaw. Oh dear, hesitate, before it is too late; draw back whilst there is yet time, from this uneven terrible struggle, a struggle that can only end in miserable disaster, and death. Think dear, you with your rank and position, hunted like a criminal, a price on your head, never knowing friend or foe, dreading every moment of each hour to hear the tramp of the Military, or feel the clutch of the traitor on your throat, or his knife in your heart.

LORD E Now, I won't listen to another word, little woman, for you would have me become what you so righteously condemn in others—a traitor. (*She makes a movement of dissent.*) Absence and your fears have depressed your spirits, you see failure ⟨when it sh'd be⟩ in success, an informer in a friend, and danger in security. Why, if I were to follow the dictates of that loving heart of yours, obloquy, deep and deserved would be mine, my name execrated and denounced, and I the worst poltroon* Ireland ever produced. No, I am the head of this rebellion, the people, the whole country look to me for guidance, for victory. They love—they trust me, and whatever comes, I'll give them back love for love, and trust for trust. Now take me to the other children.

PAMELA Pamela is with your mother, but baby is here. (*Rising.*)

EDWARD You stay with me, Papa, and Mama will bring baby.[1]

LORD E And why (*leaning back, BOY with legs on chair, ready to be lifted on his shoulder when he rises*) are you not with Grandmama at Carton?

EDWARD (*sturdily*) Because I stayed to protect Mama and baby.

LORD E (*laughing and rising with him on his shoulders*) There's a son for you, are you not proud of him? (*He stoops and PAMELA kisses him.*) Kiss him. And now bring baby. (*PAMELA exits R. To child.*) Now Ted, what shall it be, a song or a pick-a-back ride?

EDWARD Both, Papa.

LORD E Listen to the young turk; well, you shall have both. (*Aside.*) Who knows they may be the last.

Song

(*Reenter PAMELA with BABY.*)

LORD E Ah, here's Mama with baby. (*All in centre of stage.*)

PAMELA Isn't she pretty? (*CHILD still on his shoulder.*)

LORD E As a sunbeam. (*LORD E has arm round PAMELA, both looking down at the INFANT. PAMELA sobs.*) What, crying little wife!

PAMELA I—I cannot help it. Oh how happy we sh'd be if it were not for this agony of suspense—this ever present torture, the ever pervading gloom of the scaffold before our eyes. Oh God, I cannot bear it longer. (*She breaks down.*)

EDWARD Don't cry, Mama, see how brave I am. (*LORD E puts him down.*)

LORD E (*cheerfully, but with a break in voice*) There darling, let the boy's words sink into your heart—let them be the harbingers of hope and comfort.

PAMELA (*brokenly*) I feel—know, this is the last I shall ever look upon your face—feel your arms around me.

LORD E No, no, wife, no, no. Though danger lurks in our midst I shall escape scatheless, and though the cup of sorrow at your lips is overflowing, it will change, aye change to one of fullest joy.

(*Noise of clanging swords outside,* BOY *rushes to window.*)

EDWARD The soldiers Papa! (PAMELA *screams and clings to him.*)

(*Enter* THADY, TONY, *and* KITTY *door L.*)

THADY For the love of Heaven, fly masther, fly.

(*Enter* MAGAN *hurriedly door L.*)

MAGAN Impossible, every outlet is guarded.

LORD E Betrayed. Caught like a rat in a trap.

MAGAN So it seems.

THADY (*fiercely seizing* MAGAN *by the throat*) And you're the betrayer. (PAMELA *screams and faints.*)

LORD E Great Heavens, she has fainted. It is better so, better so. (*He and* KITTY *place her in the armchair.*)

MAGAN (*throwing off* THADY) Fool, I am here to save, not to betray. (*Locks door L.*)

THADY What are ye doin'?

MAGAN Keeping them out. (*Heavy knock at door.*)

SIRR Open in the King's name. (*Another knock.*)

TONY What's to be done? (*Takes sword out of box L.*)

LORD E (*drawing sword*) Fight to the bitter end.

THADY (*taking one of the swords*) Then I'll be the first to go.

(*During this, noise must be kept up outside.*)

MAGAN (*who is on sofa and has opened Picture*) Nothing of the kind. Quick my lord, in with you. (LORD E. *springs through the opening.*) Saved.

SIRR (*outside*) Open the door or I'll break it in.

THADY Thin break away, ould Sirr, for you're just too late.

MAGAN (MAGAN *has picked up* LORD E.*'s hat and cloak. To* THADY) On with them (*does so*) and stand there. (*Points to chair, he stands over* PAMELA, SIRR *keeps up the noise and just as* THADY *has assumed position, he and soldiers rush in;* MAGAN *goes to window;* TWO SOLDIERS *appear.*)

SIRR (*with hand on* THADY*'s shoulder*) Lord Edward Fitzgerald, I arrest you in the king's name.

THADY (*quietly*) Sure I'm not Lord Edward. (*SIRR jumps back amazed. General surprise.*)

TABLEAU

End of Scene 1

Scene 2

MR. O'MOORE'S HOUSE

(*Enter MR. O'MOORE, THADY, and MISS O'MOORE R.*)

MR. O'MOORE What's that you say? Another attempt to arrest Lord Edward?

THADY Thrue for yez, in Denzille Street.

MISS O'MOORE But he has escaped safely?

THADY Would I be here if he hadn't, Miss? You sh'd jest have seen ould Sirr's face when he found he'd got the wrong pig by the ear. It was like a pickled herrin' down wid a fit of the jaundice. But where's his honor? I've lashin's of news for him.

MR. O'MOORE I haven't seen Lord Edward for a week.

THADY Tare an' ouns,* ye don't say so; what if he sh'd be took afther all, an' I not to the fore. Ruination to me sowl, where is he at all, at all?

(*Enter LORD E L.*)

LORD E Why here, Thady, safe and sound, where should I be. (*Shakes hands with MR. O'MOORE.*)

THADY Daylight to me conscience, it's himself an' no other. Hurroo, Ireland for ever.

LORD E Why, what's the matter? (*Crosses to MISS O'MOORE, shakes hands.*)

THADY I thought ould Sirr had got a hould ov yer.

LORD E Not yet, Thady, not yet. (*Laughs.*)

THADY An' well for him he hasn't, or the divil w'd soon have had hould ov him. Arrah* where have you been sthrayin' to?

LORD E To Portobello, to see my faithful friends.

MISS O'MOORE Why my lord, will you run such danger?

LORD E Danger, Miss O'Moore, is my bosom companion. (*Crosses to MR. O'MOORE.*)

THADY An' ye're mighty fond ov him too, I'm thinkin'.

MISS O'MOORE (*To THADY.*) What a great big heart he has.

THADY As big as a bullock's! Sorra the haporth's* rest (*to LORD E*) ye'll give the bhoys once ye take the field.

LORD E Little indeed, till the green flag floats over every town and village in Ireland.

THADY Hurroo!

OMNES Hush.

THADY Cut it out. If ye love me, cut it, and pickle it for ould Sirr's benefit. (*Enter MAGAN L. NEILSON R.*)

LORD E Ah, Magan what of her, what of my wife? (*Goes to him.*)

MAGAN Safe in my house at Usher's Quay. There she can rest in security till you may visit her.

LORD E Which I must do to-night. (*MR. O'MOORE talks to MISS O'MOORE.*)

MAGAN Impossible, think my lord of the risk—the peril.

MR. O'MOORE The jeopardising of your liberty.

LORD E I do, but I must think of my wife as well. If I forget her in her hour of need, how can I expect heaven to succour me. I left her, ah, how did I leave her, you know (*to MAGAN*), left her with the fierce shouts of the Military paralysing her heart, her babe of a month old in her arms, her boy clinging at her side, and she heartbroken, insensible; oh Magan, I must go, I must go.

THADY And so ye shall.

MAGAN Thady's right.

THADY Begorra,* I'm never left when there's a good job to be done.

MAGAN (*Others talk aside; also aside*) I had arranged for his arrest here, but the open street will serve my purpose better, and divert suspicion from me.

THADY Ye're at it again. Ye bate Banagher* to smithereen for talkin' to yersilf.

MISS O'MOORE Thady, I thought you had news for his lordship?

THADY So I have. The curse of Mulligan's pig on me for forgettin' it. Whisht* while I tell it. If his honor hadn't made up his mind to go to Usher's Island, it's not here he could have slept to-night.

OMNES No?—

THADY That's so, in spite of yez noes.

LORD E What do you mean?

THADY That ould Sirr an' his lobsters are to pay the house a visit afore cock crow in the mornin'.

OMNES Ah!

LORD E Where learnt you this?

THADY From Tommy Tuite.

NEILSON Who's he?

THADY Me Mother's cousin on me Grandfather's side. I met him runnin' like mad in Dame Street, like a Militia man after a pint of porther. I stept, as I thought, out ov his way, an' his head stept into me stomach. The collission stopt him, an' my wind at the same time. "Is that you, Thady," says he, when he had recovered his perpendiculari[t]y from the horizontal. "It is," says I, gasping out the articulation like a say sarpent that's out of his latitude on the top of the Hill ov Howth. "What is it?" "Whisht,"* says he, "I've somethin' for yez," "I've got it," says I, thinkin' he was wantin' to repate the illustration.

LORD E For goodness sake, hurry up, you're fearfully slow.

THADY I am, bad luck to me. It's all the fault ov not havin' got my second wind. "Where's his lordship?" says Tommy. "At ould Moore's," says I, beggin' yer pardon for makin' so free wid yez age, but it was all the fault of my not havin' got my second wind, as I sad afore. "For the love of glory," says he, "get him out ov that at wanst," says he. "Why?" says I. "Because," says he, "I heard Cooke and Higgins colloquing over the masther, an' that word had been sent to Sirr to search the house when ye were all aslape an' fast awake in bed."

MAGAN Ah! (*Surprised, aside.*) Mr. Tuite must be looked after.

THADY (*To MAGAN*) Ye're at it again.

NEILSON And how came your cousin to be in the Castle?

THADY Shure he was mendin' the floors.

NEILSON That may be, but they would never talk loud enough, knowing he was there, to be heard.

THADY They didn't, they convarsed in whispers, knowin' he was present; but Tommy, the horn of plenty be his from this time out, has such long ears, by way, I'm tould, ov his mother havin' an ould donkey that was terribly fond of singin', that he overheard ivery blissid word spoken.

NEILSON Is the information to be relied on?

THADY Axe his lordship, he knows that neither Tommy nor mesilf w'd be afther disgracin' oursilves wid a lie, when the tellin' ov it would endanger his life.

MR. O'MOORE What's to be done?

LORD E (*cheerfully*) Why, quit the house. Relieve you, my worthy old friend of any suspicion of complicity in the rebellion, and of sheltering and harbouring the notorious Geraldine. Were I arrested here, even your grey hairs would not shield you from the scaffold.

MR. O'MOORE I fear not that.

LORD E I know you do not, but I fear it for you.

MR. O'MOORE There is no hurry.

THADY Not a bit ov it. Sirr won't come out till all the respectable people are in. He's like the cats, fond of night rambles.

MISS O'MOORE You will be safe (*crosses to* LORD E) at Usher's Island.

LORD E I could not be otherwise with such a friend by my side (*indicates* MAGAN). Oh, how can I repay you all?

MAGAN By trusting us always.

LORD E I do, God knows, freely and wholly. (*Shakes* MAGAN*['s] and* O'MOORE*'s hand[s].*)

[TABLEAU]

NEILSON and MISS O'M. THADY. MR. O'M. LORD E. MAGAN.

MISS O'MOORE Which way will you go?

THADY By Dirty Lane an' the Quays.

MAGAN (*aside*) Good.

MISS O'MOORE Then Mother and I will go with you. (*Crosses to* LORD E.) Our presence will tend to disarm suspicion, and our honour, my father's honour, demands that we leave you not till we see you safe and secure under Mr. Magan's roof. (LORD E *bows and shakes her hand.*)

THADY Hurroo! When the women talk like that, there's hope for the country yet.

MAGAN I'll leave you now; at midnight I shall expect you.

LORD E I shall be there. (*Bows to* MAGAN *and then talks to others.*)

MAGAN (*aside*) I am afraid not. (*THADY crosses to L. MAGAN exits L.*)

THADY (*indicating MAGAN*) The divil's cure to ye, for a one horse spaker.

MR. O'MOORE And now before you leave if your lordship will honour my humble table with your presence, some refreshment may not be out of place.

LORD E I've an excellent appetite old friend, and what's more, good digestion waits upon it. (*To MISS O'MOORE*) Permit me. (*Offers her his L. hand, they exeunt R. NEILSON follows.*)

MR. O'MOORE (*to THADY*) You know the road to the kitchen Thady?

THADY No one betther, I've thravelled it often. Biddy and mesilf are great friends.

MR. O'MOORE Then I need have no fear on your account.

THADY Not a haporth.* I'll look afther Biddy, an' Biddy'll look afther me, an' the refreshment won't be out ov place, afther I've interviewed it. (*MR. O'MOORE shakes his stick and exits R.*) Good night sir, an' may yer ould head never grow bald till I pluck the hairs out ov it. (*Exit L.*)

End of Scene 2

Scene 3

STREET NEAR USHER'S ISLAND

(*Enter HIGGINS and MAGAN L.2E. PAMELA at window as Scene opens, MAGAN at door.*)

PAMELA Will, ah will he never come? Oh Edward, husband, how my heart hungers for you and your love.

MAGAN (*at door*) She's there waiting for th' man she'll never see again.

(*Enter HIGGINS hurriedly. MAGAN closes door quickly. PAMELA startled.*)

HIGGINS Tare and agers,* who are you?

MAGAN (*in suppressed tones*) Can't you speak low?

PAMELA (*alarmed*) Who's that? (*KITTY appears at window.*)

HIGGINS (*recognising MAGAN*) Oh, it's you, is it?

MAGAN Yes, hush!

KITTY Sure it was your fancy darlin'.

PAMELA No, no, I heard voices.

KITTY It must have been the cats.

HIGGINS Who's that?

MAGAN Hush!

KITTY Close the windy darlin', or ye'll be catchin' yez death of cold. Sure sittin' there won't bring the Masther any quicker.

PAMELA Ah, will he ever come?

KITTY Ov coorse he will. Isn't it all arranged? Come. (*They disappear.*)

MAGAN (*who has looked through door*) She's gone.

HIGGINS Who's gone?

MAGAN A woman—

HIGGINS That's no loss. They're a bad lot, ivery blessed mother's son ov thim.

MAGAN A woman, now a wife, but who, if Sirr but does his duty, will soon be a widow.

HIGGINS Thrust him for that, if it's the rebel Geraldine ye're manin'.

MAGAN Will he, Sirr, be here?

HIGGINS He will, for Mr. Major Sirr is gettin' mighty surly at havin' to alter his plans agin. He's beginnin' to show his teeth.

MAGAN So much the better, so long as he shows them on the right game.

HIGGINS D'ye tell me that? What's the rayson ye don't want the rebel taken at O'Moore's?

MAGAN Because he's not at O'Moore's to be taken. Is that sufficient?

HIGGINS It is; by jabers if he's not caught to-night I'll have to try my hand at the work.

MAGAN You had him once. Why did you let him go?

HIGGINS To plase you, an' put money in yer purse; aye there was no £1000 reward out thin, me bhoy.

MAGAN And you wanted your share of it?

HIGGINS I'd be a gom* if I didn't, I think I'll stay an' see the fun.

MAGAN Are you fond of cold steel?

HIGGINS Only at male times, in the shape ov a knife an' fork.

MAGAN Then take my advice and leave as soon as Sirr appears.

HIGGINS D'ye mane that?

MAGAN Lord Edward is bold to rashness, he knows not what fear is.

HIGGINS Like mesilf, my disposition to a T.

PAMELA (*PAMELA re-appears at the window.*) I cannot rest, anywhere, anywhere. (*Looks out.*)

MAGAN The rising is to take place within a few days. His liberty, therefore, is absolutely essential to its success. He will make a determined, desperate resistance. Will sacrifice even life itself sooner than be taken prisoner.

HIGGINS Will there be many with him?

MAGAN Half a dozen at least.

HIGGINS (*slightly upset*) Ye don't say so.

MAGAN The encounter, rely on it, will be sanguinary in the extreme. The place here (*indicating street*) will be like the shambles for blood.

HIGGINS I've a rooted objection to seein' blood out ov place.

MAGAN You're not alone in the objection.

HIGGINS D'ye think I'm afraid ov it? not a bit; no, not a bit. Instead, the effect it has on me is like that a red rag has on a bull. It makes me fearless of consequences; so, as my life is ov some importance to the state, I'll take yer advice an' leave the capture of the rebel to my friend the Major.

PAMELA (*hearing footsteps; excited, yet pleased*) 'Tis he! 'tis he!

(*Noise of MEN outside C.*)

HIGGINS What's that?

MAGAN They're here.

HIGGINS (*in alarm*) The rebels?

MAGAN No, the soldiers.

HIGGINS (*in bold tones*) I'm glad ov that, for I was beginnin' to see blood.

PAMELA (*alarmed*) Great Heavens! 'Tis Sirr and his bloodhounds.

(*KITTY appears at window.*)

KITTY What is it darlin'?

PAMELA The Military. Your Master is betrayed again. He must be warned. Oh who will do it?

KITTY I will.

PAMELA Bless you! Come! Come! (*They disappear. The above must be spoken in low but distinct tones.*)

(*Enter* SIRR, RYAN, *and* SOLDIERS.)

SIRR (*to Ryan*) Place your men. (RYAN *does so; to* HIGGINS) So you're here.

HIGGINS I am, Major.

SIRR Is it the right locality?

HIGGINS It is.

SIRR Who is that? (*Points to* MAGAN.)

HIGGINS One who would prefer his identity kept [unrevealed] even from so true a servant ov the Government as yersilf, Major.

SIRR Just so, one of those sleek, slimy things, with a man's form and a serpent's heart.

HIGGINS Major, your severity borders on insult.

SIRR As such I intended it. Let him clear out of this at once, for I have a thorough detestation of vermin in such close proximity. (MAGAN *is about to speak.*)

MAGAN Sir—

HIGGINS (*stops him*) Tut, tut, man. Don't make a fool ov yersilf, there's truth in every word ov it.

MAGAN (*to* SIRR) You shall pay for this.

SIRR If I do, it will be in very different metal from that you are accustomed to receive. Mine won't be Government gold, but (*touching sword*) Government steel. (*Exit* MAGAN.)

HIGGINS (*chuckling*) Bedad, Major, ye hit him hard that time, but he desarved it. He's a great rogue entoirely.

SIRR (*looking at* HIGGINS) Then he's a credit to his master.

HIGGINS (*in a rage, right up to him*) Sir, what d'ye mane by that?

SIRR My meaning was sufficiently conveyed, not to require a repetition.

HIGGINS It was, sir, an' I'll give you to understand (SIRR *draws his sword.* HIGGINS *jumps away*) that I'll report such conduct to the Government sir, to the Government sir. (*Exits L.*)

KITTY (*opening door quietly*) Bad luck to thim sodgers they're all round the Quay; they're not lookin', now's me time to give them the slip. I wondher where ould Sirr is—

SIRR (*turning round*) Ould Sirr's here. (*MEN seize her.*) Whom have we here?

KITTY Let me go, will ye? (*Struggling.*) Let me go, ye midnight thaves an' robbers.

SIRR (*to Kitty*) Who are you?

KITTY A dacent respectable girl, that's who I am. (*To soldiers.*) Let me go.

SIRR What are you doing out here?

KITTY Tha[t]'s my business, Mr. Major, Colonel Sirr, sir.

SIRR Ye're after no good I'll be bound.

KITTY (*struggling*) If yer say that agin, ye white wigged ould villain, I'll not lave a tooth in yer head to ate yer dinner wid.

SIRR Ah you're a bit of a tartar, I see.

KITTY I'm not, I'm rale Wicklow, every inch ov me. Let me go, will ye, an' deliver me message? (*Struggling with soldiers.*)

SIRR So you have a message on you, have you? Well, as you have no right to be out at this hour of the night,[2] and the message may be of use to the Government, oblige me by handing it over.

KITTY I won't, neither to oblige you or the Government.

SIRR Where is it?

KITTY Where you can't find it.

SIRR (*to SOLDIERS*) Search her. (*She throws them off, stands defiantly C. of stage.*)

KITTY Search me, will ye, ye dirthy ould lobster, not if I know it, come a step closer if ye dare, an' I'll give yer a taste ov me ten virgins.

SIRR (*furious*) Seize her, men. (*TWO SOLDIERS do so. KITTY drops note. SIRR sees it and picks it up.*) Ah, here it is. (*Reads*) What's this? (*reads aloud*) "Do not come to Usher's Quay to-night, the house is too closely watched. The street and the lane behind are lined with Military, Your devoted but distracted Pamela."

KITTY Ye dirthy ould thafe ov the world* to rade a lady's letter out that way.

SIRR It's fortunate you've been captured, you baggage.

KITTY Baggage! baggage yersilf, yer delapidated ould cock robin. (*Struggling with* MEN.) Let me go.

SIRR Had this reached Lord Edward he would again have escaped, intercepting it is a stroke of genuine luck. (*To* MEN) Bring her here till I see if she has any more such valuable documents about her.

KITTY Ye gallows' birds, ye, ye'll do nothin' ov the kind.

SIRR (*savagely*) Bring her here!

KITTY Let me go. (*Struggles with* MEN, *throws them off, is escaping when* SIRR *pulls her back, he turns her round,* MEN *are about to seize her again.* KITTY *meanwhile crying out*) Help! Thady! help!

SIRR But Thady isn't here to help you.

(*Enter* THADY *R.*)

THADY Ye lie, ye divil, he is. (*Throws* MAJOR *off R. She rushes into his arms. Picture.*) Have yer taken to arrest women now, ye blayguard, when ye can't get hould of men?

SIRR So much the better, two birds instead of one, seize them both. (TWO SOLDIERS *rush up,* THADY *knocks them both down. The* TWO SOLDIERS *who have been quiescent at their posts till now rush from behind, one seizes* THADY *and the other* KITTY. THADY *turns his man and knocks him on top ov [sic] the others, then seizes the other struggling with* KITTY *and sends him sprawling too. They are rushing R. when* SIRR *stops them with pistol. They turn to escape L. when* TWO SOLDIERS *step on with bayonets at the charge.* SIRR *follows, seizes* THADY *by the shoulder, but is turned round and thrown off to L. They are then escaping,* SIRR *fires at* THADY *and is following with his men when they are stopped by the entrance of* LORD E, MRS. *and* MISS O'MOORE, GALLAGHER, PALMER, NEILSON, *and* MC CABE.)

SIRR Lord Edward!

LORD E (*amazed*) Major Sirr, betrayed.

THADY Fly! fly!

SIRR Too late, you are my prisoner.

LORD E I am no man's prisoner, while this arm (*raises R arm*) is able to strike a blow.

SIRR Then, thus I disable it. (*Fires pistol, it misses fire, drum rolls at wings.*)

LORD E And thus I punish you for such unsoldierly behaviour. (*He attacks* SIRR. *During fight* SIRR'*s sword breaks, and* LORD E *is about to run him through, when* THADY, MR. *and* MISS O'MOORE *stop him, they cry "Fly! fly!" Others meanwhile engage in fight, they are all escaping when Military enter in force.* MC CABE *a prisoner.*)

SIRR Fire! (SOLDIERS *fire.* LORD E'S PARTY *give a cheer.*)

LORD E (*flourishing sword*) Follow if you dare.

SIRR Charge.

TABLEAU

(PAMELA *at window crying.*)

End of Act III

ACT IV

Scene 1

MR. MURPHY'S HOUSE [EXTERIOR], ST. THOMAS STREET

(*As scene rises,* NEILSON *out of archway, knocks at door. Then passes back to the archway, and as* THADY *opens door, he appears again, both cautious.*)

NEILSON Is he safe?

THADY Yis.

NEILSON (*earnestly*) Are you sure?

THADY I am; begorra* he's on the pig's back this time.

NEILSON Thank Heaven.

THADY If ye love him, don't, for the love ov glory, be hangin' about the house this way.

NEILSON I cannot help it, something tells me the net is being drawn closer and closer, and when the bloodhounds seize him, I must be there to strike a blow in his defence.

THADY Man alive, an' do yer think it is as bad as that?

NEILSON I do; Treachery is active in our midst and I want to find the cursed informer. (*Looks keenly at* THADY.)

THADY (*returning* NEILSON'*s look*) An' so do I, an' when I do find him— (*Noise of* SOLDIERS *outside.*) Whisht!*

NEILSON The Patrol, escape.

THADY Too late, we're nabbed, an' all through yer jabber. (*NEILSON knock[s] loudly at door.*) Murther alive man, are yer mad, or what?

NEILSON That will alarm them, and give them time to hide him, in case they search the house. Only a bold front can save us now.

(*Enter SWAN with SOLDIERS R. others L.*)

SWAN Halt! (*SOLDIERS halt. To NEILSON.*) Who are you sir?

NEILSON A respectable citizen.

THADY An' I'm a dis-respectable one, Captain.

SWAN (*to NEILSON*) Your name.

NEILSON Maurice O'Neil.

THADY An' mine's Mickey the Grinder.

SWAN (*to THADY sternly*) Is it?

THADY Yes, Major, It's been in the family ever since Adam was a bhoy.

SWAN No doubt. (*Turns to NEILSON*) What were you loitering here for?

THADY He was givin' me a copper for me poor wife an' children, ten ov them alive in this blessed minute, Major, Jewel.

SWAN Giving coppers, eh? More like hatching treason.

THADY I haven't strength to hatch A chicken let alone trayson, general.

SWAN (*not heeding THADY, to NEILSON*) Do you hear?

NEILSON (*proudly*) I have no reason to disguise my errand, I was intending to make a call on my friend here, Mr. Murphy.

THADY Begorra,* the fat's in the fire now.

SWAN As I thought (*sternly*). Were not you two last night with the rebel Lord Edward Fitzgerald in Dirty Lane?

NEILSON I was not. (*Aside*) May that lie never be recorded in Heaven against me.

THADY Is it me? me, arrah* man, what would I be doin' wid his lordship? It's jokin' ye are, sure he wouldn't look at the likes ov me in a nine acre field, so he wouldn't, no Major, Lieutenant, General, I was at home boilin' the stirabout for the children at that hour.

SWAN Where do you live?

THADY In Puddin' Lane, yer honour.

SWAN I know the place.

THADY Then drop in any time ye're passin' General, an' ye'll be as welcome, as I'll be mesilf, an' that's no lie.

SWAN I will when I want—

THADY A dhrop ov the Mountain Dew, eh Major? (*Laughing.*)

SWAN No, sir, to hang you. (*SOLDIERS seize him. Knocks at door.*)

THADY Thanks, Major, for the rise in the world ye're so anxious to give me afore I lave it. But yer won't be vexed if I'm not at home when yer call? for I wouldn't like to disappoint yer.

SWAN I'll look after that. (*To NEILSON*) You will remain here, sir, in charge of my men (*TWO SOLDIERS stand beside him*) till I have thoroughly searched this house. If, as I suspect, it contains the rebel chief, you and this blackguard, here, (*indicate THADY*) will have to bear him company to Newgate.

NEILSON As you will, I fear not the result. (*SWAN and SOLDIERS exeunt into house.*)

THADY What grand times we live in to be sure, I'm terribly fond ov the army bhoys.

(*KITTY enters L.*)

THADY Oh murther, here's Kitty, what'll I do now at all?

KITTY Oh Thady darlin', is that yersilf? (*To SOLDIERS*) What are yer doin' to him at all, men?

THADY Whisht,* I'm just kapin' them company awhile, I want yer to go home and tell me wife.

KITTY (*in surprise*) What?

THADY Me wife.

KITTY Ye gallows bird, ye, ye haven't one.

THADY I have, bad luck to me, an' tin poor childher.

KITTY Oh, yer villain yer, an' ye tell me that, me (*goes up to him*) that ye've been coortin'—

THADY (*aside to her*) Whisht,* unless yer want to ruin me entoirely. (*Aloud*) I'm a blayguard, I know I am, but will ye go an' do as I axe yer?

KITTY I will. What is she like? does she squint?

THADY Wid both eyes.

KITTY An' has she a wooden leg?

THADY She has, two ov them.

KITTY Then I know her. (*Crosses to R.*) I'll tell her, an' if it wasn't for her and the childher, I wish they'd hang yez twice over. (*Sees* SWAN *re-enter and exits hurriedly.*)

NEILSON (*aside*) Thank Heaven, They have not discovered him.

THADY (*aside*) He's free still. (*Aloud*) Hurroo! (SWAN *looks at him.*)

SWAN (THADY *looks confused.*) Is that for his lordship?

THADY No, for yer honor.

NEILSON (*to* SWAN) Are you satisfied?

SWAN I am, that he is either in that house, or in the vicinity.

NEILSON With that I have nothing whatever to do. I presume I am at liberty to take my leave.

SWAN (*with marked deliberation*) You have my permission, Mr.—Mr.— (NEILSON *looks at him*) Neilson. (NEILSON *starts.*) You see I know you. As however your detention is of no further use to me, you can go.

NEILSON For which courtesy I thank you. (*Bows and exits R.* THADY *is going but is hauled back by* MEN.)

THADY Sure if he can go, I can go too.

SWAN You and I have met before.

THADY Then it must have been in a Pawn shop.

SWAN No sir, in a very different place.

THADY You don't tell me, I disremember all about it, so I do. Where was it General?

SWAN The first time in Paris five or six years ago (THADY *starts*) and more recently in Leinster House. As I know that man, so I know you; you are in Lord Edward's service.

THADY I was, but not now, he kicked me out for stalin' his shavin' brush.

SWAN You lie like truth.

THADY It's the truth that sounds like a lie, that's the lie ov the whole truth, so it is.

SWAN Your fidelity to your master does you infinite credit, but—take my advice—keep clear of this rebellion, it can only end in one thing, the drop.

THADY Well, as long as it is a drop, an' a good long one too, of potheen,* sure I don't mind it at all. (*Laughs.*)

SWAN I'm afraid you're incorrigible.

THADY I don't now what that is yer honor, but I'm afraid I am.

SWAN Fall in. (*To* SOLDIERS.) Quick March! (*Exit L.*)

THADY I'm thinkin' that Swan's a bit ov a goose. Well, I won't say anythin' agin him, for he's not a bad heart undher his jerrymentals. (*Exit R.*)

End of Scene 1

Scene 2

ROOM IN MR. O'MOORE'S HOUSE

(*Enter* THADY *and* KITTY *L.*)

THADY That was a narrow squake, Kitty.

KITTY It was, indade, an' bad luck to me, I was nearly spoilin' it all.

THADY Ye was, but I say darlin' how's the wife an' the childher?

KITTY Ye'd betther be goin' an' axin' them, yer rogue. Where's his honor?

THADY That's a saycret I'm afraid to trust yer wid.

KITTY Indeed, an' why may I axe?

THADY Because women have such terrible long tongues.

KITTY Is that so? an' d'ye mane to insinuate that mine's long?

THADY Sorra the haporth* more or less. It's like a knocker on a doctor's door, never done clanging.

KITTY That'll do yer now. (*Is going L.*)

THADY Where are ye goin'?

KITTY To Usher's Quay.

THADY (*taking hold of her*) Come here me girl, an' don't be afther runnin' away like that.

KITTY If me tongue's so long, I'm not the girl for such a gentleman as Mr. Thady McGrath.

THADY Sure isn't it mesilf knows how to stop it.

KITTY D'ye now, an' may I axe how ye know?

THADY By closin' the door this way. (*Kissing her.*) Whisht,* I was only jokin', sure the masther's safe enough.

(*Enter* MAGAN *L.*)

MAGAN I'm glad to hear that, Thady.

THADY An' so yer may, for it's no thanks to you, that he is.

MAGAN True, but I cannot be in two places at once.

THADY No, but ye're seldom in the right place when ye're wanted.

MAGAN Well, I'm here at all events. (*Crosses to R.*)

THADY An' ye're not wanted.

MAGAN Then I'll leave you, I can always take a hint.

(*Exit R.*)

THADY An' it's not the only thing yer can take, I'm thinkin'.

KITTY I don't like that man, Thady, he's got an evil eye.

THADY An' an evil heart too, me girl.

KITTY He has, bad luck to him. But how did yer escape from Sirr? ye never tould me?

THADY Didn't I? Well that's quare, now, I thought I did.

KITTY No, ye didn't.

THADY Well, afther the fightin' we all bolted into the Dog and Duck Inn, in Puddin' Lane; yer remimber the place?

KITTY I do, well.

THADY Ye've been there often, I suppose?

KITTY Oh, I have, hundreds ov times. (*THADY looks at her.*) No, ye gom,* I don't mane that at all, but that I remimber the house and the locality.

THADY So it appears, me girl, too well I'm thinkin'.

KITTY Arrah* go on wid yer story, an' don't blather so much.

THADY Well, we've smuggled the [masther] in at ould Murphy's.

KITTY What, Paddy Murphy, the gardener?

THADY (*indignantly*) No, but Mr. Murphy's the feather merchant.

(*Enter MISS O'MOORE, NEILSON, and MAGAN.*)

MISS O'MOORE Yes, thank Heaven, he is safe, at all events, for a time.

KITTY That'll be grand news for her ladyship; an' bless himself, he'll have plenty ov soft beds to lie on anyways.

THADY Begorra,* last night he preferred the inside ov one to the outside.

KITTY That'll do yer now, me bhoy, dont be thryin' to mulvather* us that way.

THADY May I niver sin more, if it's not the Gospel thruth.

MISS O'MOORE Pray explain Thady.

THADY Well, ye see Miss, it was this way. When Swan was interrupted by Neilson an' mesilf outside the house, ould Murphy was in a terrible fright insoide.

MISS O'MOORE Yes, yes, and what did they do?

THADY Well first he hurried his lordship up on the roof, but as that was too exposed, he hurried him down agin into a cellar that was full of goat skins. Well the outside ov the skins were too much for the insoide of his honor. He says the smell ov them skins was enough to take the varnish off a mahogany counter.

NEILSON Never mind that, go on.

THADY So as there was no other place handy, he was compelled to get inside a feather bed.

KITTY That'll do ye now.

THADY An' there he was for four mortal hours, an' the sight he was when he crawled out, it w'd have made a pig laugh. He was the finest two-legged bird I ever clapt me two eyes on. "Come an' pluck me, Thady," says he, when he could spake for the laughter. "I will," says I, an' for two good hours was I at the job pluckin' the feathers from him; an' I left him moultin' the rest.

NEILSON Are you perfectly sure he's safe there?

THADY Perfectly, unless I turn traitor.

NEILSON Ah, would you. (*Hand on pistol.*)

THADY Or yersilf. (*With meaning.* NEILSON *removes hand from pistol.*)

NEILSON Ah. (*With a sigh of relief.*)

THADY Or may be Mr. Magan, here.

MAGAN No fear of that Thady, I'm the bearer of a message to him now from Lady Edward.

THADY Then give it to Kitty, she has another.

MAGAN No, I prefer to deliver mine, myself; I'm going to him now.

THADY Then bad luck's on the road to him. (*Crosses to L.*)

MAGAN (*aside*) It is, and this time it shall overtake him. (*Exit L.*)

THADY (*to* NEILSON *who crosses to L.*) An' where may you be goin' to, sir?

NEILSON (*with meaning*) To follow Mr. Magan, I also have business with his lordship. (*Exit L.*)

THADY I'd give me right hand, aye, me very life itself, if I could rade the hearts ov thim two men.

MISS O'MOORE Surely you do not doubt them, Thady?

THADY May me lips never tell a lie, Miss, but I do; an sorra's the day I sh'd have to say it.

MISS O'MOORE (*reassuringly*) No, no, both are to be trusted.

KITTY Ov course they are; ye're head's full ov nonsense so it is.

THADY An' me heart's full ov love (*She looks at him*) for yersilf darlin' an' the masther.

MISS O'MOORE Rely on it, both are faithful, both are true. (*Exit R.*)

THADY I hope so, or their bodies will soon be widout their black sowls. Come Kitty and let us folly them both. (*Exeunt L.*)

End of Scene 2

Scene 3

ATTIC IN MR. MURPHY'S HOUSE

(LORD EDWARD *discovered at small table reading.* NEILSON *standing C.*)

NEILSON And has Magan not been here?

LORD E No, not yet. (*With book in hand.*)

NEILSON Strange. (*Partly aside.*) What can it mean?

LORD E How strange, what can what mean? (*Looks at him.*)

NEILSON Nothing, my lord, nothing.

LORD E (*rising, putting his arm round him affectionately*) But that nothing of yours means something, and that something, something unworthy of your straightforward honest self. You doubt Magan, suspect him again?

NEILSON To be honest then, I do.

LORD E I knew it. Why Neilson (*with a smile, laying his L. hand on his shoulder*), you suspect, then, all that is most pure and noble in human nature. His virtues surround his manhood with a halo of glory. At this very moment my wife and children are beneath his roof, sheltered and supported at his expense. Where you are all so good, so generous, so self-sacrificing, it is unmanly to select him for special praise; but if you love me utter no word of disparagement, of infidelity against Magan. He is honest, believe me, and true to the core of his heart. (*Sits down and takes up book.* NEILSON *crosses to R.* THADY *enters.*)

THADY (*to Neilson*) I see ye're afther comin'.

NEILSON Yes, I'm here.

LORD E Well, Thady, is that you?

THADY It is, yer honor. Where's Mr. Magan?

LORD E Not here.

THADY Well, that's strange anyways, what does it mane at all?

LORD E What, another unbeliever! (*Looks at* NEILSON *and laughs.*) What's strange, Thady?

THADY Why, Mr. Magan said he was comin' straight to see yez.

LORD E I assume he had reasons, excellent ones, no doubt, for keeping away.

THADY No doubt he had, grand raysons, golden raysons.

LORD E (*slightly irritated*) What do you mean?

THADY I'm thinkin' the sooner yer change yer residence the safer yer'll be.

LORD E And do you suspect him too?

THADY Savin' yer honor's presence, I do.

LORD E I tell you, I would trust him with my life.

THADY An' I wouldn't the length ov me nose.

(*Enter* KITTY *with suit of clothes.*)

LORD E Ah Kitty, just in time to dispel the clouds of suspicion and distrust. Why, what have you there?

KITTY An' ould woman was afther lavin' it awhile ago wid insthructions ye were to resave it at once.

LORD E Well, open it and let us see what it contains. (KITTY *does so.*) Ah, I thought so.

KITTY (*admiring it*) Oh, isn't it grand?

THADY It is.

KITTY An' is this yer jerrimentals?

THADY Arrah,* hould yer whist* woman an' let his honor spake.

NEILSON Who sent it?

LORD E Why the man you both distrust—Magan.

NEILSON Ah!

THADY Ye don't say so?

LORD E (*with enthusiasm*) It is the signal that all is ready for the rising.

THADY The divil fly away wid me for an ignorant bosthoon.*

LORD E When the next is given, the die will be cast; no turning back then. It will be either victory and Ireland free, or defeat and the scaffold.

THADY Hurroo! for Ireland.

LORD E And now, as I feel somewhat tired, will you kindly leave me for a while?

KITTY Ov coorse we will, is the bed all right? (*Rushes to it and begins to arrange clothes.*)

THADY (*following her*) Lave it alone, I made it mesilf. It's grand an' soft.

LORD E (*to NEILSON at door*) Good bye. (*Shaking his hand.*) And if you love me do not let that heart of yours harbour evil thoughts of friends.

NEILSON To please you I will try.

LORD E And no man can do more. (*NEILSON exit. To KITTY.*) Have you no message from your mistress, Kitty?

KITTY Oh, oh, may I sup sorrow every blessed day ov this month for forgettin' it.

THADY That all comes of yer upsettin' the bed, ye've gone and spoilt it so ye have.

KITTY (*finding it*) There it is yer honor. (*Hands letter.*)

LORD E Thanks, Kitty, in an hour's time come up for the answer.

KITTY An' yer won't let me tuck yer in, you wid that bastely cold on you?

THADY An' so will you have one if yer kape yer mouth open as wide as that; shut it, me girl, and shut yersilf out ov this room at the same time. His honor wants to be alone. (*Drawing her towards door. Exeunt talking.*)

LORD E How rich I am in faithful hearts. (*Takes off coat and vest, looks at suit.*) Emblem of the future, What canst thou tell me. Is it death or victory? Ah, who knows, who knows. (*Turns away.*) I'll leave it to that Divinity that does shape our ends, rough hew them [h]ow we will. (*Drinks from cup on table at bedside, lifts dagger, puts it down again with a sigh. Then lies on bed, draws coverlet over him.*) And now to read the words of love breathing in every syllable of this sweet letter. (*Opens it.*) Ah, my darling, wife of my heart, once the dark clouds disperse, and the sun shines out again bright and warm over our unhappy land, how happy will I make thy life, how happy—how happy. (*Voice lost as his attention becomes absorbed in the letter.* SWAN *enters quietly.* LORD E *looks up, sees him and then rises on his elbow.*)

SWAN Lord Edward!

LORD E Ah you. (*Seizes pistol.*)

SWAN Surrender in the King's name.

LORD E Never. (*Pistol misses fire.*)

SWAN You see, resistance is useless; you are my prisoner.

LORD E Not yet. (*Seizes dagger, and springs from the bed.*)

SWAN (*levelling pistol and with determination*) Will you surrender?

LORD E I'll die first.

SWAN Then die. (*He fires, and* LORD E *falls back on the bed. He immediately recovers himself and rushes at* SWAN, *who catches the dagger as it descends in his hand; they struggle.* LORD E *stabs* SWAN *in left breast.* SWAN *staggers.* LORD E *rushes to door L. where he is met by* RYAN *who enters.* RYAN *thrusts at* LORD E *who catches the sword stick with his left hand, twists it out of* RYAN*'s, and breaks it.* RYAN *draws pistol.* LORD E *seizes* RYAN*'s R. arm with his left and stabs him with the dagger.* RYAN *drops pistol and staggers L.* SWAN, *who has slightly recovered, raises the butt of the pistol to stun* LORD E, *when the latter suddenly turns, seizes him and stabs him.* SWAN *drops, catching hold of* LORD E*'s leg as he does so.* RYAN *then seizes* LORD E *who stabs him.* RYAN *staggers back, and just as* LORD E *is about again to stab* SWAN, SIRR, *who has entered, fires, and dagger falls from* LORD E*'s hand to stage.* RYAN *then seizes him as* LORD E *struggles to escape, but is stabbed by* DRUMMER. LORD E *drops his head.*)[3]

TABLEAU

End of Scene 3

Scene 4

FRONT STREET. THE DOG AND DUCK INN[4]

(*Enter* MAGAN *and* HIGGINS *R.*)

MAGAN Well, have I kept my word?

HIGGINS Ye have, he's fast the rebel, in Newgate by this.

MAGAN I hear he made a most desperate resistance.

HIGGINS He did, the blood thirsty monster, hanging's too good for him. He ought to be hanged, drawn, and quartered.

MAGAN Hush! (*Looks R.*) Who's this?

HIGGINS That blayguard Thady McGrath, an' a woman.

MAGAN (*alarmed*) His servants, I must not be seen with you.

HIGGINS No or yer life won't be worth much.

MAGAN Hide here, till they pass. (*They hide behind wing.*)

(*Enter* THADY *and* KITTY, *latter weeping.*)

KITTY Oh wirrasthrue!* wirrasthrue! what's to become ov us all, at all, at all?

THADY Sorra a bit* ov me knows, darlin'.

KITTY Only to think ov it, an' hour ago, an' the masther all smiles, an' jokes, an' laughter, an' now he's murthered entoirely.

THADY Whisht* darlin', sure he's not dead yet.

KITTY No, but he will be, for they'll never let him out aloive till he's a corpse.

THADY They won't, the curse ov Cromwell on 'em. But didn't he fight?

KITTY He did, bless him, like Brian Boru.

THADY Betther nor that; sure ould Sirr's got a hole through his nose that's spoilt his smell for the rest ov his dirthy days. An' Swan's massacred all over, an' Ryan's got his quietus.

KITTY What's that?

THADY His mortal death blow.

KITTY An' is he kilt?

THADY He is.

KITTY Think ov that now.

THADY An' isn't it his livin' to be kilt? Isn't that what soldiers is paid for? Faix* they can't be expecthin' to be drawin' their money for nothin' at all.

KITTY That's thrue, so it is, but what's to become ov us all Thady? an' the misthress, an' the poor childher?

THADY Sure his mother will take care ov them darlin', an' I'll, I'll take care ov yez. (*Putting his arm round her.*)

KITTY Oh, yer unfeelin' blayguard to be talkin' ov love an' sorra drownin' the lot ov us in salt tears this blessed minute.

THADY Sure I never mentioned love at all; an' how am I to talk? I can't marry the misthress, or faix* I would wid a heart an' a half.

KITTY Would ye? aye, I daresay ye would.

THADY Ye know I would, but if I can't marry the widdy, I can the maid, an' bedad I'm afther waitin' long enough for her, haven't I darlin'?

KITTY Troth yer have, too long.

THADY An' if we wait any longer we'll both be too ould entoirely for marriage felicity altogether. (*Arms around her.*)

(*Enter* NEILSON *hurriedly R.*)

NEILSON Is this the way I find you? (*Speaks angrily.*)

THADY An' what's wrong wid the way at all, man? It's a very good way, I'm thinkin'.

NEILSON (*more angrily*) Joking and love making when your master the Geraldine is dying in jail. (*KITTY gets away from THADY.*)

THADY An' if we are love makin', sure isn't it the only bit ov comfort we have in our sorrow.

KITTY That would die for him.

THADY Aye, more willingly, I'm thinkin', than thim that blather so much about it.

NEILSON Do you apply that remark to me?

THADY No, but if the cap fits ye're welcome to wear it.

NEILSON Then I don't, for if ever man were true to his oath, I am. Even now I am on my way to arrange for an attack on Newgate and a rescue of Lord Edward.

THADY Light ov happiness to me sowl, is that thrue?

NEILSON Do you think I'd let him die and rot in jail without lifting a hand to his escape. No, to-night he shall either be a free man or I a prisoner by his side.

THADY Ye've the thrue heart in yez afther all, an' I'm wid yer to the end.

NEILSON Meet me then in an hour's time at the Dog and Duck Inn. You'll be there?

THADY Ayther there or in Heaven. (*To KITTY.*) Begorra* (*exit NEILSON L.*) That's grand news, we'll have him out agin, or

I'll never dance at anodher wake. Hurroo! but whisht,* what's that? the divil's luck to me, if it's not Magan an' the Shamado, they're colloquing together. (*To* KITTY.) Away wid yer to the poor misthress an' the childher till I see what villan's work they're afther.

KITTY Ye'll folly me?

THADY Wid the fleetness ov the angel's wings in me brogues. (*Exit* KITTY. *Looks off R.*) They think I'm off too, but there's more ways into a house than by the front door, me bould gentlemen. (*Exit L.*)

(*Re-enter* MAGAN *and* HIGGINS *R.*)

HIGGINS (*to* MAGAN *who has crossed to L. and looks off*) Is he gone?

MAGAN Yes.

THADY (*appearing at window over door.* [*Aside.*]) That's a lie.

HIGGINS Ye seem terribly afraid of that gom.*

MAGAN I have reasons. He and that black fellow, Tony, are the only two who suspect me, and of whom I go in constant dread.

THADY [*aside*] Ah!

HIGGINS Remove the blayguards then, out ov yez way.

MAGAN But how?

HIGGINS Nothin' asier. Shoot them, an' rid yersilf an' the country ov the divils at one an' the same time.

THADY [*aside*] How kind ye are.

MAGAN But that would be murder.

HIGGINS Not at all, only justifiable homicide.

MAGAN Ah!

HIGGINS Ye see it now, do ye? The Government can't do without you; it can without them. Shoot them, an' I'll see yer through it.

THADY (*aside*) Thank ye for nothin'.

MAGAN I'll think of it.

THADY (*aside*) An' so will I.

HIGGINS Do, an' don't be afther lettin' a thriflin' matther like that throuble ye. I'm off. (*Is going.*)

MAGAN Stay, you've forgotten the balance.

HIGGINS Oh, the blood money.

THADY (*aside*) Ah!

MAGAN (*fiercely*) Curse you, speak low can't you or some one will overhear you.

THADY (*aloud*) An' someone has. (MAGAN *and* HIGGINS *start back.*)

MAGAN Ah, you, Thady McGrath.

THADY Yes, who now knows you, Magan, in your thrue colours.

MAGAN But not for long. (*Raises pistol.*)

HIGGINS That's right, shoot the ruffian. (MAGAN *fires,* THADY *gives a groan, falls back, window closes.* HIGGINS *fires.*) Begorra* ye've settled him, an' a dacent job ye've made ov it. It'll save the Government the expense ov hangin' the rascal.

MAGAN What did you fire for?

HIGGINS For very good raysons. Here comes the Patrol, that's why I fired. (*Enter* SOLDIERS *with* SERGEANT.) Ye're just in time, Sergeant, you'll find a rebel in there. (SERGEANT *tries to open door.*) Lord Edward Fitzgerald's servant man; he fired in the most wanton and bloodthirsty manner on this gentleman, who was reluctantly compelled to return his fire. (SERGEANT *cannot open door, so breaks it open with butt end of gun.*) That's right break it open, it must be a regular den—a rendevous for the villyans. Bring him out at once, and take him to Newgate. In wid ye. (SOLDIERS *exit into house. To* MAGAN.) There, ye're rid ov one blayguard. (*Crossing to L.*)

THADY (*who has stealthily entered R.*) Is he?

HIGGINS An' now to get rid ov the other in the same way. (*Exeunt L.*)

THADY (*looking after them*) Not so asily done, me bouchal,* Thady McGrath still lives, and will, till vengeance overtake ye both. (*Re-enter* SOLDIERS *from house.*) The blayguard ye're lookin' for is gone that way, and the gentlemen runnin' like mad afther him. Folly them quick. (SOLDIERS *exeunt rapidly R.*) That's right, quick, ye divils, quick, and ye'll never overtake them. (*Exit L.*)

End of Scene 4

Scene 5

ROOM IN MOIRA HOUSE

(PAMELA *discovered seated L. of table R.*)

PAMELA How strangely silent the house appears. Thady and Kitty still absent, and Tony with a look of sorrow in his face whenever he enters the room, that chills the blood in my veins. (*Rises and pulls bell.*) Even his presence is better than this awful stillness, this unbearable solitude. No answer. (*Goes to door L., opens it.*) All's quiet. Why will [h]e not come? this dreadful coldness at my heart, what does it portend? what calamity forbode? Ah, Edward, my husband, he's taken, I know it, I feel it. (*Rings bell violently.*) I must, will end at once this terrible suspense.

(*Enter* MAGAN *door L. She rushes to him, then seeing his head is bent, pauses, and gasps out the words.*) My husband, Edward, what, what of him, tell me, tell me?

MAGAN Do you not know?

PAMELA (*with anguish*) Nothing, nothing, but what my heart foretells, the intense agony it feels, the torture it suffers. What, oh what does it all mean?

MAGAN (*with an effort*) I, I dare not tell you.

PAMELA You must, you shall; ah, he is dead.

MAGAN No, no, not so bad as that.

PAMELA Then he is a prisoner? In pity's sake tell me, all—all.

MAGAN He is, and—

PAMELA Yes, yes.

MAGAN And wounded mortally.

PAMELA Ah! (*Faints, he receives her as she falls in his arms.*)

MAGAN (*fiercely exultant*) Fainted, and in my arms, with mine holding her closely to my throbbing heart. Now for the kisses my soul has longed for, hungered for. (*Kisses her.*) [H]ow pale, how beautiful, and she is mine, mine from this to the portals of the tomb. (*Kisses her again.*)

PAMELA (*recovering*) Where am I? where am I? (*More sensible.*)Ah, I know, I know, I know. (*Releases herself from his arms and staggers to chair.*) How dead my heart, how hopeless my life. (*Sits and sobs.*) How shall I bear it all, how live through it all. Oh Merciful God, how! how! how!

MAGAN (*in former tone of voice*) My heart bleeds for you, would I could have spared you the blow, have suffered in his place.

PAMELA (*lifting her face*) Is there no hope? No hope at all?

MAGAN None. (*She bows her head on her arms which she outstretches on table.*)

PAMELA Oh husband, darling, take me with you, take me with you.

MAGAN Summon to your aid fortitude and strength. As I have been his friend, so will I— (*she looks at him*) be yours.

PAMELA Oh who could have betrayed him, done so foul a deed to one, whose heart and hand were open as the day to all?

MAGAN One you little dreamed of.

PAMELA Ah!

MAGAN Thady McGrath.

PAMELA Thady, false! Then hope is indeed dead for us and Ireland when such as he prove unfaithful. (*Sits.*)

MAGAN I've suspected him for months. (*She looks at him.*) How could the Government have obtained such reliable information if not from one of your household?

PAMELA True, true.

MAGAN Not half an hour ago the villain attacked me on my way here; fired at me repeatedly, and would no doubt have killed me had not the Patrol fortunately appeared on the scene and captured him red handed. But dismiss him from your thoughts. (*Places few biscuits and wine on table.*) Take a little wine and a biscuit, you require nourishment. (*Pours out wine for her.*) I will return to Newgate, and if I cannot devise a means of escape, I will at least obtain permission for you to see him.

PAMELA (*rising*) Heaven will reward you, truest and best of friends; how, how can I thank you?

MAGAN (*pointing to wine, etc.*) By keeping up your strength; the time will come when you will need it all.

PAMELA I will, I will. (*Nibbles at biscuit.*)

MAGAN (*aside*) If she takes the wine, I shall have no trouble with her till I get her on board ship. If not, I must trust to that fortune that as yet has never deserted me. (*She looks at him. Aloud.*) Higgins is the only man who can arrange the interview for me, and he, the mercenary wretch, must have his price.

PAMELA (*rising*) Pay it whatever it is. Here take this (*hands purse*) one hundred pounds. It is all I possess at present; but here are my jewels (*obtains them*) take all, all, if it will buy that man over.

MAGAN No, no. (*In injured tones, declines both.*) Think not so badly—so ill of me as that, I have more than sufficient to satisfy even his avaricious greed.

PAMELA How good, how noble you are. Go then, go. It will seem an eternity till you return.

MAGAN I will not lose a moment. (*She returns to table, he at door.*) Now, to ascertain if Mr. Thady McGrath is dead or safely laid by the heels in jail, and then to sweep the other obstacle out of my path. It must be done if I am ever to feel safe. (*Exit L.*)

(*KITTY knocks at window C.*)

PAMELA (*alarmed*) What's that? (*KITTY knocks again.*) Who's there?

KITTY (*outside*) It's me, me lady, Miss. Ma'am.

PAMELA What are you doing there?

KITTY Thryin' to get in.

PAMELA Go round to the door then.

KITTY Sure it's locked; so is the back one, an' we can't get in at all, at all.

PAMELA Locked! Who's with you?

KITTY Tony, and—

PAMELA What fresh mystery is this? (*Opens shutters and KITTY, TONY, and THADY enter.*) Ah! (*Seeing THADY.*) You here?

THADY An' a dale ov throuble I've had too, to manage it.

PAMELA (*fiercely*) No doubt you had, you black hearted wretch. (*THADY starts back, others surprised.*) You traitor, are you not satisfied with having sold your master to the blood hounds, but you must thrust the blight of your presence on me?

THADY Poison to me sowl, what does she mane at all?

PAMELA That I have at last discovered your real character; the depths of your baseness.

THADY Oh, sorrow's disthracted her entoirely.

PAMELA No, only opened my eyes to your ingratitude and treachery.

KITTY But Misthress, darlin', dou—

PAMELA (*not heeding her*) You ingrate, to sting the hand that fed you, stab the heart that loved you, and taken the life that w'd have yielded its own for your perjured sake. Quit my sight, before I sully this bright blade with your traitor's blood.

THADY For the love of Heaven, woman, will ye tell me whom I've bethrayed?

PAMELA As if you didn't know, the man who lies bleeding to death in Newgate.

THADY Ah!

PAMELA Your master.

THADY Daylight to me sowl, an' ye belave that? that I would bethray him? him ov all men? The man I would die a thousand deaths to save one moment's pain—the man who has drawn life from the same breast. Oh, woman, woman, ye don't know me, ye don't know me at all, at all. Strike (*referring to knife*) aye, a hundred times deep in this heart if that's the only good ye can think ov my thruth and love.

TONY Miss[y], Missy, you are wrong.

KITTY Sure sorrow must have turned yer brain darlin' to think so ill ov the poor bhoy.

TONY Who told Missy that?

PAMELA Mr. Magan.

THADY That mountain ov iniquity. 'Tis himself is the informer, not me. What did he lock us out for? bekase he's afraid; bekase he knows vengeance swift and sure is on his track.

PAMELA (*mystified*) Is this true?

THADY As Heaven's light.

PAMELA In what a maze of mystery and deceit am I enveloped. In whom, whom am I to believe?

KITTY Your ould friends and servants.

THADY An' not a sarpent, who has bethrayed to his death, the best of all the Geraldines, in hopes to gain your love.

PAMELA (*as if waking to the real truth*) Ah, a light dawns in upon me, his friendship then was a mockery, his devotion a sham, done for his own hateful, selfish ends. Oh, that such a specious villain sh'd be allowed to befoul the earth. Let us escape.

THADY No, no, not yet, not yet. Here from his vile tongue, ye learnt what was false, and here ye shall learn the truth. Whisht*! he's comin' an' wid him ould Higgins. (*Opens door.*) In wid yer, he'll never suspect ye're there. Tony will be near at hand to protect ye, an' I will go for a few ov the bhoys. Take that (*gives dagger*), ye may want it. It's done sarvice already this day, an' is fit to do more. (*Closes door—to* KITTY.) Come wid me, an' mind the door to let us in. (*To* PAMELA.) In five minutes I'll be back; then Mr. Magan, make yer pace wid Heaven for sorra the bit* ov marcy will yez git on earth. (PAMELA *hides,* TONY *hides in room R.* THADY *and* KITTY *get behind screen, and as* MAGAN *and* HIGGINS *enter they exeunt through same door.*)

HIGGINS Ye're in a mighty big hurry for that money.

MAGAN (*who has entered first and looks round the room*) Hush! (*Goes to door R.* TONY *evades him.*) Right. (*Locks door.*) She's not here.

HIGGINS (*who overhears him*) Who's not here?

MAGAN (*slightly surprised*) Why my sister of course.

HIGGINS Well, that's a blessin' anyways, for by me sowl she's no Vanus.

MAGAN Never mind her, sit down here (*points to chair L. of table*) and out with the reward, I have immediate use for it.

HIGGINS So it appears. (*Sits.*) There ye are, ten fifty pound notes, and now for the receipt.

MAGAN (*who is standing R. of table hands the receipt across*) There.

HIGGINS Ah, already made out I parceive.

MAGAN Yes (*sitting*), for I have not time to lose. I leave as you know, by order of the United Irishmen (*laughs*) for France to-night. There are my despatches, and there (*indicating another paper*) but no, that is marketable goods, and must be paid for.

HIGGINS Ye're an out an' out divil so ye are, me bhoy. What's the price?

MAGAN One thousand pounds.

HIGGINS What!

MAGAN Not a penny less.

HIGGINS Bud an' ages,* is it worth it?

MAGAN Twenty, nay fifty times that amount to the government. Every detail of the rising, three days hence, namely on the 23rd May, is here. (*Points to paper.*)

HIGGINS (*excitedly*) Thunder an' turf,* yer don't say so?

MAGAN Look at it. (*Hands it across,* HIGGINS *scans it rapidly.*)

HIGGINS But it's in cypher, man. (TONY *crosses to screen R.*)

MAGAN (*laughs*) Yes, and I possess the key. Is it a bargain?

HIGGINS Yes.

MAGAN I must have the cash before I sail to-night.

HIGGINS You shall have it in an hour.

MAGAN Then a duplicate of this (*touches the document*) shall be yours.

HIGGINS Have ye heard about the Geraldine?

MAGAN Dead, I hope—

HIGGINS No, but I hear he's at his last gasp.

MAGAN So much the better. (*Aside.*) Both for him and myself.

(*HIGGINS takes up decanter and pours out wine.*)

MAGAN With the satisfaction of knowing that he, the cursed fool and enthusiast is out of my way for ever. (*HIGGINS is about to drink wine.*) Don't drink that man; it's drugged.

HIGGINS (*spitting it out*) The divil it is, Bud an' ages,* what's it doin' there at all? (*Jumps up and goes L.*)

MAGAN In case I wanted it.

HIGGINS Not for yersilf, I suppose?

MAGAN Oh, dear no, for a companion who accompanies me to France, but who at the last moment may object to leaving Dublin.

HIGGINS Ho, ho, I smell a rat; a lady companion, eh? (*MAGAN laughs.*) Mr. Magan, ye're as sly an' as deep a villyan as I ever had the honor to meet, an' I salute you. (*Does so.*)

MAGAN Well, to take the taste of that (*points to glass*) out of your mouth, I'll treat you to a bottle of very rare old vintage. It's not often I do so.

HIGGINS No, yer thrates are like the vintage very rare, me bhoy.

MAGAN (*at door where PAMELA is*) We'll drink a rapid destruction to the rebels, and a speedy death to Lord Edward. (*Opens door, when LADY EDWARD appears; he starts back amazed.*) You!

PAMELA (*advancing*) I. (*MAGAN at corner of table, he hangs his head.*)

HIGGINS Ho, ho, so this is the companion, eh? Bedad, me bhoy, ye've gone in for high game, while ye'r were about it.

PAMELA (*points to door*) Go.

HIGGINS Wid pleasure, me lady; oh, I quite understand the situation, two's company an' three's none. Bad luck to it, though, me dhrink's gone anyhow. It's so rare, I'm not goin' to see it at all.

PAMELA Will you go, ye wretch?

HIGGINS So me Lady Egalité,[5] ye've got rid ov yer husband, have yez? for the sake ov yez lover? Well, I must say it's a very nate female arrangement, and I wish ye joy. (*Bows, TONY pulls him up and throws him right out of the room. MAGAN has still his head bent in shame.*)

PAMELA (*motions TONY out of the room. To MAGAN*) Now we stand face to face, with the truth revealed at last. You viper, trickster, knave, coward. You sordid hound, and it is you who, for filthy lucre, have sold the noblest heart that ever beat for Ireland's good; would out of very wanton baseness, seduce the wife from her love and duty.

MAGAN Enough of this, you know all. Well it's better so. Henceforth we shall understand each other and there can be no mistake. (*Crosses to door L. and locks it.*) You are in my power, alone in this house; the man who has just left will hold his tongue; if he speaks at all, it will be to besmirch and ruin your reputation, not vindicate it. I have loved you for years. (*She makes a movement of disgust.*) Aye, for years, and till latterly, have had naught but insults and contumely from you in return. I had hoped to gain your love through gratitude. I have failed. Well, I am not the first man who has had to admit he has suffered defeat. But if I have lost your love, I have not lost you, nor is it my intention to do so. (*Advances threateningly.*)

PAMELA Back. Pollute me with your touch and this dagger that my husband has used to-day with such terrible effect on his enemies, shall reach your dastardly heart. (*Raises dagger.*)

MAGAN (*starting on seeing dagger*) Where did you get that?

PAMELA From one your lying tongue sought to traduce, your coward's soul to kill. Thady McGrath.

MAGAN Curse him, and he is dead, or a prisoner.

PAMELA Neither one nor the other.

MAGAN Ah! (*In alarm.*)

PAMELA But alive and free. Open that door. (*Points to door L.*)

MAGAN Never, till I have gained my end. For you I have eternally damned my soul, and now I intend you to pay the price. (*To put her off her guard, he pretends to see a person behind her, and exclaims in trepidation.*) Ah, who are you? (*She turns her head, he seizes her, exultingly.*) Ah, my beauty, did you think to measure wits with me? You are mine, mine now, alive or dead. (*She screams, he takes the dagger from her.*) Silence! or I'll (*raising dagger as if to strike*).

PAMELA (*defiantly*) Better that, than worse. (*Screams, "Tony."*)

MAGAN (*seizing her, they struggle.* TONY *batters at the door.*) Is it death, or my love?

PAMELA Death, a thousand times.

MAGAN Then death be it. (*Is about to strike when* TONY *breaks in, and seizes him, turns him round and throws him off. Noise of*

PEASANTS heard, increasing in volume as the business proceeds.) Ah, you black divil. It's you, is it? Then you have just come in time. (*Rushes to TONY, they struggle, he stabs TONY, who falls. He then rushes to door L.*) Ah, the hounds are on me, then there's no way but this. (*Rushes to window, pulls back the shutters. THADY appears.*) You!

THADY And vengeance.

MAGAN (*fiercely rushing at him*) Then vengeance be it. (*Strikes at THADY who seizes his arms, noise louder. THADY turns him round so as to be able to stab him.*)

THADY This (*stab*) for your lies. This (*stab*) for your treachery, and this (*stab*) for the masther. (*MAGAN gasps, totters back, and falls apparently dead. Noise increasing through this, till, as MAGAN falls, they rush on.*)

NEILSON Escaped?

THADY No, he lies there. (*All cheer.*)

TABLEAU

End of Act IV

ACT V

NEWGATE GAOL, INTERIOR

(*LORD EDWARD discovered in chair dying, others [HIGGINS, SIRR, PAMELA, LORD HENRY FITZGERALD, LADY LOUISA CONNELLY] as per diagram [missing from manuscript].*)

HIGGINS (*to SIRR*) How is the rebel?

SIRR He cannot last much longer.

HIGGINS That's good news, though I would rather he'd have gone out ov the world by the way of the Scaffold.

SIRR Quiet man, quiet,

HIGGINS For what? Ryan's dead, d'ye know that? (*SIRR bows.*)

LORD E (*rousing himself, and much startled*) Ryan! dead! my God! who, who says so?

HIGGINS (*crosses to LORD E*) I do.

LORD E Dead! no, no.

HIGGINS Ye've wiped him out clane enough anyways.

LORD E I, I am indeed sorry to hear it.

HIGGINS An' so ye ought. (*Noise outside, murmurs and clanging of irons.*)

LORD E (*in anxiety*) What's, what's that?

HIGGINS An execution.

LORD E No, no.

HIGGINS Yes, Clinch's. Ye may shake hands with yersilf that it is not yer own. (*Murmurs etc. Louder.* LORD E *sinks back.*) D'ye hear them now? Fine music isn't it?

PAMELA (*crosses to him*) Oh man, man, your heart must be made of stone.

HIGGINS An' so it wants to be, when ye have to dale wid a pack of rebels.

PAMELA Pitiless wretch.

HIGGINS (*with venom*) Shall I tell him what I saw in Moira House—with your lover?

PAMELA Would you dare—dare to lie in the presence of death?

HIGGINS Aye, if only to revenge what you an' yer blayguard servant did to Magan. Ye thought ye killed him; but he's alive, an' will live in spite ov yez. (*Crosses to* LORD E. PAMELA *goes round chair to former position.*) There's the will yer wanted. (*Throws it on table.*)

LORD E (*faintly*) Thank you.

HIGGINS And much good may it do yer. Every stick and pin yer have will go to the King, forfeited to the State. Ye'll die convicted of High Treason. (*Crosses to L.C.*)

LORD E You speak according to your lights, I do not—cannot blame you.

HIGGINS I spake as ivery right minded Irishman sh'd spake agin the enemies of his country.

LORD E (*with an effort*) Enemy! why man, I have devoted myself wholly to her emancipation. Sacrificed wife, children, fortune, even life itself in her cause.

HIGGINS The more fool you.

LORD E And I would rather be here wounded as I am, dying of neglect in this miserable dungeon, than be Pitt at the head of the British Empire. (*Falls back.*)

HIGGINS Bedad, I wouldn't.

LADY CONNELLY (*to HIGGINS*) Oh, Go, go!

L[ORD] H[ENRY FITZGERALD] If you have one spark of pity in your heart, leave us.

HIGGINS I am here by ordhers from the Castle, and here I remain.

LORD E Oh, to know that the green flag of liberty waved above our shores.

HIGGINS Ye'll never see it, only rebels hanging like kites from every tree and post.

SIRR Can't you let him die in peace?

HIGGINS (*furiously*) No, I can't.

SIRR Don't snarl and snap at me like an angry cur.

HIGGINS Then do yer duty, like a man.

SIRR My duty, sir, ended with his capture.

HIGGINS Did it? How falin' we've become all at once. It won't pay, for the grass will never grow above yer grave, me bhoy.

SIRR And yours, when once you occupy it, will be an object of hatred and contempt, for every passerby to cast a stone at.

LORD E (to *LADY CONNELLY*) The sight of you is like a glimpse of Heaven. Ah, Henry (*takes his hand*) how good of you to come. Take care of her (*indicating PAMELA who is kneeling at his feet*) and the children. How cold it is! How cold (*shivers*).

HIGGINS It's death ye're feeling. (*LORD E shivers.*) It's comin' nigh ye now, an' whin it grips ye hard and fast in its icy grasp, the Rebellion will die wid you, will die wid you.

LORD E (*to PAMELA, LORD HENRY, and LADY CONNELLY*) Do not weep for me. To live in the hearts of those we love is not to die. Farewell, beloved wife, partner of my life's aims, joys and sorrows. Farewell brother, Aunt and trusted friend. Farewell all. Farewell! (*Dies.*)

TABLEAU

END

Plate 13. Pictorial advertisement for Whitbread's *Wolfe Tone* (1898) portraying scenes as staged at the Queen's Theatre. Outside the frames we see Peggy and Shane, Tone solo, and Tone with Susan. *Top center:* Soldiers arresting Turner during a meeting of the United Irishmen, all swords drawn from a confrontation between Tone and Turner. *Second row, left:* Hans and his men have Peggy tied up; Turner and Rafferty confront Susan. *Second row, right:* Bonaparte, Josephine, Tone, and Susan watch Rafferty and Turner being arrested for deceiving Bonaparte. *Third row, center:* The firing squad for traitors to the cause of liberty. *Bottom:* The embarkation of French troops for Ireland as the band plays. Courtesy of Séamus de Búrca, print courtesy of Pat Johnston, Curator, Dublin Civic Museum.

WOLFE TONE

Irish Romantic Drama

J. W. WHITBREAD

[Transcribed with minor silent emendations from MS. 372, Lord Chamberlain's Plays, British Library, Manuscript Collection]

[1898]

CAST

WOLFE TONE	
SAMUEL TURNER	Barrister, United Irishman and informer
JOEY RAFFERTY	An attorney at law, In castle pay
[RAFFERTY'S MAN]	
MR. FANNING	Grandfather to Mrs. Tone
MR. WITHERINGTON	Brother to Mrs. Tone
THOMAS RUSSELL	Friend to Wolfe Tone
SHANE MC MAHON	
[LEONARD] MC NALLY	Barrister, United Irishman
[JOHN] MC KEOGH	[a United Irishman]
[HENRY] JOY MC CRACKEN HAMILTON ROWAN [JOHN] SWEETMAN [THOMAS ADDIS or ROBERT] EMMET[1]	United Irishmen
MAJOR SANDY	[does not appear in the drama]

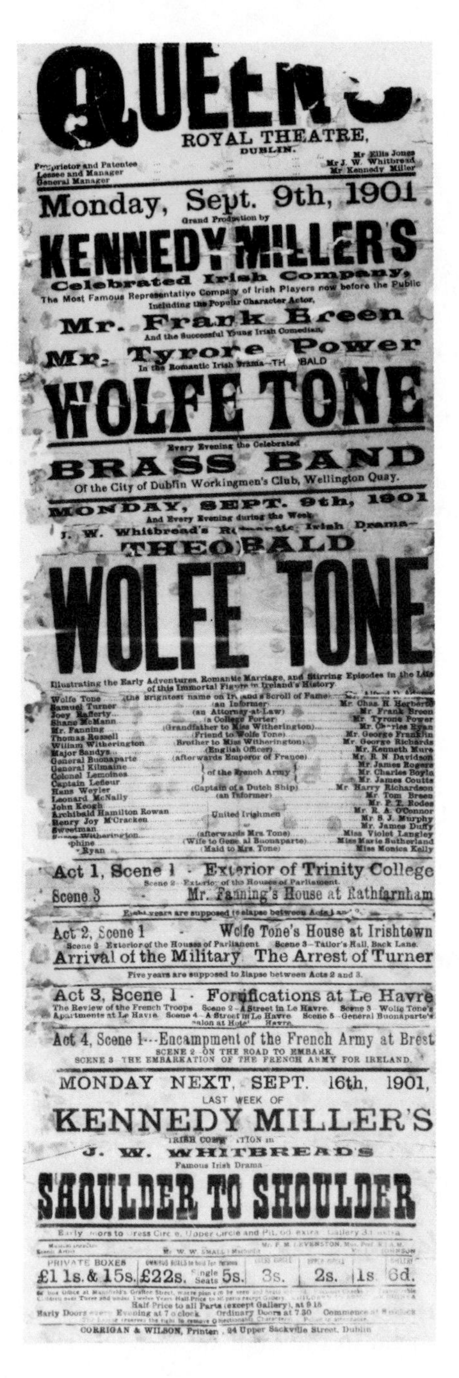

Plate 14. Daybill for Whitbread's *Wolfe Tone.* Daybills were twice the length of ordinary playbills and were displayed in shop windows, as were the playbills, next to pictorial advertisements. Courtesy of Séamus de Búrca.

GENERAL BOUNAPARTE	
GENERAL KILMAINE	[French officer]
COLONEL LEMOINES	[French officer, also identified in play as General Lemoines]
SUSAN WITHERINGTON	afterwards Mrs. Wolfe Tone
JOSEPHINE	Wife to General Bounaparte
PEGGY RYAN	Maid to Mrs. Wolfe Tone
[THREE TRINITY COLLEGE STUDENTS]	
[SAMUEL NEILSON]	[a United Irishman]
[OLIVER BOND]	[a United Irishman]
[SIM(M)S]	[probably Robert Simms, a United Irishman]
[BARTHOLOMEW TEELING]	[a United Irishman]
[MC CONNELL]	[possibly McCormick is intended]
[RICHARD MC CORMICK]	[a United Irishman]
[BROTHER]	[probably Matthew Tone, Wolfe Tone's brother]
[HANS]	[Dutch Captain bound for South America]
[HANS'S MEN]	
ENGLISH SOLDIERS	
PEASANTS	
FRENCH SOLDIERS	

ACT I

Scene 1

FRONT OF COLLEGE (TRINITY) OUTLINE[2]

(*Enter* STUDENTS *from C. Some pass R., some L. Enter* SHANE *dressed as a College Porter C. He sings quietly as he comes down. He looks R. and L., then up. Enter* TWO STUDENTS. *One knocks his cap over his face.*)

SHANE Murther alive! what's that? (*Other* STUDENT *hits him in the stomach.*) Oh! I'm kilt. (*Dances about with hand on stomach.*) Murther, thaves! (STUDENTS *laugh and exeunt R. Enter* RUSSELL *L.*)

Plate 15. Theobald Wolfe Tone wearing the uniform of France. This engraving is the frontispiece to volume 1 of the *Life of Theobald Wolfe Tone,* edited by his son William Theobald Wolfe Tone (1826). It is copied from a portrait by Katherine Sampson Tone, engraved by W. Harrison.

RUSSELL Hullo, my friend, what's the matter with you?

SHANE Ye omadhaun* can't ye see what's the matter? (*Raises hat by this time and sees* RUSSELL.) Oh, I beg your pardon, Sir, I took ye for one a thim blayguard students.

RUSSELL Student!

SHANE Yes, the divil's in thim entoirely; they're the greatest rapporees* at mischief ye ever came across; they won't let a paceable bhoy alone at all, at all!

RUSSELL Oh, there's no harm in them. (*Another* STUDENT *enters.*)

SHANE An' no good nayther. I'm sore from one end ov me to the other. No ye don't! (*as* STUDENT *attempts to hit*) me fine fellow; away out ov that now, or I'll report yez to the Provost. (STUDENT *laughs and exits R.*)

RUSSELL Who's that?

SHANE Blayguard ov the name of George Hill—(*shaking fist after him.*) Ye villain, ye, ye'll make poor Ireland shed many a bitter tear or my name's not Shane M' Mahon.

RUSSELL It's only the exuberance of youth.

SHANE Ye can call it what ye loike, but the less I get ov it the bether (*rubs himself*).

RUSSELL (*laughing tending him coins*) Perhaps that may tend to heal your wounds.

SHANE Well, it's an ointment that'll aise thim any way.

RUSSELL Do you know Mr. Wolfe Tone?

SHANE Is it Mr. Theobald Wolfe Tone? (RUSSELL *bows.*) No one bether. Whether at larnin', dhrinkin' or larkin' wid the petticoats, he's always to the fore.

RUSSELL Can you deliver that note to him? (*Hands it.*)

[SHANE] It's mesilf can & will. (*Enter* PEGGY *R.*) Ah, who have we here? Be me sowl she's a purty colleen; an' stands well in her brogues. (*She stops and look[s] through the gate.*) Are yez lukin' fer anyone me dacent girl?

PEGGY I am, a bether man than yerself.

SHANE Indade, an' who may the gintleman be?

PEGGY Mr. Wolfe Tone!

SHANE An' won't no one less sarve ye?

PEGGY No, no one less will.

SHANE (*to* RUSSELL—*aside*) Didn't I tell ye he was a divil wid the petticoats.

Plate 16. Leonard McNally. By kind permission of the National Library of Ireland.

PEGGY Spake out and don't be afther whisperin' there as if ye were ashamed ov yer voice.

SHANE Well ye're not ashamed ov yer own any way.

PEGGY No, nor no rayson to be. I don't live by blackmailin' young gentlemen out ov their pocket money.

SHANE Ye insultin'—

PEGGY Aisy, me fine fellow, aisy. Always clean yer tongue when ye address a lady.

SHANE What!

PEGGY Take that letther to Mr. Wolfe Tone. An'—at once!

SHANE The divil take you—an' your letther.

RUSSELL Better oblige the lady, my friend; and you can deliver mine at the same time.

SHANE Well, to oblige you, Sir.

PEGGY Ye oblige no one ye spalpeen.* You're here to wait on yer shupariors. Be off wid ye, an' when ye bring me back the answer, I'll give ye a copper penny for yez throuble.

SHANE Ye can kape yer copper penny agin ye want it yourself I wouldn't [d]emane myself to touch it. (*Exit C.*)

PEGGY No silver's more in your line, me bhoy!

RUSSELL (*to her*) Don't you think you were a little too hard with him?

PEGGY Sorra a bit* sir, they're all rogues in thim jirry mintals.

RUSSELL Haven't I seen you before?

PEGGY I belave ye have, sor; my name's Peggy Ryan.

RUSSELL Of course it is, and you're maid to Miss Susannah Witherington.

PEGGY Not another word, sir, the times are too dangerous almost to spake at all. Hist! (*She turns suddenly as if to tie her shoe. Enter* WITHERINGTON. *He looks at her then exits R.*) That's her brother, the villain, He's worse than the whole lot ov them. He's dead agin her havin' Mr. Tone as her swateheart—oh, the bad cruel heart's widin him so it is!

RUSSELL An' that note?

PEGGY Was from her to Mr. Tone; the poor darlin' frettin' her life away for luv ov him; an' they've taken to lock her up in her room for fear he'd break into the house and carry her off. (*Looks through gate.*) Whist!* here comes the villain they want her to marry, an' wid him is that imp ov inequity the little attorney, Joey Rafferty. I'll just step round the corner till they've gone. (*She goes R. Enter* TURNER *and* RAFFERTY C.)

RAFFERTY Stop! (*Holds up stick.*) Runnin' away won't hide yer identity me girl.

PEGGY No, but it'll take me farther away from bad company.

RAFFERTY Manin' us ov course.

PEGGY I never conthradict the truth.

TURNER What are you doing here?

PEGGY That's my business.

TURNER And mine, too, you're assisting to carry on a clandestine correspondence between your mistress and a beggarly fellow student.

RAFFERTY A disreputable young scamp.

RUSSELL If you are speaking of Mr. Wolfe Tone—I deny the imputation.

TURNER Oh, you do, eh? and may I presume to ask who you are, sir?

RUSSELL A friend of the man whose character you are assailing.

RAFFERTY Oh, indade! Well I don't think much ov the company you kape.

RUSSELL If you refer to yourself you are right; it is not a very brilliant sample.

RAFFERTY Your wit is like your appearance, nather worth much nor acceptable.

TURNER And we object to both.

RUSSELL Rogues generally do.

TURNER and RUSSELL Sir!

RUSSELL If my language is not sufficiently clear, I have a friend here (*touching his sword*) who will make it more so. It is at your service whenever you feel disposed to take a lesson.

RAFFERTY The divil take you and your sword.

TURNER And give us more of your room and less of your company.

RUSSELL Why don't you take it—the City's large enough.

RAFFERTY An' you won't leave us?

RUSSELL Certainly not, I prefer you to leave me.

PEGGY There's yer answer, ye little dirthy jackeen* ov an attorney; swally it if ye can.

TURNER (*to her*) Follow me to my office.

PEGGY Not me! I'm too sharp a fly for a spider like you.

TURNER Then go home at once to your mistress.

PEGGY I will, when I like, and widout your permission or lave either.

TURNER You'll get no answer to that letter.

PEGGY Won't I?

TURNER No, because I intircep[t]id it (*shows letter*).

PEGGY Ye robber, ye.

TURNER And you can tell your mistress that it will all depend upon himself whether she or her father receives it this evening.

PEGGY And did that thafe ov a Porther give it to yez? (*Enter PORTER.*)

RAFFERTY He did.

SHANE Ye lie, ye monkey faced villain, ye, ye esthracted them both from my possession by bare faced du[p]licity; ye said ye were goin' to Mr. Tone's chamber an' would save me the throuble. Hand thim over before I lave the stamp ov me knuckle on yer ugly nose.

PEGGY (*patting him on shoulder*) Ye're a betther man than I thought ye were. Hit him hard!

SHANE Hand thim over! (*Shows fight.*)

RAFFERTY Lay a finger on me, ye rascal, an' I'll give ye a touch ov this. (*Draws sword. They work round to R.*)

TURNER And so will I with this (*also draws sword*).

RUSSELL (*stepping before SHANE—sword drawn*) Not while I'm here.

[TABLEAU]

PEGGY RAFFERTY TURNER RUSSELL SHANE

RUSSELL Put up your swords! (*They do so.*)

PEGGY What brave gintlemen they are.

SHANE They must belong to the yeos. They're so quick at the job.

TURNER You'll answer for this affront, sir.

RUSSELL Had you been gentlemen nothing would have afforded me greater pleasure; but as you appear to be only two rascally thieves I decline the very questionable honour. Return those letters to that man (*pause*). Do you hear? (*Half draws sword.*)

TURNER And if I decline?

RUSSELL You won't. Fear always teaches men like you discretion.

TURNER (*Enter* WOLFE TONE.) There's your own. (*Throws it down.* SHANE *picks it up.*) But this is from a lady and neither you nor Mr. Tone shall ever have it. (TONE *takes it.*)

TONE But Mr. Tone has it. Isn't that remark somewhat premature—hastily expressed. (*Recognises him, changes tone.*) I beg your pardon. (*Is handing back note when he sees the superscription.*) Why it is addressed to me. (*Sternly to* TURNER.) How came you to have it in your possession?

PEGGY The villan stole it. (*He sees her and then* RUSSELL.)

TONE What, Peggy, and you Russell (*shakes hands with each in turn.* TURNER *and* RAFFERTY *are quietly leaving L. when* SHANE *stops them.*)

SHANE No, ye divils, Ye'll not lave this stool till ye've cleansed my character ov the slur ye've cast upon it.

TONE Quite right, Shane, (*to* TURNER) I know you to be a bitter enemy of mine, simply because I have succeeded in winning the affections of a young lady who prefers me to you. But why that should influence you to descend to the contemptible meanness of intercepting any communication she may honour me with requires explanation.

SHANE He got it from me by the dirthy pretence ov being your friend.

TONE Heaven forbid I sh'd ever to be so unfortunate as to have to number him among my friends. (*To them.*) You can go and if you are wise you will let this be the last time that you meddle in my affairs.

TURNER And if you are wise you will not further insult my affianced wife with your attention.

TONE Affianced Wife! How can that be when she is mine?

TURNER I have her father's and her brother's consent.

TONE And I have her own. And, as she is the party most vitally concerned I prefer her sweet consent to that of a dozen fathers or brothers.

TURNER And do you imagine she will ever be allowed to marry you a beggar without a pound to bless himself with?

RAFFERTY He owes me twenty already.

TONE Which you shall have without fail to-morrow.

RAFFERTY I wish I may get thim.

TURNER (*to* TONE) And what have you to keep a wife on?

TONE Nothing at present. Love and courage, however, will find the way.

TURNER (*sarcastically*) You mean find the way to her fortune. That's what you're after; that's a bait that never fails to tempt penniless adventure[r]s like you.

RUSSELL My friend, hadn't you better use a little more discretion in the selection of your language?

TONE Oh, let him finish. It doesn't hurt me, and the outburst may do him good.

TURNER There is an assignation in that letter.

TONE (*calmly*) Very likely.

TURNER But she will not be permitted to keep it.

TONE Indeed! Can you prevent it?

TURNER I mean to; and I give you warning that if I find you prowling in the grounds I'll shoot you down like a dog.

TONE And I give you warning that if you attempt it I'll split you as I would a fowl. I have listened to you quietly so far, on account of the relationship existing between you and Miss Witherington, but as I do not feel disposed to further submit to your abuse, please take my advice and your departure at the same time.

RAFFERTY We'll go when we like.

TONE And that's at once. Russell, your sword. (*RUSSELL hands it. They look at TONE and then exeunt L.*)

RUSSELL What a pair of Rascals.

SHANE None greater in Dublin.

TONE True both of you. (*Reads letter.*)

PEGGY (*to* SHANE) I'm thinkin' ye're an honest bhoy afther all.

SHANE So does me mother.

PEGGY What do ye get here? (*Indicating College.*)

SHANE More kicks than ha'pence.

PEGGY Why de ye stop thin?

SHANE Ah, that's a tale longer than any cow's got. Whisht,* come here an' I'll tell ye all about it. (*They talk aside.*)

TONE (*who has read the letter*) What, What abominable treatment! Why they've actually placed her under lock and key. Have threatened her with no end of pains and penalties, and purpose removing her this evening to Rathfarnham.

RUSSELL Then why subject her to it, Why not run away with her?

TONE What, Elope!

RUSSELL Precisely!

PEGGY Yes, do it! an' I'll help ye. Sure the darlin'[s] dyin' ov luv for ye.

TONE But will she consent to such a step?

PEGGY Will she consint? Arrah!* Will a kitten laps cream? What a gom* ye are, Sir, to ax such a question.

TONE But how am I to set about it? That fellow spoke the truth when he said I was a penniless beggar. I'm the poorest wretch in Dublin this minute.

PEGGY An' are yez goin' to let a thrifle like that stand in yer way?

TONE What am I to do?

SHANE Borry ov yer friends, sir, ov course.

RUSSELL Excellent advice.

SHANE An' may be the young lady won't moind it at all, at all.

PEGGY Not a little bit, sure she'd prefer startin' that way to any other.

TONE Yes, but who has the money to lend?

RUSSELL Well, I'm good for all I'm worth (*hands out purse*).

PEGGY (*pulling out old stocking*) An' so am I!

SHANE (*pulling out a large stocking*) An' so am I!

RUSSELL (*handing over purse*) Twenty pounds—Take it!

PEGGY (*who has taken out hers*) An' there's mine. A golden guinea a crown piece an' five copper farthin'. Take them an' wilcome. (*She t[h]rusts them into* TONE*'s hand, then to* SHANE.) Bedad that's a longer stockin' than mine.

SHANE Aye, an' there's more in it too, me girl. If the young blayguards are liberal wid their kicks they're aqually liberal wid their money. (*To* TONE.) How much'll do ye, sir.

PEGGY Arrah,* man, give him the lot.

[TONE] Thanks my friends, but I shall have quite sufficient here. (*Touching purse.*)

RUSSELL (*laughing*) I don't think that'll go far, Tone!

SHANE Bedad an' it won't.

PEGGY Sure how can it on an illigant runaway match; isn't there the ring to buy, a bran new suit ov clothes to get fer yerself, all the Hotel expenses, an' the post chaise to hire.

SHANE An' thim post boys are worse than lawyers at extorthion—they're rogues every one ov them.

TONE I shall never be able to pay it back.

SHANE Don't let that throuble ye at all; when ye have it, I'll get it. There's twinty guineas in that bag. (*He has taken it out of the stocking.*) They're yours wid a heart an' a half.

TONE Well I won't wound your kind hearts by refusing to accept your assistance. It shall be returned with interest. (*Shakes hands with each.*)

SHANE Sorra* the interest I want, sir.

PEGGY Nor me nayther, except the interest I'll get in nursin' the little wolves whin they come. (*All laugh.*)

TONE Well, as my marriage now is only a matter of hours and everything has to be arranged, no time is to be lost.

PEGGY True for yez; away wid ye both to yer lodgin's an' I'll folly.

TONE We'll circumvent the enemy yet. ([*Crossing*] *to L.*)

PEGGY Throth an' we will.

TONE Come, Russell! (*Takes his arm and they exeunt L. saying*) Good day Shane!

SHANE Good day to ye both! (*To PEGGY.*) There's a dale ov pleasure in lendin' muney to a gintleman.

PEGGY De ye tell me that?

SHANE Yes, ye see ye make a friend an' a safe investment at the same time.

PEGGY Are ye worth much?

SHANE A thrifle!

PEGGY A thrifle! does that mean a hundher or two?

SHANE May be it does an' may be it means more. Listen I'm worth a tousand golden guineas this minute.

PEGGY The lord save us, man, ye don't say so?

SHANE Yes's!

PEGGY Are yez married?

SHANE Not yit.

PEGGY Thin its time ye were.

SHANE (*looking at her*) I'm thinkin' so, mysilf.

PEGGY A thousand golden guineas. An' de ye kape it all in that ould stocking?

SHANE (*mimicking her*) Do I kape it all in me ould stockin'. Arrah,* woman what do ye take me for at all, at all?

PEGGY Well, I did take ye for an impudent, lazy, impty headed gosson* but I made a mistake an' I apologise.

PEGGY What's yer name?

SHANE McMahon at your sarvice; an' yez own?

PEGGY Peggy Ryan.

SHANE Yer name's as swate an' as nate as yersilf. I say Have yez any bhoy at all—Meandherin' around ye?

PEGGY Meandherin! What's that at all?

SHANE Swateheartin' ye know.

PEGGY Oh, I've a dozen ov thim sort.

SHANE A dozen is it?

PEGGY Yes, when I'm in the humour.

SHANE Have yez any bhoy particular that's a sort—ov—a particular bhoy?

PEGGY Arrah* man they're all particular bhoys or they wouldn't be givin' me their attention.

SHANE Now, do ye know I never thought ov that. Well, I'm a particular sort ov a bhoy mesilf so would yez mind puttin' me along wid the rest ov the blayguards—I mane—particular bhoys?

PEGGY Ye may come on thrial.

SHANE May I! Well that's somethin' anyways; an—the—address?

PEGGY Time enough for that me bhoy when I know more about yer anticedents. Good day! (*Is going L.*)

SHANE An' de ye think I'm goin' to let a purty dacent respectable lady go through the streets ov Dublin unescorted?

PEGGY Well, ye can come wid me as far as Mr. Tone's.

SHANE I bether or may be, as your so good lukin', he might be runnin' away wid the maid instid ov the misthras. Will yez wait a moment till I lave the word inside that I won't return till I come back. (*Exit C.; she struts across stage.*)

PEGGY I wondher if it was all blather whin he said I was good lookin'. (*Enter* TURNER *and* RAFFERTY *L.*)

TURNER I tell you it will have to be done. (*Sees her.*) What, you hanging about here still?

PEGGY Yes, whin your hanging it'll be in a different place.

TURNER Confound your insolence, your master shall know of this.

PEGGY What a grand spy ye'd make.

RAFFERTY We're in luck, me bhoy, Here he is! (*Enter* WITHERINGTON.)

WITHERINGTON (*to* PEGGY) What are you doing round here? (*Enter* SHANE *C. without cap.*)

SHANE Waitin' for me!

WITHERINGTON Do you hear?

TURNER Need you ask, carrying love messages from your sister to that cub Wolfe Tone.

WITHERINGTON Is this true?

PEGGY Do ye doubt yer foine gintlemin friends so much that ye have to axe me?

WITHERINGTON No quibbling, girl, answer.

PEGGY I won't. All the infermation ye want ye can exthort from thim blayguards there. (*Takes* SHANE*'s arm and is going L.*)

WITHERINGTON Stop fellow.

SHANE Felly yersilf. Don't ye see I'm busy.

WITHERINGTON I want that girl.

SHANE Then want must be your Masther.

PEGGY An' thaves yer companions. (*Exeunt laughing L.*)

RAFFERTY What's the world comin' to at all whin servants spake to their shupariors in that disgraceful fashion!

WITHERINGTON What are they after?

TURNER I sh'dn't be at all surprised if Wolfe Tone did not get some of the students here to break into your house to-night and kidnap Miss Witherington.

WITHERINGTON Do you suppose for one moment they would dare with such a proceeding perpetrate such an outrage?

RAFFERTY Dare is it? They'd dare the divil himself if they thought they would; oh they're a gallows lot ov bhoys, I know them. I was one myself, once!

WITHERINGTON What do you suggest?

TURNER Remove her at once to Rathfarnham; the farther away the better.

WITHERINGTON It shall be done. Come! (*Crosses to L. and exits L.*).

TURNER Now Mr. Tone if you should take it into your head to visit the house in Grafton Street to-night you'll find the cage empty and the bird flown. (*Exeunt with* RAFFERTY *L.*)

End of Scene 1

Scene 2

HOUSE OF PARLIAMENT, EXTERIOR

(*Enter* RAFFERTY *and* TURNER *R.*)

RAFFERTY I consider that an exceeding nate piece ov business.

TURNER No fear of her escaping now, eh? she's virtually a prisoner and will remain one till she becomes my wife.

RAFFERTY Which I'd advice ye to do without any further delay.

TURNER Oh, I defy that scoundrel Tone to rob me of her now.

RAFFERTY Get the knot tied me bhoy before the week's out; ye're never safe till ye have possession.

TURNER I know that; but I have that confounded old grandfather to consider; she's his favorite. If I force the marriage on too quickly he may kick over the traces and I can't afford to lose the money he intends to give her.

RAFFERTY No, ov course not, money's the root ov all evil so it is. If ye want the goold through [though?] marry the girl an' ye'll get both. Once yer wife the ould fool will soon knock under. An' if he dosn't why what's the use of being Members of the law if we can't find a way to make him.

TURNER You're right. Delays are dangerous. We'll decoy the old man into Dublin tomorrow on a fool's errand and before he can get back to Rathfarnham the marriage shall have taken place.

RAFFERTY An' Mr. Wolfe Tone left out in the cold. Meanwhile, me bhoy, we must not forget our appointment at the Castle.

TURNER Curse it, yes, I say Rafferty, I don't altogether relish this blood money business.

RAFFERTY Ye'll soon get over that; the Government's too good a paymaster for thim qualms to remain long wid ye, and Government goold is an excellent antidote to patriotic sentiment.

TURNER Confound it, yes; and I am so deep in the mire that I can't now do without it.

RAFFERTY Precisely! If there were no pathriots there would be no informers. It's a wise dispensation ov Providence, the one was created for the other. The pathriot, the fool—the informer, the wiseman. The pathriot schemes, works, delves, builds for the regeneration of his country, the informer steps in and reaps the reward; the pathriot is starved, exiled, bayonetted or hanged; the informer retires to his country seat a rich gentleman, respected by the cumunity at large and there ends his day, peacefully and quietly like the honest man he is. (*Exeunt L.*)

(*Enter* SHANE *R.*)

SHANE Whativer's kapin' that Colleen at all? Here have I been wearin' out me brogues for a full hour thrampin' round these ould houses of Parliament an' not a sign ov her yet. (*Looks at Scene. Enter* PEGGY *hurriedly L.*)

PEGGY Oh, ye're there, are yer.

SHANE Yes, its mesilf, only ouldher.

PEGGY What are yez lukin' at?

SHANE Just at the place where they hatch trayson.

PEGGY What, against England.

SHANE No, against Ireland (*turns round*).

PEGGY Is it jokin' ye are?

SHANE No, its rale earnest an' well poor ould Ireland knows it; well, me jiwel, have ye settled iverthing?

PEGGY We have, an' the wind'll be taken out ov their sails completely. I must hurry along to the darlin' at once. (*Crosses to R.*)

SHANE May I come wid ye?

PEGGY Ye may as far as the corner.

SHANE No farther.

PEGGY Not a step, I have me character to look afther.

SHANE Let me luk afther that fer yez?

PEGGY It wouldn't be worth much if it was left to you, me bhoy; I tell ye ye'll have to lave me at the corner.

SHANE Well, may I come out to see ye to-night at Rathfarnham?

PEGGY It's an impudent blayguard, ye are.

SHANE An' isn't that the kind ye like best?

PEGGY Indade an' it's not.

SHANE Indade an' it is. Spake the truth, now; ye know it is. Sure isn't impudence in the bhoy the spark that lights the fire ov luv in a girls heart? May I come now? (*Wheedling up to her.*)

PEGGY For what? To deludher me out ov the house into catchin' could? not me, ye rascal!

SHANE Arrah* now, won't the warmth ov my luv, cumbined wid me top coat kape us both warm?

PEGGY Yer coat'll be the more reliable ov the two, I'm thinkin'.

SHANE May I come?

PEGGY Well I'll take pity on yez this time.

SHANE That's right; come undher me hoxter.* (*She does so.*)

PEGGY But mind, ye'll conduct yersilf.

SHANE Oh, ov course, I will. I'll naythur squaze ye, nor kiss ye till ye axe me.

PEGGY Ye Rogue ye! (*Exeunt laughing R.*)

End of Scene 2

Scene 3

GARDEN OF HOUSE AT RATHFARNHAM

Gate Tree House

Diagram A

(*Moonlight—Music to open*)

[TABLEAU]

FANNING PEGGY RUSSELL and SUPERS discovered.

FANNING (*at gate*) The hour is getting very late, and still there is no sign of them. I think she has left the old nest for good.

PEGGY (*R.*) Is it leave you an' it widout as much a word ov partin' or blessin' from your lips? Arrah,* sir, don't be wrongin' the darlin' that way.

FANNING (*coming C.L.*) I trust I have done right.

PEGGY Of course ye have, Hark! (*runs up to gate*) there's the shay stoppin' at the foot ov the hill; she leaps from it wid her heart in her feet to hasten thim on. Hark, at her laugh! the very sound ov it does one good. Here, here she is.

(*Enter* SUSAN WITHERINGTON *L.C.*)

SUSAN (*embracing* FANNING *who meets her* C.) Dear old grand dad. I've kept my word, I'm back again.

FANNING Yes, my darling, but not for long—not for long. But where is he—your—

SUSAN My—Mr. Tone, oh, he's coming; the lazy fellow couldn't run up the hill as fast as I could. (*Enter* TONE *L.C.*) Ah here he is.

TONE (*to* FANNING) How can I express my grateful indebtedness to you sir, for your kind help and co-operation.

FANNING By keeping her life free from all regrets.

TONE You can trust me, sir in that, as in all things else. (*Sees* RUSSELL.) What Russell!

FANNING Your friend is here to do honour to the occasion.

RUSSELL How kind of you. (*Shakes his hand.*)

TONE Dear old friend. (*d[itt]o*)

FANNING Come and let us partake of the good things provided—there is no time to be lost. (FANNING *exits into house;* RUSSELL *and others follow.*)

PEGGY (*to* SUSAN) Just a kiss, darlin!

SUSAN A thousand (*embracing her*) oh, you dear good soul.

TONE And a thousand thanks Peggy for your good services. (*Shakes her hand.*)

PEGGY Ah, don't be afther thankin' me; sure am I not hers to the very sthrippins ov me heart. (*To her*) Go in Acushla,* and may yer bright eyes never have more sorrow in thim, than they have at this moment.

SUSAN They never will, Peggy. (*To* TONE) Will they?

TONE Not if I can help it, darling. (*Exeunt laughing into house.*)

(*Enter* SHANE *cautiously R.L.*)

PEGGY (*L.C.*) My blessins' on ye both, an' may [earthier?] care never knock at the door ov ayther ov yer hearts. It's a handsome pair so they are. (*Sighs.*) Ah, me! Luv has a dale to answer for.

SHANE (*aside at back*) It has!

PEGGY It plays old harry* wid us women, entoirely.

SHANE It does.

PEGGY I'm thinkin' I'm afther gethin' a touch ov it mesilf.

SHANE So am I.

PEGGY I haven't had that gosson* out ov me hid the whole blessid day.

SHANE That's a good sign any ways.

PEGGY He seems a dacent sort ov a bhoy.

SHANE Oh I am.

PEGGY An' I may do worse.

SHANE Ye may.

PEGGY Now I wondher (*turns and sees him, she starts*). Ye Spalpeen!* is that yersilf?

SHANE Wait till I see (*comes down*).

PEGGY Did ye hear any thin?

SHANE Divil a word—of what?

PEGGY Well, it's a good job ye didn't.

SHANE I'm much to be thankful for.

PEGGY You've come too early so ye have.

SHANE Sure one can never be too early for a good ting.

PEGGY Ah, I suppose ye're hungry after yer walk from Dublin.

SHANE Me stomach, impty so it is.

PEGGY An' that manes that ye want me to fill it.

SHANE Well, a w[e]isha* taste ov somethin to ate wouldn't go amiss.

PEGGY An' a dhrop ov somethin' nate to wash it down wouldn't go amiss ayther?

SHANE Bedad, an' it wouldn't.

PEGGY Ah, ye're just like the rest ov the min, think ov nothin' but atin an' dhrinkin! Ye're all blayguards entoirely.

SHANE We are bad luck to us.

PEGGY I've just a good mind to sind ye back to Dublin impty as ye are.

SHANE Sure ye wouldn't be so cruel as all that darlin'.

PEGGY Wouldn't I. Ye don't know me yet me buchal!*

SHANE Well, me heart's full ov luv anyways; ye've filled that me girl, an' if ye won't fill the other place I must just draw on luv to supply the vacuum (*handles pistol*).

PEGGY Arrah* man what's that at all?

SHANE Just a pistol I picked up at the fut ov the hill, beyant.

PEGGY Throw it away.

SHANE Arrah,* why should I? it may come in handy on me way home to-night to fill somebody else's vacuum.

PEGGY Ye gallows bird! ye. Put it away an' come in.

SHANE Lade the way an' I'll folly.

PEGGY Folly! I'm thinkin' its folly altogether takin ye in at all.

SHANE Yes, the folly that makes us all wise in toime (*Exeunt L.*)

(*Enter* TURNER *and* RAFFERTY *L.C. Behind* TURNER.)

TURNER What's that post chaise doing at the bottom of the hill?

RAFFERTY Arrah* man how do I know! may be it's there to take Tone and the girl away. I'd laugh if the pair ov thim had stolen a march on ye.

TURNER No fear of that. (MEN *laugh inside.*) What's that? (*going to window.*)

RAFFERTY The Buneens* gruntin'. (TURNER *looks through window.*)

TURNER Why, he's there!

RAFFERTY Whose there? (*Quickly and crossing to window.*)

TURNER Wolfe Tone! (*Crosses to R.C.*)

RAFFERTY The divil he is! (*Looks in.*) An' hobnobbin' with ould Fannin', too. Begorra* judgin' from the atin an' dhrinkin' it luks like a weddin'. Supposin' they're married?

TURNER Impossible!

RAFFERTY Well, he's there anyway!

TURNER Curse it yes!

RAFFERTY An' there's the guril, instead ov bein' locked up, smilin' up in his face as if she never could get enough ov him. What are ye goin' to do now? (*Crosses to him.*)

TURNER (*furiously*) Kick him out.

RAFFERTY Are ye? thin ye'd betther go inside & do it.

TURNER (*is going—then pauses*) Wait!

RAFFERTY Ah, second thoughts are always best. He may kick you out instead. A severe Castigation, me bhoy, is never an agreeable adjunct to one's personal comfort.

TURNER Confound it what's to be done? (*Crossing and crossing.*)

RAFFERTY Invoke the aid ov the law.

TURNER How?

RAFFERTY He owes me twenty pounds. It was due two months ago. He can't pay so I'll arrest him for the debt.

TURNER You will?

RAFFERTY Aye, will I. The man will be here in time for the job. You see I always like to be prepared for any emergency; an' while Mr. Wolfe Tone will be kickin' his heels in the Marshalsaes prison, Dublin, you'll have a fair field to carry out your plans with the girl. Whisht!* Some one's comin'. (*They hide behind tree R. Enter* TONE *and* SUSAN *from house.*)

TONE Just a few moments, darling, in this dear old garden before the inevitable parting comes.

RAFFERTY (*aside to* TURNER) Did ye hear that? Ye're safe, they're not married.

SUSAN Ah, how happy we have been in it, haven't we? You will often think of it, won't you?

TONE Next to the window at which I first saw your winsome face memory will give it the dearest place in my heart. Ah shall I ever forget that day when I first beheld you?

SUSAN You were a very bold young man, Sir.

RAFFERTY (*aside*) What twaddle.

TONE Was I. But you have forgiven me?

SUSAN Oh long since, and now (*nestling up to him*) I'm more than happy.

RAFFERTY (TONE *embraces her. Aside*) How do ye like that?

TONE And you will never regret?

SUSAN Never as long as life lasts.

TONE Bless you.

SUSAN Dear old grand dad. Hasn't he been good?

TONE The very best in the world.

SUSAN Oh, what should we have done without his love and assistance.

TONE Ah, what! (*She shudders.*) You are cold dear, I will get you a wrap.

SUSAN No, never mind.

TONE But I do mind, I won't be a minute. (*Exit into house.*)

SUSAN (*crossing to L.C.*) What a dear, dear, kind good fellow he is, and I mean to be the very best wife in the world to him.

TURNER (*aside*) Do you? Not if I can prevent it.

SUSAN (*who slightly overhears, startled*) What's that? (*Re-enter* TONE *with cloak. He throws cloak so as to envelope both of them in it.*)

TONE Why what's the matter little woman? What has alarmed you?

SUSAN That man! I thought I heard his hated voice.

TONE It was only fancy, dear; and even had it been he himself, he could not harm you now. Within this cloak with my arm around you you can defy even worse villain[s] than Mr. Samuel Turner. (*They wander off R.*)

SUSAN How brave you are. (TURNER *and* RAFFERTY *come down.*)

RAFFERTY Did ye hear his opinion ov ye?

TURNER Curse him, yes. (RAFFERTY *is going up C.*) Where are ye going?

RAFFERTY To see if that man is anywhere about.

TURNER Can't we place some incriminatory document upon him?

RAFFERTY Arrah* man, how can we? Hasn't he got all his clothes on his back this minute; it's far too early for that; only wait an' we'll have him ornamentin' a gallows yet. But I thought ye said ye'd shoot him if ye found him prowling around here.

TURNER So I would if only I had my pistol.

RAFFERTY Where is it?

TURNER I must have lost it on the way here.

RAFFERTY Ah, that's ayther awkward or convanient. (TONE *and* SUSAN *reenter;* TURNER *hides behind tree.*)

SUSAN I shall sorrow to leave the dear old place.

TONE To go with me?

SUSAN No, you foolish boy, for that I shall be glad.

TONE Very glad.

SUSAN (*softly*) Very, very glad.

TONE And have you no fear for the future?

SUSAN Why should I? Shall not we be always together?

TONE Yes, but I am so miserably poor little woman.

SUSAN Well, what of that? does not poverty strengthen love and bind hearts closer to each other?

TONE But hard times may come.

SUSAN And if they do shall I not share them with you?

TONE But if they should weaken your love—your faith?

SUSAN They never will, come weal, come woe, you'll find me ever by your side, ever brave, ever true.

TONE Bless you. (*Kisses her;* RUSSELL *enters at door.*)

RUSSELL Do you two turtle doves purpose cooing out here the whole evening?

TONE (*laughing*) No, you stupid fellow. (*TURNER escapes L.C.*) Take her in I'll follow directly. (*She turns, he kisses her hand, she exits.*) Hist! Russell! (*RUSSELL turns.*) Your pistol.

RUSSELL For what?

TONE There's a rat in the grounds, and I want to kill it.

RAFFERTY (*aside*) Then I'm not that rat. (*Exits R.U.L.*)

RUSSELL Be careful. (*Exit RUSSELL.*)

TONE Have no fear. (*Goes C.*) There he goes. I thought that would frighten him. (*Comes down.*) There's no fight in a cur like that. (*Takes off cloak.*) I may as well leave them here. If the darling sees this (*indicating pistol*) it will add to her fears. (*Leaves both on table and exits. Enter* SHANE *and* PEGGY *from behind house.*)

PEGGY I tell ye it's time ye were goin' back to Dublin.

SHANE Arrah* woman, dear, sure we've done no swat[e]heartin' yet at all.

PEGGY Ye've had a good supper an' that's bether nor any swateheartin'.

SHANE Well, ye ought to know for ye seem to have had plinty ov exparience of both.

PEGGY ([*SHANE*] *is going to window*) Where are yez goin' to at all?

SHANE To have a pape at the quality.

PEGGY Ye'll do no such thing, come away out ov that now. (*Crosses to R.*)

SHANE Oh, certainly (*sees cloak and pistol*) a nice dacent pair ov companions. And [One?] to kape the cold out and the other to let it in, I'll borry one (*takes up cloak*) an' swap this (*own pistol*) for the other; exchange is no robbery.

PEGGY Arrah,* whatever are yez doin' there man?

SHANE Nothin'.

PEGGY Are yez goin?

SHANE No, I['m] comin'. (*Crosses to L.C.*)

PEGGY What's that? (*Meaning cloak.*)

SHANE Just somethin' to kape us both warm a bit. Come undher me girl.

PEGGY Not me, me bhoy.

SHANE Faix* ye take a dale ov persuadin'.

PEGGY Will yez go if I come?

SHANE Will a canary sing? (*Holds out cloak.*)

PEGGY There then. (*She gets under.*)

SHANE Closer.

PEGGY I can't.

SHANE Ye can, ye know ye can. (*She gets closer.*)

PEGGY Ye take a dale ov plazin' so ye do?

SHANE Throth that's true me girl.

PEGGY Are yez satisfied now?

SHANE No I am not; gives us a kiss, an' then I'll be.

PEGGY Ye'll get no kiss from me, me fine fellow.

SHANE Hold up yer head till I thry. (*She does so, he kisses her suddenly.*)

PEGGY Oh, ye blayguard ye, let me go (*struggling*).

SHANE Didn't ye want it.

PEGGY No I didn't.

SHANE Thin what did ye hold up yer face for?

PEGGY It's a mulvatherin'* villain, so ye are; an' ye've no manners at all.

SHANE Well, come along me girl & tache me bether. (*They exeunt R.L.*)

(*Reenter* TURNER *and* RAFFERTY *L.C.*)

TURNER Is the man there?

RAFFERTY He's follyin' me up the hill this minute (*goes to door*).

TURNER Good! (*Sees* SHANE *and* PEGGY.) Ah, there he is again.

RAFFERTY (*who has taken up pistol*) An' makin great runnin' wid the girl, too. Bedad! luk at that! Did yez ever see such luv makin' in yez life?

TURNER I'd shoot him down without a particle of remorse if I but had a pistol.

RAFFERTY Here's one ready to hand. Give him a dose to cool his spirits. Hist! someone comes! (*They hide in front of house. Enter* TONE.)

TONE On second thoughts I'd better take these in—not here, Why where can they have gone? can that scoundrel have returned and taken them. (*He goes up C. and looks off and then exits L.C.*)

TURNER Who's that?

RAFFERTY One ov the guests maybe; now yer time! luk at him! luk at him!

TURNER What if I sh'd hit the girl?

RAFFERTY Ye won't ye're too good a shot for that, man, did ye see that?

TURNER Curse it, yes. (*Fires—he puts pistol back and they exeunt quietly L.C.* PEGGY *screams—*TONE *re-enters quickly L.C.* FANNING, RUSSELL, SUSAN, *and others from house also* PEGGY *&* SHANE *R.C.*)

OMNES What's the matter! (*Re-enter* TURNER *and* RAFFERTY *L.C. Man L.C.*)

SHANE Murther's the mather, who fired that shot?

Diagram B

FANNING That's what we want to know.

TONE Are you hurt?

SHANE I am in the full front ov me back; but nothin to spake about.

RAFFERTY (*aside*) You've hit the wrong man. (*They come down R.*)

TURNER (*aside*) Curse it, yes; but I see a way out of it yet.

SHANE I want to know who fired that shot!

TONE And so do I!

TURNER (*going up* R.C.) You do?

TONE We all do.

TURNER Then it was yourself, Wolfe Tone. (*RAFFERTY gets round to L.*)

TONE (*amazed—also all the others*) I?

TURNER Yes, you! You thought I was watching you, and Miss Witherington there; you sent her in and then asked that man for his pistol, saying you wanted to kill a rat; I was the rat you intended to kill. Not finding me you left the pistol there (*points to table*) [against] you returned; you did so a moment ago, saw me as you thought and fired that shot.

TONE It's a lie.

RAFFERTY Is it? then here's the pistol to give back the lie in your teeth!

RUSSELL (*takes pistol*) But this is not mine!

OMNES No!

TURNER Then whose is it?

RUSSELL Your own, Here's your name on the butt of it (*touches it*).

SHANE An' here's that gintlemans' (*holds up pistol*).

TONE You see! your cowardly scheme has fallen through.

SUSAN And your soul saved from the stain of murder.

FANNING I only regret that the same blood runs in our veins. Leave the grounds at once, both of you!

TURNER I decline to go!

RAFFERTY And so do I!

(*Enter WITHERINGTON* L.C.)

TURNER Ah, you're just in time.

WITHERINGTON For what?

TURNER Can't you see? Your sister making a fool of herself with that penniless scoundrel (*TONE makes a movement, she restrains him; she is on his R.*), disgracing his family, and that old man aiding and abetting her.

WITHERINGTON (*to TONE*) Had you not sufficient warning to cease annoying her and us with your insolent attentions but that I find you intruding them on us even here? (*To her.*) And you, are you lost to all sense of decency? That is no place for you.

SUSAN It is my right place and here I intend to remain.

WITHERINGTON You graceless hussy! an end to this mad folly! Let go of that viper before I drag you from him. (*He goes to her but* TONE *puts her round to his L.*)

TONE (*quietly*) Did you not hear what your sister said? she declines to obey you.

WITHERINGTON Since when you—

TONE Since [she] ⟨yielded up⟩ transferred the right to me—Became my wife.

TURNER and RAFFERTY His wife!

WITHERINGTON Your wife, you mercenary hound! since when?

TONE Since this morning.

WITHERINGTON You lie! she never left the house till she was brought here; she was locked up the whole morning.

PEGGY Bedad an' she wasn't for I let her out.

WITHERINGTON You traitor. (*Makes a movement towards her,* SHANE *intercedes.*)

SHANE Hands off, me buchal!*

WITHERINGTON Married, It's a lie, I say, hatched for the occasion! who married you?

FANNING I did
WITHERINGTON You
TURNER Ah
RAFFERTY Hoo hoo
(*together*)

FANNING Yes, and I am proud to have made them what they are—man and wife.

RAFFERTY Thin I mane to spoil the honeymoon. (*To man.*) Arrest that man.

TONE Fiend
WITHERINGTON All
FANNING For what
RAFFERTY For debt
(*together*)

SUSAN You, you cannot mean it.

RAFFERTY But I do, Oh, it's my turn now. (*To* TONE.) You'll spend this night my newly made Benedict in jail. (*She shudders and clings to him.*) Do ye hear? in jail, unless ye can pay what ye owe me. (*Savagely.*) Can ye?

TONE Heaven help me, no! (*Bows his head; she turns to her grandfather.*)

RAFFERTY I thought as much!

FANNING What, what is the amount?

RAFFERTY Twinty pounds is the sum borrowed; interest an' expenses ten more; thirty pounds the lot! (*TURNER and WITHERINGTON get down R.*)

FANNING I haven't as much money in the house.

RAFFERTY I thought ye wouldn't.

FANNING But my word.

RAFFERTY It's not words I'm wantin' but money; money in legal golden soverigns; can ye pay them now, this minute?

FANNING I cannot!

RAFFERTY Perhaps some ov his rich friends here can. (*To RUSSELL.*) Can ye?

RUSSELL You divil, No.

SHANE But I can!

OMNES You! (*All animated.*)

SHANE Yes, and will! there it is! (*Throws it down.*) They shall have their honeymoon in spite of yez!

TURNER Damnation! (*Quietly. As RAFFERTY stoops to pick it up, SHANE gives him a kick; he falls flat on his face—Laughter and cheers. An act drop falls.*)

End of Act I

ACT II

Scene 1

WOLFE TONE'S HOUSE AT IRISHTOWN

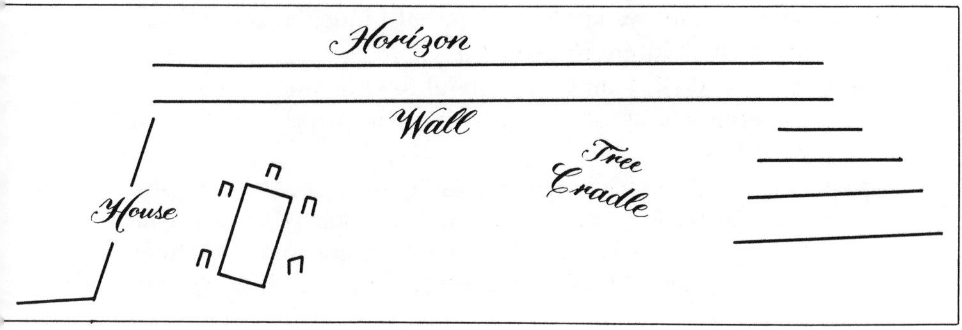

Diagram C

(*Music to open*)

(RAFFERTY *discovered disguised as an old woman, crouching, rocking.* RAFFERTY *croons an old song. Enter* TURNER L.U.C.)

TURNER Confound, that fellow, Rafferty! He promised to meet me at the corner (*indicating L.*) there and though I have been waiting this half hour not a sign of him is there anywhere. Deuce take it where can he be?

RAFFERTY (*rising*) I'm here!

TURNER (*surprised*) You, and in this garb!

RAFFERTY Yes, I thought it safer when in this vicinity; divil a soul would take me to be a castle attorney in this disguise; even Mrs. Wolfe Tone couldn't penetrate it for she axed me to mind the child while she stepped down bayant there (*laugh*). Fancy Joey Rafferty rockin' a cradle. (*Changes tone.*) But I have had a good squint round inside, and have got these (*shows papers*) for me trouble.

TURNER (*intimated [?]*) What are they?

RAFFERTY What should they be but papers belongin' to the United Irishmen!

TURNER Let me see!

RAFFERTY Not till I've examined thim first. But ye mustn't stop here. Will yez go before the she Wolfe returns? (*He hast[ens] him off R. to E., then hobbles back chuckling, to the cradle & rocks it looking at child.*) Drownin' too aisy a death fer ye, my boy, only lave ye alive an' the hangman'll do it bether for yez. (MRS. TONE *enters L. to E. She goes to him.*)

MRS. TONE Oh, it was kind of you to stop and mind baby.

RAFFERTY Not at all Ma'am.

MRS. TONE But it was; now go inside and you shall have something to eat.

RAFFERTY Thank ye kindly ma'am but I must be gettin' back to my own children. (*Is going L.*)

MRS. TONE Well, I am very grateful to you; and there's something to assist you back to town. (*Gives coin; she turns to go in.*)

RAFFERTY All the blessings ov this life folly ye. (*and changing tone—aside*) An' never over take ye. (MRS. TONE *exits into house.*) Mr. Wolfe Tone, I think I have got somethin' here (*touching papers*) that'll hang ye! (*Exit L. to E. Noise of whip cracking,* SHANE'S *voice heard outside saying "Steady! there!"* PEGGY'S *also heard sayin')*

PEGGY I'm kilt, Will yez let me off. It's breakin' my neck you'll be.

SHANE (*outside*) Are yez right now?

PEGGY I am. (*They enter L. to E.*)

SHANE That baste is just like the rist ov ye ***.

PEGGY Be civil if ye can. (MRS. TONE *appears at door.*) Or ye'll come no farther.

MRS. TONE Ah, Peggy, is that you?

PEGGY All that is left ov me.

MRS. TONE (*crossing to cradle*) Then you're back from town.

PEGGY Thanks be to goodness, yes, darlin! an' wid all me bones whole too; that's the greatest rapparee* at drivin' I ever saw in my life.

SHANE Sure the mare's only a bit fresh and skittish.

PEGGY Fresh and skittish, was that all?

SHANE Well maybe like yersilf, a bit onraysonable.

PEGGY Ye're a gom* so ye are! (*Goes up.*)

SHANE I am, swate bad luck to me, or I wouldn't be wastin' me time and me substance dangling' afther ye as I do.

PEGGY Danglin' indade. (*Goes to cradle—*MRS. TONE *comes down L.C.*)

MRS. TONE And if I were you, Shane, I would not submit any longer to such tyranny, it's abominable.

SHANE Bedad it is, ma'am; she's worse than the English government so she is; an' nothin'll suit her ladyship but the very best horse an' kyar, to drive about wid.

PEGGY Don't drive me any more than. (*To Baby*) Cushy! Cushy!

SHANE I won't, Cushy! Cushy!

MRS. TONE Don't you two quarrell over Baby. (*Laughing.*)

PEGGY As if I would, the darlin'. Cushy! Cushy!

MRS. TONE Shane, I have been married seven years to-day.

SHANE Glory be to goodness an' is it as long as that, ma'am?

MRS. TONE Yes, doesn't time fly? only fancy, three children too.

SHANE Begorra that's true; an' if Peggy there had only been sinsible we might have been married an' had three, too.

PEGGY (*curtly*) Might we? (*MRS. TONE goes up C. looks off then comes to cradle.*)

SHANE Ye know we might (*goes up to cradle*).

PEGGY Well, spake fer yersilf.

SHANE Isn't that what I'm doin', me girl. (*Kneels L. of cradle.*) Cushy! Cushy.

PEGGY Lave it alone. (*On L. of cradle.*)

SHANE Arrah,* woman, de ye think I'll break it? Cushy! Cushy!

(*MRS. TONE puts baby in his arms. Enter TONE and RUSSELL R. to L., sees picture.*)

TONE (*laughing, coming down R. C.*) There's a family picture for you Tom. Ah, Shane taking a lesson, eh?

SHANE (*with baby in his arms*) Just a weisha* one Sir, not that it'll be any good to me if things go on as they are (*MRS. TONE comes C.*)

PEGGY Come here & don't be afther makin' a fool ov yersilf that way. (*They all laugh.*)

MRS. TONE (*to TONE whom she meets C.*) Home again, dear?

TONE Yes, and I've brought Russell with me as usual. I knew he'd be welcome.

MRS. TONE (*crossing to RUSSELL*) Dear friends are always welcome.

RUSSELL Or I wouldn't have come. (*They talk.*)

TONE (*going up L.C.*) You see, Shane, we can't keep the wolfe from the door.

SHANE No, nor the tone of it ayther whin it cries. (*They laugh.*)

PEGGY (*singing [?] baby*) Here lave go ov it; I'll have no jokin' over the darlin!

TONE (*to SHANE*) Why don't you get married Shane?

SHANE Why don't Pigs fly—because I can't. (*TONE laughs.*)

MRS. TONE (*crossing to TONE*) Why Tom tells me that you invited some friends to dinner. (*PEGGY raises her head to listen.*)

TONE So I have, but I had quite forgotten it.

PEGGY Friends, an' there's not a scrap in the house worth atin'.

TONE Don't be worried about it, little woman, they must just take pot luck.

PEGGY Pot lick he manes. (*RUSSELL sits on the edge of table.*)

MRS. TONE Who are they?

TONE Keogh, McCracken, Rowan, and Turner!

PEGGY Four ov thim, what'll I do at all? (*Kneels over cradle.*)

MRS. TONE Turner! And you know I dread—distrust that man.

TONE He has forgotten all that folly of seven years ago; and so must you. He is one of our best friends now.

MRS. TONE I doubt it, dear, I doubt it. (*SHANE plays with whip and looks first at one and then the other.*)

TONE A woman once suspicious always suspicious.

MRS. TONE It's instinct, dear, instinct that rarely plays us false; but dinner is the question now, and must have all my attention.

RUSSELL And I'll come and help you. (*He makes a movement to follow her—TONE accompanies her to the door.*)

MRS. TONE Hinder, you mean; no, you must stay here and keep this good but thoughtless husband of mine company. (*TONE kisses her hand.*)

TONE (*coming down*) Poverty's an awful nuisance, Tom. (*She exits.*)

RUSSELL Awful. (*They talk.*)

SHANE (*to PEGGY*) Any money in the house?

PEGGY (*rising*) Not a shillin' an' the credit's gone entoirely.

SHANE Never mind, take that! (*Gives money.*) Get all ye want & say nuthin'.

PEGGY Ye're a darlin' so ye are; forgive me all the cruel hard words I said to ye; an', here, Shane (*he turns*) there's a kiss for ye. (*She gives him a very loud one. TONE and RUSSELL look around—SHANE falls on his knees at the cradle.*)

TONE What was that?

PEGGY What was what? (*Crossing to door.*)

TONE Why— that— that— (*rising, laughing and going up C.*)

SHANE Oh, that—Sure that was the bhoy here sucking his thumb.

PEGGY (*to TONE*) Are ye satisfied.

TONE Oh, perfectly. (*Looks off L. to E.*)

PEGGY An' so am I. (*Exits into house.*)

TONE Ah, here they are. (*RUSSELL rises.*)

(*Enter MC KEOGH, MC CRACKEN, ROWAN, and TURNER.*)

TONE (*heartily*) Welcome, friends, all. (*They all shake hands.*)

TURNER Then we have not preceded it?

TONE No, nor will you outstay it; my house is not a mansion but hospitality reigns within it—my table is anything but a ⟨tempting⟩ sumptious one but what it is friends are ever welcome to. (*They seat themselves.*) By the way what do you say to a glass of sherry before dinner? I'll call for it (*at door*). Peggy! here!

PEGGY (*At door, her face floured, also hands.*) Well, what's are yez wantin'?

TONE Will you bring a decanter of sherry and some glasses Peggy?

PEGGY Ye can have the glasses, but sorra* dhrop ov wine de ye get till dinner time. There's only just what'll do for the male itsilf.

[TONE] Ah, that's awkward Peggy. Well we must do without it that's all, the gentlemen don't mind (*to them*) do you? (*Exit PEGGY.*)

OMNES Certainly not. (*All laugh.*)

SHANE (*Coming forward with bottle of whiskey; he has either taken it out of his pocket or he exits at PEGGY's speech and goes out to his car for it.*) Perhaps the gentlemen wouldn't mind a dhrop ov the craythег*? It's a grand thing for givin' one an appetite.

TONE Why, Shane, where ever did that come from? (*PEGGY enters with glasses.*)

SHANE Oh, it's just one ov half a dozen the Misthress got me to ordher for her.

PEGGY (*aside*) The lyin' blayguard!

SHANE I'm takin' the other round to the back door.

PEGGY Are ye? (*She puts glasses on table—TONE pours out whiskey.*)

TONE Shane you're a genius, you always seem to know what's wanted.

PEGGY (*sniffing*) Whiskey! Who gave ye that? (*To gentlemen.*)

SHANE Don't be axin' impertinent questions, me girl, but go an' attend to your culinary department. (*They go up to door.*)

PEGGY Ye'll die in the poor house yet.

SHANE I will, unless ye take pity on me an' marry me. (*They talk.*)

TONE Here's success, to United Irishmen!

SHANE United Irishmen. (*They all drink; PEGGY slams door in SHANE's face; he stumbles back to C.*)

TONE What! has Peggy turned you out Shane?

SHANE Begorra* she wouldn't let me in; she says she's no Peg for me to hang me hat on.

TONE Don't mind her. Have a glass of your own whiskey instead, I'll keep your better company [it'll keep you better company?].

SHANE My head's too wake for that stuff, sir. (*Finger to nose.**) Ye'll find me round the corner at the ould place sh'd you be wantin' me. Good day, Sir, Good day gintlemen.

(*Exit L. to E.*)

TURNER Who is that fellow? I seem to know his face!

TONE Why he's the man who came to the rescue on my wedding day at Rathfarnham.

RUSSELL Paid his debt to that villainous old Rafferty.

TURNER Ah, I remember him now.

TONE (*with fervour*) And may my right arm wither in its socket when I forget him. Many a stile has he helped me over since; many an obligation discharged; and I am honoured in calling him friend. Here's to his health, an Irishman loyal and true to the core of his heart. Well gentlemen what news bring you from Dublin?

MC KEOGH Curran's speech last night on the Penal laws fairly electrified the house.

TURNER And dismayed the Government.

(*Enter MC NALLY L. to E.*)

MC NALLY God save all here. (*All rise.*)

TONE McNally! This is good fortune indeed.

MC NALLY Say rather ill, for it is ill news I bring (*TURNER R.C.*)

OMNES (*startled*) What?

TURNER Ill news! They travel fast. (*Crosses to L.C.*)

MC NALLY And I have travelled fast to bring them.

TONE What are they?

MC NALLY All friends here?

OMNES All.

TONE Not a traitor within three miles of us.

MC NALLY (*with a laugh*) Unless I'm he—(*Looks at TURNER.*)

TURNER Or I. (*Hand on sword.*)

TONE (*coming between*) A truce gentlemen to this badinage. It is neither the time nor the place for it. (*To* MC NALLY) What ill news have you to impart?

MC NALLY Jackson has been arrested.

OMNES Arrested!

MC NALLY Yes within the hour. Suspicion has also fallen upon you.

TONE Upon me!

MC NALLY And that you are the next on the list for government care and attention. On Jackson was found a document of yours of the most incriminatory not to say revolutionary description. (*TURNER crosses to RUSSELL, others talk aside to TONE.*) Have you got that proclomation safely back in your possession?

TONE No, you have it, I left it in your charge.

MC NALLY And I lent it yesterday to Turner to read; he promised most faithfully to return it to you last night without fail. Did he not do so?

TONE No!

MC NALLY Then if I were you I'd look to the safety of my neck. (*TONE looks at TURNER*) For the government will have got it for a certainty.

TURNER What has disturbed you? (*MC NALLY goes up and talks to rest.*)

TONE Only this, McNally gave you a paper of mine yesterday to peruse, a paper on which my liberty—perhaps my life depends. If you are not a traitor where is it? (*MRS. TONE enters, speaks to gent[lemen] who exeunt into house.*)

TURNER (*crossing to L.C.*) If I were a traitor I shouldn't be here. If you want to find the article look nearer home for it (*looks at RUSSELL*). I came down last night with it as promised—You were not here but Russell was—as usual. (*MRS. TONE who has crossed to cradle listens.*)

TONE What do you imply by "as usual."

TURNER Well, he's your bosom friend isn't he? I gave it into his keeping; perhaps he can explain.

TONE He can. (*To RUSSELL.*) Tom, where is that paper Turner left with you last evening.

RUSSELL Oh, as you were so late in getting home I left it with Mrs. Tone.

MRS. TONE (*coming down*) And I put it in your desk with the rest.

TURNER (*aside*) And Rafferty's got it now.

TONE (*to TURNER*) You hear?

TURNER I do, but sometimes we entertain a serpent in the guise of a friend.

TONE You're quite right we do (*looks at him*). My wife has never succeeded in eradicating her old dislike to you; she distrusts you still.

TURNER She has reason (*looks at MRS. TONE and RUSSELL who are at door*). She sees that I perceive the game she is playing. (*MRS. TONE exits.*)

TONE There is no mistaking the offensive character of your observation.

TURNER Tut, man, I am not your enemy—but your friend. (*RUSSELL comes down.*)

TONE A pretty friend to malign a woman to her own husband. Russell if I am arrested within the next twenty-four hours call this (*looks at TURNER*) gentleman out and run him through. If I'm still at liberty I'll have the satisfaction of doing it myself. Go!

TURNER Most husbands are not so hard to convince; but I'll produce proof that shall satisfy even so pronounced a sceptic as you as to the falsity of her loyalty and truth. (*Exit L.*)

RUSSELL What has upset you?

TONE Could you believe a man could fall so low as to try and poison a man's heart against his wife?

RUSSELL Some men fall so low that they merge into vermin and exist only to desecrate the earth.

TONE That man, Tom, said in language that the most obtuse could not mistake that you—you—were my wife's lover.

RUSSELL The hound! but you, you do not believe it?

TONE A thousand times no; my trust in you, Tom, is laid on too too sacred a foundation for any cursed Iago's venom ever to undermine it.

RUSSELL (*with hands clasped*) And no act of mine, Tone, shall ever cause you to say otherwise. (*Enter MRS. TONE; she comes down; they meet her. Enter PEGGY who crosses to cradle and takes up child.*)

MRS. TONE Are you idlers coming?

PEGGY Are yez comin' to-day at all at all?

TONE Yes Peggy, yes.

PEGGY The dinner's spoilin' so it is. (*Crosses to door.*)

TONE It'll be more spoilt directly, Peggy.

PEGGY Will it? I'm thinkin' ye'd joke even on the gallows.

TONE Choke, you mean Peggy.

PEGGY Ah, yer incorrigible so ye are. (*Exit into house.*)

TONE (*going up*) Am I not well blessed?

MRS. TONE For being in disgrace.

TONE No, for possessing so good a wife and so excellent a friend.

(*Exeunt into house. Enter* RAFFERTY *L. to E.*)

RAFFERTY The divil fly away wid ye for a useless lot. I suppose me bould Turner's inside there gormandisin' wid the rest ov thim. The felly's improvin' so he is. He'll sup now wid his best friend one minute an' sell him to the castle the next. I'm gettin' rale proud ov him so I am. (*Enter* TURNER *L.U.E.*)

TURNER What are you muttering about?

RAFFERTY Bury me dacent, is that yersilf? An' I afther thinkin' ye were in the house with your dear friend Tone (*chuckling*).

TURNER No, the friendship dodge has come to an end at last.

[RAFFERTY] Ye don't tell me so. An' the rayson?

TURNER Hintin' at his wife's faithlessness.

RAFFERTY Is that all? An' ye mane to say he belaves in her still?

TURNER More than ever.

RAFFERTY Poor divil, an' I don't belave in one ov thim; their's not a woman brathin' I'd give a ha'porth* ov butthermilk for.

TURNER If I could only bring conviction home to him that she is frail and that Russell is her lover, the agony of mind and heart he would endure would compensate me more than anything else.

RAFFERTY Even to the government hanging him?

TURNER That's a pleasure I also intend to participate in when the time is ripe for it.

RAFFERTY Ye must have the divil's blessing on ye for being a good hater. Ye want to convince him, eh? Well, wait an' see how aisly I'll do it fer ye. Among those papers I got inside, I came across these (*produces a bundle of papers*) a bundle of her old love letters. Just imagine the gosson* kapin' them all these years & tied up with green ribbon too. Here's one (*taking one out*) that'll suit the occasion down to the ground. (*Reads*) "My darlin mate me to-night at the old place. I'm dyin' to fale yer arm around me again an' yer swate kisses on my lips." (*Speaking sarcastically*) Dying to fale yer arm around me an' yer swate kisses on my lips. What blitherin' nonsence the ijiots do write to be sure. (*Reads*) "As he has friends dining with him to-night I shall not be missed Don't fail to come, Susie."

TURNER Is there any date to that?

RAFFERTY Arrah,* did ye ever know a woman date a letther at all?

TURNER Nothing could be better, and if we can only contrive for him to find that in Russell's possessions, further belief in her innocence is impossible.

RAFFERTY Lave it to me. Whisht,* someone's comin'. Hide yersilf at once. (*He does so. Enters* MRS. TONE.)

RAFFERTY Is that yersilf, ma'am?

MRS. TONE What have you returned for?

RAFFERTY Whisht*! Spake low. I hurried back to tell ye that the military are out & that they are on their way here.

MRS. TONE (*agitatedly*) On their way here—for what—for whom?

RAFFERTY For whom—the masther—for what—Trayson!

MRS. TONE Great Heaven, I must save him! (*Is going to house.*)

RAFFERTY If ye go that way ye'll hang him; they can't be here for an hour yet; listen! have ye a friend ye can trust?

MRS. TONE Yes, yes, the best, Russell.

RAFFERTY Call him out thin, but don't let your husband hear ye; if he does he's lost.

MRS. TONE (*at door softly*) Peggy, Peggy!

RAFFERTY Mind yersilf now—for there's a traitor among them there.

MRS. TONE Ah, can it be McNally!

RAFFERTY Whisht!* (*He hides R. Enter* PEGGY.)

PEGGY What is it darlin'?

MRS. TONE Send Mr. Russell to me at once, Peggy, at once!

PEGGY (*startled*) Whatever's the matther at all?

MRS. TONE And don't let the master hear you tell him.

PEGGY And why?

MRS. TONE Because he's in danger; the military are on their way here to arrest him!

PEGGY There sorrow's, knocking at the door at last!

MRS. TONE It is, it is, oh, hurry, Peggy, hurry!

PEGGY I'll not be a moment darlin'. (*Exit into house. MRS. TONE crosses to L.*)

RAFFERTY (*coming down—aside*) The bait's takin' beautifully so it is. (*To her aloud*) Go down to the arbour there an' I'll bring him to ye.

MRS. TONE Why cannot we talk here?

RAFFERTY Bekase the spy inside may folly him out; an' see, there's another ov thim there! (*Points off L. to TURNER.*) In the arbour ye're safe. Arrah* why do ye hesitate like this! If ye want to save your husband's life ye'll do as I tell ye. Will yez go?

MRS. TONE Yes! yes! (*Exits L.U.E. Enter RUSSELL from house.*)

RAFFERTY (*to him*) Ye're just in time, sir! ye're wantin' Mrs. Tone.

RUSSELL How do you know?

RAFFERTY Bekase she told me to sind yez to her; she's beyant there agin the arbour. (*He is going.*) An', here's a bit ov a note I want yez to give Mr. Tone; but for the love of Heaven, don't let a crature percave yez givin' it!

RUSSELL (*suspiciously*) But why this secrecy?

RAFFERTY Is it why? Bekase danger is closin' round him like a sea fog, round a ship on sea & that (*points to paper*) shows him the way of escape. But go to her, say I'll be wid you directly. (*Exit RUSSELL L.U.E.*) The train laid—now to explode the mine. (*TURNER, whom he has beckoned out as RUSSELL exits, enters—knocks.*) I lave this all to yersilf. (*PEGGY appears.*) Send yer masther out immediately.

PEGGY An' who are you at all, to give such an ordher?

RAFFERTY Niver mind, me girl, who I am. Do as your bid.

PEGGY I'll— (*Enter TONE from house.*)

TONE What's the matter, Peggy? (*Sees RAFFERTY.*) Who are you? (*Then sees TURNER.*) Ah, I thought I gave you to understand that your presence here was no longer desirable—

TURNER You did, and I gave you also to understand that when I returned I would furnish you with undeniable proof of your wife's ⟨falsity⟩ fraility (*goes up a little*). Look there!

TONE You demon!

TURNER They meet by appointment; her love letter's in his breast at this moment. See how she clings to him, your dear friend Russell. How lovingly she gazes up into his face, how passionately she kisses his hand. (*Turning to him.*) Do you believe me now?

TONE No, you scoundrel, I do not. Defend yourself lest I become your murderer.

TURNER You mean it then? (*Draws sword.*)

TONE I mean to kill you.

TURNER Will nothing convince you?

TONE Nothing but that you are a slanderer—a spy—an informer.

TURNER Then have it. (*He lunges at TONE who, taken unawares steps back then drawing his sword rushes at TURNER. PEGGY screams. RAFFERTY stabs TONE in the back. PEGGY pulls him off and knocks him down R. and stands over with jug or chair. TONE staggers up C. and drops his sword—TURNER follows and is about to run him through when SHANE enters and pulls him round to L. He recovers and is rushing forward again when MRS. TONE, who has entered with RUSSELL, picks up sword and stands before her husband—RUSSELL holds up TONE—RUSSELL can pick up sword and MRS. TONE can assist her husband, whichever is most practicable; others rush on and form tableau.*)

RUSSELL What outrage is this? Would you kill him?

TURNER Not more than you have done. His eyes (*pointing to TONE*) are open at last—You—

TONE Silence—

TURNER Why don't you ask him for the letter?

TONE (*quietly*) You have a letter for me.

RUSSELL Yes, but—

TURNER You see, he hesitates.

TONE (*firmly*) Give it to me! (*RUSSELL does so—TONE deliberately tears it up and throws it at TURNER's feet.*)

TONE That is my answer to your vile aspersion!

End of Scene 1

Scene 2

HOUSE OF PARLIAMENT

(*Enter TURNER and RAFFERTY R.I.E.*)

TURNER Could you believe any man could be so infatuated, so proof against such damning evidence of guilt?

RAFFERTY Bedad I couldn't. All my nicely laid trap to go for nothin'. It is too bad so it is.

TURNER The love sick fool.

RAFFERTY The disbelievin' blayguard.

TURNER It's no use attacking him in that quarter.

RAFFERTY No, nor in any other I'm thinkin' an' if the counthry had only a few more like him there wouldn't be a livin' at all for men like you an' me. Here's McNally, mind yersilf now. (*He goes L. Enters* MC NALLY *R.*)

MC NALLY Ah, is that you Turner? A word with you. (*They talk R.*)

RAFFERTY (*aside*) There's a pair ov the grandest blayguards that iver drew blood money from a disthracted government; each thinks the other's a true patriot an' each is a rascally informer.

MC NALLY Well, that's understood, but take my advice and don't play any more such ungentlemanly tricks upon Wolfe Tone.

TURNER As to that I shall please myself.

MC NALLY If you do you will certainly get yourself into disfavour with the heads of the Society.

TURNER My private affairs have nothing whatever to do with them.

MC NALLY That I do not pretend to dispute, but such a display of bitter hatred against one whom all love and admire is decidedly calculated to raise doubts in their minds as to your fidelity to the cause.

TURNER You think so?

MC NALLY I do, my warning, believe me, is well meant; who is that?

TURNER Some old hag or another.

MC NALLY Or old Rafferty, which? (TURNER *starts.*) Oh, you needn't deny it, I recognised his voice well enough at Irishtown. It looks suspicious his being there—and with you.

TURNER Oh, the old fool followed me there about a loan, that's all.

MC NALLY (*meaningly*) I hope it is all. By the way I want to see him about a similar piece of business; you'll be at the Meeting tonight.

TURNER Without fail.

MC NALLY (*crossing to L.*) Good night then.

TURNER (*hand on sword—gruffly*) Good night. (*Crosses to R.*)

MC NALLY (*hits* RAFFERTY *on the back. He jumps.*) Well, old money bags any cash to spare? (*Change of tone.*) You see I know you, listen. I'll give you a £100 if you'll tell me if Turner is in the pay of the Castle.

RAFFERTY What do ye want to know for?

MC NALLY Because I'd pick a quarrell with him and run him through with pleasure.

RAFFERTY Divil doubt* ye, I suppose ye want all the field to yersilf?

MC NALLY Precisely, too many in it are dangerous.

RAFFERTY Then ye nadn't fear him. There isn't a bit ov the informer about him.

MC NALLY Ar ye speaking the truth?

RAFFERTY Gospil.

MC NALLY Then, good night! (*Exit L.*)

RAFFERTY Good night, and may all the gould ye've robbed the governmint of lay like lead on yer chist this night.

TURNER (*crossing and meeting* RAFFERTY C.) I say, do you think the castle has got hold of McNally?

RAFFERTY Tut man no! you informers are the most suspicious mortials breathin'.

TURNER Well, I have had my doubts of him for a long time—and if I had but a tittle of evidence to go upon—

RAFFERTY Ye'd call him out an' run him through!

TURNER I would.

RAFFERTY Ye nadn't for he's an honest bhoy is that same McNally, what had he to say to ye?

TURNER Oh, war[n]ed me, confound him!, to exhibit less animosity to Tone—

RAFFERTY An' it's a warning ye cannot afford to ignore. Neilson, Rowan, Emmet, and a few more of them suspect ye already, and if the word goes round a bullet fired from some dark corner will quickly stop your career. Ye must rehabititate yersilf in their good graces; restore their confidence in you—without a moment's delay. Ye're goin' to the Matin'?

TURNER Yes.

RAFFERTY Thin I'll arrange that before it breaks up, ye'll be more established in their favour than ever.

TURNER You will, how?

RAFFERTY Lave it to me, me bhoy, lave it to me. Good night for the present an' if ye've any since left thry and presave yez timper. (*He leads him off L., turns.*) Ah, it's a good job he's gone for here comes Wolfe Tone himsilf. Had they met their would have been wigs on the green here to-night. (*Enter TONE R.*)

TONE (*sees him*) Stop! (*RAFFERTY takes no notice.*) Do you hear? Oh, disguise won't help you now. Where are those papers you stole from my house?

RAFFERTY I didn't stale thim man.

TONE Then who did—

RAFFERTY Turner!

TONE Ah (*throws him off—he falls L. Enter RUSSELL R.*)

RUSSELL Here you are! (*Sees RAFFERTY.*) Who's that? Why it's that scoundrel Rafferty.

TONE Yes a castle leech that gorges itself with the blood of its victims.

RAFFERTY (*who has risen*) Ye'll pay dearly Mr. Wolfe Tone for this nights work so ye will. Only to see ye dancin' a jig in mid air will satisfy me now— (*backing L.*) will satisfy— (*Enter SHANE hurriedly L. seizes him by the back and rushes him across stage and off R.; the others laugh quietly. SHANE reentering R.*)

[SHANE] What do ye mane ye dirthy ould swape by runnin' up agin a gintleman that way for. Go home out ov that and wash the pigs.

TONE You gave him a surprise that time, Shane.

SHANE Begorra* if the river had been a bit handier I'd have given him a greater. Wasn't I standin' by & heard what he said to ye—Arrah* why didn't ye let out some of his bad blood.

TONE Because I wish to reserve my sword for worthier foe—not to sully it with such as he.

SHANE Thrue for yez—He's only fit for the crows.

TONE Good night Shane.

SHANE Faix,* it won't be good night till I see ye safely home at Irishtown. I'll be waitin' for yez wid the car whin the Matin's over.

TONE I'm greatly afraid I shall never be able to discharge my obligations to you, Shane.

SHANE Wait till yer axed, Sir.

TONE Is it to take me home or to see Peggy, eh?

SHANE Both, and there's your answer.

TONE With which I am perfectly contented. Well good night for the present. (*Exit L. with* RUSSELL.)

SHANE (*looks R.*) Who's this comin'! Tundher & turf*—it's the Patrol, an' ould Rafferty with it, Now for squals.

(*Enter* PATROL *R. also* RAFFERTY.)

RAFFERTY There's the ruffin that assaulted me; off to Newgate with him.

[SHANE] Is it me assault you? Arrah,* woman! dear! ye must be either mad or dhrunk!

RAFFERTY I'm no woman ye scoundrel, but a respictable attorney at law.

SHANE Thin more shame to ye, for it's always respictability like yours that gets into such a disgraceful condition, Ye poor misguided creature, ye.

OFFICER Why Shane, my man is that you?

SHANE Mysilf sir, an' no other.

RAFFERTY (*to* OFFICER) Will yez do your duty an' arrest that Villian?

SHANE Sure Gineral, dear, you know me too well for an honest bhoy to belave a miserable object like that?

OFFICER Yes, I think I'd rather take your word than—

RAFFERTY (*quickly*) Am I to tache you yer duty, sir?

OFFICER No, but if you don't behave yersilf I shall teach you yours.

SHANE Ah, General don't be too hard upon the poor deluded Ijiot.

RAFFERTY (*to* OFFICER) Do ye know who I am, Sir?

OFFICER I know you are a nuisance. What do you mean by perambulating the streets in this fashion and creating this disturbance?—

RAFFERTY I'll report yer sir, for insolence, for insubinordination, for dereliction ov duty.

OFFICER If you don't keep a civil tongue in your head—You'll find yersilf in the wrong box.

RAFFERTY Will I Sir, I dare ye, Sir, to put me anywhere that I don't want to go.

OFFICER That is quite sufficient. (*Pushes him between two men who step forward to enable him to do so.*) Get in there, and consider yourself my prisoner.

RAFFERTY Prisoner, Sir, How dare ye! (*He keep[s] up exclamation till—*)

OFFICER (*to* PATROL) Forward! Quick march! (*They exeunt L.*)

SHANE Begorra,* that was a knock down blow for ould Mr Attorney at law. More power to your four bones General. Ye're not a bad sort though you do wear a red coat.

(*Exit dancing L.*)

End of Scene 2

Scene 3

CHAMBER IN BACK LANE

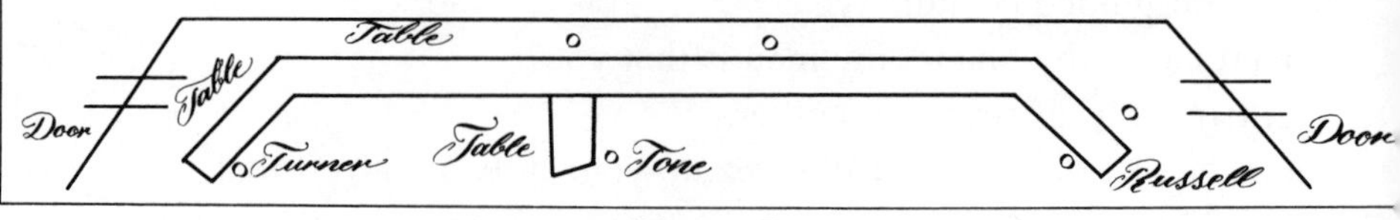

Diagram D

(*MC KEOGH, HAMILTON ROWAN, NEILSON, JOY MC CRACKEN, OLIVER BOND, SIMMS, TURNER, TONE, RUSSELL, MC NALLY, and TEELING discovered. All sit round table as per diagram. Papers, desk etc. on table, BROTHER, SHANE, MC CONNELL [MC CORMICK?]*)

MC NALLY Are we all here?

OMNES All!

MC NALLY Now to business. Here are letters from Lewins from Paris, from Napper Tandy from Hamburg, and from O'Connor from Brussels. All urge the vital importance of our dispatching at once an accredited envoy to De-La-Croix the minister of France. Now on whom shall devolve this important duty—On whom fall the honor?

OMNES Wolfe Tone! (*TURNER does not speak.*)

MC NALLY (*to TONE*) You hear. The most perfect unanimity exists with regard to the selection. Are you willing to accept it?

TONE (*rising*) No man in Ireland more willing—more sensible of your kindness or who appreciates more fully the great honor you would confer on him, but gentlemen I'm too poor a man to occupy so high a position. Select one from among you—One whose wealth will enable him to undertake the embassy with credit to himself and to the country.

TURNER (*with sarcasm*) And is this the return for all the confidence reposed in you? I suppose you would accept the post if the money were found you.

TONE (*quietly*) Certainly! For the one and only obstacle in the way to my accepting it would be removed.

TURNER And have you no shame in making such a statement?

TONE None whatever.

TURNER Just as you would have no shame in takin' the money—

TONE No possible shame could nor can lie in taking money when it will be used for Ireland's good. The shame lies in taking it for betraying her.

TURNER Do you imply that I betray her?

TONE I imply that a man who can stoop to steal—spy on a woman to rob her of her good name will not hesitate to sell either friend or country.

TURNER (*Jumps up. Both place hands on their swords.*)

MC KEOGH Peace gentlemen, peace.

TURNER Who sent in my name to the castle to be the next after Jackson for arrest?

TONE Probably yourself, for who amongst us but yourself would know that it was ever sent in. (*TURNER turns his head—TONE to assembly*) I fear no man's criticism, no man's censure. But gentlemen I must live, must support wife and family and the salary I receive from the society to enable me to do so is known to you all. Is there I ask any degradation in receiving such an honorarium. I say no, the degradation is with those who live and [b]atten on cursed blood money.

TURNER Do I live on blood money?

TONE Ask your conscience—not me. If that satisfies you then I am content.

MC NALLY It frequently occurs Mr. Tone that those who are the most violent in their denunciations of others are invariably the least to be trusted.

TURNER Methinks gentlemen, Mr. Tone doth protest too much. It wouldn't surprise me to learn that under the outward garment of such intense patriotism he wears himself the garb of a spy.

TONE Enough, if any one among you here, has the slightest doubt of my fealty—my truth and honour, let him sheath that sword (*throws it on table*) in my body. I leave it to time to wipe out the stain—clear my character before the world.

TURNER And erect a monument to your name.

TONE The only monument I require is to live in the hearts of all true Irishmen. Is there no one here to strike the blow? No one who believes me false?

TURNER (*jumping up*) Yes, I do. (*Picks up sword, all rise hastily. RUSSELL draws his sword and as TURNER makes a thrust at TONE he knocks it out of his hand.*)

RUSSELL You coward! would you strike an unarmed man?

TURNER I would if he were a traitor.

RUSSELL He who calls Wolfe Tone traitor must answer to me for the lie.

MC KEOGH And me!

OTHERS And me! (*Swords up raised.*)

TURNER Be it so! McCormick as honest men's lives are not safe when rogues are to the fore (*RUSSELL restrains TONE*) I will take my leave. (*To MC NALLY and MC KEOGH, who have resumed their seats*) Should you by chance elect me to undertake this journey to France I am ready to depart at a moment's notice—And though I am also a poor man I shall require no subsidy from the society to defray my expenses.

TONE Devil!

TURNER Meanwhile I prefer an atmosphere less impregnated with the presence of a Castle hireling. (*Is going when drums beat, trumpet sounds; SHANE rushes in R., another in L. shouting*) The military!

OMNES (*jumping up with swords raised—one leg on the table*) The military. (*SOLDIERS rush in R.U.L.—and form—OFFICER enters.*)

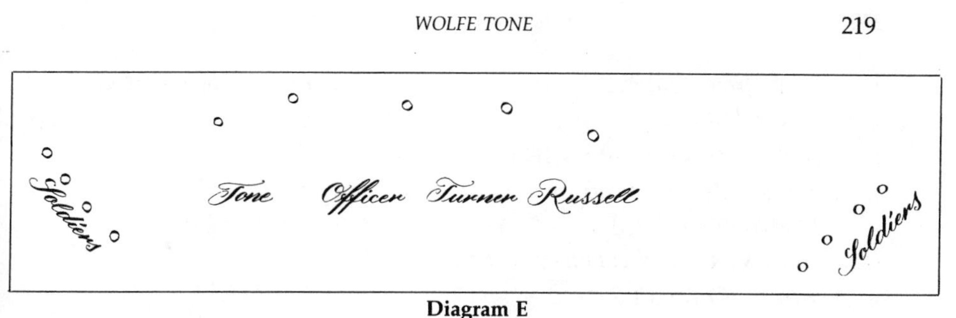

Diagram E

(*Two soldiers also appear at window R. and L. and point rifle down.*)

OFFICER Put up your swords gentlemen, I want but one man here.

TURNER And that is you (*to* TONE). Your time is come, I shall see you hanged yet.

OFFICER I have here a warrant (*producing it*) for the arrest of—

TURNER Wolfe Tone!

OFFICER No, Sir, for Samuel Turner (*places hand on his shoulder*). And you are the man! (TURNER *amazed.*)

[TABLEAU]

End of Act II

ACT III

Scene 1

ENCAMPMENT OF PART OF THE ARMY OF INVASION AT LE HAVRE

Back Cloth
French Flag
Lieutenant
Sentry

Diagram F

(*Music to open—Bugle Call—Drums*

FRENCH SOLDIERS—*cross from L.U.E. to R.U.E. Enter* COLONEL

LEMOINES *from Tent R.2.E. Meets* GENERAL KILMAINE *who enters at same time R.U.L. C.)*

KILMAINE Ze General wishes to see you.

LEMOINES Zen I attend on him at once. (*Both salute. Exit* LEMOINES *L.1.E.*)

(*Enter* TURNER *and* RAFFERTY *L.U.E.*)

KILMAINE Qui va la?

RAFFERTY Glance yer eye over that an' perhaps that'll satisfy yer wid yer—

KILMAINE From Ze Ministers ov War—(*who has taken paper—reading it*).

TURNER And mine! from General Bounaparte. (*Hands pass.*)

KILMAINE (*Reading it*) Quite correct Zhentlemen! You are at perfect liberté to go whenever you please. (*Returns paper, salutes and retires L.*)

TURNER (*looking round*) And so this is part of the army for the invasion of England.

RAFFERTY An' I'm thinkin' this is about as far as it'll get on the road—Bouniparte's heart is not in the job.

TURNER No, he prefers frying other fish—

RAFFERTY Supposin' we sh'd fall across Mr. Wolfe Tone here?

TURNER The possibility is too remote even for thought—He is safe at Hamburg.

RAFFERTY I don't know so much about that, me bhoy, Duckett told me he was either at Rouen or here. If ye meet he'll make yez sup sorrow fer yez tratement to him in Dublin. Had I not got the government that night to arrest ye, to throw thim blayguards of society bhoys off the scent, yer own life would have paid the penalty.

TURNER It was a bold stroke and a surprise to me as well as to the others.

RAFFERTY Aye, a stroke that reinstated ye in the good opinion of the United Irishmen, and kept thim suspicious of Tone.

TURNER When Jackson died in Court—

RAFFERTY An' spoilt the hangman ov a job—

TURNER Why wasn't Tone arrested? The warrant was issued for it.

RAFFERTY Because the spalpeen* had the good word ov friend and foe alike. Every one was fond ov him so they was.

TURNER Except you and I.

RAFFERTY Ye see he was one ov the upright sort an' not to be bought.

TURNER Curse him, Yes.

RAFFERTY Well, ye'll be lavin' him alone now anyways?

TURNER I never will, I'll hunt him down till the French shoot him as a spy or I see his head grinning on a spike on one of Dublin's bridges.

RAFFERTY Who's that?

TURNER (*looks L.*) Why I believe it's Tone, himself.

RAFFERTY (*looks L.*) Belave, man, Bedad I'm sure of it, an' as I have no particular desire to be tickled wid could steel this fine mornin' I'll thravel a bit farther. (*Crosses to R.1.E.*)

TURNER I suppose I had better go too. (*Crosses to R.*)

RAFFERTY I suppose ye had! (*Exeunt R.1.E.*)

(*Enter* TONE *L.U.E. Salutes* SENTRY. *He has papers.*)

TONE What glorious news! The best I have heard this many a day. The Minister for War has at last made up his mind—definitely decided to dispatch another army to Ireland. (*At tent R.*) Shane! Shane.

(*Enter* SHANE *dressed as a French soldier—a corporal.*)

SHANE Yes, yer honour. (*Salutes.*)

TONE I'm bursting with good news. We shall soon be on our way to the dear old country.

SHANE The sooner the betther I'm tired ov this one altogether.

TONE (*slapping him on the shoulder*) And Shane; what do you think?

SHANE Peggy, the wife, has twins.

TONE What (*laughing*). Won't one be sufficient?

SHANE (*in excitement*) Ye don't tell me it's come?

TONE It has, ye've got a son and heir.

SHANE For the luv ov marcy, whin?

TONE Seven weeks ago.

SHANE Sure?

TONE Quite, there's a letter from Peggy herself (*hands it*).

SHANE (*delighted*) Begor* that's grand, I'm a father at last. Hurroo! for the old stock! (*Crosses L.C.*)

TONE And what's more Shane, she and Mrs. Tone may be here at any moment.

SHANE Tundher & turf* ye don't say so, what's to be done at all?

TONE I'll tell you.

SHANE Good man! (*Kisses letter.*)

TONE You must go into the town and secure rooms.

SHANE How many—A dozen?

TONE No, you foolish fellow, three will suffice.

SHANE Ov coorse two fer yersilf, and the misthress, an' one for me and Peggy. Are they bringing the childher wid them?

TONE No, that was impossible.

SHANE Sweet luck to me, that's too bad entoirely. Here am I afther becomin' a father and I didn't know it.

TONE Never mind, Shane, as long as you get your wife, that should satisfy you.

SHANE Bedad it should. (*Enter* LEMOINES *L.U.E.*) I'm off (*exits L.1.E.*)

LEMOINES (*to* TONE) Good morning! (*Salutes.*)

TONE Good morning, Sir. (*Enter R.U.E.* TURNER *and* RAFFERTY.)

LEMOINES Ze General has received an order from ze General Bounaparte imtimating zat he vill be here zis morning to review ze troops and ze fortifications.

TONE (*in surprise*) General Bounaparte!

LEMOINES Zat is so.

TONE (*sotto voce*) Then I may, nay, will, find the opportunity I have so longed [long?] waited for to approach him on the subject of Ireland's wrongs. (*A bugle call—drums.*)

LEMOINES Ze army is assembling; he will be here shortly.

TONE Then if you will excuse me, I will leave you. (*Salutes.*)

LEMOINES Zont mention it—(*Salutes;* TONE *exits into tent.* OFFICER *goes up.*)

TURNER (*meeting* LEMOINES C.) Pardon, Colonel, may I ask who that gentleman is who has just left you.

LEMOINES Zat, Oh, zat is Ze General Smeeth.

RAFFERTY We know him at home in Ireland as Wolfe Tone.

LEMOINES Var likely.

TURNER Why has he assumed that name?

LEMOINES Zat is his business, you had bettar ask him.

TURNER Is he liked?

LEMOINES No man bettar, far, in zee whole armee (*bows stiffly and exits L.U.E.*)

RAFFERTY Evidently puttin' the comither* on thim here too, me bhoy?

TURNER Yes, but we must undo all that; what's more we must set about without further delay now we know he's here.

RAFFERTY How?

TURNER Bounaparte is indebted to me for many a favor, I have therefore the advantage of knowing him, a whisper of a suspicion in his ear and he strikes relentlessly. (*Exeunt L.1.E.*) (*Re-enter* WOLFE TONE *R.1.E.*)

TONE Now I am ready for my first interview with the arbiter of Ireland's destiny—If I succeed in obtaining it. How will it end? (*With a shrug.*) The future will tell. (*Enter* MRS. TONE *and* PEGGY *L.U.E.*) What Susie and Peggy. (*He embraces* MRS. TONE.) And so we meet again after months of weary separation?

MRS. TONE And such dreary, weary months, too, dear, I thought they would never end. How brave you look in your uniform.

PEGGY An' handsome, too.

TONE Complimentary as usual Peggy. (*Shaking her hand.*) But if I'm handsome you should see Shane. He eclipses me completely.

PEGGY Where is he? Let me see him? (*Enter* TURNER *and* RAFFERTY *L.U.E.*)

TONE He'll be here directly. (*To* MRS. TONE.) We're expecting Bounaparte every moment, so you will have an excellent opportunity of seeing France's greatest general. (*They turn up and see* TURNER *and* RAFFERTY; *they start and return;* TURNER *and* RAFFERTY *raise their hats with offensive politeness.*)

MRS. TONE That man, again! He seems to ever dog our footsteps. He is like a black shadow in our path; ever keeping life's warmth from our hearts.

TONE Be brave dear, He cannot harm us here, you are nervous, tired with your long journey. Come and rest awhile (*Leads her to Tent R.E.*)

TURNER (*with a sardonic laugh*) I think I have thrown a damper on the felicity of that meeting, eh? (*Comes down,* RAFFERTY *follows.*)

RAFFERTY No lie in that, she shook badly as any blayguard rebel dangling at the end of a hempen rope. (*Exeunt R.U.E.*)

PEGGY (*who has watched them*) Ye dirty scum ov a dirty society's boilin'! so ye've followed us here, have yez? The curse ov Cromwell on ye both. (*Coming down.*) What's to be done at all, at all. (*Re-enter* SHANE *L.1.E. They look at each other.*) Shane! (*They rush into each other's arms—Bus[iness].*)

SHANE Peggy! Ah, It does me heart ov hearts good to see ye once again.

[PEGGY] An' mine too, I've be dyin' for this moment, so I have.

SHANE An' so have I. (*Embrace again.*)

PEGGY Oh let me look at you in your Frinch Jerrymintals (*She does so.*) Oh, they're grand they're georgeous, they're lovely, so they are.

SHANE They are. But they're a thrifle too tight for comfort.

PEGGY Ah, no matther. It's beautiful they are. Oh, Shane, it's a fine, sthrappin' big soldier ye make an' no mistake.

SHANE Much too fine to be shot at, me gurl.

PEGGY Not at all, Oh. It'll be a grand thing to be ye're widdy.

SHANE Here! What's that? What's that?

PEGGY The widdy ov a hayro!

SHANE Will it, me gurl.

PEGGY Ah, come to me arms again, acushla* (*embrace*).

SHANE Am I worth more to yez did than livin'.

PEGGY Not at all, ye gom;* sure it's jokin' I was.

SHANE Well, it's a kind of jokin' that's mighty unpleasant for the bhoy.

PEGGY Ah, never mind it at all. What would I want yez did for whin I've made yez a father.

SHANE Are ye sure ov that?

PEGGY Am I sure ov it? Ov coorse I am. Didn't I lave the blissed darlint all alone wid himself, this day week in Parrhee.

SHANE Is that so? I say, Peggy, What's the youngster like at all?

PEGGY (*tossing her head*) Youngster indade. He isn't a youngster at all. He's a born beauty so he is.

SHANE Oh, ov coorse. He couldn't be any other wid such a woman as yer silf for his mother. Is he like me at all?

PEGGY The very spit ov yez.

SHANE Yez don't say so.

PEGGY I niver saw a handsomer baby in the whole coorse ov me life. He has as much hair on his head, as yer silf has.

SHANE Ye don't tell me. Bedad that's grand. Can he talk yet?

PEGGY Arrah,* man, how can he talk whin he's only siven weeks born.

SHANE Ov coorse, I was forgettin'. I suppose they'll be afther callin' him a french man?

PEGGY A Frinchman indade. There isn't the very laste bit ov a Frinchman about him at all, at all. He's thrue Leinster ivery inch ov him.

SHANE On both sides?

PEGGY Ov coorse!

SHANE Faix,* Peggy, I fale as proud this moment as a paycock wid two tails. Can he walk yet?

PEGGY No, but he can kick his legs about as good as any playactor fellow.

SHANE Ye don't tell me; Begobs he must be a great bhoy intoirely.

PEGGY I niver saw his aqual, though I say it mysilf that shouldn't.

SHANE I say, Peggy, do I look like a father at all? Have I that important expression ov fature—that—magistirial air ov responsibility that all fathers have?

PEGGY Ye have, Shane, ye have, an' ye ought niver to sthop rememberin' for fear ye'd be afther forgittin' it, that it is mysilf that has placed ye in the proud position ov bein' the immagiate progenitor ov my child.

SHANE Shure I won't. Come along till we talk it all over again.

(Exeunt L.1.E. Drums. At end of which BAND *begins to play, piano then increases to forte. Enter* TONE *and* MRS. TONE *R.1.E.* PEGGY *L.1.E.* TURNER *and* RAFFERTY *R.U.E.* BAND *enters L.U.E. Then* SOLDIERS, *they march around stage and take up position at back. Then enter* BOUNAPARTE, JOSEPHINE *and* LEMOINES, KILMOINE *[?],* KILMAINE, FRENCH OFFICERS. TONE *salutes.* BOUNAPARTE *looks at him then speaks.)*

BOUNAPARTE Your name, sar!

TONE Wolfe Tone, General, at your service.

BOUNAPARTE Known in the armee as Smeeth!

TONE (*bows*) Yes.

BOUNAPARTE I do not like a man viz two names, Sar. (*They speak.*)

JOSEPHINE An' Zes i[s] Madame Wolfe Tone (*to* MRS. TONE).

MRS. TONE (*curtsees*) Yes, Madame.

JOSEPHINE I, I did zink so; you have ze beautiful eyes ov ze Ireland—aise—

BOUNAPARTE (*brusquely to* TONE) What benefit can accrue to you, sar, from an interview viz me?

TONE None to myself, General; to Ireland, much.

BOUNAPARTE When zat England, whose white clifes are almost in sight, is at my feet, and Pitt my prisoner, zen I will give my attention to your Ireland.

JOSEPHINE Madame, you have aroused my interest—my sympathy.

MRS. TONE You confer too much honour upon me, madam.

JOSEPHINE No, no, ze honour is mine; now mind I sall call and see you in Parhee.

PEGGY An' I'll show ye the finest baby ye iver clapped yer two bright eyes on.

JOSEPHINE Ah, is zat zo?

PEGGY Divil a lie in it.

JOSEPHINE Well, he zall grow up to fight ze battles ov La Belle France.

PEGGY Will he? He'll grow up to mind his father's farm in the ould country that's what he'll do, me lady.

JOSEPHINE (*laughs*) Vell, ve zall zee, vell ve zall zee.

BOUNAPARTE France gave you, sar, a grand armee—with Hoche at its head and a fleet magnifique—and what became of both?

TONE I organised victory—your generals through incompetency courted defeat.

BOUNAPARTE Vell. I will send you instructions vhen I can receive you.

TONE For which Ireland in my person thanks you. (*BOUNAPARTE goes up, surveys men—stops a[t] SHANE, beckons him out.*)

BOUNAPARTE France? (*Laconically.*)

SHANE No, Ireland! County Wicklow!

BOUNAPARTE Vhy you here, sar,—

TONE He followed my fortune, general, and to be near me, became a soldier of France—

BOUNAPARTE Ah, Belle France is one fine Country.

SHANE Ireland's a finer.

PEGGY [T]hat's thrue.

BOUNAPARTE Fight?

SHANE Like the divil!

BOUNAPARTE Zen you zall go to the Rhine. (*Motions him back.*)

SHANE (*aside*) Bedad I won't, I'll go to Ireland or I'll desart.

BOUNAPARTE (*to* LEMOINES)—Now for ze fortifications. (*He takes* JOSEPHINE *who bows to* MRS. TONE *who curtsies, then exits, followed by* OFFICERS, BAND, *and* SOLDIERS. *Scene changes as last* SOLDIERS *disappear—through the above* TURNER *and* RAFFERTY *are not seen by* BOUNAPARTE.)

End of Scene 1

Scene 2

FRONT CLOTH: STREET IN HAVRE

(*Enter* TURNER *and* RAFFERTY *R.1.E.*)

RAFFERTY (*who enters first*) So the redoubtable Bounaparte has condescended to mate Mr. Wolfe Tone. Ye'll have to be careful me bhoy or the spalpeen* will be after puttin' yer nose out ov joint.

TURNER The corsican's word is not his bond. There's as much honesty about him—

RAFFERTY As there is about yersilf, eh?

TURNER Tone will accomplish nothing with him—

RAFFERTY And if he does it will but tighten the rope that's waitin' to hang him.

TURNER Or drop into the musket the bullet that'll reach his miserable heart. I hinted to the Corsican the last time I had an audience of him that it was well known in Ireland that Tone was in Pitt's pay. (*Cross to R.*)

RAFFERTY Ye did? That's good.

TURNER And the seeds of distrust once sown in the fertilizing soil of his suspicious mind will fructify so plentifully that not even Tone's ⟨masterly⟩ eloquent sophistry will be able to render ineffective the crop.

RAFFERTY I wondher where he's left the petticoat part ov him?

TURNER We must find out, for she shall suffer as well as he.

RAFFERTY What, ye still mane to wreak yer vingeance on her?

TURNER Aye, to the bitter end on both ov them.

RAFFERTY Thin I have a man that'll do the job for ye. A dutch captain that's bound with his ship to South America. Ye'll have to entice her aboard his craft—that done the rest will be aisy.

TURNER How?

RAFFERTY He'll either drop her overboard some stormy night in the Atlantic whin divil a cry can be heard, or he'll sell her on arrival for a slave to some up country black—whichever ye like.

TURNER The very thing. Hush! Here's the French Colonel I spoke to this morning. Probably he may know where she hangs out. (*Enter* COLONEL *R.*) I beg your pardon, Colonel, but I sh'd esteem it a favor if you could furnish me with Mrs. Wolfe Tone's address in the town?

COLONEL Why not you obtain it from her husband, sar?

TURNER I have a reason.

COLONEL Exactly, I understand. Zen, sar, if you have a reason for not asking zee address from ze lady's husband, I have a reason, too, for not giving it. Bon soir. (*Exit L.*)

RAFFERTY The Ill-natured, concated Jacknapes. (*Enter* SHANE *R.*)

SHANE Shure, that must be ould Rafferty's croak. I'd know it anywhere. (RAFFERTY *turns & speaks to* TURNER.) Musha,* it's himself, an' that must be the odher blayguard he's spakin' to, what are they doin here at all, at all? (*Puts pad over eye.*) I must thry & find out.

RAFFERTY (*who then sees him*) Here's a French gossoon,* ask him?

TURNER (*beckons him*) Can you speak English—parler Anglais?

SHANE Oui.

TURNER Do you know General Smith?

SHANE Oh, oui! (*Crosses to C.*)–

RAFFERTY Thin perhaps ye can tell us where his wife—Mrs. Tone—I mane Smith is stayin?

SHANE Oh, oui.

RAFFERTY Thin where?

SHANE Oui!

RAFFERTY Is it French or English ye're spakin?

SHANE Oh, oui! (*RAFFERTY turns L. in disgust, TURNER R.*)

TURNER Oh, the fellow's a d—d fool.

SHANE [*aside*] An' you're a d—d rogue. (*Both TURNER and RAFFERTY turn suddenly. Aloud*) Oui.

TURNER (*to RAFFERTY*) Did you speak.

RAFFERTY Divil a worrd! The gom* doesn't underherstand us at all, at all. We'll have to seek the information elsewhere so we will.

TURNER And when we do get it—let the she Wolfe look to herself—Mercy I'll show her none. (*RAFFERTY takes SHANE by the ear and leads him to L.1.E.*)

RAFFERTY That's your way, me bouchal.*

SHANE Oui!

RAFFERTY Will I tell yez what ye are?

SHANE Oui!

RAFFERTY Ye're a blitherin' ijiot.

SHANE An' yez are a d—d ould thafe. (*Both surprised.*) Put that in yer mouth an' chaw it Mr. Joey Rafferty. (*Exit L.1.E.*)

RAFFERTY (*with rage*) Ye, villain, ye blayguard, ye frog golloper. (*Then to TURNER.*) Who is he at all? He knew what we're afther sayin' all the time. Bad cess to it,* that's the worst ov bein' out ov Ireland, ye don't know whether ye're talkin' to a christian or a haythin; who can he be at all?

TURNER I don't know, unless he's that fellow Shane McMahon.

RAFFERTY The double dyed scoundrel to desave us in that way; the curse ov the crows on him—

TURNER Hush, Someone's approaching. (*Enter HANS R.1.C.*)

RAFFERTY Swate luck to me if it's not the man I spoke to yer about. Now's your time to arrange. (*To HANS*) Ah, Hans, me bhoy! ye're just the man we're wantin'!

HANS Goot, I am here mid you, what want you wid myself?

RAFFERTY My friend requires a delicate piece of business executing.

HANS Mein Gott. He coms den to de right parties for beesiness, wot is eet?

TURNER When do you sail?

HANS De winds is fair, den I sails myselfs to night if I mistooks me not.

TURNER Then no time is to be lost, I require you to receive on board a woman whom you will dispose of either on your voyage to South America or on arrival there—whichever is the easier or more agreeable way—you understand?

HANS Aeh! I do understands myself mid you perfectly, you do want me, mid myselfs, to murder (*they both enterpose quickly, hush*) to settle her leetle ash or to sell her all by herselfs to de planters?

TURNER Yes.

HANS Vell, if de winds do blow wid violence to make de watair rough, she may herself drown—overboard falls—if not den I know myself a friend who vill buy her from me wid plazaire. I have sold him monny fine vomans pefore, and he vill zhust zhump at anodher von.

TURNER Then you don't object? I will pay you well!

HANS Objects! Mein Gott, I vould sell my own mudher for monies; vot are vomans for?

TURNER (*looks off R.*) We're in luck's way and no mistake. Here she is—and with her husband, too.

(*Enter* MR. *and* MRS. TONE *R. She starts on seeing them.*)

TURNER Good day, Mrs. Tone (*raises his hat*).

RAFFERTY The same to you, me lady (*raises his hat*).

TURNER This is an unexpected pleasure.

RAFFERTY Yes, a pleasure we didn't expict.

TONE (*with curt emphasis*) Then the pleasure is all on your side; stand aside and let us pass.

TURNER Won't you forget old sores? (*Holds out hand.*)

RAFFERTY An' be ould friends agin! Sure bein' strangers in this haythen counthry sh'd bind us the closer together; come now Mrs. Tone, shake hands, (*holds out his*) like the dacint forgivin' lady yez are.

MRS. TONE I would sooner die than touch willingly a hand of either of you.

TONE You hear what my wife says; her sentiments are mine. Let us pass. (*Hand on sword.*)

RAFFERTY Oh, certainly! (*He stands aside.*)

TURNER A lady's wish is law. (*He does the same.*)

TONE (*to her*) That's right, show a brave front, dear; you see even a little woman like you can cow such curs.

(*Exeunt L.1.E.*)

TURNER (*to Hans*) That's the woman! Follow! See where they go and then come to me to this Hotel. (*Gives address.*)

HANS I have de sights of dem, I vill not lose myself, nevair fear, undhtell I do run myself to earth. (*Exit L.1.E.*)

RAFFERTY Bedad, me bhoy, we're having the divil's own luck.

TURNER We are, and if it will only hold to us a little longer Mr. and Mrs. Wolfe Tone will have learnt that Samuel Turner never forgets or forgives. (*Exit L.1.E.*)

End of Scene 2

Scene 3

HOUSE OVERLOOKING THE HAVRE HARBOUR, NIGHT

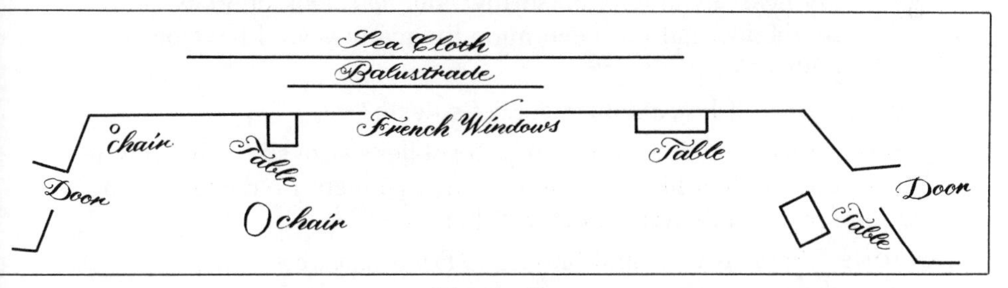

Diagram G

(*MR. and MRS. TONE discovered at back looking out. SHANE at table L.*)

SHANE I'm thinkin' (*looking at them*) that they'd sooner be alone— (*sighs*). Ah, what times we do live in to be sure, they're that bad, bad luck to thim, that they won't bear thinkin' about at all, at all. (*Crossing turns to them.*) Hiven bless thim both! (*Exit R.*)

TONE What a magnificent night little woman.

MRS. TONE But not for long I'm afraid. See how rapidly those clouds are rising in the East. They will soon blot out from sight yon deep eternal blue; those myriads of stars, Heaven's own bright sparkling eyes—leaving all as dark and gloomy as our own poor lives.

TONE (*They come down.*) As quickly as the clouds gather dear, so as quickly will they disperse; never was the horizon of our hopes brighter than at present—our fortune more assured of realization. The directory, as you are aware, have decided upon another expedition to Ireland. With England worried on every side, hampered, almost overwhelmed with difficulties she cannot possibly surmount, success is certain—

MRS. TONE You, you will be careful—run no risk—

TONE You would not have me a coward?—

MRS. TONE No, no!

TONE The more a soldier courts death dear, the more it holds aloof. Have no fear for me.

MRS. TONE I will be brave for your sake (*closer to him*). I will cast aside all doubts, gloom and despair, and look only on the sunny side of things—consider only the noble, unselfish work you are accomplishing for old Ireland's good. Deep down in my heart I will bury all sorrow—all fear, look only, live only on the joy that has been mine the many years I have been your wife.

TONE And if I *should* die a soldier's death?

MRS. TONE I will mourn you as a soldier's wife sh'd. Glorying in the fact that like thousands of Irishwomen, I have yielded up for Ireland's weal another of her sons.

TONE Spoken well, and bravely— (*They embrace as* SHANE *enters; she goes up.*)

SHANE Here are some Dublin papers, sir, I thought yez like to see thim.

TONE (*in pleased tones*) Dublin papers! Shane! (*Meets him.*)

SHANE Aye, an' ill news, too, they contain.

TONE (*who has taken them*) No, no, don't say that! (*Sits R. of table L. quickly opens one—* MRS. TONE *comes down and leans over him.*)

SHANE Yez are not wantin' me?

TONE No, Shane, no! (SHANE *looks at him—he is immersed in the paper—then exits R.*) Great Heavens! the English government has arrested the whole committee of United Irishmen in Leinster (*lets paper fall on his knee; in despairing ⟨voices⟩ tones*). Every friend I knew and loved in Dublin. (*She kneels at his feet.*) See (*he points to paper*) Emmet, McNeven, Sweetman, Bond, Jackson and others; Lord Edward Fitzgerald is not to be found though they've searched the city high and low for him. This is the most terrible blow poor Ireland has yet sustained. My heart is torn in twain at the news. (*Rising and walking up and down.*) What is to be done! What is to be done! (*She rises and meets him.*)

MRS. TONE All is not yet lost. Keep up your heart still!

TONE I will; but France must move—must act at once. (*Enter SHANE with COLONEL LEMOINES; he salutes—SHANE goes up.*)

LEMOINES Le General Kilmaine desires your presence at once, sar.

TONE I will obey his commands instantly. (*LEMOINES salutes and exits—To her*) If only it sh'd be the order for the embarkation, God in Heaven grant it may. (*She gets his hat and sword—places the latter in his belt.*)

MRS. TONE God grant it may, dear. If it is, no spartan woman of old ever sent her loved ones more willingly to the fray than I will send you to fight, ould Ireland's foes. (*She leads almost pushes him to the door; he kisses her.*) Go, dear, and God be with you! (*He exits—she crosses painfully to chair L. and lets her hand fall heavily upon it.*)

SHANE Heaven send ye glory ma'am for that speech; it was grand, courage in ivery word ov it. It'll put strength into his honour's heart.

MRS. TONE And leave, Shane, only cruel anguish, to wring my own (*sinks into chair head in hands and arms on table. Enter PEGGY R.*)

PEGGY Darlint, there's a lady below who's afther callin' on yez.

MRS. TONE A lady! (*Turning to her.*)

PEGGY The same who spoke to yez to day, she says she's Madame Josephine Bounaparty. (*MRS. TONE rises quickly and dabs her face with handkerchief as if she had been crying.*)

(*Enter JOSEPHINE R. also OFFICER: latter Exit[s].*)

JOSEPHINE Ah, my tear Madame, you zee I do come before my times. I am here to zee you.

MRS. TONE (*curtsey*) An honour, Madame of which I am unworthy.

JOSEPHINE No, no, I vill not listen to you, if you will persist in talking like zat; you are one soldier's wife like myself. What is zis. (*She has taken her hand.*) You, have been weeping—shedding tears to dim those bright eyes of yours. For shame for shame, I must—vill scold you.

MRS. TONE We have had news—sad news from home—news that has distressed both my husband and myself.

JOSEPHINE Ah, from Irelandais—that distressful countree of yours; she is always in trouble, trouble—trouble.

MRS. TONE Her misfortune, Madame, not her fault. Will you not be seated?

JOSEPHINE Wiz plaisair! (*Is about to sit when PEGGY darts forward rubs seat violently with apron.*)

PEGGY I beg yez pardon Ma'am, one moment!

JOSEPHINE Zank you, var much, you are so var—what you call it—zinkful—zoughtful—kind! (*Sits—MRS. TONE goes round to L.*)

PEGGY (*curtseying*) Not [at] all ma'am, not at all. (*To MRS. TONE as she crosses to door.*) I suppose I can lave yez together darlint.

MRS. TONE Yes, Peggy, yes.

PEGGY (*to SHANE*) Who is she at all? (*Meaning JOSEPHINE.*)

SHANE Shure she's the wife of the little corporal.

PEGGY Little corporal (*with disgust*). Is that all her man is?

SHANE Yes.

PEGGY Faith thin, if I'd known that I wouldn't have been in such a hurry to dust the sate for her. Sure, you're a corporal yersilf.

SHANE That's so; but though they call her man the little corporal he's the biggest general in the French Army, an I'm not, an' that's the whole ov the differ between us.

(*Exeunt R.*)

JOSEPHINE (*to MRS. TONE*) Yees, I have come to tell you that I have after so much persuasion, got ze general Bounaparte to grant an audience to your husband.

MRS. TONE A thousand thanks, madame, for your generous intercession on his behalf. He feels confident that an interview would enable him to convince the great commander in chief that help to us would mean victory to him.

JOSEPHINE Ah, my heart, my sympathies are with you; but ze general is so var deficult to deal wiz. He stands like von great rock—immovable—like ze sphinx unfathomable. He vill hear all—he vill look fierce and frown, zo (*attempts to frown*) but if it does not please him to speak he vill say nozzing, even I cannot manage him.

MRS. TONE Ah, if you will only plead our cause, success must crown your efforts.

JOSEPHINE No, no, you do not know him as vell as I do, or you vould not say zat. Oh, he loves me to distraction; but for all zat he vill not let me have my own vays unless it does please him zat I should have zem. (*PEGGY's voice heard in altercation with HANS outside—LADIES rise expectantly.*)

PEGGY I tell yez, ye can't go in!

HANS Mein gott, but I must! (*Enter HANS, [with] PEGGY trying to pull him back.*)

PEGGY What de ye mane ye gin drunkin' spalpeen* disthurbin' two ladies in this outrageous manner? Well for yez that my man was out [or] ye'd niver have got in. Take off yer dirthy night cap (*snatches it off*) whin ye're in the prisence ov your shupariors!

MRS. TONE (*advancing to* C.) What is the meaning of this intrusion?

HANS I vant myself mid von vomans by ze name of Smeet or Wolfe Tone.

MRS. TONE I am she! What do you require?

HANS I have mit me, von leetle message from [mysther? mynher?] your husband.

MRS. TONE (*startled*) What, what is it?

HANS He sends mit me to say dat de general Bounaparte has him ordered to sail mit me by mine sheep at once to Brest.

MRS. TONE To sail at once to Brest?

HANS Dat is zo. He alreadys is on board of mine sheep and wants you to come mit me to says Good bye to himself. (*He goes to balcony and looks over, gives signal.*)

MRS. TONE Yes, yes, I will go at once. (*Is going L. JOSEPHINE stops her.*)

JOSEPHINE Stay, cherie! (*To HANS with energy.*) Come you here, Sar. (*He comes down.*)

[TABLEAU]

HANS JOSEPHINE
PEGGY MRS. TONE

What general did you mention sar, zat gave zat order to ze's Lady's husband?

HANS (*in doubt*) Vot General?

JOSEPHINE (*stamping her foot*) Zat, sar, is what I did say to you.

HANS De lettle Corporal—General Bounaparte.

JOSEPHINE Sar, you do lie in von barefaced manner; ze General Bounaparte gave no such instructions. Ze's lady's husband is at zis moment wiz General Kilmaine, Kivand, and Colonel Lemoines. Zis is a plot, sar, to ensnare zize lady avay from her home.

HANS (*confounded*) Mein gott, Dis no plot is, On mein honour it is de truth; who mights you be?

JOSEPHINE Who might I be, sar.

HANS (*blustering*) Yah, Dat zo! who mights you be?

JOSEPHINE I am ze vife of ze General Bounaparte.

HANS (*a bit frightened*) The tousand debbils I have put mein heads in my mouth.

JOSEPHINE Go sar, before I have you laid by ze toes of your boots and put in prison.

PEGGY Ye've got yer ordher, yer dirthy Dutch haddock (*flourishes broom*). Go! or I'll spiflicate yez.

MRS. TONE Call Shane, Peggy.

PEGGY (*aside*) Whisht* darlint, he's out. (*To* HANS *hitting him with broom.*) Will yez get out of that when yez are told? (*When he is in the doorway she pushes him out with broom.*)

MRS. TONE (*to* JOSEPHINE) Madame, my feelings deprive me of the power of expressing how deeply thankful I am for your timely intervention. I shudder to think what might have happened had you not been here.

JOSEPHINE You would have gone to a fate vorse zan many deaths. Ah, I know zees Dutchman; Zey should be all guillotiend ze wretches. Nevair you trust strangers again, cherie, and above all nevair zes diables of Dutchmans; now I must from you take my leave.

MRS. TONE Memory, madam, can never rob me of the thoughts of this day—or make me forget the immeasureable debt I owe you.

JOSEPHINE Tut, tut, you do owe me nozzings. Because I do love all you Irish ladies. I love your eyes, your complexion, your figure. Zey are grand—perfection. You must return zis visit—you vill?

MRS. TONE I shall feel honoured (*curtsey*).

JOSEPHINE No, no, no honour, plasair! (*MRS. TONE bows.*) Zat is right zat is right and vhile your husband does lays his plans before ze general you sall converse—talk wiz me. (*Enter PEGGY.*)

PEGGY The French officer, me lady, ma'am.

MRS. TONE Permit me to escort you to the door. (*Enter OFFICER, he salutes.*)

JOSEPHINE Zank. (*They talk and then exeunt.*) You must all attention pay to what I do say—(*OFFICER exits after them, PEGGY after him.*)

PEGGY Begorra* there's a dale ov starch in the French quality.

(*Lights down to half—music. HANS appears above railings at back; looks cautiously round. Then throws rope ladder over; TURNER appears, also RAFFERTY; latter after looking round goes to table at back L. opens desk and looks among papers. TURNER opens door R. then closes it again—MEN gradually climb over railings and hide R. & L. As the action of piece proceeds.*)

TURNER (*at door R.*) Not here, so much the better, we can secure you quietly my fine lady—no noise—no trouble, and no fear of your husband returning. (*To RAFFERTY.*) What are you doing?

RAFFERTY Seein' if there's anythin' worth takin'. (*TURNER beckons.*)

TURNER (*to HANS*) You're ready to sail the instant she's aboard.

HANS Yah! dats zo.

TURNER Stand there! (*TURNER crosses to door L.*) What place is this? I'd better explore it. To prevent a surprise or flank attack. (*Exit L. Enter PEGGY R. musing; HANS gets behind door.*)

PEGGY Here, I haven't seen Shane for six mortial months an' he's gone & left me. If it hadn't been for that fine French officer turning up, I sh'd niver have got rid ov that Dutch blayguard.

RAFFERTY (*who has been reading paper and doesn't know that* PEGGY *is in the room*) I'll pocket this. (*She starts.*)

PEGGY The Lord save us what's that? (*Turns and sees* RAFFERTY.) Ye gallows bird ye, what are yez doin' there at all? (*He turns.*) Ould Rafferty! (*She dashes at him and pulls him C.*) Ye, ould robber, ye! ye thafe ov the worrld,* ye!

RAFFERTY (*struggling*) Let go, will yez?

PEGGY Not till I choke the dirthy life out ov ye.

RAFFERTY Help! there! help! (TURNER *appears L.* TWO MEN *down C.* HANS *seizes her by the waist, turns her round so that the* TWO MEN *can get hold of her, she recognises* HANS.)

RAFFERTY (*pulling himself straight*) Ye female divil, ye!

PEGGY (*to* HANS) Ye dirthy lump ov mouldy Dutch cheese; so yez are back again are yez?

HANS Yah, dat is zo, you prake my head von time twice—You prake him no more my tear.

PEGGY I'll break yer back if I get a hould ov yez, ye blayguard. (*She sees* TURNER.) You! (*They both advance—she struggles then cries*) Help, Shane, Help!

TURNER Stop her cries. (HANS *get[s] behind her.*)

HANS (*placing handkerchief over her mouth*) How likes you dat? Dat stops yer tongue, eh? Yah, I sall cut your claws for you when I gets you mit myself on board mine sheep. You sall not prake my heads for noddings. (*During this another has tied her legs together; they place her in chair R. of table L. then tie her hands to chair, all done quickly.*) You sits dare wit yourselves, den tell I dakes you avays.

TURNER Confound you, that's not the one. (*Goes to door R. to listen.*)

HANS Nein, dats zo, ze order von I dakes to please you—dis von I dakes to please meinself.

TURNER If you do you'll spoil all.

HANS I don't care von d—d leetle ting, I dakes dis von too or I dakes noddings.

TURNER Curse you, just as you please. Hush, she's coming. (*He hides behind the door;* RAFFERTY *falls L. of table L.;* ONE MAN *gets under table;* OTHERS *exeunt quickly C.*)

(*Enter* MRS. TONE. *As she enters* TURNER *closes door.*)

MRS. TONE Surely I heard Peggy's voice calling for help. (*Sees her—she starts.*) Great Heavens! What is the meaning of this?

TURNER (*locking the door*) It means that as the mountain would not come to Mahomet, Mahomet has come to the mountain. (*RAFFERTY has quickly got to door L. and locked it.*)

MRS. TONE (*To RAFFERTY*) Ah, you, too? (*TURNER R., MRS. TONE C., PEGGY L.C., RAFFERTY L.*)

RAFFERTY (*elaberatily bowing*) At your sarvice, me lady.

TURNER At last you are in my power.

MRS. TONE Not while I can raise my voice to cry for help. (*Rushes up C., HANS and ANOTHER MAN appear R. and L. off C.; she staggers back.*) Ah. (*ANOTHER MAN leans over table L. with pistol to the head of PEGGY.*)

TURNER Raise but your voice loud enough to attract attention and that pistol will be fired.

MRS. TONE Are you human at all? (*TWO MEN hold her.*)

TURNER I am what you have made me.

MRS. TONE I or your own evil heart, which?

TURNER No matter which. Do you know what I am going to do with you (*with suppressed passion*). In an hour you will be on board that man's (*points to HANS*) ship bound for South America. When you arrive you will be disposed of—Sold—to a man half nigger–half spaniard who lives fifty miles up the country from Buenos Ayres. He is waiting to receive you with open arms. What a prize you will be. Do you like the picture?

MRS. TONE You demon, so surely as there is a Heaven above, so surely will your deeds find you out.

TURNER You would have done better to have married me, eh?

MRS. TONE Married you! I would sooner prefer the death in life you say you have meted out to me, than endure the ignominy of being for one single instance your wife.

TURNER Oh, don't imagine it's love, —love slighted and spurned that has prompted me to this. It's hate! do you hear, hate? Hate for you and your cur of a husband. I strike at him through you. His agony will be my joy—your ruin part and parcel of my revenge—(*TONE's voice heard faintly R. then louder then—*)

TONE (*knocks at the door*) Where are you? Are you there?

MRS. TONE Husband!

TURNER Away with her. (*During this the man under the table who is SHANE disguised has, unseen by the rest, untied the rope that binds PEGGY, and as TURNER['s] speech ends and TONE's voice is heard, she pulls the handkerchief off, seizes poker which must be placed under table before scene commences.)*

PEGGY (*She starts up.*) Stir a step an'll brain yez! (*Knocks at door L. also door R.* TONE'*s voice heard.*)

SHANE (*throwing over table and tearing off beard and cap*) An' I'll do ditto. (*Points pistol—*TABLEAU. MAN *at table goes to door,* RAFFERTY L.U.E.)

Rafferty
Man Mrs Tone Man Peggy
Hans Shane Man
Turner

Diagram H

PEGGY and MRS. TONE Shane!

TURNER and RAFFERTY You!

SHANE Aye, mesilf. (*To* MEN) Let go that lady or I'll blow yez to Timbuctoo.

TURNER (*furiously*) Seize them both. (*Knocking kept up at both doors.*)

TONE (*outside*) Let me in!

(*Struggle and Business till end of scene.*)

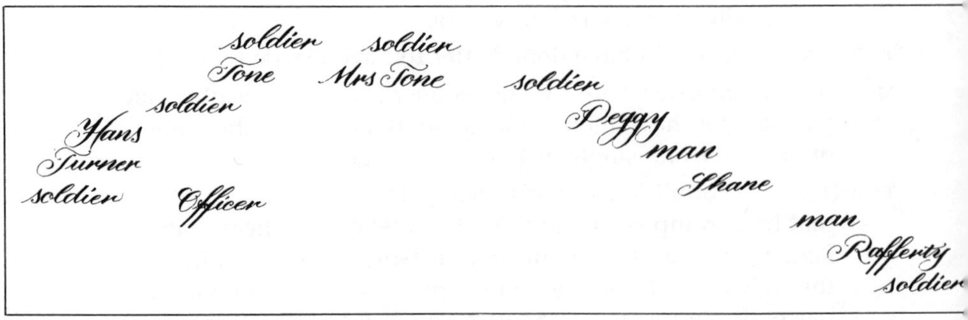

soldier soldier
Tone Mrs Tone soldier
soldier
Hans Peggy
Turner man
soldier Officer Shane
man
Rafferty
soldier

Diagram I

TABLEAU

End of Scene 3

Scene 4

STREET IN LE HAVRE

(*Enter* RAFFERTY *and* TURNER *L.*)

RAFFERTY The divil fly away wid us, but that was a tight corner—

TURNER Yes, only Bounaparte's safe pass averted our arrest.

RAFFERTY An' bein' marched off to prison wid the rest ov the blayguards. I'm thinkin' we're safer in Ireland than in this country.

TURNER (*fiercely*) Quiet, curse you! (*They retire L.1.E. Enter* PATROL *with* HANS *and* OTHERS *as prisoners—they march from L. to R. and exeunt.*)

RAFFERTY Murther alive, an' to think I was saved by the skin ov my teeth from bein' among thim. (*Cross to R.*)

TURNER If you don't keep that confounded tongue of yours in better subjection French bullets will do it for you.

RAFFERTY What the divil thin did ye tempt me to lave Ireland for at all? Wid Dublin Castle at my back I'd dare any Frenchman to shoot me.

TURNER Well, you're not in Dublin now.

RAFFERTY No, worse luck. (*Cross to L.*) But I'll hire a boat an' sail at once so I will.

TURNER Easier said than done. Now if we could only ring the changes so as to turn that defeat into a victory all might yet be well.

RAFFERTY Begorra* I have it. See Bounaparty yersilf at once. Explain that the attempt at the abduction was but a ruse to enable ye to secure proof ov Wolfe Tone's connection wid the English Government. Tell any tunderin' lie ye like only get us out ov this scrape.

TURNER The corsican is not the man to be hoodwinked so easily—Something more tangible—more substantial than bare lies must aid us now.

RAFFERTY Thin give him the papers ye intended for Pitt. Swear by all that's holy ye got thim from Tone's desk.

TURNER Ah!

RAFFERTY Here they are (*hands them*). Oh murther, who's comin' at all.

TURNER (*sees* BOUNAPARTE) Hush, If you value your life keep quiet. It's the corsican himself. (*Enter* TWO OFFICERS *and* BOUNAPARTE.) Good night, General! (*Salutes.*)

BOUNAPARTE (*curtly*) Good night, sar. What report is this I hear of your attack on ze household of ze Adjutant General Smeeth—or as you call him Wolfe Tone?

RAFFERTY Och Murther I'm a did man.

BOUNAPARTE Explain, and be brief in ze explanation.

TURNER (*hands papers*) Those General will afford an explanation more than sufficient.

BOUNAPARTE What are zeez?

TURNER Documents that plainly show Wolfe Tone's complicity as a spy in the service of Pitt.

BOUNAPARTE Ah! Where and how did you get zeez?

TURNER Your constantly repeated [expressions] of doubt as to his being other than he represented himself to be, left me no alternative but to secure [incontestable] proof of his baseness.

BOUNAPARTE And so, sar, you stooped to robbery to serve your ends.

TURNER I did so, that I might convince you, General.

BOUNAPARTE Convince me, sar!

TURNER Yes, as well as to save my own life.

BOUNAPARTE Sar, what mean you?

TURNER I saw that you were entertaining suspicions of my own veracity—my own position here, and though the step was, I admit, somewhat contempt[i]ble, still my own safety demanded that it sh'd be taken.

BOUNAPARTE And is it customary with you, when you wish to save your life, to make war on womans?

TURNER It is not, the attack was but a ruse de guerre to distract their attention from the point at issue. No harm was intended them none inflicted.

(*Enter* SHANE *and* PEGGY *L.1.E.*)

SHANE Holy fly! Here are the two blayguards thimsilves.

PEGGY (*hitting* RAFFERTY *on the head*) Ye ould villaine, ye, take that and that, an' that!

RAFFERTY How dare ye touch me, ye amazonian ruffian.

PEGGY Dare! If ye dare me, I'll squaze the soulless life out ov ye ye miserable Dublin jackeen,* ye.

RAFFERTY (*stuttering in a rage*) Ye, ye dregs ov the gutter, ye.

PEGGY Ye scums ov Dublin Castle, ye. (*SHANE sees BOUNAPARTE.*)

SHANE (*in alarm*) Hould your whisht,* sure there's Bounaparty, himself.

PEGGY Ye don't till me. (*Curtsies to BOUNAPARTE.*) I beg your honour's pardon, I hope ye'll excuse me. I'm afther comin' across this dirthy apology ov a gentleman here, an' it has quite upset me so it has, I trust your honour's good lady, an' the childher are all well an' enjoyin' good health.

SHANE Arrah* woman, hould yer whisht.*

PEGGY Arrah,* man, let me spake. (*She curtsies.*) Yer honour's glory—(*She catches his eye. Then stops suddenly and backs round to L. of SHANE.*)

SHANE That's the kind ov man ye want me guirl to put ye in order.

PEGGY The divil's in that eye ov his, Shane, Hould me tight for the love of Heaven.

BOUNAPARTE (*to TURNER*) What is zat man (*indicating RAFFERTY*) in ze Dublin Castle?

TURNER He was an attorney—a notary under the government (*BOUNAPARTE looks fiercely at RAFFERTY*) but when they discovered that he was in league with the United Irishmen and furnishing them with valuable information they summarily dismissed him. (*BOUNAPARTE partly turns away.*)

RAFFERTY How dare you!

TURNER If you value your neck, curse you, keep still.

BOUNAPARTE What evidence have I beyond your word that zese were abstracted from ze bureau of ze General Wolfe Tone?

TURNER As good fortune will have it that woman can corroborate my statement, she saw my friend here take them.

BOUNAPARTE Ah. (*To PEGGY.*) Come you closer. (*She hesitates.*) Quick!

PEGGY The Lord save us, what I'll do at all?

SHANE Arrah* woman, stir up the Irish blood widin ye; sure the man can't ate yez. (*He pushes her forward.*)

BOUNAPARTE Listen did you zee zat man (*points to RAFFERTY*) rob ze desk of your master?

PEGGY I did, yer honour, the curse ov Cromwell on him for an ould thafe.

BOUNAPARTE Did you zee what he took?

PEGGY Faix* it was a bundle ov papers, neither more nor less—the ould villain hadn't time to take more. (*To* RAFFERTY.)

BOUNAPARTE Zat will do!

PEGGY Ah, ye ould blayguard ye, I've put a spoke in your wheel so I have.

RAFFERTY (*aside*) Or in your master, which? (*She goes to* SHANE.)

TURNER (*to* BOUNAPARTE) Are you satisfied?

BOUNAPARTE (*to* ONE OFFICER) Zee zese gentlemen to their hotel—Zen rejoin me without delay. (OFFICER *salutes—aside*) Place a guard around it so zey cannot escape. (*To* TURNER *and* RAFFERTY) Go, zare, but hold yourselves in readiness in case I sh'd require you. (TURNER *is about to speak.*) Not anozzer word. Go. (*They exeunt; to* SHANE) Come here, sar, do you want to be shot before ze sun rises in ze mornin'.

SHANE Bedad I don't. (SHANE *close to him.*)

BOUNAPARTE Zen speak ze truth, who is zat leetle man?

SHANE A thafe ov a lawyer, General, in the service ov the government at Dublin Castle.

BOUNAPARTE Ah, say you zo! Zen he is not what you call a United Irishman?

SHANE Arrah* man, no, nor niver was—nor niver will be—sure they wouldn't have the like ov him among thim at all, at all.

BOUNAPARTE Zhust zo. How came you in zese? (*Indicating clothes.*)

SHANE I overheard thim two blayguards arranging wid a Dutch Sailor man to kidnap the misthress an' sind her to South America—So I just enticed one ov his dirthy crew into a sort ov Sheebeen* place, made him dhrunk, stole his clothes & thin took his place among the rist ov the robbers.

PEGGY An' lucky it was for us all, ye did, or it's on the salt say we'll have been this minute.

BOUNAPARTE Zat is sufficient! You can go. (*They are crossing.*) No, no, back to ze apartments of your master and, listen, do not move out for ze rest of ze night.

SHANE Bedad, if that's the ordher of the day I won't.

BOUNAPARTE If I want you I will send an officer for you, Go! (*They exeunt L. crossing to R.*) Now to find out who is ze true and who is ze false—Ze loyal soldier and ze traitor (*Exit R. followed by* OFFICER.)

End of Scene 4

Scene 5

(*As curtain rises all leave the room except* JOSEPHINE *and* MRS. TONE *who comes down.*)

JOSEPHINE Yes, cherie, I do your husband like much, He has ze grande air ov command; ze mannare, zat compels respect, love, admiration— (*They cross to couch L.C.*) He has done much for your Ireland? (*They sit.*)

MRS. TONE His whole life, Madame, since our marriage has been devoted to her cause. For her he has sacrificed career, home, friends, fortune, —for her he has suffered ignominy, exile, poverty. For years the prison, the gallows and a felon's death cruelly—relentlessly stared him in the face. The victim of petty intrigues—of studied malevolence. He has still unselfishly—unflinchingly worked on. The one motive ruling and ennobling his life justice to Ireland—the enfranchisement of her people.

JOSEPHINE Ah, zen great vill be his reward.

MRS. TONE He desires no reward, [Madame], but the love of his countrymen. (*They rise and walk down L.*)

(*Enter* BOUNAPARTE *and* WOLFE TONE *R.C.*)

BOUNAPARTE (*curtly*) Ze French Directory— (*He stops abruptly seeing* JOSEPHINE *and* MRS. TONE*—to* TONE) Silence! (*To* JOSEPHINE *who has met him.*) Leave us!

JOSEPHINE (*playfully*) No, no! (MRS. TONE *meets* TONE *L.C.*)

[TABLEAU]

BOUNAPARTE JOSEPHINE TONE MRS. TONE

TONE (*to* BOUNAPARTE) General! will you permit me? (*Introducing her*) My wife—(MRS. TONE *curtsies; Bounaparte does not move.*)

BOUNAPARTE (*brusquely—looking first coldly then almost rudely at her and then turning to* JOSEPHINE) Well, zend her away! (MRS. TONE *starts;* TONE *amazed.*)

JOSEPHINE No, no she sall remain—here—viz me. (*Goes to her.*)

BOUNAPARTE Zen keep you both quiet— (*MRS. TONE and JOSEPHINE sit L.C. BOUNAPARTE motions TONE to seat R. of table; he, himself sits L. of table R.*) You were saying?

TONE That as your minister of war—bestowed upon me the commission I at present hold that that should be a sufficient guarantee of my bon a fides.

BOUNAPARTE Bah, Ze Minister you mention—even the whole French Directory may be liable to imposition.

TONE But my credentials!

BOUNAPARTE (*shrugging his shoulders contemptiously*) May every one ov zem be forged!

TONE (*rising with haste; LADIES also rise*) I did not seek this interview to be insulted!

BOUNAPARTE (*insolently*) No insult was intended!

MRS. TONE (*slightly advancing*) Then why address him in such language?

BOUNAPARTE (*with cold contempt*) Silence, woman if you wish me to listen to your husband.

MRS. TONE No wife, sir, can remain silent, when that husband's honesty is being impugned.

BOUNAPARTE Diable! I do not decide the fate of nations wiz irresponsible women—Leave us!

TONE General, you forget yourself. (*Crosses to MRS. TONE; JOSEPHINE crosses to BOUNAPARTE.*)

BOUNAPARTE I forget nozzing, but that you are wa[s]ting my time.

MRS. TONE (*to TONE*) And can you—must you suffer this?

TONE (*aside*) Yes, dear, yes, Be patient for my sake—for our country—Remember he is all powerful—and that Ireland needs his friendship!

BOUNAPARTE (*rises*) If you cannot submit to my questions ze interview is at an end.

JOSEPHINE No, no, forgive zem and listen!

BOUNAPARTE (*to TONE*) Madame intercedes for you; be seated. (*TONE crosses; MRS. TONE goes L. to JOSEPHINE.*) Take zat woman avay—at once. (*Enter KILMAINE.*)

JOSEPHINE (*crosses to MRS. TONE; to KILMAINE*) Will you escort zis lady to ze salon. (*To MRS. TONE*) I vill join you directly. I vill zhust stay to throw a leetle oil on ze troubled waters.

BOUNAPARTE (*to TONE*) You want a French army dispatched to Ireland?

TONE The directory has already decided that one shall be sent.

BOUNAPARTE Whether that Armee goes or not rests wiz me. Do you hear, sar? viz me! Listen, you may be an English spy—an emissary ov Pitt. I have papers here that prove such is so. (*Tone starts.*) You are surprised.

TONE I am at the audacity of the attempt to malign and ruin me. May I ask how they came into your possession and from whom?

BOUNAPARTE Zat, I cannot disclose.

TONE Precisely, because the fellow, being a scoundrel, prefers to stab in the dark. He may be a spy himself.

BOUNAPARTE He may, But zat is not ze question. Him I have known for years. You—only today—He comes furnished as an ambassador sh'd wiz money to uphold his position—You have plenty of zese (*touches papers*) but of money—none!

TONE Am I any worse for being poor?

BOUNAPARTE You do not understand. I do not apply ze remark to you as a man but as a representative of a people aspiring to independence.

TONE I perceive you are determined not to believe in me.

BOUNAPARTE On ze contraire, I have ze one desire to trust you.

JOSEPHINE Zat is so.

BOUNAPARTE But England is a power, a nation of ze first rank, and France must nevair strike in vain.

TONE Then strike at her through Ireland—I have news that she is on the eve of a rebellion—that Lord Edward Fitzgerald assumes command.

BOUNAPARTE Zen why are you not there, sar, instead ov wearing the uniform of France.

TONE I am here in her interest.

BOUNAPARTE Or your own. I'm much afraid, sar, you are an adventurer.

TONE An adventurer. (*BOUNAPARTE bows.*) And if I am what are you? An adventurer also. You a corsican, I an Irishman. Force of circumstances alone necessitated my application to the French Directory for employment. They offered money—I declined— preferring instead of taking it as alms, to earn it. We are both aliens, but we are both Officers in the French army; and though you are the Commander in chief I must request from you that courtesy due from one officer to another.

BOUNAPARTE You speak boldly, sar.

TONE My honour demands I should.

BOUNAPARTE What if I send you to ze Rhine.

TONE You have but to command, I to obey.

BOUNAPARTE You are sanguine, sar.

TONE I tell you, that Ireland's necessity is your opportunity. Seize it and you attain to a pinnacle of greatness unknown since the day of Alexander and Caesar. Neglect it and you push aside the foundation stone on which to rear an edifice of power as unassailable as imperishable—a power, sir, that will make you an Emperor and France, for centuries to come, the foremost nation of the world.

JOSEPHINE What enthusiasm, what nobility of thought, what expression!

BOUNAPARTE (*puts up his hand as if to stop her*) You speak plainly, sir, hesitate not to speak more plainly still.

TONE Then, sir, give up your plans on Egypt (*BOUNAPARTE starts*) on Switzerland, on the Rhine, concentrate your troops at various points, Brest, Boulogne—the Te[x]el. Simultaneously attack England, north, south, east and west, and, with the greater portion of her army engaged in Ireland, she will be unable to resist you, and in a month you will be in London, with Pitt at your feet, suing for mercy.

BOUNAPARTE Ah, you zen zink I can beat zese English bulldogs—crush zis boastful England?

TONE I do, if carried out now, as I suggest.

BOUNAPARTE And if I zink otherwise?

TONE Then England will as surely crush you.

BOUNAPARTE (*with energy, rising*) Nevair! Ze nation is not born zat can crush ze might of zis brain—ze force of zis arm—ze power of La Belle France. Nevertheless I will considair—ovair—what you have said. Meanwhile, Adieu! (*TONE rises; BOUNAPARTE crosses to L.*)

JOSEPHINE (*meeting TONE C.*) An he so sall considair it zat you sall have your desire. Trust me! (*Goes up with him; he bows and as he exit[s]*) I will join you anon. (*She comes down, meets BOUNAPARTE C.*) What say you—

BOUNAPARTE Zat you must also leave ze room, I wish to be alone. (*They go up—Bows—she curtsies and exits R.C. He returns, opens door R. Enter* TURNER *and* RAFFERTY. *Latter stealthily examines papers on table—to* TURNER.) You heard? (RAFFERTY *R.* TURNER *R.C* BOUNAPARTE *L.C.*)

TURNER Every word.

BOUNAPARTE And you still assert he is in ze pay of England's prime minister.

TURNER The papers I gave you sh'd alone be conclusive evidence of that fact.

BOUNAPARTE Ah, zem papers! (*Is going to table when* JOSEPHINE *laughs, he changes his mind, goes up and looks off R.*)

RAFFERTY (*aside to* TURNER *in alarm*) Tundher an' turf.* Ye gave him the wrong ones—Every one of these (*indicating them on table*) has got your name on them.

TURNER (*aside*) Then the game's up.

BOUNAPARTE Zem papers! I have not examined yet, I must do so. (*Still at back.*)

[TURNER] (TURNER *and* RAFFERTY *give a sigh of relief.*) Quick, change them, while I distract his attention. (*Goes up.*) That general is not like you. (RAFFERTY *changes papers; as he puts them down* BOUNAPARTE *turns quickly, points pistol.*)

BOUNAPARTE Leave zem papers alone, sar, or I fire. (*Levels pistol,* RAFFERTY *puts them down.*)

RAFFERTY Pardon, general, for the moment I forgot where I was. (JOSEPHINE *laughs again—*BOUNAPARTE *looks off. —Aside to* TURNER *who comes down*) I've got them. (*Gives them—*TURNER *goes L.*)

TURNER Saved! (*Puts them in breast.*)

BOUNAPARTE Such curiosity, sar, is dangerous. Much of it may lead you to a stone wall—a platoon of soldiers and a volley of bullets. (*Enter* JOSEPHINE *R.C.*)

JOSEPHINE I vill not stay any longar avay. (*Sees* TURNER, RAFFERTY.) Ah, how comes zeze two men here? I tell you I vill not stay avay ven you know zat you leave for Egypt tonight. (*He stops her suddenly.*)

BOUNAPARTE (*angrily*) Diable! Silence! (*She looks amazed—then in soft tones.*) Pardon, cherie, pardon, yes you sall remain. (*Re-enter* MRS. TONE *R.C. As* BOUNAPARTE *speaks she stops and stands as if petrified—to* TURNER.) As zis Volfe Tone is a countryman of yours vhat do you suggest I should do viz him?

TURNER Order his immediate arrest and execution.

JOSEPHINE (*startled*) No, no.

TURNER If madam will pardon the seeming brutality of the remark a fitting end for all spies.

JOSEPHINE (*with energy*) He is no spy, sar, but a brave Irish Zhentleman.

MRS. TONE (*to JOSEPHINE*) I thank you, madame, for those words. (*To TURNER*) Yes, Samuel Turner, as much an Irish gentleman as you are an infamous renegade.

(*Enter TONE hurriedly R.C.*)

TURNER General—this woman—

BOUNAPARTE Silence! (*Angrily to TONE*) Again, sar, What means zis intrusion?

TONE News of the utmost importance. (*Sees TURNER*) Ah, you, here!

[TABLEAU]

(RAFFERTY R. JOSEPHINE R.C. TONE C. BOUNAPARTE L.C. TURNER L.)

TURNER (*to BOUNAPARTE and JOSEPHINE; going up*) I will bid you—

TONE Stay!

TURNER What have you to say to me?

TONE (*to BOUNAPARTE*) Is this the man whose name you declined to divulge?

BOUNAPARTE What if it is, sar?

TONE Only this (*crosses to TURNER*). Coward! Liar! Thief!

BOUNAPARTE (*to JOSEPHINE*) Go! Go!

JOSEPHINE No, no, I vill stop. Ze truth is coming out now, and I sall love to hear it.

TONE Do you hear! Coward! Liar! thief! (*TURNER with hand on sword. —RAFFERTY making off L.C. but BOUNAPARTE stops him.*)

[BOUNAPARTE] Bah, this is not the place for that, outside if you have the courage you can draw it with pleasure.

JOSEPHINE Zis is grand, Magnifique!

TONE I ask you again, General, Is this the man whose name you decline to divulge?

BOUNAPARTE Zat is ze man! Is he not an agent of your country?

TONE He is!

BOUNAPARTE Zen what have you against him?

TONE That his whole life has been a living lie. For years he has been my bitterest—deadliest foe, his vile vindictive nature ever at work to encompass my ruin. Not only has he betrayed me to the British Government—nearly brought me to the gallows, but this very night he has endeavoured to abduct my wife—to consign her to slavery—to a fate worse than death.

JOSEPHINE Ze monstar! I understand all now. (*BOUNAPARTE crosses to table R.*)

TURNER It's a base fabrication—a tissue of lies.

TONE (*to BOUNAPARTE*) You taunted me with poverty—the neglect of my country to supply me with funds—with this man's affluence. You accused me of being a creature of Pitt—an English spy. I turn round on you now, and say, there stands the man, the man whose wealth has been bought with Irish blood—whose gold has been poured out like water from the coffers of the English Government.

BOUNAPARTE (*taking up papers*) But here are your papers?

TONE Stolen by that villain from my desk to-night.

BOUNAPARTE But which condemn you.

TONE (*amazed*) Condemn!

BOUNAPARTE As being in communication with Pitt—as being a traitor to your country and to France. Zere they are. (*Hands paper.*)

TONE (*to TURNER*) You fiend incarnate, this then is also your work.

BOUNAPARTE (*who has gone up a little to OFFICER*) Close every door! Let no one pass either in or out.

(*SOLDIERS appear at every entrance. TURNER and RAFFERTY get very uneasy.*)

TONE I demand no more—no less. Let truth prevail—this conspiracy be exposed and the guilty punished.

BOUNAPARTE (*to OFFICER*) Bring in zat man, and see you guard well every exit. (*OFFICER exits and returns with HANS and TWO SOLDIERS.*)

TONE (*to TURNER and RAFFERTY*) You cringing curs, you have overreached yourselves—your villainy recoils on your own heads.

BOUNAPARTE (*to HANS*) Is zis ze man (*points to TURNER*) who hired you to abduct zat lady? (*Points to MRS. TONE.*) Ze truth, sar, and nothing else!

HANS Ten tousand debbils dake him, yah! that's him. (*SHANE and PEGGY ha[ve] entered at the same time as HANS. TONE has glanced at the papers.*)

BOUNAPARTE Enough! (*Waves him back.*)

TONE These are parts of my journal—my diary—breathing through every page devotion to my country. Search me, my desk, my house, and if you can find but one single line implicating me as being in England's pay, then hang me for the vile wretch you would have me be. I shall deserve no better fate. But the [i]gnominy you mete out to me—mete out to those men as well.

BOUNAPARTE It sall be done! Zearch zem! (*OFFICER goes to TONE, KILMAINE to TURNER and RAFFERTY, who hastily get C. They draw their swords.*)

TURNER I protest against this abuse of privilege—this insult.

RAFFERTY Lay a finger on me and England shall pulverize ye to atoms.

(*FOUR SOLDIERS on steps at back, make ready to fire.*)

BOUNAPARTE Give up your swords, or zeze (*meaning MEN*) fire. Do you hear? (*To MEN*) Ready! (*TURNER and RAFFERTY throw down their swords.*) Zearch zem! (*KILMAINE to TURNER, LEMOINES to RAFFERTY.*)

SHANE Twig ould Rafferty! (*OFFICER hands paper.*)

OFFICER (*who has searched TONE*) Nothing, sar. (*Salutes.*)

BOUNAPARTE (*looking at papers, to TURNER*) Here is your name, Turner, on zese, your letters addressed to Pitt—and zeze (*to RAFFERTY*) yours to Dublin Castle, you, (*to TURNER*) and not he, are ze spy—you are traitors both. Avay viz zem.

KILMAINE And their punishment? (*Saluting.*)

BOUNAPARTE Shot at sun rise.

TABLEAU

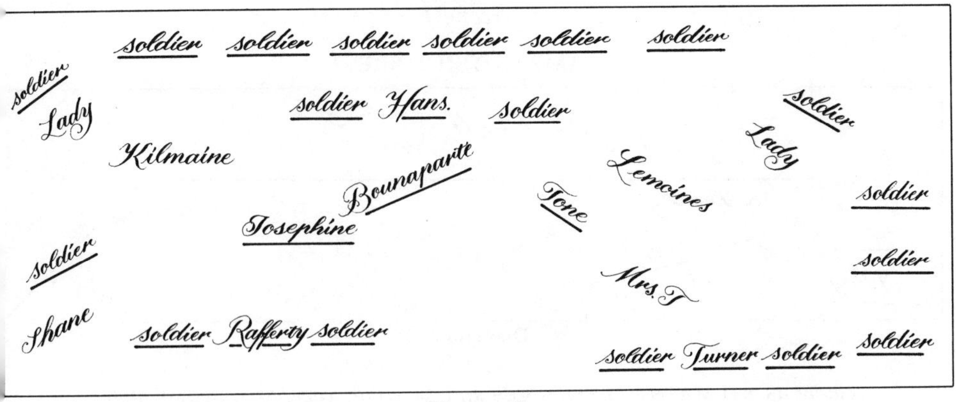

soldier soldier soldier soldier soldier soldier
soldier
Lady
soldier Hans. soldier
soldier
Kilmaine
Lady
Bounaparte
Lemoines
soldier
Tone
Josephine
soldier
soldier
soldier
Mrs. T
Shane
soldier Rafferty soldier
soldier Turner soldier soldier

Diagram J

TABLEAU

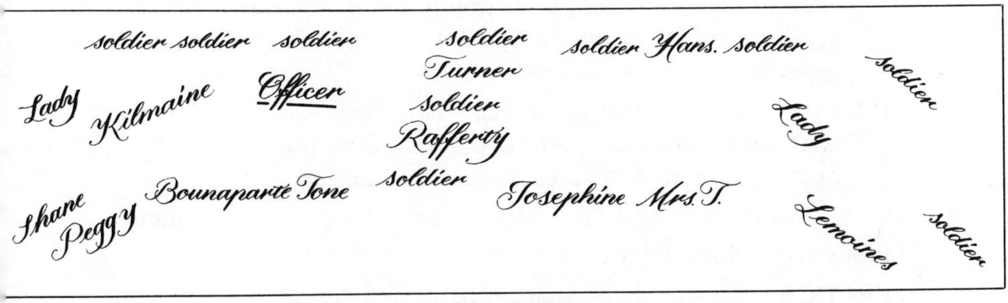

soldier soldier soldier soldier soldier Hans. soldier
Turner
soldier
Lady Kilmaine Officer soldier
Lady
Rafferty
soldier
Shane Peggy Bounaparte Tone Josephine Mrs. T.
Lemoines
soldier

Diagram K

End of Act III

ACT IV

Scene 1

CAMP OUTSIDE BREST

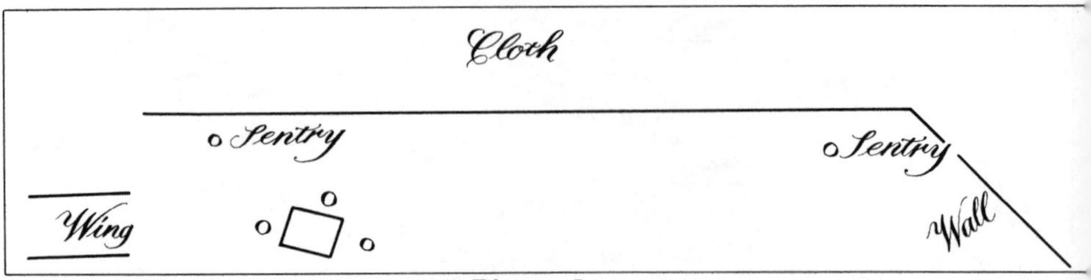

Cloth
Sentry
Sentry
Wing
Wall

Diagram L

(*Generals* KILMAINE, LEMOINES *and* TONE *discovered seated at table. Sentries at back, walking up and down. Drums beating; Trumpet-calls.* SIX MEN *march across from L.1.E. to R.U.E. Enter* OFFICER *with despatches L., crosses and hands them to* KILMAINE, *salutes & exits R.U.E.*)

LEMOINES When do we sail?

KILMAINE To-night.

TONE Only a week and beloved country I shall see you once again. Once more feel your green turf beneath my feet, breath again your life-giving air. (*To* KILMAINE) Who commands the expedition? (*Sits L. of table,* KILMAINE *C.,* LEMOINES *R.*)

KILMAINE General Hardy. (*Looking at another dispatch.*) And here is an order from the general commanding for ze instant execution of ze two spies Turner and Rafferty.

TONE Ah then there's no possible hope of a pardon for them?

KILMAINE None whatever.

LEMOINES General Bounaparte postponed zes sentence at your interposition—zat is ovar six months ago. Sufficient grace in which to prepare for death. If zey are not ready to die by zis zey never will be.

KILMAINE (*to* TONE) Will you zee zat ze sentince is duly carried out?

TONE (*rising*) No, no, you must relieve me of that unthankful task; though they are such vile wretches, they are still my countrymen.

KILMAINE I forgot zat. (*To* LEMOINES) Vill you attend to ze ordar?

LEMOINES Why, where we troubled viz zeme all zee way from Havre here? (*Rising*) Why not have shot zem zer?

KILMAINE Zat is not our business!

LEMOINES Where shall I carry out the sentence? (*Crosses to L.*)

KILMAINE Any where! Here if you like—(*rises.*) It is as good as any—Zat is an excellent wall for ze purpose. Only use dispatch. (*Enter* MRS. TONE *R.1.E. followed by* PEGGY *and* SHANE. LEMOINES *L.1.E.*) Ah, madame, we have news for you. We leave for Ireland to-night.

MRS. TONE (*anxiously*) To-night.

TONE Yes, dear, to-night! Is it not glorious news?

MRS. TONE (*with an effort*) Yes!

TONE At last the triumph of my life approaches—the goal I have longed for is in sight. (*She clings to him and sobs.*) Why, what is the matter?

MRS. TONE The parting that I have dreaded is come at last.

TONE (*reassuringly*) But only for a time, three months hence and you will be with me in dear old Dublin once again.

MRS. TONE Never! never! this parting, oh, I know it dear, is final—our last in this world. The presentiment that has hung like an icy pall round my heart all these weary months now closes in upon it with the cold chill of death.

TONE You are weak, unstrung, morbid; you must put aside these vague foolish fears—cast from you all unreal shadows—look only to the bright side of things—to our meeting in dear old Ireland.

MRS. TONE I do, I do, and though I know I am sending you to your death I send you, though my heart is breaking, willingly, willingly for Ireland's sake.

TONE Bravely spoken!

MRS. TONE You—you will die a soldier's death?

TONE I will die no other; no hangman's rope shall ever close around my throat; of that have no fear!

MRS. TONE Kiss me! (*He does so. Enter* JOSEPHINE, SHANE, *and* PEGGY.)

JOSEPHINE Ah, here I am! All zee way from Parhee to vish you bon voyage, to see my brave troops sail for your country.

TONE Madame, your very words are heralds of hope.

JOSEPHINE And I sall take zis vife of yours back viz me; oh, I sall take care of her till you return, —covaired wiz glory. (*Roll of drums.*)

MRS. TONE What is that?

TONE A sight, dear, you must not behold, the death of two traitors.

MRS. TONE Ah, I know; is there no—no hope for them?

TONE None! (*JOSEPHINE and he lead her off R.1.E.; PEGGY follows.*)

TONE (*to SHANE*) Have you your pistols?

SHANE There they are— (*He hands them—TONE places them in his belt. Enter SOLDIERS, then RAFFERTY and TURNER—both stripped to the shirt—both are livid, haggard; they form up L. SOLDIERS R.*)

RAFFERTY (*to TURNER*) Man! man! what are they going to do to us?

TURNER Wait and see!

LEMOINES (*to men*) Ready! (*SOLDIERS get ready.*)

TONE Permit me one word with them.

LEMOINES Be quick zen.

TONE (*to them*) Your time has come. I have tried to save your lives and failed. If you have any last message—last word to send to Ireland I will take it for you?

TURNER Curse you! none! my only one regret is that I did not kill you when I had the chance. If I have to die—I'll die game!

RAFFERTY (*in terrified tones*) Die! who says die? I'm not fit to die. (*[To] the MEN who are fixing him to chain*) Kape off, I won't die, I won't die I tell yez, help! help! (*Enter OFFICER R.1.E. with paper.*)

OFFICER Stay! here is a reprieve, a pardon for ze prisoner Turner, from General Bounaparte. (*SOLDIER unbinds TURNER.*)

RAFFERTY An' for me, too, for me, oh, say for me, too.

LEMOINES No, you die ze death still.

TURNER (*to RAFFERTY*) And I shall live—do you hear live—live to enjoy your money, your wealth. Your will's safe here (*touches breast*) old boy, lucky I got you to make it, eh? It was a narrow shave, but (*with a laugh*) I have won by a neck. (*To TONE*) You and I, curse you, shall meet again. (*To RAFFERTY*) Ta, ta old fellow don't be afraid! I won't forget to put a stone above your grave.

RAFFERTY I see it all, I have been your dupe, your catspaw, to save your own life, you have sold mine, but if I have to die you shall die, too. (*He has been struggling fiercely. He gets free,* TURNER *laughs and says*) Not yet, old boy! (*Seizes pistol from* TURNER*'s belt and fires at* TURNER. TURNER *falls* R.C. *then he jumps upon him more like a maniac than a human being.*) You would enjoy my money would you? but you shan't, you would live would ye but ye shan't. ye'd rob me would ye but ye shan't. Where is it? (*Has been searching for Will—gets it.*) Here it is. (*Tears it up.*) Curse ye! curse ye! enjoy it now! enjoy it now! enjoy it now! enjoy it now! (SOLDIERS *have been pulling at him and at end of speech they drag him back to wall, others raise* TURNER.)

LEMOINES He is not dead—Let him lie.

(RAFFERTY *breaks away from men and rushes to* TONE. *He clings to him.*)

RAFFERTY Save me.

TONE Nothing on earth can save you now.

RAFFERTY If you've any soul at all in ye, save me. If ye've any heart at all in ye, save me. If ye've any hope of Heaven, oh, save me, save me, save me!

TONE The blood—the innocent blood of those you have sent to death cries aloud for vengeance.

RAFFERTY (*shudders*) No! no! no!

TONE The men you have sent to the gallows; the fleshless heads grinning on government spikes—the bones rattling in their chains now stare you in the face.

RAFFERTY No! no! no! save me! I'll give ye goold—every pinny. I have in the worrld 20,000 pounds!

TONE 100,000 wouldn't save you now—If you cannot die like an Irishman, at least try and die like a man.

RAFFERTY I am not fit, I am not fit— (*They drag him away and bind him to chain—handkerchief placed over his eyes, he struggles crying all the time*) Save me! save me! 2[0],000 goolden guineas! save me! (OFFICER *signal to* MEN; *they raise their guns and fire; he falls with a scream, dragging chain and all from the wall on to stage.*)

TONE So perish all traitors!

(BAND *plays, they march across—followed by* SOLDIERS *then* CHARACTERS, *then* SOLDIERS *again, change of scene, all discovered forming* TABLEAU*—or they march on—whichever is found to be the most effective.*)

END

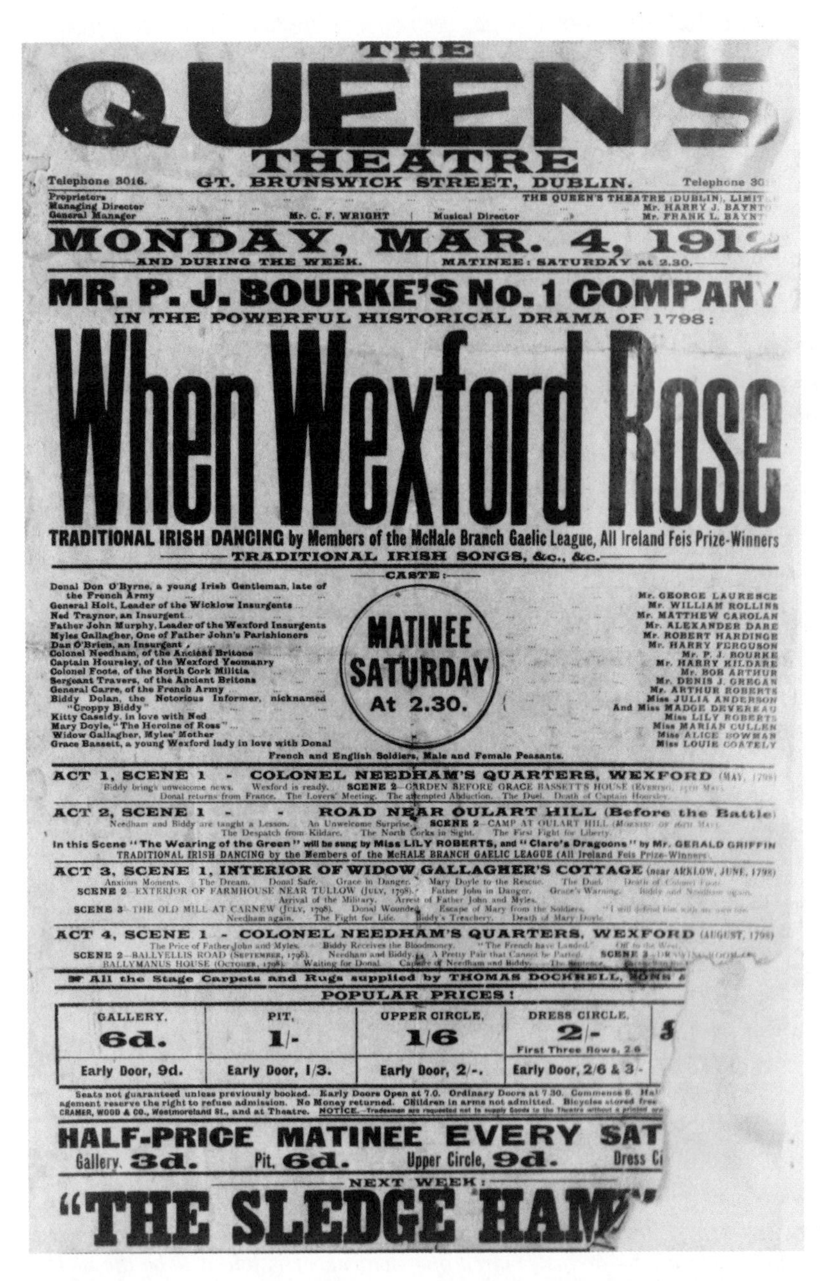

Plate 17. Playbill for Bourke's *When Wexford Rose.* By kind permission of Dr. Cyril Cusack.

WHEN WEXFORD ROSE

P. J. BOURKE
[1910]

A Romantic Irish Drama in Four Acts. Dealing with the Wexford Rebellion in 1798. [MS. B: An Historical Drama in Four Acts. Dealing with the Irish War of Independence 1798.]

CAST

DONAL DON O'BYRNE	A young Wexford Gentleman in the service of France [MS. B: A young Irish Gentleman late of the French army. In love with Grace.]
GENERAL JOSEPH HOLT	Leader of the Wicklow Insurgents
FATHER JOHN MURPHY	Leader of the Wexford Insurgents
NED TRAYNOR	Servant man at the Manor [MS. B: An insurgent. In love with Kitty.]
MYLES GALLAGHER	One of Father John's faithful friends [MS. B: One of Father John's parishioners]
DAN O'BRIEN	An Insurgent [not in script]
COLONEL NEEDHAM	Commander of the ancient Britons
CAPTAIN HOURSLEY	Of the Wexford Yeomanry [MS. B: Grace Bassett's guardian]
COLONEL FOOT[E]	Of the North Cork Militia
SERGEANT TREVORS	Of the ancient Britons

Plate 18. Original cast for the first production (1910) of *When Wexford Rose. Back row, far right:* Peadar Kearney; *front row, third from right:* P. J. Bourke. Courtesy of Séamus de Búrca.

GENERAL CARRIE	Of the French Army [called FRENCH OFFICER]
BIDDY DOLAN	A [MS. B: The] notorious informer. Nicknamed Croppy* Biddy.
KITTY CASSIDY	In love with Ned
WIDOW GALLAGHER	Myles's mother
MARY DOYLE	The heroine of Ross
GRACE BASSETT	A young Wexford lady in love with Donal
ENGLISH SOLDIERS	
MALE AND FEMALE PEASANTS	
[MS. B: SERGEANT AND OFFICER	Of the French Army]

SYNOPSIS OF SCENERY

Act I

Scene 1. Room in Colonel Needham's quarters at Wexford
Scene 2. The garden and ground before Grace Bassett's house

Act II

26th May, 1798

Scene 1. Road near Oulart Hill
Scene 2. The Insurgent Camp, Oulart Hill

Act III

Scene 1. Interior of widow Gallagher's cottage
Scene 2. Outside farm house, near Tullow
Scene 3. The Old Mill, near Carnew

Act IV

Scene 1. Room in Needham's house
Scene 2. Road near Ballyellis

Scene 3. Drawing room in Ballymanus

First produced at the Queen's Theatre, Dublin, Week of 4 March 1911 by P. J. Bourke, No. 1 Company, Irish Players [An earlier production occurred in 1910 at the Father Mathew Hall in Dublin]

ACT I

Scene 1

FRONT CHAMBER CLOTH

(Room in Colonel Needham's house, Wexford. Table, centre, chairs at right and left of table. NEEDHAM *seated writing. Pens, ink and papers and map on table.* HOURSLEY *standing on the right of the table. Music to take up curtain.)*

NEEDHAM And so, Captain Hoursley, you want more money already? What the devil did you do with the £200 I gave you last week?

HOURSLEY My Dear Colonel Needham, the cursed cards were against me. But you need have no fear. When my niece, Grace Bassett, is your wife, you will have a fortune of a full Twenty thousand.

NEEDHAM True, when she is my wife. I seem to be making very little progress, though. By Heavens, if you should be playing me false!

HOURSLEY Psha, man. How can I play you false? Of her fortune of £40,000, I have already spent half. If any other man should marry her, he would demand a strict account of her fortune, and I would find myself convicted of embezzlement. But I am safe with you as her husband, as you have already given me your bond to pay me £20,000 on the day she becomes your wife. I will thus be safe as regards the money I have spent, and you as her husband will get what remains.

NEEDHAM But how can I be sure that anything remains? You may have made away with it all.

HOURSLEY Curse it, I couldn't. Her father made me her guardian until she is twenty-five. But since she became twenty-one the lawyers have refused to accept any mortgage that has not her signature as well as my own.

NEEDHAM And you could not get Grace Bassett to sign? Are you not acquainted with certain *gentle* means of persuasion?

HOURSLEY That would be too dangerous. If I drove her too far, she might in desperation marry the first man she met. No, it is my business to see that she marries you, and nobody else, before she is twenty-five.

NEEDHAM And has she never had a sweetheart?

HOURSLEY I believe she has one now. I have learnt that her childhood's playmate, Donal Don O'Byrne, has returned to Ireland.

NEEDHAM I have heard of him and of his return. But he is a rebel, and could not proceed against you for her fortune.

HOURSLEY If he were only a rebel, I would be safe. But he has been many years in France, and rumour says that he is both a French citizen and a French officer.

NEEDHAM But we are at war with France.

HOURSLEY Peace may be arranged at any time, and then he would be more dangerous to me as Grace Bassett's husband than would be any Irishman, for he would have the French Government to back up his claims. No, you must see that I cannot play you false, so like a good fellow, now, let me have the money I ask.

NEEDHAM You shall have it. (*Writes and hands paper to HOURSLEY.*)

(*Enter BIDDY DOLAN L.*)

NEEDHAM Good evening, Miss Dolan.

BIDDY Good evening, Gentlemen. I have just dropped up to let you know that a party of rebels have attacked and defeated the yeomanry, and are now encamped at Shelmalier, under the command of some unknown clergyman of that neighbourhood.

NEEDHAM How many are there, do you know?

BIDDY There are about three hundred, but they are badly armed.

NEEDHAM Aye, but their infernal pikes are dangerous weapons at close quarters.

BIDDY Troth, and if that's the case they'll be heard from, for every man jack of them is armed with a good pike.

NEEDHAM (*to HOURSLEY*) Take all the available troops and proceed at once to the rebel encampment. Give no quarter!

HOURSLEY Rest assured, if the rebels show fight it will be their last battle. (*Bows and exit R.*)

NEEDHAM Now, my good girl, what news?

BIDDY I've been keeping an eye on Miss Bassett as you told me, and there's no doubt about the story that Donal Don O'Byrne has returned and is paying her his attentions. And faith he'll have to be a stout lad that wishes to marry that girl against her will.

NEEDHAM Where there's a will there's a way, and her receiving this arch-traitor places her in the hollow of my hand. I'll engage she will prefer to live as my wife than to share O'Byrne's fate.

BIDDY Since you are satisfied with my work, I'd like to get my hire. I've been very useful to the Government in keeping it informed of the rebels' proceedings.

NEEDHAM Don't be uneasy, you shall be well paid. Those in high places are shelling out royally, and you shall have your share.

BIDDY There's an important prisoner on the road below. The Dragoons, acting on my information, arrested him. They are waiting for you to sign the warrant for his execution.

NEEDHAM Good! Here's a cheque to go on with. Trevors of the Dragoons will cash it for you.

BIDDY And here's a list of all the leading men in this county. You can have them all at your pleasure. Good-day.

NEEDHAM Good-day. (*Exit* BIDDY.) First to get rid of the rebels and traitors; then we'll give short shrift to Miss Croppy Biddy and her associates. (*Exit* NEEDHAM.)

Black out Scene 1

Scene 2

(*The Gardens before* GRACE BASSETT'*s House L. Balustrade opening in Centre. Music till* DONAL *on. [MS. C: Landscape at Back Garden, Balcony runs from R. to L. of stage, steps centre. House stands on the R. of stage. Wood Wing on left. As scene opens up,* DONAL DON O'BYRNE *enters L. and comes down steps to L.C.]*)

(*Enter* DONAL *R.C. Looks off L.*)

DONAL I have been obliged to make a circuit to avoid those men, one of whom, if I mistake not, was indeed a foe—a bitter foe! The other man I well know as Grace's uncle. Now to see if Ned is about. Ah me! (*Enter* NED *humming "The French are on the Sea." He starts at the sight of* DONAL. *Then advances to L.C.*)

NED Eh, is it? No! yes! it is—it must be—and it's yourself [MS. C: Master Donal,] that's the grand gentleman (*shakes hands*). And before I tell you any more let me bid you, Céad Míle Fáilte go hEirinn!*

DONAL Yes, Ned, when I received the glad news that Ireland was ready to strike, I left Brest accompanied by several other officers. We feared that we would be unable to arrive in time to take part in the rising, and on our arrival in Dublin we found it impossible to have an interview with the commander-in-chief, Lord Edward Fitzgerald, and had to leave without seeing him on account of the strict watch kept on him. But tell me, who is the young lady I saw going down the road before Needham?

NED Sure that's Biddy Dolan, bad luck to her! She's arm in arm with the Government in Wexford.

DONAL Biddy Dolan! Who is she? I never heard of her before!

NED Didn't you? Faith, and it's she that's well known about here. Well, [MS. B: an'] I'll tell you who she is. You knew ould Pat Dolan the thatcher below in the town of Carnew. He was as dacent a poor man as ever pulled a faning of straw, so I'm sorry to have to tell you that that's his daughter and there isn't a woman or child about the neighbourhood that's not in dread of their lives of her, for she goes round in the dead of the night with a troop of soldiers, and if there's any man about the place that she has anything against, she'll have them called out of their beds and shot or hanged, or maybe burned in their beds to save expense. Sure only she's a woman she'd be shot long ago.

DONAL Do you really mean to tell me that she is as bad as all that? Great God! Such a viper in human form!

NED Bedad, she's worse than the Devil himself, and you better mind she doesn't see you, or the fat's in the fire, for to-night the boys are to assemble.

DONAL Good, good! Tell me, Ned, is Miss Bassett here or can I see her?

NED She's gone down to Jim Byrne's below at the cross. Jim's wife Mary never got over the fright the yeos gave her the other night, and I'm afraid she's done for. Will I go and tell her that you are here?

DONAL No, no. I shall go and meet her returning. (*Looks off L.*) Look! who are those coming yonder?

NED It's Croppy Biddy coming back with Needham and Hoursley. Surely they couldn't have been in Wexford since? Will you answer the blackguards now?

DONAL Their answer is in my scabbard. Shall I draw it?

NED On second thoughts, not until later on; it might cause a hitch in the signal [MS. C: for the risin']. You had better leave them a little more time to make their souls. Come away before they see you. Biddy has an eye like an owl, that can only see when she wants to seek her prey at night. Here they come all smiles as if they were going to their wedding instead of to their funeral.

DONAL Good-bye, boy, you know my mind. I will leave them to their gossip. Those people Hoursley and Needham both shall hear from me before the moon shall rise to-night, and till then peace be yours. ([MS. C: *Exit* DONAL *up steps C. and disappears L. followed by* NED, *who disappears R. Enter* COLONEL NEEDHAM, *L.C. followed by* BIDDY DOLAN, *and* HOURSLEY.])

NEEDHAM Curse the jade! Once more she has given us the slip.

BIDDY Well, you know, she has an idea you are after her and so keeps out of the way.

HOURSLEY Well, there's no use discussing our failure. Better luck next time. I want your services, Miss Dolan, and if you carry out my orders you shall be liberally rewarded.

NEEDHAM I cannot remain. Urgent business awaits me. Therefore, I wish you a very good night. ([MS. C: *Crosses up steps, turns and bows.*])

HOURSLEY This niece of mine has compromised herself by holding communication with Donal Don O'Byrne and if the authorities become aware of her criminal conduct her estate will be confiscated.

BIDDY Which wouldn't suit you at all, Captain.

HOURSLEY Ah, I have made myself too useful to the Government to be forgotten. With yonder minx under lock and key and O'Byrne dangling from the gallows, I shall enter into possession of the fairest estate in Wexford.

BIDDY Well, captain, the Devil's own children have the Devil's own luck. But I'm told that the estate is none the fairer for your guardianship.

HOURSLEY (*aside*) This jade knows too much! (*To* BIDDY) My surmise is that my niece is not at home yet. To-night a party of soldiers shall pay her a visit. You'll be there, denounce her as a rebel and have her placed under arrest.

BIDDY And my reward?

HOURSLEY One hundred pounds when your prisoner is under lock and key in Wexford gaol.

BIDDY Hush, some one is coming. Let us not be seen together.

(*Exeunt L.C. Enter* KITTY *R. with milking pail.*)

Music

KITTY Well, the milking is done with, thank God, & now to help Miss Grace to get ready to start. Faith the soldiers will be disappointed this blessed night when they find the house empty. Bad luck to ould Needham, how dare he have the cheek to make up to Miss Grace. (*Enter* NED. KITTY *starts.*)

NED Bedad Kitty, you're a powerful spaker entirely. Faith, you'd bate Grattan himself at servin' out the pay. You bothered me, anyhow.

KITTY You ought to be proud of yourself, Ned Traynor, to be dodgin' about listenin' to people.

NED Faith, & I was lookin' too, Kitty agrah.* And troth I'd do a lot of dodgin' to be lookin' at your purty face.

KITTY The cheek of you, Ned Traynor.

NED You often told me that before.

KITTY Dickens a much good it seems to do you.

NED Why, if it goes to that, I can't help myself for when you're knockin' around my head goes astray, & as the Docthor says, I'm not responsible for my actions. (*Attempts to embrace her.*)

KITTY Now Ned, behave yourself.

NED By this night of the twenty-third of May—

KITTY Now Ned, quit humbuggin'.

NED There's not a girl in the whole county—

KITTY Don't be makin' a fool of yourself. Isn't the country disturbed enough without his Riverence catchin' us like this.

NED Lave it to me to watch that, & as for makin' a fool of meself, I'd do more than that for you Kitty darlin'.

KITTY [MS. B: This is no time for that kind of talk. We] have both got a dale to do before the moon rises tonight.

NED That's the reason, Kitty, I want to talk what you call foolish. It may be a long time before we stand here together again, & I want to know will you have what's left of me when the war is over.

KITTY Did you ever doubt me, Ned? (*Kiss.*) Here's Master Donal & Miss Grace. Two is company.

(*Exeunt,* KITTY *singing "I wish that the wars were all over / I wish that the wars were all over / for when Ireland is free, my true love an' me / will be wed, when the wars are all over." Enter* GRACE *and* DONAL.)

GRACE How beautiful the sun is setting! The clouds are piled up like palaces of fairy-land and the golden beams come shooting out thro' the bright chinks as if the halls were illuminated for the merry-making. But it is the King of the storm who will hold its feast amongst them. For that bright sunset looks troubled. Soon all those bright and glowing clouds will be scattered by the storm, for to-night Donal the great struggle is to commence—Oh! how I envy you men who shall be in the midst of it.

DONAL You too, dearest, shall find work to do in a sphere of action more suited to your strength; for in the struggle for life & home the women of Ireland must aid their struggling brothers in every way.

GRACE When I left you last I doubted if I should ever see you again, for in these dreadful times one is never safe. I have much to tell you of suffering & grief, but troubles crowd too thickly upon us to spend our last few moments in sorrow.

DONAL Fear not, darling, the dark clouds of care are about to break in a glorious and resplendent dawn. Be assured I know all about the nefarious machinations of Needham, for which I shall exact a summary account. My God! to think of you as the wife of that scoundrel almost drives me mad. To-night you must come with me to Father John, who will receive you with open arms.

GRACE While you are near, Donal, I shall fear nothing. Together we shall endure whatever trials God wills that are in store for us, and it is I shall be proud when I wed the free soldier of an independent nation.

DONAL And my arm shall be doubly strengthened and my steel shall be doubly keen when I remember that the best little woman in Ireland is waiting & praying for me and my cause.

I must go now, darling, I shall return to-night. Good-bye till then (*kisses her hand and exits*).

(*Enter* KITTY.)

KITTY Is he gone, Miss Grace?

GRACE He is, Kitty, did you want to see him?

KITTY You had better come inside, Miss. (*Enter* NED.) Croppy Biddy is knocking around & there's no knowing what mischief she'd be up to. [MS. B: *Enter* NED.]

NED Let everybody get inside! Here's Croppy Biddy coming up the avenue.

KITTY Come on, Miss Grace. You can stay here to meet her, Ned; you're the boy to talk to her. (*Exeunt* KITTY *and* GRACE. NED *sits on stone. Enter* BIDDY.)

BIDDY Oh, good evening, Ned. I hope all are well. There's no need to ask you how you are, because you never looked better. I was passing & I thought I'd drop in to see if there were any messages for the town. On my way up I saw a strange gentleman along with Myles Gallagher; I don't remember seeing him before in these parts.

NED Maybe it's the Docthor. We've a new Docthor now you know.

BIDDY Docthor? Why, who's sick?

NED I am—very sick.

BIDDY You, Ned? Why, there's not a feather out of you.

NED Bedad & I'm sick all the same. I'm sick of people tryin' to get news out of me, and I'm goin' to get well an' give them no more news.

BIDDY Ha, ha, you were always a funny lad, Ned.

NED [MS. B: Always, faith. Well it's time to get serious, so you can try your hand at getting information somewhere else.]

BIDDY I think, Ned, you are carrying your joke too far, or else you misunderstand me.

NED Devil a bit. I know you to the veins of nicety, my lady.

BIDDY If the captain were here I would have you punished for your insolence. Ha, here come the soldiers.

(*Enter* HOURSLEY, NEEDHAM, *and* SOLDIERS.)

NEEDHAM Where the devil is everybody. Oh, you're here, Miss Dolan—and in company with that ruffian Ned Traynor! I am surprised.

NED Faith & *I'm* surprised at myself to be found in such low company. Why, if my poor father thought that I'd come so low he'd turn in his coffin, God rest him (*exit*).

NEEDHAM Well, of all the devils—

BIDDY And of all the impudence—

HOURSLEY Come, come. It will never do to be wasting time like this.

NEEDHAM Correct. I shall proceed with my business. You remain, Hoursley. Now men, forward, quick march! Good night, Miss Dolan. (*Exit with* SOLDIERS.)

HOURSLEY Now, Miss Dolan, have you seen any strangers in this neighborhood?

BIDDY Only one, at least I can't recollect seeing him before.

HOURSLEY Describe him.

BIDDY A strong well-made gentlemanly fellow with a slightly foreign appearance.

HOURSLEY Then I have made no mistake. That must have been Donal O'Byrne, commonly known as Donal Don.

BIDDY Do you really tell me that he's in these parts? I heard a rumour of his return from France, but I attached no importance to it.

HOURSLEY Is he really a French officer?

BIDDY Exactly. He was seventeen years of age when he went to France. He joined a Military school in Paris and from that rose to be Colonel. I have heard that he was decorated for bravery on the field of battle by Bonaparte himself.

HOURSLEY He may pay Miss Grace a visit, and one pistol shot shall remove him from my path forever. Come into the house. (*Exeunt.*)

(SENTRY *crosses stage followed by* NED.)

NED By the 'tarnal, Donal has bound & gagged the sojer. More power to your elbow, my boy.

(*Enter* KITTY *and* GRACE.)

GRACE We are safe so far.

KITTY I'll keep watch at the back.

(*Enter* MYLES *and* PEASANTS.)

MYLES Come this way boys, the soldiers are all at the back. (*Exits with* PEASANTS.)

(*Enter* DONAL, *embraces* GRACE.)

DONAL I am come to carry you safely from [MS. B: here.]

GRACE Quick, Donal, they are coming.

(*Noise inside. Exeunt* KITTY *and* GRACE.)

HOURSLEY (*inside*) To arms, men, the rebels have surrounded the house.

(NEEDHAM *and* BIDDY *rush across stage.* NED *fires after them without effect. Enter* HOURSLEY *and* TWO SOLDIERS. DONAL *seizes* HOURSLEY. *Exeunt* SOLDIERS *and* PEASANTS *after them.*)

HOURSLEY Donal O'Byrne! You rebel scoundrel, how dare you lay hands on an Officer of his Majesty's forces.

DONAL I am the man and you should know by this that Donal Don O'Byrne dares everything! You escaped me last night when you were carrying out your fiendish work at Boulavogue, but you shall not escape this time, for you have men to face, not old women. (*Draws [MS. B: sword].*) Defend yourself. (*Duel.* HOURSLEY *killed.*) So perish all who hold this land in bondage!

[CURTAIN]

[*End of Act I*]

ACT II

Scene 1

FRONT CLOTH

(*Road near Oulart Hill. Morning, 26 May 1798. Enter* NEEDHAM *and* BIDDY *in haste R.*)

NEEDHAM A pretty mess the rebels have made of us.

BIDDY A pretty mess, indeed and all through your stupidity.

NEEDHAM How the Devil do you make that out?

BIDDY If you had come to my assistance we had them and without a shot being fired.

NEEDHAM Why did you not tell your men to fire on them?

BIDDY How could I, and that ruffian Ned Traynor with a pistol on full cock at my ear. What could I do but make off as fast as I could.

NEEDHAM How pale you are, girl! Here, have some brandy.

BIDDY I almost fell into their hands and I owe my life to the quickness of my pony. (*NEEDHAM looks off left.*) Are the rebels in pursuit of us still, Colonel?

NEEDHAM No, no, they are not. We are out of their reach now.

BIDDY How many of your men escaped?

NEEDHAM But two have come back alive.

BIDDY Hoursley was laid out anyhow. It was a good job he paid me before he took his departure.

NEEDHAM Yes, it was. What of Grace Bassett? Did she escape?

BIDDY She was gone from the [first]. After we had entered the house she and her maid ****** out while you were posting the soldiers around the house.

NEEDHAM I am sorry I missed her and I am doubly sorry for poor Hoursley. He was a goodhearted fellow.

BIDDY I warned him that O'Byrne was the better swordsman, and he should not have accepted O'Byrne's challenge.

NEEDHAM I will settle with O'Byrne yet, curse him!

BIDDY Not in single combat. These French officers are too swift and sure with their swords for your sort.

NEEDHAM What! do you mean to imply that I am—

BIDDY A coward and would not meet any man face to face. Why, I should not fear to meet you and cross swords with you myself.

NEEDHAM Hush girl! Here comes Colonel Foote.

(*Enter FOOTE.*)

FOOTE I have been in search of you, sir. Good day, Miss Dolan, you will pardon my intrusion. I have been informed that a party of your men have been set upon and brutally slaughtered by a party of rebels led by some unknown clergyman of the neighbourhood. Who can he be?

NEEDHAM We know not, but unfortunately we were trapped.

FOOTE I thought so. Could the rebels win otherwise?

BIDDY It will take some time to put down this rebellion.

NEEDHAM I fear so. This party that attacked us last night have succeeded at Camolin before in overthrowing Colonel Bookey. The rebellion is yet in its infancy and already two of King George's officers have been slain.

FOOTE Who is the second officer?

NEEDHAM Captain Hoursley, who was killed last night at his niece's residence in a duel with a French officer named Donal O'Byrne.

FOOTE And where were your men?

NEEDHAM Flying before the rebels, and but two got away.

FOOTE May I ask your strength and that of the enemy.

NEEDHAM There were 2,000 rebels and only 50 of ours.

BIDDY Well, better luck next time. I shall leave you now, gentlemen. I will go towards Oulart Hill. I may learn something of the rebels. (*Exits left.*)

NEEDHAM Well, thank God we are rid of your company for a while. She has rendered us some good service, but you can never rely on a woman.

FOOTE I have received an important despatch from Lord Mountjoy. (*Takes papers from belt and reads*) "The rebels are encamped on Oulart Hill. Proceed at once with all your available forces and may God aid you in holding the right of our King to rule in Ireland." What do you think of that?

NEEDHAM Why, my dear Foote, while you have such a regiment as the gallant North Corks I think you have a capital opportunity of crushing the rebellion and making a name for yourself.

(*Enter* BIDDY *L.*)

BIDDY My soul to glory! I have just walked into the hands of Father John Murphy and a party of his men. Look, see, they are marching towards Oulart Hill.

FOOTE And so this is the unknown clergyman.

NEEDHAM If we are caught here our lives won't be worth much.

FOOTE I have left some of my men on the bend of the hill. I'll make off for them and go round the other road to Oulart Hill. You get some of your mounted men and come up by the Wexford road and cut off the rebels' retreat. Now, Father Murphy, to-day it will be success to the North Corks and confusion to their enemies.

BIDDY Keep up your courage, Colonel, your men will soon **** your ******.

NEEDHAM Tis well to be cautious. These are no times to run idle risks.

BIDDY From what I have seen and heard the rebels will be encamped on Oulart Hill yonder, and it will be a capital opportunity for you to take them by surprise. (*During this speech* MARY DOYLE *and* KITTY *enter and listen.*)

NEEDHAM That I will do and ere morning shall dawn the rebellion shall be begun and ended in Wexford.

BIDDY Come, Colonel, it's time we were moving from here, for life is precious, as the tailor said when he was running from the gander.

(*They turn sharply and start on seeing* MARY *and* KITTY. *[MS. B: Chord.]*)

NEEDHAM The Rebel hussies.

MARY At your service, Colonel. (*Bows mockingly.*)

KITTY An' the top of the mornin' to ye both.

NEEDHAM You meddlesome jades, you have followed us and you shall pay for it. (*Half draws sword.*)

KITTY Did anyone ever hear such cheek from a blind ould lobster like that.

MARY (*presenting pistol*) I neither feared nor sought your company, Colonel Needham. Go on your way, yourself and your precious companion. Your time has not yet come. (NEEDHAM *and* BIDDY *cross to R.,* MARY *and* KITTY *to L.*)

NEEDHAM I call upon you two to surrender in the King's name.

MARY To the Devil with yourself and your King. Pass on, leave here, or I will fire. That will settle the question.

BIDDY The two of you can settle in Wicklow jail tonight.

MARY If you threaten again I will call Father Murphy and his men, who are near at hand.

BIDDY Come Colonel, don't be foolish, as we are alone. But I shall never know true content until I see you at the foot of the gallows in Wicklow jail.

MARY That rests with God and not with you.

NEEDHAM I swear by Heaven I will yet lay you by the heels. (*Exeunt* NEEDHAM *and* BIDDY.)

MARY Ha, ha, well they won't come back here in a hurry.

KITTY The sight of that pair was makin' me sick.

MARY I've come all the way from Kildare. I thought Colonel Aylmer's despatches would never be delivered. Come, let us not delay. Now for Oulart Hill, to bring the great news of the

Kildare men to Father John. As for you, Colonel Needham, when you arrive from Wexford with your army of soldiers, you shall meet with a warm reception. (*Exeunt L.*)

Black out, Music til opening of Scene 2

Scene 2

(*Camp at Oulart Hill. Full Set.* NED, MYLES, *and* PEASANTS *about.*)

NED There's some hot work before us, boys, that will make all our fightin' up to this seem very small, though I suppose most of ye feel ye're war-scarred veterans. Maybe it's medals ye're wantin'.

MYLES Faith Bookey doesn't want a Medal, anyhow.

1ST PEASANT Who's talkin' about Bookey.

MYLES I am, Dan, God forgive me for that same.

1ST PEASANT Faith, I'm thinkin' he's mortial hot this minute, who ever knows it.

NED And so he ought, for he earned hell anyhow, though our Pastors tell us to judge not lest we ourselves may be judged. But I think it's no harm to judge a man by the life he leads on this earth.

MYLES Aye Ned. Faith it's a pity he couldn't bring his friends along with him.

1ST PEASANT Isn't Hoursley gone to keep him company.

MYLES Aye, Master Donal settled his hash.

1ST PEASANT Faith, Boney is great for makin' sogers.

NED If the lads we have here were under Boney for a while we'd bate the world, so we would.

MYLES You're right, Ned. There's truth in every word he's sayin', boys.

1ST PEASANT I wonder how are things in the city.

MYLES Did ye not hear the news, boys.

1ST PEASANT What news? We've heard no news at all.

MYLES Ned, tell them.

1ST PEASANT Is it bad news?

NED Couldn't be worse. Lord Edward has been arrested.

OMNES Lord Edward arrested!

MYLES Aye, but he made them that took him pay dearly for their capture.

NED His Lordship was stoppin' with a man named Murphy in Thomas Street. One evenin' he lay down to rest himself & he was just dozin' off when the door was burst open & a yeoman Captain named Swan rushed into the room. Lord Edward sprang from the bed & snapped a small pistol he had on the table in Swan's face. The pistol, bad fortune to it, missed fire, or there might have been a different story to tell. Swan then discharged his pistol at his Lordship, woundin' him in the shoulder. Then they grappled with each other & the Geraldine struck the soldier twice with a small dagger; & Swan fell, still holding on to Lord Edward. A soldier named Ryan then rushed in & attacked Lord Edward with his sword. His Lordship struck Ryan several times & he too joined his comrade on the floor. There was every chance of Lord Edward's escaping, only for Major Sirr—Hell's flames to him—who, standin' like a coward outside the door, fired at the Geraldine who sank severely wounded on the Red Coats. Before he could recover himself a dozen soldiers threw themselves on him &, weak from his wounds & the rough handlin' he received, he fainted. The few people who saw his Lordship bein' brought out were sure he was dead & so the sogers had a safe journey to Newgate.

MYLES God help us in our terrible loss & God be good to brave Lord Edward.

OMNES Amen!

MYLES I have to go & see Father John. He'll be wantin' to see me.

2D PEASANT An' I'll go across & get somethin' to ate.

(*Exeunt* MYLES *and all but* NED *and* 1ST PEASANT.)

NED That's the worst of knowin' all about sojerin'. Gettin' left on outpost duty.

PEASANT Begor,* aye, & it's a mighty could job, too. It must be about six o'clock now & we'll have a glorious day.

NED Aye, this is Whitsunday; & if God wills we'll make it a day to be remembered in Ireland for all time.

PEASANT Plase God. —Here's Father John.

(*Enter* FATHER MURPHY *reading*.)

FATHER MURPHY Well, boys, nothing disturbed your watch during the night.

NED Dickens a ha'porth,* your Riverence.

PEASANT Might I make so bould, your Riverence, as to ask, do you expect a visit from the red coats to-day.

FATHER MURPHY I'd prefer not to fight on Whitsunday, though if the yeos come here we are always ready.

PEASANT Long life to your Riverence.

NED Here's Miss Grace ridin' up the road. I wonder where's Kitty.

(*Enter* DONAL *and* GRACE.)

FATHER MURPHY My poor child. Thank God you are safe.

GRACE I am safe, Dear Father, thanks to the timely arrival of my dear friend here. Had he been late, I would not have been here to speak to you.

FATHER MURPHY All praises to him who helps the weak. Come up to my cabin, where you shall receive some refreshment. Come Grace, come child. (*Exeunt.*)

(*Enter* MYLES *and* PEASANTS.)

MYLES You're to go to your breakfast, Dan & Ned.

NED Troth & it's nearly time. We're wallfallin' with the hunger. (*Exeunt* NED *and* 1ST PEASANT.)

(*Enter* MARY DOYLE *and* KITTY.)

MARY God save all here! Where's his reverence. I want to see him.

MYLES He's gone up with Miss Grace to his house.

MARY I'm afther tramping all the way from Kildare, & there's great news, aye & great deeds too boys.

KITTY Yes boys, Kildare has been victorious.

(*Enter* NED.)

NED Kitty darlin' is that yourself.

KITTY Aye, all that's left of me, though we were nigh not bein' here at all.

NED How's that, Kitty.

KITTY Ask Mary there, she'll be able to tell you.

NED Oh, Miss Doyle, you'll excuse me, for I didn't see a bit of you. Maybe it's because I'm in love that I'm losin' me sight.

MARY Are you really in love Ned. Well, if you are it must be the first attack, for I never thought you'd love anyone.

KITTY He in love! [MS. B: sure Mary, he hasn't enough love in him to smother a kitten.]

NED Ah, Kitty, don't be too hard on a poor boy. But you didn't tell me what happened to ye.

MARY Well, we were coming along the road to here when who should we see plottin' & plannin' against Oulart Hill but Croppy Biddy & that ould thief of the world* Needham. So we frightened them off with this empty pistol. If I hadn't had the courage to do so, we would have been landed off to Wicklow jail & this despatch from Colonel Aylmer of Kildare would be far from a letter of recommendation [MS. B: for me].

NED A despatch from Kildare, you don't tell us. Ah, go on!

MYLES Will I go for his Reverence to read it for us?

KITTY No you won't go for his Reverence to read it for us. We went to school & learned to read.

MARY I'll read it for you myself.

NED Oh don't, Miss Doyle. Maybe his Reverence would be displased for it's he that has the quare ways about him betimes. Now I'll tell you what happened me when I was goin' to school to ould Shemus Byrne beyant at the cross. You all knew Shemus, or at least any of you that didn't he made them feel him very quick. Well one day I was comin' from school & the boys said to me, "I bet you a penny, Ned, you won't kiss Kitty Cassidy." "Done" says I, & I did.

KITTY Oh, you thief of a liar, I'll box your ears.

OMNES Ha—ha—ha!

NED Well, his Reverence got to hear of it & if he didn't lash me with his whip! That's the sort of a man Father John is.

MARY Well, you got off safe. If I was Father John I'd have made an example of you before all the parishioners, for darin' to do such a thing & you with no sinse at the time. An' Kitty was worse to let you.

NED Ah, you're too hard on me. Well, gather round, till Miss Doyle reads it for us. Here get upon this bank where we can all hear you.

(MARY *gets up on embankment C. facing audience.*)

NED Gather round, boys.

MARY "Early on the morning of the twenty-third of May, mail coaches were stopped at Santry. This was the first signal for the risin'."

OMNES Hurray!

MARY "And on the twenty-fourth of May the Kildare men opened an attack on the enemy near Ross."

OMNES Hurray!

MARY "And after a furious and desperate encounter the Kildare men succeeded in routing the enemy and taking possession of the town."

OMNES Hurrah, Hurrah, Hurrah!

NED Go on, Miss Doyle.

MARY I can't go on, Ned. There's no more in it.

NED Well read it again for us.

KITTY No, no. Don't be makin' a fool of yourself.

(*Enter* DONAL *C.*)

MARY Some letters from Colonel Aylmer. (*Gives them.*)

DONAL This is glorious news. Mary, you are a trump and deserve the praise of your countrymen, and for your reward I give you this sword, and with it you may do good work for your country. (*Gives her sword.*)

MARY With this sword I swear to stand for Ireland.

NED Long life to you, Mary.

MARY With song and with story shall I ever endeavour to encourage my countrymen on. Listen, Boys, while Kitty relates a verse of an old song.

(*Concert turns here.*)[1]

(KITTY *sings. At end of song, enter* GRACE *and* FATHER JOHN *C.*)

FATHER MURPHY I am glad to see you all merry and let us go forward with our hearts light to meet the foe. Too long have I preached peace to one and all of you, but peace shall never again be restored until an Irish Republic is declared.

GRACE God may guide the hand and success may crown our arms.

DONAL And God will hear your prayer, my brave little one. Come here, Mary. You must go with Grace and take her to the Widow Gallagher's, where she can remain in peace, until God sends better times. Adieu.

(PEASANTS *and* NED *gradually leave stage.*)

GRACE Adieu, dearest Donal and I shall never cease to pray for your safety.

DONAL Keep up a brave heart and all will be well for God will watch over the destinies of our land. Adieu, and always remember me in your prayers.

FATHER MURPHY God bless you, my children and send that we may all meet together on a happier occasion when the war clouds are banished and Ireland is free.

DONAL Again goodbye and I may see you sooner than you expect.

MARY Come now, Miss Grace, we have lost too much time as it is. The patrol may be on us at any minute.

DONAL Yes, Grace, Mary is right. Delays are dangerous. (*Exeunt GRACE and MARY L. Exit KITTY R.*) If you come here a moment, Father John, I will show you those plans I was telling you of. (*They converse in a whisper. Enter NED and PEASANTS.*)

NED Begorra,* boys, that's a great piece of a stone wall out there. If some of our Shelmaliere lads were posted behind it they could inflict a power of damage on an advancing army.

(*FATHER MURPHY comes to centre of bank.*)

FATHER MURPHY Now, men, the time for action has come and we must realise our responsibilities as soldiers of Ireland and a greater or holier cause no nation ever had than the cause that calls on you Wexfordmen to-day. Each one of you has a duty to perform, and I hope each of you shall acquit himself as a man and as a soldier.

OMNES True for you Father John. (*Enter KITTY in haste R.*)

KITTY The North Corks are marching this way. Look, you can already see them turning the bend of the road below.

FATHER MURPHY That wall yonder will shelter a large body of pike men and we can line the hedges with as many musketeers as we can get together. The rest is simple. You take command on this side, Donal. I will take charge on the far side of the hill. (*Exit C.*)

DONAL Everything is ready; the signal is arranged and not a shot is to be fired until our musketeers can see the eyes of the military. (*Shouting and cheering of approaching SOLDIERS heard and a voice.*) Now lads, not a move until I give the word.

Now. Ready, present, Fire. (*Draws sword.*) For Ireland, boys, and Liberty. (*All charge out cheering and shouting.*)

CURTAIN

End of Act II

ACT III

Scene 1

Kitchen Set, Window C. and Door R. and L.

(*Widow Gallagher's Cottage between Arklow and Gorey. The* WIDOW *discovered sweeping floor.*)

WIDOW It bates all where Myles, Donal & his Reverence are this three weeks, to say they never darkened the dure to see Miss Grace, & she convinced they're kilt out & out, & faith maybe they are, God between us & all harm. And Kitty hasn't been here aither. It's a quare idea she has now goin' round fightin' like a man. I suspect meself that it's seein' afther Father John she is. But sure if we're out of the track of everybody here faith we're clear of the soldiers too. I used to be lamentin' me loneliness. God forgive me, but I'm glad of it now.

(*Enter* GRACE *R. and sits at table.*)

GRACE No news yet. This waiting is weary work. God grant that Donal is safe. If I could see any one to tell me of him how glad I would be.

WIDOW Wisha,* don't be wearin' yourself away fretting avourneen.* Sure they're in the hands of God & his blessed Mother where ever they are.

GRACE Oh, what horrors War brings in its train!

WIDOW Sorra* worse, a cailin',* than what we had before War started. We should have had War years ago.

GRACE I have been dreaming—

WIDOW They're all stuff & nonsense them same drames. Put them out of your head alanna* & don't annoy yourself with them.

GRACE Oh, this one left such a vivid impression on my mind that you must listen to it. I saw in my dream thousands of men led by Donal and Father John. They were charging on some town like New Ross. The noise of the cannon and musketry and the hoarse shouting of the thousands was terrible. Hundreds were falling dead and dying. Then I heard Donal shout "One more charge, men, & Ireland is free!" Then the British broke and fled, hotly pursued by the insurgents and there was great joy on the faces of Father John and Donal. Then the scene changed. I saw before me a large plain covered with heaps of slain. On every side was blood blood blood and then I came upon two torn and mangled bodies—they were Father John and Donal. (*Weeps.*)

WIDOW Don't cry, alanna,* sure God's help is nearer than the door. (*KITTY heard singing outside.*)

WIDOW That's Kitty. She's singin' to show the coast is clear. Now if she has good news that's your drame out.

(*Enter KITTY D.R., embraces GRACE.*)

GRACE What of Donal, Kitty?

KITTY Safe & sound. Dickens a feather out of him. He'll be here himself immediately & I just came to prepare you.

(*Enter DONAL, embraces GRACE.*)

DONAL Grace!

GRACE Donal!

DONAL I have but a little while here, Dearest, for tomorrow we march on Arklow, where if we are successful Wicklow and Wexford are ours.

(*Exeunt WIDOW and KITTY D.L.*)

GRACE Oh, Donal, I wish it were all over and we had never to part again.

DONAL Patience, sweetheart, patience. While struggling to banish Ireland's troubles we must strive to forget our own. The tide of War is in our favour and cannot be long delayed. One more brave effort and Ireland's troubles and ours, darling, will be at an end. The men who fought at New Ross are men who in spite of the sad ending will yet bring freedom to Ireland.

GRACE Were you in command of New Ross, Donal?

DONAL No, I was on General Harvey's staff. We were drawn up on a sloping plain on the Three Bullet Gate side of the town, in full sight of the enemy, who were splendidly entrenched behind strong stone walls with several batteries of artillery. One unfortunate affair made havoc of the General's plan and put all chance of an organised attack on New Ross out of the question. That was the shooting of young Furlong, who was sent with a flag of truce to General Johnston. He had almost reached the gate when a volley rang out and he fell riddled with bullets. This was all in sight of our men, who were awaiting the word to advance. A shudder of horrified surprise passed along the insurgent ranks, as if not realising what had happened. There was a pause of dead silence. Then with a roar like the crashing of breakers on a rockbound coast the whole mass of men seemed to spring down the slope, deaf to commands and throwing discipline to the winds. They only knew that the walls of Ross lay between them and vengeance. No trained troops could have attacked Ross in such a manner, no trained troops could have taken Ross in such a manner, but our men were insane for vengeance and as often as they were driven back by the dreadful fire from the enemy's artillery they came charging on again. Through the whole forenoon the fight went on and the men who made the final charge on the Three Bullet Gate looked more like demons than human beings, with the sweat coursing down their powder blackened faces. I need not describe the scene when Ross was taken—it was terrible. Our men dashed in among the gunners, piking and slashing while others chased the flying cavalry and infantry through the town. The streets of Ross ran red and then as the shades of evening were falling, the relapse came. Such a body of men, after fighting the length of a broiling summer's day, could not possibly hold out against a fresh force. And the fresh force came. We officers did our best to rally our men, but they not having had anything to eat through the day, the temptation to drink was strong. Foot by foot we were driven back from the town and forced to retire, and thus Ross was won and lost in a day. But training and discipline must eventually triumph over mob bravery and for that reason the English are now in possession of New Ross. When we organise, drill, and inculcate a spirit of discipline into our men, the beating of the English soldiery will be a mere bagatelle.

GRACE Great God, Great God, beaten again. (*Enter* WIDOW, *D.L.*)

WIDOW There's a cup of tay ready in the room, Master Donal, for yourself & Miss Grace. (*Exeunt* OMNES. *Enter* NED, *sits at fire.*)

NED They must be all in the room. Bedad I never was so tired in all my life. I wonder whirs Kitty. I'll have a smoke. After Kitty there's nothing like a pull at the pipe. (*Enter* KITTY.)

KITTY Is that yourself, Ned? Are you long here?

NED Just after arrivin', Dickens a more.

KITTY I must get a cup of tay for you, you'll want it.

NED I'd be glad of that same, Kitty, though I'd go without tay for the rest of me days to see you & Mary Doyle fightin' the yeos. Faith I won't forget New Ross as long as I live. It's many a life the pair of you saved & Master Donal himself wouldn't be here only for your bravery.

KITTY Oh, Na Bock Lish.* Who wouldn't fight the cowardly yeos after seein' the way poor Furlong was shot & he the bearer of a flag of truce. Bedad the same shootin' cost them dear.

NED Aye, poor Furlong, God rest him. Ah, but we made them pay for his death. (*Enter* WIDOW *L. and* MYLES *R. and* MARY DOYLE.)

WIDOW You're lookin' well Myles. Is that yourself Ned? You're welcome. I'll have a cup of tay for the pair of you in less than no time. Tay is scarce in these times, for one can't go near New Ross at all.

MYLES Faith Mother you'd scarcely know New Ross there's so little of it left.

KITTY Faith & there'll be less when we're done with General Johnston & his scarlet runners.

MYLES Begorra,* mother, you'd hardly believe it if I was to tell you the great work these two girls did at New Ross.

MARY Now Myles don't be talkin' nonsense.

MYLES It's no nonsense at all. Would you believe it, Mother, that Mary Doyle, lookin' so simple & innocent there, proved herself as half a dozen men at the battle of New Ross.

MARY Musha,* never mind him, Mrs. Gallagher.

NED Faith it's nothin' but the truth.

(*Exeunt* KITTY *and* MARY *D.L.*)

WIDOW Tell us all about it.

NED When we were attackin' New Ross, we had made a breach at one point, after wipin' out a regiment of soldiers who held that part & then another regiment occupied a position above and swept the pass with their bullets. The General ordered the pikemen to charge across & commanded our riflemen to cover the charge with their fire & we found that the riflemen had no ammunition left. But what does my bould Mary do? Bravin' the storm of bullets from the redcoats above, she leaped into the pass of death and cutting the ammunition belts from the dead bodies of the fallen redcoats, she flung the belts back to our men. I never saw anything so quick. She got over fifty ammunition belts in about five minutes. The bullets were flying' around her all the time, but the favour of God protected her & having done her work she leaped back to the safety of our lines. Then our riflemen, makin' good use of the ammunition she gained for them, fired at the soldiers above & dislodged them, our Pikemen charged through the pass, and Ross was ours.

WIDOW It was a grand piece of work. Musha,* I'm sorry I'm not a bit younger meself. An' so you captured Ross.

MYLES Aye, but we lost it again, bad fortune to it. We sent the redcoats flyin' helter-skelter out of the town, but reinforcements came to them, the flyin' regiments were reformed, and all comin' back, took us by surprise & drove us out of the town.

NED But even there Mary Doyle proved herself the colleen she is. The boys in their hurry were leavin' behind a small cannon we had brought with us & that proved very useful. But my bould Mary sat herself on the barrel & declared she wouldn't stir a step from the place unless we brought her dear little gun along with us.

(*NED and MYLES take their tea. Enter KITTY D.R. with rifles and ammunition, which she puts on other table.*)

KITTY That much is ready for to-morrow anyhow, whoever lives to see it. (*NED goes to her.*) I'm gettin' ready my plans for to-morrow.

NED (*examining guns*) They're fine plans anyhow Kitty. You got these from the yeos?

KITTY Faith they threw them away so as they could run aisy.

NED It's time for us to be goin'. Come along, Myles & take some of Kitty's plans. I'll carry the rest.

MYLES Well, good bye mother till we meet again. (*Exeunt NED and MYLES D.R. Exeunt KITTY and WIDOW D.L. Enter DONAL and GRACE D.L.*)

DONAL You can now understand, dearest, that if we get the slightest assistance from France, the Irish Republic is assured.

GRACE Oh Donal, what a day that will be and how the people of Ireland will praise the brave men of Wexford who fought the battle of Independence so bravely and so well.

(*Enter* WIDOW *R. and* HOLT *after her.*)

WIDOW Here's General Holt to see you sir.

HOLT (*bowing*) You will pardon me if I have intruded upon your conversation, but in time of war we have to be rough and ready to all. (*GRACE bows and then talks aside in whisper with WIDOW.*) The following is a copy of a despatch received from General Tone. (*Reads.*) Paris, May 28th 1798—a small French force commanded by General Humbert left Brest this morning. The[y] have received instructions to land if possible on the coast of Wicklow or Wexford. Humbert is accompanied by my brother Matthew and several other Irish Officers. T. W. Tone.

DONAL That's good news anyhow.

HOLT We must hold a council of war at once.

GRACE (*aside to WIDOW*) Thank God, the French have sailed at last.

DONAL (*looking at maps*) General, we must first capture Dublin. The capital once in our hands we would have the remainder of the country with us within a week. Here we find a large and well provided garrison comprised of infantry, cavalry and artillery under command of General Needham at Arklow to intercept our march to Dublin. But a few days ago Arklow was unoccupied by the Royal troops and I urged upon Father Michael Murphy and his friend Esmond Kyne the necessity of a quick march on Dublin after our victory over Walpole's troops at Tubberneering. But they said no, that it would be impossible without aid from France, and now they have all mobilised against us. They swore to crush us once and for all. We must meet them one against a host and to-morrow we will either again be masters of Wicklow and Wexford or beaten back until the French do arrive.

HOLT We must fight our own cause, we cannot wait for the French. There is danger in delay.

DONAL Then let us order an attack upon Arklow at once. Let us make straight for Needham's centre, cut them in two, drive the yeomanry and cavalry into the sea and the infantry back upon Rathdrum, then unite with the Wicklow forces and on for Dublin. If we fail to unite with them we are lost.

(*Distant artillery heard.*)

HOLT There goes the first shot from our artillery. Come, Donal, come, there is no time to be lost.

DONAL Very well, General, I shall not leave your side until Dublin is ours. (*Exit* HOLT *R.*)

DONAL My time is up, dearest. I must get back to my post. You must pray for our victory. Take this pretty stilletto, it came from the sunny land of Italy. It will remind you of me. (*Gives stilletto.*)

GRACE I will take it Donal, though God knows you are always in my thoughts. (*Horses heard.*)

DONAL Our mounted men have departed. Now to organise a victory that shall shine in the annals of Ireland and freedom—a star of hope to struggling people the world over. Goodbye Grace, goodbye and when next we meet it may be in a free Ireland. (*Exit R.*)

(GRACE *looks out of window. More artillery.*)

GRACE God guide you, Donal.

WIDOW Sure he will. God's help is always nearer than the door.

(*More artillery and distant cheering.*)

GRACE God help us, will this war be ever ended?

WIDOW I'm afraid not, alanna.* The fight for Ireland will be long & sore. (*Horse heard approaching.*) We had better put out the candles, they'll only attract the soldiers. Go into the room, there, Miss Grace, some horsemen are coming.

GRACE Donal, Donal you are beaten. What will become of us. (*Bursts into tears.*)

WIDOW (*bolting Door*) They come nearer. Take my advice & go into the room. 'Tis sure to be strangers they are. (*Knocking heard at Door R. Exit* GRACE *D.L.*)

FOOTE (*outside*) Open the door, do you hear? (WIDOW *opens Door. Enter* FOOTE *and* SERGEANT.) What means the delay in opening the door for the King's officers? Do you know you are breaking the law, my good woman, by having candles lighted at this hour of night.

WIDOW I didn't know the time, your honour.

FOOTE Ah, indeed. Well, let us see who you have in the house (*seizing her*). Are you a loyal subject or not? (*To* SERGEANT.) Bolt that door and let no one into this house. (*To* WIDOW.) Do you hear, old hag?

(SERGEANT *makes for Door. Enter* GRACE *from Room L.*)

GRACE Take your hand off that poor old woman, Sir. Shame on you.

FOOTE Ha! There's a pretty wench. Then you come with me.

(*Throws* WIDOW *aside and makes at* GRACE, *who draws stilletto.*)

GRACE Touch either one of us if you dare.

(*Struggle. Enter* MARY DOYLE *R., seizes* FOOTE *and throws him left.*)

MARY Ha, my gallant Colonel, we are face to face at last. (*Goes to door.*) Come in boys, he's here.

(SERGEANT *makes off L.*)

FOOTE You pair of devils, I will show you no mercy now.

MARY I'm ready any time. Come, deliver up those despatches you have in your possession to me. You coward, you fled from the field of battle to meet a worse fate, for but one of us leaves this house alive. (*They fight.* FOOTE *drops sword and is run through and falls centre.* MARY *takes despatches from belt and holds them up with left hand.*)

MARY These despatches will mean the saving of General Humbert's plans.

CURTAIN

Scene 2

Exterior of farmhouse between Tullow and Hacketstown.

(*Enter* FATHER MURPHY *and* GENERAL HOLT *R.*)

FATHER MURPHY Good news, good news, General. Each succeeding day brings our mission nearer to a close. Thank God my forced inactivity is at an end and I am sufficiently recovered to take my place in the field again.

HOLT I hope you shall be able to join us tonight.

FATHER MURPHY With God's help, General. I hope to be able to join you tonight. Were our losses at Arklow heavy?

HOLT Yes, very heavy, Father John. One of the first to fall was the gallant leader of the Shelmaliers, Father Michael Murphy.

FATHER MURPHY God rest him, he did his best for his country and showed his flock the way.

HOLT True. I never saw his men fight better. One would think they had been fighting all their lives to see the cool manner the[y] received the charge of the heavy cavalry. They were simply irresistible, no troops could withstand their terrible onslaught. And yet their bravery went for nothing before the enemy's artillery.

FATHER MURPHY Hush, someone is coming. (*Looks off L.*) It's Ned.

(*Enter* NED *L.*)

NED How do you feel to-day, your reverence?

FATHER MURPHY Very well, Ned, thank God.

NED Amen, your reverence. The boys are all longin' to see you back again. I was forgettin' that I had somethin' for you, General (*gives letter*).

HOLT (*reads in silence*) Very well, Ned, I shall join them immediately. Good bye Father John, we shall meet tonight.

(*Shakes hands and exits L.; enter* WIDOW *R.*)

WIDOW Well Ned, did you get back? Did you remember all I told you to get in Tullow.

NED To be sure I did. Here's the lot for you. (*Hands parcel.*) I forgot nothin'.

WIDOW Did you call for the coat for his Reverence?

NED I have it here under my arm as snug as a thrush in a clump, & a grand article it is too. Wait till you see it. (*Opens coat.*)

WIDOW Oh, isn't it grand? Have a look at it your reverence.

FATHER MURPHY Yes, it will do nicely and help to throw off the suspicion my clerical garb would surely bring on me.

NED It's your only chance, your reverence. When I was comin' down the main street of Tullow who should I see at the barrack gate talkin' to Major Sandys & Colonel Needham but Biddy Dolan, bad luck to her, God pardon me this blessed & holy day. I turned back when I saw her & took the fields instead of the road home.

FATHER MURPHY Are you quite sure you have not been followed?

NED The divil a fear, your reverence. I don't believe they saw me at all, at all.

FATHER MURPHY Very good. Let us hope you are right.

WIDOW Well, you'd better come inside, your Reverence, & change your coat at once. (*Exeunt all into house R.*)

(*Enter* BIDDY DOLAN *and* COLONEL NEEDHAM *L.*)

BIDDY So far, so good. One of those men I am almost sure is the man we saw in Tullow today. The other is a stranger to me.

NEEDHAM You must be gifted with remarkable sight, Miss Dolan. Personally, at the distance I could not distinguish one from the other.

BIDDY I must again remind you, Colonel, not to use my name aloud. Trees have ears.

NEEDHAM Quite right, Miss Dol— oh, dash it all, there it goes again! By the way, did you remark the horses in the farm yard?

BIDDY I did, they seem to have travelled far. However, we had better get back for a company of Dragoons and make a thorough search through this neighbourhood.

NEEDHAM Stay a moment. You were saying something to Major Sandys in Tullow about O'Byrne. Have you seen him lately?

BIDDY Yes, I have. He has been wounded and if you wish to get rid of him we can pounce upon him in his hiding place.

NEEDHAM This is news. Tell me his whereabouts.

BIDDY You know the old mill at Carnew.

NEEDHAM Yes, I do.

BIDDY Last night I was passing along and I stopped my pony to give him a drink in the mill race, and as the moon threw her broad beamy light above the mountains I saw the form of a wounded man scramble in through the door of the mill. He stopped suddenly and turned his face around towards where I was. The moon's rays fell full on his pale face. Then in the silence of the night there was a faint whistle and a man came running up and he says "Master Donal, are ye there?" So I mounted my pony and soon showed them the full front of my back.

NEEDHAM Good, good. I wish you could have let me know before now.

BIDDY Well, I was waiting for the Governor to issue a reward for his head [and] I saw it in Tullow this morning posted up on the Barrack wall. Here is a copy of it. The Government are getting short of money I'm thinking and they have no wish to part with the money or pay for the work done for them. There is £150 offered for O'Byrne dead or alive.

NEEDHAM You are clever—too clever. You must take no heed of what the Government does. We must get O'Byrne out of the way at any price. You can do it if you like. I must have the girl, you understand—Grace Bassett.

BIDDY Surely, Colonel; you don't want me to win honour for you to wear. We can do the job ourselves, then no one will be the wiser.

NEEDHAM Villain, would you entrap me?

BIDDY Only in the same cage as myself and that is fair when life is to be risked.

NEEDHAM Be it so. You make haste. Send me all the available troops you can get together. I shall await them. You then proceed to the mill and await me there. This time it shall be a case of "'Walk into my parlour,' says the spider to the fly." (*Exit* NEEDHAM *L.*)

BIDDY Take care, Colonel, that you don't be the fly. But whether he fails to catch the rebels, I'll make sure I get my money all the same. (*Exit L.*)

(NED *looks out through window and then enters.*)

NED I thought I heard some one talkin'. I must have been dramin' at the fire. I wonder what the mischief has happened to Kitty. Anyhow I'll have a smoke. After Kitty there's nothing in the world like a pull at the pipe. (*Sits down and smokes.*)

(*Enter* GRACE *R.*)

NED (*rising*) Musha,* Miss Grace, is that yourself. How is every inch of you?

GRACE Well, thank you, Ned. Is Father John here?

NED He is, Miss. Wait till I give him a call. (*Calls.*)

(*Enter* FATHER MURPHY *in civilian dress.*)

GRACE My dear Father John, forgive me for not coming to see you sooner, but the strict watch kept on my movements in Tullow made it impossible for me to visit you. Are you quite recovered?

FATHER MURPHY Completely, my child, thanks to Him who decrees life and death.

GRACE Thank God you have your strength, because I risked all to come here to tell you to leave this place at once. A search party may be here at any moment. Miss Dolan is at the bottom of it all.

FATHER MURPHY I have already made preparations to leave at nightfall. What is this coming across the field?

GRACE It's a man, and my goodness he's carrying a girl.

NED It's Myles, it's Myles. I'll go & give him a hand.

(*Exit. Enter* NED *and* MYLES *carrying* KITTY. *Seat her on bench.*)

FATHER MURPHY Good gracious, what has happened?

KITTY The sogers— (*she sinks back.*)

WIDOW Here's somethin' that will do the crathur good.

NED Kitty darlin'!

WIDOW She's comin to, now, avic.*

KITTY I met a party of dragoons comin' from Hacketstown & one of them made a cut of his sword at me. Luckily I was struck with the flat of it, but the wound I got at Ballyellis startin' to bleed, I lost my senses. The sogers, thinkin' I was dead, mounted their horses & rode away.

MYLES I found her about three miles this side of Hacketstown lyin' across the road & brought her here.

GRACE What of Donal, Kitty? Have you seen him lately?

KITTY He's finely, miss, considerin' himself & the boys are havin' a busy time skirmishin' round the country. But now—

GRACE What, Kitty? Tell me.

KITTY He's been wounded, miss. But it won't be much.

FATHER MURPHY (*to* WIDOW) You had better go and attend to him. You go with her, Grace. Ned will escort you.

GRACE Donal wounded! My God, my God!

FATHER MURPHY Be of good cheer, my child. God in his goodness will bring us safely through. We must part now and God knows if we shall ever meet again. May God and his angels guard you all and bring you safely through the troubles of the coming time.

NED Come along now before night falls. (*Exeunt* NED, KITTY, WIDOW, *and* GRACE *R.*)

MYLES Now for the road, your reverence.

FATHER MURPHY And the tented field, Myles. To-morrow Tone may arrive from France, then ho for Dublin Town. (*Both go into house.*)

(*Enter* COLONEL NEEDHAM *and* SOLDIERS.)

NEEDHAM Guard every door, let no one pass, in or out! (*Knocks.*) Open in the King's name. (*Enter* FATHER MURPHY.) Pardon me, sir. You are a stranger in these parts.

FATHER MURPHY I am an Irish gentleman.

NEEDHAM Search the house, Sergeant. (Exit SERGEANT.) Here, you fellows, search this Irish gentleman. (SOLDIER *takes stole from* FATHER MURPHY'*s pocket and holds it up.*)

NEEDHAM A mass-monger, by the Lord! Here's luck!

(*Enter* SERGEANT *and* MYLES.)

NEEDHAM Ha, this man is a peasant, money may tempt him. Come here, my good fellow. Bring him here, men. (SOLDIERS *drag* MYLES *across stage.*) Now, my good fellow, I'll give you ten pounds to tell me who this gentleman is.

MYLES I wouldn't betray him for £10,000, let alone £10.

NEEDHAM Thank you, you have betrayed him by that speech. Bind the brace, men. Now for Tullow and our sport to-night shall be roasting rebel priests. Right turn, quick march!

(*Exeunt.*)

BLACK OUT

Music

Scene 3

OLD MILL AT CARNEW

(*Door L. Large opening at back with platform in front and rope hanging behind. Only one door. Enter* GRACE. [*MS. B.: One of the compartments of an old water mill. Near Carnew. The only means of entrance is by a door L.3.E., a large opening in back through which is seen the open country, a rope hangs from C. of opening in front of opening, on stage is a platform with steps from R.C. to R. supposed to lead into another compartment in the Mill. Above lights down, the recess must be kept very dark. Enter* GRACE *as scene opens up, cloaked and with lantern.*])

GRACE Here is the place he was last tracked to, and in this old mill, of which so many fearful tales are told, it is such a lonely place. But what of that, the whole world would be lonely without my beloved Donal and why should I not venture into the deepest cave to seek him. (*Examining.*) I see some footprints here and here and up to the old broken window. There seems to have been a struggle here. Oh Heaven, if he should have been betrayed! Ned told me of rooms upstairs. I will seek him and with God's help I shall find him. (*Exits up steps R. A pause, then enter* NEEDHAM *and* BIDDY *L.*)

BIDDY There's no one here at all, at all. He mustn't have arrived yet.

NEEDHAM So it would appear, but he might be here and we could not see him until the moon rises above the mountain. You understand what we are to do?

BIDDY Yes, to arrest Donal O'Byrne, a desperate villain that has loyal subjects like you and me in dread of our lives, and if he resists to blow his brains out.

NEEDHAM No, no, the report of fire arms might attract notice and we want to do the job as quietly as we can. Better leave that pistol of yours aside, lest you might be tempted to shoot me—I mean by accident. Put it down anywhere. Leave it on the steps there. You saw General Johnston give me this letter.

BIDDY That I will take my oath on.

NEEDHAM Well now I put it in your hands and as a sworn servant of His Majesty George III you will arrest the man I will point out to you as [one of] the two persons described in it. You know whom I mean—Donal O'Byrne and the girl Grace Bassett, whom we saw enter the mill a few moments ago.

BIDDY Well, it will be they or I for it, if I don't. By the way did not General Johnston give you something for me?

NEEDHAM Oh, yes he did, some money. So now we have an equal share in the responsibility and can work without fear of betrayal on the part of one.

BIDDY I was told that this old mill was haunted by the ghost of a croppie* who was hanged here by some of your men early in this year because he would not betray the secrets of the United Men.

NEEDHAM Oh, what stuff and nonsense. My dear girl, when a man leaves this world of sorrow and joys he does not trouble to come back again.

BIDDY But Colonel, don't you think that we had better have your men near at hand. I feel fainting already. Have you got your flask of brandy with you?

NEEDHAM No, unfortunately, in the hurry I have forgotten it. Are you in need of it?

BIDDY Yes I am, a drop might steady my nerves.

NEEDHAM Unsteady you mean. Remember you work for money and shall have plenty of gold in your pocket to-night if all goes well.

BIDDY That's enough. I'll not flinch and the long sought prize shall be ours.

(*Voices heard outside.*)

NEEDHAM Hush. Footsteps and voices. Let us conceal ourselves until we see who comes. (*Exeunt up steps and disappear left. Enter* NED *and* DONAL *L.* DONAL*'s arm in sling and head bandaged.*)

NED An' so this is your hidin' place until you are strong enough to leave it. Bedad you'll not be troubled with much company here for fear you might be proud takin' tay wid the ghost.

DONAL Oh, I don't expect a visit from the poor boy though if he came I would strive to make him welcome.

NED You would? Oh, so would I, provided he came in the day time. But I wouldn't like to stop here all night by myself in case he might mistake me for the North Corks that hanged him & take a fancy to do me an evil & tell m[e] my days were numbered & the exact time I'm goin' to die.

DONAL You don't believe in ghosts, do you? You, a man who has been through all the big engagements.

NED Well, I know some men don't or purtend they don't. But what you learn to believe as a child, it's hard to forget or disbelieve when you grow up. I had a great respect for my granny, & she believed in ghosts & taught me to believe the same & out of regard to her memory I stick to it. But anyhow this is a grand hidin' place as there's more than one way of gettin' off if you were tracked or pursued.

DONAL Indeed. I have not observed. Where are they?

NED Well, in the first place if you were followed up by that path leadin' to this door you've only to go up to this openin' that was once a window & by the aid of the rope hangin' from the crane drop yourself down on the bank of the river not far from the ferry where there's always a boat ready to take you across.

DONAL That's worth knowing. Is the rope secure do you think, Ned?

NED Well, I dunno. It has been so long exposed to all weathers, it may be rotten. (*Hangs out of it.*) It's all right; it's as sound as a bell.

DONAL And the other road to escape.

NED Well, it isn't a road, although it's a way. It's by raising a trap door that's just inside this door here & takin' a dive down the chute that leads to the mill wheel & into the race, which will carry you down the river a long ways off.

DONAL In how many pieces? For of course I should be crushed to death by the mill wheel.

NED Oh, sure the wheel isn't workin' now. Just before the mill was desarted the wheel was lifted up above the current & there's now plenty of room to pass under it. When I was a boy I done it more than once for a bet. (*Going to Door.*) Well, I must be goin' on my errand to tell his reverence you are safe & out of danger. Will I come back after for you to come home with me to my cabin? You'll be safe there & the mother'll take care of you.

DONAL That might involve you as giving shelter to an outlaw.

NED Oh, never mind that.

DONAL I thank you Ned for the kind hospitality you have offered me, but I do not wish to place the rope round your neck for the sake of saving my own.

NED Well, if you won't come with me, I can bring you a shakedown of straw & a blanket & quilt. Then if the ghost does come you can do as the childher do, put your head under the blankets & bid him do his worst. Let me think. This will be my shortest way (*going down rope*). It's a long way to drop, but though it's mortial hard to go up, it an aisy matter to go down in the world, isn't it. (*NED goes down.*)

DONAL So again I seem to stand in danger of a slip twixt the cup and the lip. Ah, Grace, better to have died far away with your image shining in my heart than to come back here and be obliged to tear it thence (*goes up steps*). There are soldiers outside! Some one is coming. It's a girl, she must have escaped from the soldiers. I shall wait here until I see who she is. (*Hides. Enter* MARY DOYLE *L.*)

MARY Ha, how neatly I gave them the slip. What will ould Needham say when he finds I'm gone. While the soldiers were jiggin' away in the guard room, faith it was other steps I was takin! What a night of it I've had. But poor Father John & Myles. I wonder will they escape. It must be late now, & the martial law out & the soldiers out too, & maybe they're hard upon my track. Bedad, if they catch me this time my bread is baked without an oven & the divil of it all is I can't get out of here for fear of meetin' the soldiers. Whist,* what's that. Be the vartue of my oath, it's the soldiers. I know their tramp. Bad luck to them, couldn't they go some other way but this. Whist,* they're comin', then I had better be goin'. No, second thoughts are best, I won't. I'll hide here. (*Goes towards platform.*)

DONAL Mary, is that you? Come here. What did you say of Father John and Myles?

MARY They have been arrested. I escaped. For God's sake, man, go & hide somewhere. You are weak, you are wounded. See, Needham is coming.

DONAL I won't leave you to be arrested again.

MARY You go. You escape. If I am taken it matters little about me. You are a great man & can live to revenge those who suffered & died on the scaffold in defence of their country. Go, escape while you have time. Give me your sword. They may not find me and you are unable to use it.

DONAL I will, Mary, but if I hear any noise, I shall come to your assistance. (*Exits R.*)

MARY I will defend him with my own life.

(*Enter* COLONEL NEEDHAM *on platform L.*)

NEEDHAM You here, Mary Doyle and escaped. Then I arrest you in the King's name.

MARY You shall never take me alive.

(*They fight.* BIDDY *comes on platform and shoots* MARY, *who falls R. Enter* SOLDIERS *L.*)

BIDDY I saved your bacon that time, Colonel.

NEEDHAM She is out of our way at last, Ha ha!

BIDDY (*looking at* MARY) She is not dead, she lives. Here men, pitch her into the mill race, that will finish her. (*SOLDIERS go to take up MARY. Enter GRACE on platform.*)

GRACE Hold, you murderers.

BIDDY The ghost. The ghost of the murdered croppie.* (*Faints.*)

NEEDHAM Ghost be damned, it's a woman (*drags her centre*). What, Grace Bassett.

GRACE You cowards, do you call yourselves men?

NEEDHAM Hold your tongue, or you shall quickly join your friend Mary Doyle in the millrace. You will remain here with me till I can get a clergyman to marry us and make an honest woman of you.

GRACE Marry you sir. I would advise you to play your part more like a man and less like a beast.

NEEDHAM Hold your tongue I tell you.

GRACE Marry you. No. I'd prefer death first. (*Seizes her, she wrests away.*)

NEEDHAM Then death be it. (*GRACE screams.*) Seize her, men, her screams will bring the rebel army swarming upon us. (*GRACE shoots SERGEANT, DONAL enters R., NED and PEASANTS L. SOLDIERS overpowered.*)

TABLEAU

CURTAIN

ACT IV

Scene 1

Needham's quarters, Wexford. Three weeks elapse.

(*Same as Act I, Scene 1. NEEDHAM seated.*)

NEEDHAM Well, of all the beastly countries I was ever in, this is the [MS. B: worst]. Though we have the rebellion almost crushed as far as Wexford [MS. B: is] concerned still the cost was heavy and King George's Ministers [MS. B: will] remember it for some time. If the rebels had been properly led [MS. B: deuce knows] how it would have gone. (*Enter SERGEANT.*)

SERGEANT Lady to see you sir.

NEEDHAM Show her in, Sergeant.

SERGEANT Certainly, sir. (*Enter* BIDDY *veiled. Exit* SERGEANT.)

NEEDHAM Whom have I the honour of addressing? (BIDDY *removes veil.*)

NEEDHAM Oh, Miss Dolan! Be seated.

BIDDY I just dropped in for a little money and to tell you that a French force has landed at Killala.

NEEDHAM French troops in Ireland! Impossible!

BIDDY Nothing is impossible to the little Corporal.

NEEDHAM Surely you don't mean to say that Bonaparte is with them.

BIDDY So I heard. But anyhow it's a matter of indifference to me whether he is or not. I want £150 for the arrest of Billy Byrne and £350 for [MS. B: Father] John Murphy and his friend Myles Gallagher who were hanged at Tullow. The job was done very cheap, considering I have Mat, Davis, Doyle and [Dinio?] to pay out of it. Those are the fellows who swore against Billy Byrne at Wicklow Gaol, and they *must* be paid.

NEEDHAM I haven't the slightest intention of paying you such huge sums. [MS. B: Even if you] were the principal cause of bringing those people to the gallows, [MS. B: you can't] bring them to life again.

BIDDY (*drawing pistol*) I came prepared for such an answer. My motto [MS. B: is make] hay while the sun shines. Tomorrow the rebels may be on top and you [MS. B: won't be] in a position to pay. Now is the time.

NEEDHAM Surely you wouldn't murder me?

BIDDY There's thousands in Ireland would bless me if I did.

NEEDHAM Well, I can give you £300 and an order for the balance. (*Gives her [MS. B: notes].*)

BIDDY That's more like business. (*Counts notes.*)

NEEDHAM (*writing*) By Gad, I shall yet strike a sore balance with you, [MS. B: my lady,] but just now you are useful.

BIDDY What's that you say, Colonel?

NEEDHAM I was wondering where Miss Bassett is. Have you any idea?

BIDDY None save that she has been with the rebels ever since the hostilities. Beat the rebels, Colonel, and you have Grace Bassett.

NEEDHAM Yes, by Jove, you are right and I will beat them. Make them fly like sheep.

BIDDY You have a very short memory Colonel. What about Ballyellis, where, thanks to a good horse, you were the only one to escape.

NEEDHAM I think, Miss Dolan, your business here is finished. Good day.

BIDDY Good day, *Colonel* Needham. (*Exits.*)

NEEDHAM [MS. B: Well,] of all the devils I ever met she is the worst.

(*Enter* SERGEANT *with letter.*)

SERGEANT Despatch from General Lake, sir. (*Exits.*)

NEEDHAM From General Lake (*reading*) "March with all possible speed to intercept French force near Castlebar." Fighting French is not in my line; however, orders are orders and must be obeyed.

CURTAIN

Scene 2

Road near Ballyellis [Ms. B: Hill], Three weeks later.
(*Enter* NED *and* KITTY *R. Front Cloth.*)

NED Bedad, Kitty, that's great news entirely. I suppose it'll be no time now until you see me goin' round dressed up in a grand French uniform with a grand sword hangin' by my side & a big cocked hat & then I'll be General Ned Traynor, eh, what do you say, Kitty?

KITTY Sure, Miss Grace was readin' it out of the paper for me today—last week's paper it was—& this is what she said. That Frinch General—what's this his name is—oh its the quare name it is—Hubert I think it was.

NED No no, Kitty; it's Humbert, long life to him.

KITTY How well I knew it was spelt with a H— well, as I was sayin' there were thousands of English & only a handful of the French, & the French beat the English. Sure wasn't it a great battle. That all happened at a place called Castlebar.

NED Aye & I'm tould that they'll soon be here. Tell me, Kitty, when is Miss Grace to be married?

KITTY In the mornin' Ned & I'm to be bridesmaid & I've a grand new dress, oh wait until you see it. Come on Ned, I've such a lot to do & I want you to milk the cows & I'll give you a kiss.

NED You will. Begorra* then I'll do that same for you Kitty. Come on now, hould up your sweet little lips.

(*Kisses her. Enter* DONAL *R.*)

DONAL Now Ned that's not fair.

NED All's fair in love & war, sir.

KITTY It's meself that's glad to see you, Master Donal. (*They both shake hands with him.*)

NED Bedad you're nearly as strong as ever you were, though you were nigh as dead as a maggot.

DONAL Yes, I am as strong as ever, thank God, but my heart grieves for those brave hearts that sleep beneath the sod. Poor Father John & Myles Gallagher in Tullow & bravest of all Mary Doyle who tried to save my life in the old mill & in doing so poor girl lost her own. But I will avenge them & show no mercy.

NED Tell me, how did you get back out of the mill race?

DONAL When I had recovered myself sufficiently I dropped through the trap door you had previously shown me and had just reached the water when I heard a cry for help. I scrambled back again and just reached the platform in time to keep the soldiers at bay until your arrival with the boys.

NED Bedad the ghost stood a good friend to you & all of us for when Biddy Dolan fainted it cowed the soldiers & it was then an easy task to overpower them.

KITTY Oh, but poor Mary Doyle! They set the barn on fire when they were running away from Scullabogue & then they said it was the Wexford men that did it.

DONAL It's a cowardly lie put forth by the yeomanry and their friends.

NED Everyone knows that our men had nothin' to do with it at all, at all! Here comes General Holt.

(*Enter* HOLT, *shakes hands.*)

HOLT You're just the man I wished to see. How are you after your long illness?

DONAL Strong as ever, thank Goodness.

HOLT The latest newspapers to hand contain accounts of the surrender of the French force which landed in the West six weeks ago. 'Twas an unfortunate thing they did not land this side.

DONAL Had they landed on the coast of Wicklow or Wexford we would be in possession of Dublin by this.

NED That's the worst news I've heard to-day.

HOLT Not so terrible to my mind. Humbert's small force has at least proved one thing and that is the easy manner in which a foreign army can land in Ireland in spite of England's fleet. Tone is still in Paris. You must start for the French capital at once and bring the latest news to Tone, aiding him in every possible manner to impress upon the French executive the importance of Ireland.

DONAL I thought that my wanderings were over, but I am ready to start for Ireland's sake.

HOLT Tomorrow you will be married to Grace Bassett. Your trip to Paris will also be your honeymoon.

DONAL I have a few visits to make this evening, I must be off. Come General, come Ned and you Kitty. (*Exeunt all L. Enter BIDDY DOLAN and SOLDIERS R.*)

BIDDY Halt! Who are those people going down the road? (*Enter NEEDHAM R.*)

BIDDY Well, my redoubtable warrior, you have returned from your campaign in the west?

NEEDHAM Straight from Ballinamuck, where the French surrendered after three days' fighting. We outnumbered them by five to one. We made sure by force of numbers not to have another Castlebar. Any news this side?

BIDDY Nothing particular except that Grace Bassett will be married to-morrow.

NEEDHAM Grace married—to whom?

BIDDY Donal Don O'Byrne.

NEEDHAM Impossible, impossible!

BIDDY Impossible? the word does not exist. They are in Dublin by this.

NEEDHAM Then I am finished in that quarter. Well, blessed is he that expects nothing, for he surely won't be disappointed.

BIDDY I'm glad to hear you say that, but don't despair, Colonel. You can marry me.

NEEDHAM The Devil I can!

BIDDY Oh but you must. We know too much about each other [MS. B: to part].

NEEDHAM Well, I might do worse. But, not much worse. Then come along. Now men, right turn, quick march! (*Exeunt SOLDIERS, NEEDHAM and BIDDY arm in arm.*)

Scene 3

Drawing Room at Ballymanus House, three weeks later.

(*Table L., chair beside it, arm chair R., Door C.B. and R. and L. OFFICER seated at table as curtain rises.*)

FRENCH OFFICER (*Sol[o?]*) I am surprised that Byrne has not yet returned. I sincerely hope he has not met with an accident; men of his abilities cannot be spared at such times as these. (*Enter GRACE R.*)

GRACE (*confused*) Pardon, Monsieur, I thought you were away.

FRENCH OFFICER (*bowing*) Not a word madamoiselle. I was just thinking of you as I wish to express my sorrow at your dear friend's fate. Such is the fortune of war, a soldier's life, a soldier's death.

GRACE 'Tis hard to bear. But mourning for Fathers, Brothers, and husbands is common in Wexford today.

FRENCH OFFICER Yes, your Wexford men are certainly bravehearted fellows and the making of wonderful soldiers.

GRACE 'Tis terrible to think that amongst such men traitors are found who [f]atten on their comrades' blood.

FRENCH OFFICER Not peculiarly Irish, Madamoiselle, but a trait of human nature the world over; my France, too, has had her share of treacherous sons.

GRACE (*sighing*) The lack of military discipline and military punishment amongst the Insurgents is powerful incentive to the traitor. Holt is one of few leaders who has given his men a military training.

FRENCH OFFICER (*enthus[iastically]*) Yes! Yes! Holt is [a] really splendid fellow. I was astonished at the splendid manner he handled his men. Were it not for their ordinary clothes I would say they were King George's smartest troops.

GRACE And the pity of it, Holt stands alone.

FRENCH OFFICER And there you have the weak spot in your movement. The mob is willing, but organising ability is wofully lacking. Some one is at the door. Come in.

(*Enter* KITTY *R.*)

KITTY There's a gentleman to see you, sir. He's waiting for you in the courtyard (*FRENCH OFFICER bows and exits R.*)

GRACE Stay, Kitty, I wish to speak to you.

KITTY Sure there isn't a sign of wan of them yet & I'm sick waitin'. These Frinch gintlemen inside bother me entirely with their praise of La Belle France, & though I know it couldn't be half as nice as Ireland, I wish you were there safe & sound, Miss Grace.

GRACE And so we will soon, please God. But we won't be long away, Kitty, and Ireland's day will surely come.

KITTY And I hope when you're comin' back, Miss Grace, that you'll be bringin' back a few thousand big Frinch sogers to larrup the mischief out of the murderin' red coats.

GRACE I hope so. (*Enter* NED *R.*)

NED Well bad luck to them sogers. I had the divil's own job to get here unbeknownst to them & only for Holt & his men it's as like as not I'd be in Wicklow Gaol this minute. Master Donal is close behind; he sent me on to see if everything was right.

KITTY Why wouldn't everything be right & rale Frinch Officers stoppin' in the house with us. Sure the whole British army wouldn't tackle one of thim after Castlebar.

NED Frinch Officers, Kitty? You don't tell me!

KITTY Yes I do tell you. They belong to that Frinch schooner that's out in the bay, that's goin' back to France when Master Donal & Miss Grace get on board.

(*Enter* DONAL *and* FRENCH OFFICER *Centre.*)

FRENCH OFFICER Within an hour's time we leave the coast of Wicklow.

DONAL One short hour and I shall again become a wanderer and when shall my feet again press the soil of Ireland?

GRACE Soon, Donal, the darkest hour is just before the dawn.

FRENCH OFFICER I too, ardently hope to revisit your beautiful country with the brave grenadiers of La Belle France.

NED Long life to yourself and La Belle France.

DONAL When a stranger takes such an interest in my poor country how much greater should my faith be in the ultimate triumph of our cause.

GRACE That's right, Donal. You have important work to do for Ireland in the land we are going to and a strong faith in the God of Justice will ensure success.

DONAL God in his wisdom gave me a great gift when he gave me you. Go now dearest and make ready to start.

GRACE And believe me Donal, sad as our parting from our country may be, my hopes are strong and bright and there will yet be peace and happiness in our own dear country. (*Exeunt* GRACE *and* KITTY *R. Shots heard outside.*)

NED Them devils of soldiers again. (*Makes ready pistol.* COLONEL NEEDHAM *rushes in centre, followed by* HOLT *and* PEASANTS.)

HOLT I arrest you, Colonel Needham, in the name of the Irish Republic.

(NEEDHAM *draws sword, strikes at* HOLT, *blow stopped by* FRENCH OFFICER *and* DONAL. FRENCH OFFICER *takes* NEEDHAM'*s sword.*)

DONAL Now sir, what have you to say for yourself?

NEEDHAM Nothing that can save me from the fate which awaits me. I escaped the French cannon in the West to meet my fate at the hands of a cur like you.

FRENCH OFFICER I will hear no more of this, sir. Let the prisoners be searched.

HOLT Send in Miss Dolan, Ned. (*Exit* NED C.)

FRENCH OFFICER We shall deal with traitors as traitors should be dealt with, General Holt.

(*Enter* BIDDY, *guarded.* NED *and* OTHERS *salute.*)

FRENCH OFFICER (*to* BIDDY) You, Miss Dolan, have been found in arms against your countrymen. (*To* NEEDHAM) As for you sir, your Government has executed two French officers who were prisoners of war—Matthew Tone and Bartholomew Teeling, at Arbour Hill, Dublin, and in return for these brave men's deaths we shall execute you both. Take them away, General.

HOLT And their punishment, sir?

FRENCH OFFICER In half an hour's time let a platoon be formed on the lawn yonder. Then let them be led forth and at sunset there shot!

BIDDY Is there no hope for me, Gentlemen?

FRENCH OFFICER None whatever. You must meet the fate you richly deserve.

NEEDHAM May I ask one request before I die and that is to be allowed to see Grace Bassett. You Frenchmen are generous even in your worst moods.

FRENCH OFFICER Why should we allow you to see this lady?

NEEDHAM Because I should like to ask her forgiveness.

DONAL Be it so, sir.

FRENCH OFFICER Very well. Let the interview not last more than ten minutes. Then let him be taken away. (*To DONAL*) Be ready to start at the appointed time. (*Exeunt HOLT and FRENCH OFFICER.*)

BIDDY Won't you say goodbye to me, Donal? (*Holds out her hand.*)

DONAL I refuse to hold any words with a traitress. (*Exits.*)

BIDDY Oh, how wretched a woman I am now. Not a friend to say goodbye. Curse you, Colonel Needham, you were the first man who ruined me. Where are now all the promises of your government? I hope that my death will be a warning to all who in the future may depend on the generosity of the English Government, or on such a man as you. I die the death of a traitor; no one will ever breathe a prayer for my soul's repose, nor shed a tear; all that will be known is that I shall live in the memory of my countrymen [who will] say "Here lie the remains of the notorious informer, Curse her—curse her!" (*Exit guarded by NED and OTHERS. Enter GRACE and HOLT.*)

HOLT I will be near if required. (*Exits.*)

GRACE Well, sir, what is it now?

NEEDHAM Won't you shake hands and be friends? It may be the last time in this world we will ever meet again.

GRACE There is no reason why I should. There was never any friendship between us. What have you done now?

NEEDHAM I am condemned to be shot as a spy at sunset.

GRACE What have I to do with that?

NEEDHAM Nothing, but I should like to ask your forgiveness for all the wrongs I have done you.

GRACE Forgive you, indeed, do you imagine for a moment that I could forgive you. No. Go ask forgiveness of your God, for he alone can forgive you now.

NEEDHAM Ah, Grace, do not be so cruel. A few moments ago I did not fear to die, but now the fact of seeing you again brings back all the memories of the past. I would like to live—bare life is all that I ask. I will do anything for you. You alone can save me—one word from you and they will let me go free.

GRACE Save your life! Did you hear the cries of the widows and orphans when they appealed to you for mercy? Did you try to save Myles Gallagher and Father John Murphy from the awful death they received at the hands of your unmerciful men? Did you hear my cries when I appealed to you in the old mill when you swore I should die if I refused to wed you? And the awful death you gave Mary Doyle and swore I should meet the same.

NEEDHAM I am impulsive. I did not mean it—you know it—what I say is true. I will lead a new life, be a new man—only spare me. I will leave the country—give you all I possess—only save me, save me. I cannot die, you must not see me die. Look, see, already the sun is setting. I have but a few moments more to live. Speak and I will be set at liberty—I swear to you I will keep my word—I will keep———

GRACE Yes, swear—and I swear to you as you have sworn to me in the old mill that your time would come and it has come now. Go, coward and meet your fate. (*She throws him off, he falls on his hands. Enter* FRENCH OFFICER *and* HOLT *and* NED.)

FRENCH OFFICER Time's up. Not another word. (*NEEDHAM rises.*)

NEEDHAM I am ready, Sir, and I hope that the next man to mount the gallows in Ireland will be O'Byrne. Curse him, he'll die like a dog. (*Exits followed by* FRENCH OFFICER. *Shots heard outside.*)

NED God rest them. They're gone now & I hope it's no harm to pray for their souls' repose.

KITTY Amen, Ned, & it's a long road that has no turn. Your luggage is gone to the boat, Miss Grace; that tall Frinch chap took it with him just now. (*Enter* FRENCH OFFICER *and* SOLDIERS.)

FRENCH OFFICER Time's up, Colonel O'Byrne. We must now set sail for Brest. The escort awaits you.

DONAL Thanks, monsieur. Good-bye, all, till we meet again.

HOLT Remember, Donal, we shall be keeping the heather ablaze until you return.

DONAL And I can never know true happiness, General, until I take my place once more with the men of Wicklow and Wexford in the struggle for Independence.

CURTAIN

END

QUEENS

Telephone 3016— THEATRE Great Brunswick St., Dublin

Proprietors	THE QUEEN'S THEATRE (DUBLIN) LIMITED
General Manager	Mr. CHARLES F. WRIGHT
Acting Manager	Mr. JOHN L. SULLIVAN
Musical Director	Mr. SAMUEL LEVENSTON

6-30 | Twice Nightly | 8-30

MONDAY, 26th APRIL, '20, and during the week

P. J. BOURKE'S

PRINCIPAL COMPANY IN THE GREAT HISTORICAL IRISH DRAMA

FOR THE LAND SHE LOVED

TIME—THE SPRING OF 1798

GENERAL MUNRO (of the United Irishmen)	T. MORAN
GEORGE MAURICE GRAY	J. L. SULLIVAN
DERMOT McMAHON	P. McCORMAC
SQUIRE GRAY (Governor General of Down)	LEO STRONG
COLONEL JOHNSTON	P. J. BOURKE
SERGEANT LOUTH	TED WARNER
MATT McGRATH	F. FOX
SHAMUS O'FLYNN	W. WATERS
GENERAL SIR JOHN NUGENT	J. B. CARRICKFORD
BETSY GRAY (The Heroine of Ballinahinch)	Miss FITZPATRICK
SHEELAH DE LACY (Her Maid)	Miss LENA PEMBROKE
Mrs. McGRATH	Miss MAY SWEENEY
LADY LUCY NUGENT (In the Secret Service)	Miss LOUIE GRAFTON

SOLDIERS, GUESTS, PEASANTRY.

Produced by J. B. CARRICKFORD

Scene 1	The Blacksmith's Forge at Ballinahinch	Scene 6	Exterior of McGrath's Cottage
Scene 2	Interior of Ballinahinch Barracks	Scene 7	Interior of Matt's Forge
Scene 3	Drawingroom in Ballinahinch Castle	Scene 8	A Street in Ballinahinch
Scene 4	Gardens of General Nugent's House	Scene 9	The Cross Roads near Ballinahinch
Scene 5	Court Yard in Ballinahinch Gaol		

Irish and Ensemble Dances arranged by
EILEEN LENNOX MAGEE

Songs by J. L. Sullivan and Lena Pembroke

SEATS BOOKED AT THEATRE Dress Circle 2/4 TEL. 3016

GALLERY,	PIT,	UPPER CIRCLE,	DRESS CIRCLE,	SEATS IN BOXES
6d.	1/2	1/6	2/4	3/-
			No Booking Fees	

Amusement Tax: 2d. on 6d. Seats; 4d. on 1/2, 1/6 and 2/- Seats; and 6d. on 3/- Seats

Plate 19. Playbill for Bourke's *For the Land She Loved*. Courtesy of Séamus de Búrca.

FOR THE LAND SHE LOVED

P. J. BOURKE
[1915]

CAST

[This list does not appear in the typescript]

MATT MC GRATH	A blacksmith
MRS. MC GRATH	Matt's wife
SHAMUS O'FLYNN	A blacksmith
SQUIRE GRAY	"Governor General of Down" (according to the 1920 playbill)
COLONEL JOHNSTON	Commander of the yeomanry [in history, Colonel Johnson]
GENERAL ROBERT MUNRO	A United Irishman
BETSY GRAY	The heroine of Ballinahinch
DERMOT MC MAHON	A local patriot
SHEILA DE LACEY	Betsy Gray's maid
GENERAL SIR JOHN NUGENT	Commander-in-chief of the King's troops in Ulster
LADY LUCY NUGENT	Daughter of General Nugent (and according to the 1920 playbill, "In the Secret Service")
GEORGE GRAY	Betsy's brother, a United Irishman
COLONEL BRUCE	Of the 18th Royal Regiment, Bombay
ENGLISH OFFICERS AND SOLDIERS	

8 THE HIBERNIAN. Nov. 13, 1915

"For the Land She Loved."

Great Irish Historical Play by Mr. P. J. BURKE'S No. 1 COMPANY.

Who fears to speak of '98?

Miss Peggy Courtney (as Betsy Grey)

Miss Kitty Carrickford (as Lady Nugent)

God Bless the Northern Land.

ABBEY THEATRE, DUBLIN. — 15th to 20th November.

C COMPANY, II. BATT. I.V.

GRAND CONCERT

with a short Address from Eoin Mac Neill,

SUNDAY, NOVEMBER 14th, at 8 p.m.,

IN

41 Parnell Square,

The following are among the artists who will contribute:—

Miss JOAN BURKE, Mr. BRIAN O'HIGGINS, Miss MOLLIE BYRNE, Mr. JAMES RAUL.

The MacHale Dancers.——The Celtic Glee Singers

TICKETS .. .. 6d. 1s., and 2s. each

Ticket holders are warned to secure their seats before 7.45 p.m.

YOU SHOULD JOIN

THE

"HONESTY."

An Outspoken Scrap of Paper,

Every Tuesday, One Halfpenny.

:: :: Instantaneous Success :: ::

COMMUNICATIONS TO BE ADDRESSED TO

The Gaelic Press, 30 Upper Liffey Street

DUBLIN

UNDER THE CLOCK,

99 Upr. Dorset St.

——Call and See J. T. RYAN,——

Tea, Wine, and Spirit Merchant.

GAELS—Where to get your News,

PHILIP MEAGHER

4 NORTH EARL ST., DUBLIN

John Jameson and Son's 10 years old and 7 years old Malt, and Power's Three Swallow

The Laundry which should be suppported by all is

The National Laundry Co.,

60 STH. WILLIAM ST., DUBLIN.

Special Terms to Clubs, Institutions, etc.

Eat Less Meat. Dine at THE

COLLEGE CAFE

(VEGETARIAN)

COLLEGE STREET.

The Popular Dublin Resort for Excellent Luncheons and "Select" Teas

Plate 20. Advertisement for Bourke's *For the Land She Loved,* placed in *The Hibernian* (1915).

LADIES AND GENTLEMEN OF
ANGLO-IRISH SOCIETY

IRISH PEASANTS

ACT I

Scene 1

(Matt McGrath's Forge at Ballinahinch. Large Forge. Set: Fire and Bellows stands on R. On the R.C. is the anvil at which MATT *is discovered making pikes. Large open window at back C. Door on the L. Bench at back at which* MEN *are seen working. As Curtain rises, voices heard singing: Lights down, door opens:)*

The Boys are bound for Wexford Town
And shortly so are we
But now is our time to make the blades
That sets Ould Ireland free.

MATT Aye. The boys are bound for Wexford town sure enough: and the French are on the Say too I'm tould, an' boys it's well we have plenty o' good strong pikes to charge with the true and tried soldiers of France.

SHAMUS Aye, worth waitin' on indeed, sure they might be here long ago if they liked. What's the use in your talkin' like that Matt McGrath. An' I'm thinkin' that the sorra good* they'd be even if they were here this minute.

MATT Bedad, but it's yourself that's the quare sort of an Irishman, or are you a patriot at all that you'd be for ever grumblin' over the French comin'; sure ye can't send out an army like that or it's gettin' them all kilt ye'd be. Sure if ye keep on talkin' like that ye will never be o' the rank an' file at all.

SHAMUS An' sure ye don't want me to be made a rale General, an' I only a common blacksmith?

MATT A Blacksmith did ye say? Faith I go bail that Lord Edward himself could not turn round and make a pike like that. Tho' he'd know how it should be done an' it's as like as not he'd—

Plate 21. Still from a prison scene in the 1918 melodramatic film directed by Fred O'Donovan, *Willy Reilly (and His Colleen Bawn).* The limelight on the heroine and stylized gestures suggest the prison encounter between Betsy Gray and Robert Munro in *For the Land She Loved*. Courtesy of the British Film Institute.

SHAMUS Will ye hould ye'r prate an' let us get on with the work. I was never a man to be makin' speeches for they never do us any good, no more than fightin' the sodgers: bad fortune to them. There is a lot o' lads beyant in College Green in Dublin in the ould parliament House, that's speech-makin' an' what good do they do us, we still have to work. We are still the blacksmiths makin' pikes an' horseshoes, an' anthin' else that comes along. It's hard enough for poor men to live without goin' out to fight with the French that has no soul or no God; think o' that now.

MATT Hould your prate. I knew you wor always a milk an' water man, an' I'm not goin' to waste me intelligence conversin' with ye any more. I think ye are turnin' into a Pagan; ye are no patriot at all. (*Noise of horses hard R.B.*)

SHAMUS Whist* man—what's that. (*Listens.*) Be the powers, maybe it's the sodgers comin' or maybe it's the French, long life to them.

MATT Come Shamus, clear away these pike heads out o' the way; maybe it's strangers they'd be, an' if they wor the sodgers they'd be after hangin' us both for makin' arms. (*Going to window.*) Bedad if it's not the ould Squire an' a sodger with him. Now what will we do at all, an' we haven't the shoes made for the brown mare of his.

(*Horses now gallop up and stop. Voices heard outside.*)

SQUIRE Hold there you fellow, and don't let these horses stir for a moment.

(*As SHAMUS and MATT hammer at horseshoe, the SQUIRE, followed by COLONEL JOHNSTON, passes window at back and enters through open door.*)

MATT God save both your honours! (*SQUIRE nods assent.*)

SQUIRE Well Matt, busy as usual. What are you making now? New shoes, eh? (*Slapping MATT on shoulder.*) You are working late as usual. But I am indeed sorry to trouble you at this hour of the night. My mare has bad fore-shoes and as I have a damn long journey before me I must ask you to put on a new pair at once. (*COLONEL JOHNSTON looking carefully around the forge.*)

MATT Sure I will ye'r honour. An' didn't Dermot McMahon tell me all about them this mornin' an' sure here we have them ready to put on.

SQUIRE Good Matt, get them on then. We are on our way to the town of Antrim, and a considerable distance, to see General Nugent. These are troubled times Matt. I'm sorry to say there are a lot of disloyal people through the country—foreign emergency, and all such people. However get on with the work Matt. Make a good job of it, and when you call over to the Castle I shall pay the bill.

MATT That I'll do Sir, an' in regards to the payment of the bill, sure your honour is quite good enough for such a triflin' amount. Come Shamus, get up them shoes until we do the mare.

(*Taking up shoe, etc., they both exit through open door, and disappear at back R.*)

JOHNSTON Now to business, what shall we do? Search the forge for the arms we have been told about, and if we succeed in finding them, we shall have but little trouble in placing the rope around the neck of Robert Munro. Thus leaving my coast clear to claim the hand of your daughter Betsy Gray.

SQUIRE Give me your flask, Colonel Johnston; then I shall be in a better position to speak on my daughter's love affairs afterwards.

(COLONEL JOHNSTON *gives flask. They drink.*)

JOHNSTON The best Scotch: nothing like it Squire to arouse good feeling and give one more courage when the country is in a state of rebellion. (*Striking his toe against a pike-head which* SHAMUS *previously dropped.*) Hello! What the devil is this. Ah! I see, one of those infernal pike-heads—the weapon of a rebel. Look here Squire. Ah! Splendid weapon at close quarters no doubt. If the British Cavalry had something similar which could be used on horse-back. What Squire! No, not even Napoleon's dogs of war could stop them.

SQUIRE You are quite right. So information was quite correct. I always thought Matt McGrath a loyal and a faithful subject. However, on account of his old age and friendship with my family we shall pass him over. Poor old devil, he is well paid for his work. But my daughter shall not wed a rebel dog. No. Whatever respect I had for Munro has passed away when I see these weapons of rebellion, and I would sooner see her laid in her mother's grave rather than she should wed with a viper whose life is devoted to spreading unrest and rebellion against our Good King George.

JOHNSTON I am indeed glad that you have proved the scoundrel's falsehood to your daughter. Why, it is not your daughter he wants, but her money. (*DERMOT MC MAHON now appears at window.*) I may now in honour claim the hand of your daughter Betsy.

DERMOT (*aside*) Not while Dermot McMahon is here. (*Disappears.*)

SQUIRE I shall consider and give you your answer tomorrow. You see she is the only one I have left since my son disappeared some years ago. But there, I don't want to dwell on sad memories of the past. Let us not forget the work we have before us tonight.

JOHNSTON Very well then. Let us now proceed to Antrim. There we shall obtain a warrant for the arrest of Munro, and in the meantime we can send word to the Military at Ballinahinch to send a party of soldiers here tonight for the purpose of seizing the arms hidden in this forge, and then pay Munro a mid-night visit, arrest him on the charge of high treason, and it shall be easy to prove his guilt to the General and the Military Tribunal.

MATT (*outside*) It's all right Shamus; that won't come off.

SQUIRE Curse on our luck, could they have overheard us? Hush, they come—now for the road.

JOHNSTON (*aside*) While he lives he shall not consent to my marrying her. (*Aloud*) Yes I think the turnpike Road is the shortest for us to proceed by.

(*Enter MATT, at Back, carrying hammer; he stops at door.*)

MATT Ye may go home Shamus if ye like. (*To SQUIRE*) Now Sir, the job is done for your honour.

SQUIRE Alright Matt. Come Colonel, now to work.

COLONEL Yes Squire and I shall leave my flask with Matt. Good night Matt.

(*Gives flask. Exeunt both L. and R.*)

MATT I suppose he means me to drink the health o' the King. (*Voices heard, and horses galloping away.*) They are off, as they say whin ye are at a races.

(*As he sits on Anvil DERMOT enters door L.*)

DERMOT Well may sweet bad luck to the two o' ye goin. A purty pair o' blaguards and that's a quare thing for me to say o' the Squire. (*To MATT*) I overheard them spake about arms when ye wor puttin the shoes on the mare. If ye happen to have some you had better get them away from here now, an' at once, or as sure as there is a bill on a crow ye spend the remainder of the night in Ballinahinch gaol.

MATT Well let us go for a couple o' the boys to help us. Here, let's drink up this sup of whiskey an' I'll give ye a toast. (*Fills out whiskey.*) Here's to the Green above the red. (*They drink. Enter* SHEILA.)

SHEILA Well Matt, drinking again as usual.

DERMOT So am I.

SHEILA (*looking puzzled at* DERMOT) Now it strikes me I've seen that face before.

DERMOT Yes Miss, ye may have; if my memory serves me right I have got this face a mighty long time.

MATT Ha, Ha! good on ye Dermot. It's yourself should be a member of the ould House in College Green.

SHEILA Sure make that omadhaun* a member an—

MATT Sure he's no omadhaun* for he can spake like a book.

SHEILA Bedad an' it's the book that's mighty hard to close. An' if he could spake why does he not spake at the meetin' that's to be after Church on Sunday next. In memory of poor William Orr.[1] Do you know Matt, if I had a little practice I could spake, only I couldn't remember a sentence.

DERMOT I wish I could only forget mine.

SHEILA What was the last word ye said.

DERMOT Not guilty your reverence.

SHEILA I suppose it was for kissin' some colleen, ye blackguard. Well there now if I'm not forgettin' the message I was sent with. Young George Gray has returned home again, an' the young Mistress Betsy sent me over to tell ye the glad news. An' he are to come over and fix the wheel of the carriage; she is off somewhere tonight. Isn't it a quare time she is thinkin' of travelling.

MATT The ould Squire is gone to meet the English General that's to be down in Antrim town from Dublin, an' the colonel is surely gone back to the barracks whatever is on.

DERMOT Would there be word from France that they wor here or may be it's the risin' in Wexford. I heard today that there was trouble in it.

SHEILA Well there's no use mindin' trouble, there's trouble everywhere, an' I'm afraid that there is trouble with the young Mistress an'. . . . But spake of the devil, here comes Master George himself.

(*GEORGE GRAY passes window at back and enters Door R.*)

GEORGE At last Matt. I am back again in the dear home, rendered dear, yes, by loving absence. Oh God! How often have I longed for the fair hills and pleasant turf fires of the dear Irish homes. The years have rolled by since I stood in this forge before. I should say that you have almost forgotten me. Yet in that space of time in France and Spain, I have worked night and day side by side with Tone. Meeting with disappointments and reverses. Yet we have succeeded in seeing the French Directory move their men and arms to aid our suffering people and our country's liberties.

SHEILA The French comin', then old Ireland will be free. Speakin' about forgotten ye, bedad General Nugent's daughter has not forgotten you I'm thinking.

DERMOT Sure he wouldn't be marryin' a lady like that and her father wearin'a red Coat.

GEORGE Love knows no bounds neither does it know its equal; for when she gave me her love long ago, she vowed she'd be true. Oh boys, don't tell me that her love is dead.

MATT My poor boy, it's the sorry day that you have returned for they have branded you as an outlaw an' put a price on your head, because they said ye loved the ould land an' that's why ye disappeared.

GEORGE Oh, I fear not the gallows. I would gladly lay down my life for the cause I have worked for, and there is not a man in the society of United Irishmen that would not openly avow the same. Tho' there are traitors amongst us yet, there shall be no quarter shown them now that the French are on their way.

SHEILA Then here's to an ould Ireland, Hurrah!

GEORGE Sheila, in your enthusiasm you have forgotten to give Matt his message.

SHEILA Bedad, Master Gray, I did that same. Come on, Matt, an' I'll have a supper ready for you when ye come over. Good night boys.

DERMOT Are ye goin' that way? Ye wouldn't care to be after takin' a poor boy with ye.

SHEILA No, ye can go ye'r own way. On second thoughts, it's late an' I suppose it's better to have some kind of a man; so I'll let you come.

(*Runs off R. and disappears L.*)

DERMOT Alright me darlin', I'll be there.

(*Runs after* SHEILA *R., disappears L.*)

GEORGE Lady Nugent was to meet me here tonight. It is now past the time. Could anything have happened?

MATT No. But here she comes. Hide yourself and be after givin' her a bit of a surprise.

(*As* GEORGE *conceals himself on the L. behind bellow,* LADY NUGENT *enters R.*)

MATT It's yourself that's welcome my Lady. But the worst of it is I have not got a clean seat of any kind for ye to rest yourself while I have a look at your pony's foot. But I have a bit of a surprise for ye. There's someone here you would like to see.

LADY NUGENT You must be going mad Matt. Who could be here that I would wish to see? The only one in the world is Robert Munro. I love him; but he does not love me. The day shall come when I shall see him crave at my feet for mercy. He loves Squire Gray's daughter. If you mean George Gray he is many miles from here; he is a fellow with a price upon his head. He cannot—dare not return to Ireland. I used to love him when I was young, but I found it was just a passing fancy.

(GEORGE *comes forward.*)

GEORGE Lucy, Lucy, darling—

LADY NUGENT Oh! George, have you returned—

GEORGE Have you no word of welcome for me! did you not get my letters?

LADY NUGENT I received no letter, but I am glad to see you are well.

GEORGE You might so greet an utter stranger. Oh! Lucy is there none of the old love remaining in your heart?

LADY NUGENT Hush: —We have nothing to say to each other now. You must forget that you ever knew me.

GEORGE Lucy, since I returned I have learned that I am an outlaw with a price upon my head. If it's a crime to love Ireland, and [if for] that you despise me, may God in his kindness forgive you.

LADY NUGENT Again I say I cannot listen to you. I have given my heart to another, and so, you will understand I can no longer love you.

GEORGE But Lucy, you must have known I loved you in the past; I love you still. Ah Lucy, think of all I have suffered in all my years of exile; think of the love of the olden days of my youth—my boyhood, and now my manhood—think will you before you discard it like a withered leaf of an Autumn tree, a love that will make your life a long dream of joy and happiness.

LADY NUGENT I cannot hear you longer. Pluck the leaves of my memory from your heart—for henceforth our paths shall be widely apart as the poles which are at both ends of the earth. So now farewell and forever, there is but one man in this world, and from that man I shall endeavour to gain his love and friendship even at the cost of my own life: —Adieu.

(*Exit* LADY NUGENT *R.*)

GEORGE Lost: —Lost—And forever. Oh God! What a fool I have been. Yet thank God, there is but one great hope left, and that would be to die for the Ireland of a Hundred Sorrows.

(*Enter* BETSY GRAY *at back, crosses by window and enters R.*)

BETSY George, my brother, welcome. So you found your way to the forge after your years of absence. Where is Matt? He has not yet come to see to the wheel of the carriage as you know. There is going to be a wedding tonight—. But what is wrong? You seem so dull. Is there bad news?

(*Takes both his hands in hers.*)

GEORGE Betsy, my darling sister. I am proud to see your heart light and free. You are young and know but little of the troubles of this world. As for me—I have only one hope left. The only only one I have ever loved beyond my God and country has faded and gone—? Lost to me for ever— And the only thing now left to me is a soldier's death in my country's cause.

BETSY Oh yes, death would be a glorious thing. Why, I was only thinking last night of how the women of Limerick fought and died like heroes with Patrick Sarsfield but little over a hundred years ago. Don't you think that there are a few women left in Ireland still who could do as much for the land they loved as in those days. But there, I will not make a speech, it might worry you. Ah! —Here comes Robert Munro, he shall be pleased to see you—now that you are the bearer of good news from France.

(*Enter* ROBERT MUNRO, *R., who embraces* BETSY.)

ROBERT Betsy darling I missed you from the castle, and Sheila De Lacey informed me that you had come here; so I was bold enough to follow you. Oh George, I heard of your return. What is the best news you bring us? Thousands of Frenchmen I hope.

GEORGE Yes, the news I bring is of the best, there is a meeting tomorrow night. I shall expect you to be present there. There are most important dispatches from the directory. Two are company, I shall say no more—Adieu.

(Exit GEORGE *R. and disappears at back L.*)

BETSY Robert dearest, I have waited for hours, and owing to my father being suspicious of our meetings I thought it better to meet here in secret. I have arranged that we be wed, to-night if you will it. I love you more than life itself—love you so well that I would lay down my life for Ireland and you. My father wishes and wills me to wed Colonel Johnston to-morrow. Oh, Robert, if you love me, save me.

ROBERT Yes, Betsy, I will with all my heart, if you are content, I shall be proud to give you my heart and hand. But not here; we shall be wed in the little church yonder at midnight. But your father will never forgive you if you marry me because he looks upon me as a rebel, an outcast from Society and a traitor to the King.

BETSY It matters but little about my father when we two live and love each other. My first duty is to you Robert—my affianced husband.

(*Enter* LADY NUGENT *R.*)

LADY NUGENT I am more than surprised at you Betsy Gray, a squire's daughter, love-making with an outlaw. And if your father became aware of your conduct he would have you cut off from his household. Besides, Robert Munro is betrothed to me.

ROBERT This is a trick—another trick—of yours Lady Lucy Nugent. Is it not enough for your father to outrage law and order in this country but that you must dare try to take from me the girl I love.

LADY NUGENT But you pledged your love and honour to me long ago. You surely would not treat me thus now that you have found a new Betsy Gray.

ROBERT Enough of this, I—(*BETSY now crosses over to L.*)

BETSY Stop! let me speak; Lady Lucy Nugent, you were ever a welcome guest at my father's Mansions; we have always been the best of friends; if Robert Munro loves you I shall give him to you, and now, let him answer for himself and choose between us.

(*ROBERT* now crosses down to *BETSY*.)

ROBERT To you Betsy till death do us part. (*They embrace.*)

LADY NUGENT So this is to be the end. Well, I shall wait for the day to dawn. Tho' you wed him—yet I shall wait in silence for the day when my vengeance shall fall slowly but surely on both your heads. (*Aside*) Now the train is laid, next to the Colonel with the news.

(*Exit LADY NUGENT R., comes to window then disappears.*)

BETSY Now that she is gone and we are again alone let us decide what is best to be done. This is my plan: —Tonight when all are asleep I shall be ready in my bedroom, which shall be known to you by a light burning in its window. You scale the garden wall and conceal yourself by the hedge along which leads to the small gate at which I shall be waiting for you. Dermot will leave a horse ready saddled in the stable for me and before many hours will pass, with the aid of my brown mare, we shall be on our way to Dublin before to-morrow dawn.

(*At this moment SQUIRE GRAY followed by COLONEL JOHNSTON and SOLDIERS enters R., leaving two men outside window.*)

SQUIRE Stand aside from my daughter. You are my prisoner in the name of the King.

JOHNSTON And your place is here by my side Betsy Gray.

BETSY No, my place is here by the side of Robert Munro, my affianced husband.

ROBERT Lay one hand on her as there is a heaven above I shall not answer for your lives (*pistol in hand*).

SQUIRE Again I say, advance men and seize that man.

ROBERT Back I say; I demand your warrant.

JOHNSTON Here I hold your warrant and you are arrested on the charge of Sedition and Rebellion.

ROBERT 'Tis false, as heaven itself is true. Out of my way.

(*ROBERT MUNRO now rushes to break thro' soldiers. SQUIRE seizes him, they struggle and MUNRO drops pistol. DERMOT and MATT rush in, seize the SOLDIERS. COLONEL JOHNSTON knocks MATT on the head with pistol; he falls. SOLDIERS seize DERMOT. At this moment LADY NUGENT discharges pistol at COLONEL, misses him, and hits SQUIRE, who falls down dead.*)

JOHNSTON Arrest that man for the murder of Squire Gray.

BETSY 'Tis false.

LADY NUGENT 'Tis true. I saw him fire and here is his empty pistol.

(*Enter SHEILA on L. and pointing to LADY NUGENT.*)

SHEILA 'Tis false, for I saw Lady Nugent fire that shot.

ROBERT And may God give me strength that some day we may live to bring the murdered and guilty ones to justice.

CURTAIN

ACT II

Three months later

Scene 1

The guard room in the barracks at Ballinahinch. (As scene opens COLONEL JOHNSTON and LADY NUGENT discovered seated. Table, chairs C.)

JOHNSTON Now that the scoundrel Munro is safely under lock and key it will make my course easy to obtain the hand and fortune of the Squire's daughter, Betsy Gray. Tho' the Squire's death has cast a gloom over her, yet I mean to pay her a visit to-night, and if all goes well, I will soon teach her to forget her old fool of a father.

LADY NUGENT Yes, it is now three months since that fatal night. Tho' you have tried Munro for the murder, yet your witnesses have failed in their evidence. I don't doubt but if he is courtmartialed you will have enough evidence to have him shot. What is your next move? You want Betsy Gray, what is your price?

JOHNSTON Yes, and by heaven I shall have her; this is my way. I have made an application to the authorities of Dublin Castle to have him tried by the Military Tribunal on the charge of Sedition. Next we must get your father's consent as the general commanding to allow you, his daughter, to appear as a witness and—

LADY NUGENT I protest against this. I shall not appear as a witness against the man I love. No Colonel Johnston, wretch that I am, I shall not be base enough to help you to put the rope around the neck of an innocent man.

JOHNSTON What, you refuse me?

LADY NUGENT Yes, I shall leave you to pursue your villainy alone and unaided by me.

JOHNSTON What! Well as you will not aid me I demand the payment of that I.O.U. which you had from [me] some time ago, as I helped to save your good name in Society by helping you to pay off your debts. So I will now disgrace you if you cannot pay me.

LADY NUGENT And what amount do you demand?

JOHNSTON I demand £400 on account tonight and the rest to be paid to me within the week. Can you pay it?

LADY NUGENT No! heaven help me I cannot.

JOHNSTON I thought not. Now I have you in my power, help me to swear away the life of Munro so that my coast will be clear to gain the hand of Betsy Gray; or I shall place the rope around your dainty neck, instead of Munro. Your answer? (*Rings bell.*)

LADY NUGENT Would you dare—(*enter* SERGEANT *R.*)

JOHNSTON Sergeant, bring the prisoner Munro here. I wish to speak with him in private.

SERGEANT It's against the rules and regulations. My orders are from the General that no person will be allowed to converse or hold conversation with him without an order.

JOHNSTON The order does not apply to the King's officers; I command you to send the prisoner here, or I shall call a guard and put you under arrest.

(*SERGEANT salutes and exits R. Locks and Bars heard distant.*)

JOHNSTON You remain as you are. Now is your chance for love or vengeance, which now rests in your hands.

(*Enter ROBERT MUNRO followed by SERGEANT R.*) Sergeant! You may leave us for a moment. (*Exit SERGEANT.*)

ROBERT Well, what is it?

JOHNSTON My business with you has a two fold object. In the first place I have to remind you that owing to the unsettled state of the country we find that you are the leader of a dangerous conspiracy, which is found to incite people of this country to a breach of the peace by an armed force, and to overpower, if you are able, the Government in Ireland for the purpose of obtaining for the people of Ireland what they call their rights and Freedom—an act which is punishable with death.

ROBERT Yes, it is the hope of every Irishman to make her what she was; and if God gives us the strength she shall again be a nation.

JOHNSTON Believe me, Robert Munro, that I have your country's interest at heart. Now it is the decision of the General that you be tried by Courtmartial, and before doing so, I have the said power from the Authorities to set you at liberty on condition that you first disclose the names of the leaders of the United Irish Society, and also that you consent to allow Betsy Gray to become my wife.

ROBERT Colonel Johnston, this is my answer. I know nothing of the projected rebellion. But if I did I assure you, as surely as I stand here to-night, that I should suffer myself to be hanged, drawn and quartered, and to let my bones drop asunder from the gallows height, or my head to drop into the basket of the Guillotine before one particle of information should escape my lips. I am an Irishman and love Ireland, and my hope is that some day I may see her once more placed among the nations. And before I should see the girl I love tied to a scoundrel and my country's enemy, I say death—yes a hundred times.

JOHNSTON Enough, I shall give you twenty-four hours to consider and if your answer is not forthcoming in that time the law shall take its course.

(*Exit COLONEL JOHNSTON L.*)

LADY NUGENT Robert Munro, for the love I bear you, don't throw your life away on a useless and worthless girl like Betsy Gray. Give up Betsy and come and marry me who loves you.

ROBERT I refuse to hold further conversation with you. You, who have already murdered and robbed the girl I love of her father. Had I never seen you or known of your villainy I might have loved you, and—

LADY NUGENT I tell you Robert Munro that I shall see you swing, and when next I meet face to face with Betsy Gray the Assassin's dagger shall do its work.

(*Enter* SERGEANT.)

SERGEANT Fall in, Quick March.

(*Exit* SERGEANT *followed by* MUNRO*—R.* LADY NUGENT *sitting down and looking after him.*)

LADY NUGENT I shall win him yet tho' Heaven and earth were against me.

BLACK OUT

Close in Scene 1

Scene 2

(*Drawing room in Castle at Ballinahinch. Large opening in C. Doors R. and L. Windows at each side of doors. Garden Cloth at back. Table down C.L. Chairs R. and L. Lights full up. Branch of candlesticks lighted on table at which* BETSY *is discovered seated as scene goes up.*)

BETSY Oh! Robert, pulse of my heart, the joy of my very soul, how my thoughts travel to you to-night in your lonely prison cell at Ballinahinch. Would to God you had not come to the forge of Matt McGrath on that fatal night four months ago. At times my heart misgives me when I think we are parted perhaps for ever. Oh! Robert; you could not doubt my love for you, whose name is ever on [my] lips. I know you love me as truly as I do you. How happy you made the days of my childhood when we roamed through the woods hand in hand in the golden summer time of long ago. Oh! Ireland: beautiful Ireland! why are your sons so brave, shot down, because of their love for you. They say that memory is the book of God and Heaven in its own good time shall punish the wicked and drive out the tyrant from our shores.

(*Enter* SHEILA, *door in Centre.*)

SHEILA I thought I would find you in the garden Miss Betsy. All alone!

BETSY Yes, Sheila, alone, here with my thoughts and these are sad thoughts.

SHEILA Oh sure, alanna,* don't let your thoughts run on anything sad. For sure sad thoughts will never do you good.

BETSY My heart is sad to-night when I think of the man I love and who loves Ireland under sentence of death for the murder of my poor father.

SHEILA Now don't be talking like that Miss, for you may be sure as the kind angels are in heaven that he is dying an Innocent man, for poor Robert Munro never fired that shot, what good would that be doin' the poor boy and then to say that they would not hear my evidence at the trial they had in the market House. But 'tis like what the ould Colonel would do. He's afraid that Robert would be after marrying you an' doin' himself out.

BETSY Don't speak of that man to me. He whose name is cursed by the poor peasantry for his cruelty to them, led on by his brutal band of soldiers. Curse on the laws that set class against class and creed against creed, that can only rule us by sword in our disunity. But God shall give us strength that some day we shall yet be a nation free.

SHEILA Now I'll spake to ye, Miss, if it costs me my life. There is no one else about, and listen to what I'm about to tell you. I have overheard a plot being hatched in the garden outside. The Colonel is coming here to pay you a visit at midnight. So we shall be well prepared to give him a warm reception, and I overheard him say that the poor boy that never hurt a hair in his worst enemy's head would be hanged or shot in the morning or at sunset to-morrow, and may God help you if that scoundrel lays his ten commandments on you. Now what are we to do? We must save the master.

BETSY I shall proceed by the mail coach to Dublin and seek to have an interview with the Lord Lieutenant, put the case of my father's murder before him giving him your evidence and I am sure he will grant me a free pardon for Robert Munro.

SHEILA You can't do that, sure you'd want to be a bird that would fly there and back before tomorrow at Sunset. Now this is my plan for his escape.

BETSY Yes, Sheila, go on, be quick.

SHEILA Listen to me a moment. This is my plan. Tonight Colonel Johnston will pay a visit here to this house, be as friendly as you plaze with him, and tell him you shall consider and maybe accept him if he will give ye a pass to bid farewell to your own darling Robert. Then when ye are in the prison, ye can have by the way of no harm a drop of whiskey in a bottle an' give it to the Sergeant in charge of the guard, and I being acquainted with him shall keep him engaged while you yourself extract the bullets from the soldiers' muskets, which they leave in the rack outside the guard room. Then when the soldiers get the order to fire, of course the young master will fall as if shot dead, and then leave the rest to me and to your brother, George.

BETSY Oh, how lovely Sheila, yes I shall do it. But how can I ever thank you? Now to put your plan into operation and then for the liberty of the man I love.

(*Exit* BETSY *C.,* SHEILA *looking after her.*)

SHEILA God and kind angels be ever with her. Now to find that omadhaun* of mine, Dermot. 'Tis mighty hard to trust a boy like that.

(SHEILA *going to door L.,* DERMOT *runs against her.*)

DERMOT Musha,* bad cess to the bit,* but if it's not here where ye are.

SHEILA And where would you want me to be at this hour o' the night? and where were you now?

DERMOT Oh, musha,* where would I be but stravagin'* about in the dark, thinkin' what I could do to save the Master himself.

SHEILA Aye, thinkin' of the master sure enough. May the kind saints be ever near to guard him. Well sit down here till we draw up our plans of attack.

(DERMOT *sits down at the table looking at* SHEILA *and takes up a glass of wine and drinks.*)

DERMOT Begorra,* I'll sit down an' here's your health; faith, Sheila I never saw ye lookin' purtier.

SHEILA Ah, sure don't goin' on with your blarney.

DERMOT Begorra,* an' it isn't blarney at all Sheila. It was only the other day I was talkin' to the mother about you and says she, there's Kathleen Nevin, the tailor's daughter, that would make a good wife for a poor man, an', by the way of no harm, says she, if a poor boy was sick and not able to work, she could keep him while she'd be on the spree* wid her trade.

SHEILA So your mother wants a colleen to keep her lazy son, and give him plenty to eat and drink an' let him sit in the corner spakin' wid all the people who would chance come in an' you would tell them how they would free Ireland or something like that, but don't aix ye to do it.

DERMOT Easy now and don't be after misunderstandin' me. Well says she to me, she's the purtiest girl in the parish. Nonsense says I she's not a patch on Sheila DeLacey. Sure she's twopence in the pound better than any girl in County Down and a kiss from her sweet lips is as good as a drink of butter milk, says I.

SHEILA Here out ye go; I don't want ye to be after makin' little o' me, and don't think that I'd let an omadhaun* like you be after bossin' me.

DERMOT Well to make a long story short who should come in but his Reverence, an' was after hearin' what I was saying bad fortune to me. Who have you such a bright opinion of says he to me. Begorra,* Sheila DeLacey, Your reverence says I, 'tis a pity you wouldn't say that and all the rest ye have to say to herself says he. I never thought of that, says I, but I'll take ye at yer word. Good-bye says he and I won't be too hard on ye for the marriage money, says he. So here I am to ask ye to become Mrs. Dermot McMahon.

(*Stands up and straightens himself.*)

SHEILA Well, I'll think it over.

DERMOT Could ye not be after sayin' yes, me darlin', an' be after taking the ball on the hop.

SHEILA Well, I'll be after sayin' yes, if ye are able to keep a wife. I wouldn't be the one to buy a husband.

DERMOT Well, that I'll do, me darlin'.

SHEILA Well now, you mustn't drink nor smoke, nor aix me where I'm goin' if I may want to go out to the town. Give me up all the money and possessions ye have, an' I must always have my own way. Have a nice pony and trap and have nothing to do, and have a servant to help me to do it. Well, I think I would be satisfied with that.

DERMOT Are ye sure that's all ye'd be wantin'.

SHEILA Yes I'd do with that.

DERMOT Well look here, me girl its not marryin' ye should be. You should be in heaven wid all the other women who has a mind like ye.

(*Knocking hard.*)

SHEILA Who can this be at this hour. Get ye into the kitchen an' I'll have something ready for ye in a minute.

(*Exit* DERMOT *C. Enter* COLONEL JOHNSTON *at Door R.*)

JOHNSTON (*to* SHEILA) Where is your mistress?

SHEILA She's busy at present.

JOHNSTON Send her to me, I want to see her on urgent business concerning the execution of the Rebel Robert Munro. (*Exit* SHEILA *by door R.*) If I fail in persuading her to marry me I shall have her seized and brought away by force. Curse her, she is as stubborn as only a woman can be. 'Tis the money I want, not the girl. (*Enter* BETSY *door L.* COLONEL JOHNSTON *advances, she passes him.*) After years of waiting you have come to me at last, and now that your brother has again disappeared, and Robert Munro is to die in the morning, poor fellow. I did my best to save his life.

BETSY Colonel Johnston, I fear your best did not avail even when the court martial found him guilty of a crime for the murder of a man that you know died by the hand of Lady Nugent.

JOHNSTON Lady Nugent! Surely you would not think that a friend of yours, and your brother's sweetheart, would be guilty of such a crime. However if you wish to save his life, I can save him if you—

BETSY If I—

JOHNSTON If you consent to become my wife; I hold here a [new?] pardon, signed by the commander-in-chief of the King's troops in Ulster—General Nugent—and now your answer.

BETSY And so Colonel Johnston, you wish me to buy Robert's life at the price of my honour. Well then this is my answer, that I shall suffer him to be hanged, drawn and quartered rather than I should become the wife of a scoundrel like you, and now, Colonel, you may leave me. Go—

JOHNSTON Very well, remember that I am not a man to be trifled with, you jade of the devil; as you will not come with me of your own free will, I shall take you by force.

BETSY What do you mean to do? Surely you are not going to make war on a defenceless woman?

JOHNSTON Yes, by heavens, I mean to have you here and now.

BETSY Help! help!!!

(*Rushes to C.* COLONEL JOHNSTON *seizes her.*)

JOHNSTON You may shriek for mercy if you will. (*They both struggle,* BETSY *gets free and rushes to door R.* SOLDIERS *rush in and seize her again; at this moment* DERMOT *rushes in, grapple[s]* SOLDIERS, *throw[s] them.* BETSY *rushes to center,* COLONEL JOHNSTON *and* SOLDIERS *are about to rush on her when* SHEILA *appears and covers them with pistol.*)

SHEILA Stir a foot and I'll blow you and your bloodhounds to the devil.

BLACK OUT

Close in Scene 2

Scene 3

(*The Garden and grounds of General Sir John Nugent, Evening— Music continues to entrance of* LADY NUGENT, *R.*)

LADY NUGENT Well, I wonder if the Colonel succeeded in capturing his love, Betsy Gray, last night. I suppose it will be another of his well laid schemes. The girl makes good her escape; but once in our grip my course is clear. I swear to have Robert Munro, and what a women sets her mind on she will carry out, though heaven and earth stand in her way. Well I have played my cards well and have won, and now to my father; I shall seek his aid and he shall not refuse me a free pardon for Robert. (*Looks off R.*) Here comes the Colonel. What can he want? I hope he does not spoil my plans. Oh, God! if he should once come before my father and tell him I am the murderer of his old friend, Squire Gray, Oh, no, he cannot. He has no proofs.

(*Enter* COLONEL JOHNSTON *in haste, R.*)

JOHNSTON Curse on my infernal luck again, she has evaded my vigilance.

LADY NUGENT Why, Colonel, have you made another blunder? Oh! you Officers of the King, where are your brains?

JOHNSTON 'Tis easy for you to speak of brains. My plans were so well laid that I really thought they could not fail. But they have failed, miserably failed, and now she is at large and coming here to-night to put the case before your father—General Nugent—and if possible obtain a free pardon for Munro, and perhaps place the rope around both our necks.

LADY NUGENT 'Tis our business to see that she does not. This is my plan. My father is at present in the smoke room with General Lake. I shall go to him at once and tell him the whole facts of the case. You watch the grounds here, and when she makes her appearance have her seized and taken back to your quarters at Ballinahinch. You know the rest yourself. Ah! here she comes. Now is your chance and don't make a mess of it this time. I shall call a couple of soldiers to aid you. (*Exit* LADY NUGENT *L.*)

JOHNSTON Now my fine Betsy, you shall be more than surprised to meet me here. (*Enter* BETSY *R. and wearing a dark cloak.*) Well Miss Betsy, this is rather a late hour of the evening for you to be out and so far from home and unprotected, in these dreadful times, permit me to—(*offers his arm to* BETSY).

BETSY Colonel Johnston, I wish to hold no conversation with you. Please let me pass.

JOHNSTON Not 'till I know what is your business here.

BETSY My business is of an important nature with General Nugent, to save the life of an innocent man from a scoundrel like you.

JOHNSTON I cannot allow you to see the general on such an errand, so you may be content to remain as you are, here with me, till I can get a carriage to take you to my home, where you shall remain a prisoner till you consent to become my wife and forget that you ever knew Robert Munro. (*Calls off L. At this moment* TWO SOLDIERS *enter and seize* BETSY *by the arms. Enter* LADY NUGENT *R.*)

LADY NUGENT So you have got your prize at last, Colonel. Well Miss Betsy Gray, after all the years you have kept Robert Munro apart from me, you, yourself, are in our power, and I shall be his wife before this night shall pass.

JOHNSTON Yes you may as well believe now that he has deceived you all these years, and at last you shall be the wife of the man who loves you.

BETSY You may threaten as you will, but I have always believed and trusted in my Robert, and you may kill him and hold me prisoner, but you cannot change my love for him, and even till death and in the grave my heart shall be ever his. Now you have your answer, both of you, I pray you will be satisfied.

JOHNSTON You jade of the devil, before many months shall pass when you shall be in solitary confinement your precious high spirit shall be cool enough. Take her away, men, I see the carriage waiting at the gate. I will follow on immediately. Right turn, Quick—(*at this moment* GENERAL NUGENT *enters R.*)

GENERAL NUGENT Hold! Colonel Johnston, what is the meaning of your brutal conduct towards this young lady. Betsy Gray! My God! What does it mean? Release her, men, and I demand an explanation of your unsoldierly conduct.

JOHNSTON I protest against your interference for this girl who is mixed up with the rebel—Munro—in helping him and his disloyal band to overthrow the rule of our King in Ireland by holding secret meetings in her mansion, and the country under Military Tribunal and Martial Law.

LADY NUGENT And I protest, father, and I say here and now that if you set this girl at liberty your honour is at stake as Commander-in-chief of his Majesty's Troops in the North, for this girl is a spy and is aiding and abetting the Rebels, and I swear her business here now is to find out the position and strength of the Garrison.

GENERAL NUGENT I will not believe it. Squire Gray's daughter would not be guilty of such an act. I will ask the girl to give me her own version and I shall further ask her business with me.

BETSY My business here with you, General, is that I want you—I beseech you—to save the life of an innocent man, whom Colonel Johnston has sworn his life away for a crime which he is not guilty of.

GENERAL NUGENT Colonel Johnston, can this be true—

LADY NUGENT 'Tis false, and—

GENERAL NUGENT Be silent. I am not addressing you. Who is the man? What is he charged with?

BETSY His name is Robert Munro, and he is charged with the murder of my poor father. He is innocent, and I will ask you to save him from that man who wishes me to become his wife, and because I refuse him he wreaks his vengeance on me by hanging the man I love, for the murder of my father.

GENERAL NUGENT When is the execution to take place?

BETSY To-morrow at sunset in Ballinahinch gaol.

GENERAL NUGENT Then there is no time to be lost. Colonel Johnston, at once proceed to Ballinahinch. I shall follow presently. I shall go into this matter at once. General Lake is at present in my house. Come with me, Miss Gray, and we shall see if we can save your lover's life if only for my friendship with your father. Come follow me, men. (*Exeunt SOLDIERS*)

BETSY Oh thank God! Thank God! (*Exit GENERAL NUGENT, followed by BETSY R. LADY NUGENT and COLONEL JOHNSTON looking after them.*)

JOHNSTON Curse him, I'll—

LADY NUGENT There now Colonel, don't lose your temper. Of course 'tis just your luck.

JOHNSTON Come with me. As we have played this game together, we shall now go further, and trust me, I shall not rest night or day 'till I see Munro dangle from the gallows. Now to Ballinahinch. (*Exit both L.*)

BLACK OUT

Close in Scene 3

Scene 4

(*The Courtyard at Ballinahinch gaol next morning. Large stone wall across stage from R. to L. At Back Guard Room exterior stands, L. Prison on the right. Landscape at back, guns stocked on the L. as scene opens, with drum rolls. SOLDIERS are discovered seated outside Guard Room on the L. SERGEANT walking up and down, etc.*)

SERGEANT Come inside, boys, and have a drop out of the bottle that the lady was so kind as to give us. Your muskets are loaded and ready for the Croppy,* when the bell rings for execution. (*Exit* SERGEANT, *followed by* SOLDIERS *into Guard Room L. Enter* GENERAL NUGENT *and* COLONEL JOHNSTON *R.*)

GENERAL NUGENT Through the intercession of the Squire's daughter, Betsy, I, together with General Lake, have heard her evidence, and she has proved to us that Munro is not guilty of the murder and we have decided to discharge the prisoner. This is the warrant for his release.

JOHNSTON But General, there is a second charge against him. You must remember he is also charged with being an agent of the United Irishmen, who may rise up at any moment and overthrow His Majesty's troops, with a successful issue which will cost the Government all their men; they have to conquer and subdue.

GENERAL NUGENT That is so. But in the case of Munro you have failed in every effort to prove his guilt, and in that case there is no other alternative but to release him at once.

JOHNSTON What if I refuse, he is my prisoner and—

GENERAL NUGENT Rufuse at your peril, Colonel. This is the warrant signed by me as Lord Lieutenant of the country, a title which gives me full power to release all prisoners when there is not evidence of guilt against them—Now Sir, I leave for Dublin to-night on military business and I command you to hold your men fully mobilised within the next twenty-four hours. When I return I shall send you with your regiment to release the Fourth Light Dragoons now garrisoning the town of Antrim and whom I have ordered to Belfast. I shall take an escort with me of the Second Inniskillin Dragoons. I command you in the name of the King; remember and obey.

(*Exit* GENERAL NUGENT *into Guard Room L.* COLONEL JOHNSTON *watching him and gazing at warrant—then tears it into two.*)

JOHNSTON Release him, I shall not. This is how I will execute the warrant. Now Munro, your pardon shall be given you from the people in the next world.

(*[Enter]* SERGEANT *L. followed by* BETSY GRAY *cloaked.*)

SERGEANT The Squire's daughter to see the condemned prisoner by the General's orders. (*Exit* SERGEANT.)

JOHNSTON Well, Miss Gray, you come I presume to bid farewell to your lover Munro.

BETSY Your words but mock me and add more to my misery. I am here by kind permission of the General, therefore I wish to hold no further conversation with you.

JOHNSTON Very well, I shall give you an interview not to last longer than ten minutes, after which you shall remain here to witness his execution. (*Crosses to L. and calls off.*) Sergeant, release Munro, and let him come here. And now Miss Gray, this interview must take place in my presence.

(*Enter* SERGEANT *L. followed by* MUNRO *in shirt sleeves.*)

BETSY Robert! My beloved Robert! (*Rushes to his arms.*)

ROBERT Betsy, darling, you have found a means to come to bid me a long farewell—a farewell for ever.

JOHNSTON It is against the rules to allow lovemaking in prisons, particularly in the case of a Rebel. (*Catches* BETSY *and pulls her roughly aside.*)

ROBERT Scoundrel, you may thank God that my hands are chained.

BETSY Coward! how dare you insult me. It is not enough that you must put an innocent man to death but you must dare to deprive him of the liberty to speak a last parting word with his friends.

(COLONEL *advances to seize* BETSY. *She strikes him across the face.*)

JOHNSTON Curse you, you jade of the devil, you shall pay for this, for as there is a God above you he shall die.

(*Exit* SERGEANT *after* COLONEL *into Guard Room L.*)

BETSY Robert, hush, till I tell you. We are going to rescue you to-night.

ROBERT Rescue me, how?

BETSY I, together with the aid of Dermot and Sheila and a few trusty friends have all arrangements made for your escape. I shall remain here in hiding until the coast is clear. Then you see those muskets. I shall have the bullets extracted from them and when the soldiers march you in here to be shot, they will use those guns which are now here in readiness when they fire. You, of course, shall fall as if shot dead and then the rest is simple. Across this wall where we shall have a carriage in readiness to convey you to a place of safety and then for France and Liberty.

ROBERT But you may forfeit your own dear life for the sake of saving mine.

BETSY Yes, Robert, forfeit my life for the love of you. Hush, the Sergeant comes. (*Enter* SERGEANT *L.*)

SERGEANT Young Lady, the prisoner must retire.

ROBERT Good-bye, Betsy, and may God and the angels guard and bless you. (*They embrace.*)

BETSY Good-bye, Robert, forever. (*Aside*) You understand.

(*Exit prisoner* MUNRO *into Guard Room, followed by* SERGEANT *L. At this moment* LADY NUGENT *appears at the door R.* BETSY *starts, etc.*)

LADY NUGENT So you have dared to come here to bid farewell to the man you have robbed me of, and—

BETSY I do not wish to discuss him ever again with you. I pray that be your answer. (*Exit* BETSY *R.*)

LADY NUGENT 'Tis a pity we cannot do for you; but my time will come as sure as I live.

(*Enter* COLONEL JOHNSTON *from Guard Room.*)

JOHNSTON Lady Nugent, this is no place for you. The firing party is ready, and the execution shall take place within half an hour.

LADY NUGENT Not of Munro. My father has given you a free pardon and I have arranged for him to stay in the Castle to-night.

JOHNSTON I fear I shall have to upset your little arrangements. Munro will not be set at liberty. I am quite surprised at you trying to shelter a rebel and a man who despises you with a bitter hatred. Munro does not, could not, love you, even if your coast was clear of Betsy Gray. I have tried and failed, having your interest at heart as well as my own, and now I refuse to set this man at liberty.

LADY NUGENT Then you will not execute the warrant.

JOHNSTON Yes, I have already executed it, by tearing it to pieces.

(BETSY *appears at door R. and listens.*)

LADY NUGENT But you yourself shall be shot for disobedience.

JOHNSTON This is how we will act; we will march the firing party on and when he is dead, we can say the prisoner escaped, or made an attempt to do so, and the guard fired and shot Munro by accident. (*Bell heard off L.*)

LADY NUGENT There is the bell. Let us proceed and talk it over in the Guard Room.

(*Exit both L.* BETSY *advances.* DERMOT *appears on top of wall, also* SHEILA.)

BETSY Well, there's many a slip. Your plans are undermined this time. Now for the muskets.

DERMOT Well Miss, everything is ready and Sheila has the clothes here and a good hot supper for the Master.

SHEILA Get yourself over the wall and hide down behind that bit of wall, and don't be talkin' for fear they might hear ye. I'll remain here and keep watch for the patrol. Give her a hand to extract the bullets from the Soldiers' muskets.

(*DERMOT now crosses the wall and comes to* C.)

DERMOT Now to business and I'll give ye a hand.

(*BETSY and DERMOT now extract the bullets from the muskets.*)

BETSY We had better leave them in the same order as before. Now Colonel Johnston this is our revenge on you. (*Roll of Drums, etc.*) Dermot be quick to your post. Have you got your pistols?

DERMOT Yes, Miss, I have, and leave the rest to me. (*They disappear. Enter COLONEL JOHNSTON followed by LADY NUGENT L. SOLDIERS and MUNRO. SOLDIERS take muskets up and line up on the L. MUNRO is placed by SERGEANT against the wall R. SERGEANT binds his eyes.*)

ROBERT Sergeant, do not bind my eyes; I am an Irishman and I am not afraid to die, but glad to give my life for Ireland and the girl I love.

SERGEANT Ready, men! Present! Fire!

(*SOLDIERS fire, MUNRO falls. BETSY rushes to MUNRO, takes her cloak off and spreads it over MUNRO. SOLDIERS recross arms and march off L.*)

LADY NUGENT Well you may weep over your murdered lover; you may shed tears over him, but you cannot give him back life again. You have robbed me of his love and now I have robbed you of him. (*COLONEL JOHNSTON drags BETSY away from over MUNRO, etc.*)

JOHNSTON Come! you silly girl, a dead man is of little use to any of you. Now Betsy, my love, you shall come away with me NOW.

BETSY Do not touch me! you may have taken away the only man I love, but you will not outrage my honour with your villainy.

JOHNSTON This is the honour I have for a rebel.

(*Kicks MUNRO who rolls over on his back.*)

BETSY You beast.

(*LADY NUGENT now seizes BETSY at the back by her arms. COLONEL JOHNSTON attempts to embrace her, when MUNRO springs to his feet. JOHNSTON draws sword, dashes him down, then takes BETSY in his arms [and] rushes up.*)

LADY NUGENT Trickery! Trickery! Guard, guard!

(*GUARD now rushes on with gun; at this moment DERMOT, SHEILA, and SHAMUS with pikes and pistols appear at back and hold up SOLDIERS.*)

ROBERT United we stand for the land we love.

CURTAIN

Quick on Picture

End of Act II

ACT III

Scene 1

(*The outside of Matt McGrath's cottage door in Cloth C. As scene opens up SOLDIERS march on, followed by COLONEL JOHNSTON R. They halt and front SERGEANT at door C.*)

JOHNSTON Halt. Is this the home of Matt McGrath, the Blacksmith, known to the Government as the Sledge hammer?

SERGEANT This is the cottage, Sir; shall we enter?

(*At this moment, when SERGEANT is about to enter, MRS. MC GRATH comes out.*)

MRS. MC GRATH Sure if your honours wouldn't mind, I'll save your honours' generals and sergeants the trouble for that same.

JOHNSTON What is your name? Who the devil are you?

MRS. MC GRATH Sure, I'm a poor harmless creature, the wife of a poor ould blacksmith, that's well known to your honour and your Captain here, for 'tis many the good pair of shoes he was after puttin' on your honour's black Bess, that ye took from Patsy Kinsella for three pounds.

JOHNSTON Oh, never you mind black Bess or her shoes. I am here on very important business; I have received information.

MRS. MC GRATH Oh, indeed, your honour, I suppose your honour often receives information.

JOHNSTON Curse your tongue, give it a rest and listen to me.

MRS. MC GRATH Sure my tongue is at rest sure enough an' 'tis myself is at your service an' that's no lie.

JOHNSTON Listen to me, my good woman, I have received information that your husband is committing treasonable acts by sheltering and harbouring certain persons connected with United Irishmen, and that he is at the present time forging pikes for the purpose of arming his Majesty's subjects to a breach of the peace, which as we understand is about to take place here in the north and which is at the present time raging rebellion in Kildare and Wexford.

MRS. MC GRATH Ye don't tell me, your honour.

JOHNSTON Yes, it is the truth, and—

MRS. MC GRATH And they are knockin' smoke out of the murdering Scarlet Runners. Hurrah! Faith, they'll run as fast as ould Bitty Muldoon's cheap black shawl when she went to dye it.

JOHNSTON Come, come be serious or as there is a heaven above I shall have you flogged and pitch-capped for your outburst of treason. I'm not a man to be trifled with. I shall have your house searched and if I find the persons whom I am in search of within, you must remember the consequences.

(SERGEANT *now looks through door.*)

MRS. MC GRATH The Lord between us and all harm, but I have no persons in my place at all an' the poor ould man himself is just gone into the town to buy some iron.

SERGEANT Yes, there are men [is a man] hiding here, Colonel, disguised as women [a woman].

JOHNSTON Then enter the house and bring him here.

(SERGEANT *enters house and drags out* SHEILA *who has the hood of her cloak over her face, they pull it back, etc.*)

JOHNSTON What the devil have you got there, Sergeant?

SHEILA I beg your honour's pardon, I'm not the devil, but a nice young lady, the pride of the county Down.

(*Enter* GENERAL NUGENT *L. and listens.*)

JOHNSTON Just my luck, Sheila DeLacey. Now my good girl, where is your mistress in hiding and Robert Munro, who escaped from a French Frigate in Lough Swilly about a week ago.

SHEILA I am sorry I can't oblige your honour with the information.

JOHNSTON Come now, my good girl, don't you be foolish. Here is a purse of gold and it contains 500 guineas, a fine fortune for a peasant girl like you.

SHEILA It would be a fine fortune for a peasant girl as you say, but I should suffer myself to be hanged from the nearest tree in the country rather than betray those faithful sons of Ireland.

JOHNSTON Come, don't be foolish my good girl. Where is he?

SHEILA Where you'll never find him.

JOHNSTON Then as you refuse to tell, I shall find a means of making you tell. Once more, I say, will you tell?

SHEILA (*fixed*) No, I will never tell!

JOHNSTON Fix your bayonets, men. (*SOLDIERS fix bayonets.*)

MRS. MC GRATH Sure, ye wouldn't be after trying to make her a traitor, as they call it, your honour.

SHEILA He can't put in me heart, what's not in me blood. He will never tempt me with bribes or gold.

JOHNSTON Then place her against the wall and pierce her with your bayonets. (*SOLDIERS level their bayonets. GENERAL NUGENT advances.*)

GENERAL NUGENT Hold! Colonel Johnston, you are taking this too far. I am a soldier and will not stand by while my men are outraging Military law by making war on a poor peasant girl.

JOHNSTON And I refuse to obey your orders. I am within the bounds of the law. The girl is a rebel in her heart and on those grounds she is my prisoner.

GENERAL NUGENT You cannot prove she is a rebel. Besides you are wasting the valuable time of the Military. We do not wish to waste time over irresponsible women. Sergeant, take those men back to the barracks at Ballinahinch. There await my orders. I shall give you more fitting work to do than making war on defenceless women. Company attention, right turn, forward Quick march!

(*Exeunt* SOLDIERS, *followed by* GENERAL NUGENT *R.*)

JOHNSTON Curse him, again he has crossed my path. As for you, you pair of devils, I shall have your old cabin burned from over your heads to-night.

(COLONEL JOHNSTON *exits L.*)

SHEILA Well I hope, Colonel Johnston, that when next we meet that you'll be reduced to the ranks and made a full General of.

(*Enter* MATT MC GRATH *carrying iron, etc.*)

MRS. MC GRATH Well, Matt, what on this earth is after keepin' ye, sure we are after been courtmartialed by Colonel Johnston and all his blackguards and sentenced to be shot or somethin' like that.

MATT 'Tis a mighty pity that ye were not shot at. It would be a great service to me or any man who is married and tied to a woman like you. Here I'm kilt outright with hard work and haulin' this iron from the town and devil a bit of steel could I get to finish them pike-heads that's wanted for the boys and Matt McConnell tells me that it's all too little for the Government's use, an' he says he will not have any for a week or so.

MRS. MC GRATH Do you really mean to tell me that things are so bad as that. Glory be to God. Things are a terrible price, sure enough.

MATT Aye, that's the truth. Things are bad for some people, but for Ireland things are glorious, an' 'tis time we people of Ireland will have our country a heap of red ashes or she'll be free.

SHEILA Sure an' ould man like you wouldn't be thinkin' of goin' out to fight for Ireland.

MATT Is it me ye mane? Who could fight better with a pike than me, the man that made it, and that's myself for I know every spring in the handle and the way the pike should cut, an' the use of the hook and hatch. There's goin' to be a war, an' I, ould as I am, is goin' to be in the lines of the battle.

MRS. MC GRATH Be the powers of Derry,* but I'm proud of you, Matt, an' I'll go off now an' milk the goat, while Sheila herself will get the tay ready. Get inside now and I won't be a second, an' I'll be back in a minute.

(*Exit* MRS. MC GRATH *R.*)

SHEILA Come on, Matt, I'll carry your parcel.

(*Exit* SHEILA *into cottage;* MATT *lights pipe and follows her. At this moment* COLONEL JOHNSTON *enters L. followed by* LADY NUGENT.)

LADY NUGENT Again Robert Munro and George Gray have made good their escape in the shallow water of Lough Swilly. Curse on the gunner that fired the gun from his Majesty's Transport that did not sink their ship to the bottom. What is to be done now with the country in a state of Revolution? But I have secured Betsy Gray and have her held a prisoner in my father's house and she shall not escape till I hand her safely into your keeping.

JOHNSTON Good, so at last she will be my loving wife. But, how to get Munro out of the way, and another, Sheila DeLacey, her maid, is at present inside the cottage; shall we have her carried off and locked up? While these people are at liberty, I do not feel safe. I shall call a few of the men, and set this place on fire.

LADY NUGENT There is a ball to be given at my father's house on to-morrow night in honour of some officers who have returned from service in India. You will be there. Have your men at hand, and in the meantime I shall get a trusty messenger to deliver a letter to Munro telling him of the capture (SHEILA *appears at door and listens to conversation*) of his lady love; it shall so enrage him that he shall come to the house in the hopes of rescuing her from her prison.

JOHNSTON And a trusty bullet shall rid us of him for ever. Now you come to my house this evening and I shall pay you the price on Munro's head. (SHEILA *now appears and comes on to* C.)

SHEILA Not if I can prevent it, you pair of devils.

JOHNSTON Sheila DeLacey! Then you have heard us, but you shall not spread the news.

LADY NUGENT Seize her, Colonel, for she is a dangerous enemy. I shall call your men. Set the house ablaze and pitch her into the flames.

SHEILA Stir one foot and I shall brain you with this iron bar.

(COLONEL JOHNSTON *makes at* SHEILA; *she deals him a blow; he staggers.* LADY NUGENT *now fires and hits* SHEILA *in the arm; the bar drops,* COLONEL JOHNSTON *rushes up and seizes* SHEILA. *At this moment* DERMOT *rushes in, throws off* COLONEL JOHNSTON. MATT *appears at door with pike head in hand and keeps back* COLONEL. DERMOT *takes* SHEILA *in his arms.*)

MATT Stir and I'll plunge this pike-head into both of your hearts.

BLACK OUT (QUICK)

Close in Scene 1

Scene 2

(*The Ballroom in General Nugent's house, Ballinamore. Large opening in C. Windows at either side through which can be seen a beautiful garden. As scene opens, groups of* LADIES *and* GENTLEMEN *are seen.* ENGLISH OFFICERS *of the various regiments of the time. Swords waltz continues, with different coloured lime lights thrown on the dancers. As dancing ceases* GENERAL NUGENT *enters C., followed by* COLONEL BRUCE.)

GENERAL NUGENT Well, Bruce, old man, make yourself merry while you may. A great many have passed since the day you set sail for Bombay with your gallant fellows of the Eighteenth Royal Regiment, and even through all these years you, yourself, have changed a little. Come sit down and take a good view of the pretty ladies assembled.

(LADIES *and* GENTLEMEN *converse in groups.*)

COLONEL BRUCE Yes, yes, by jove, you are quite right too. Of pretty faces there are many in this quaint old Castle, the home of your loyal ancestors. By the way I was passing through the garden and I noticed there the prettiest girl I have ever seen even when we were campaigning in Egypt against Napoleon—when I saluted her, she raised her dark eyelids and passed me with the air of a princess.

GENERAL NUGENT Oh, she is a very old friend of our family and her father to you was well known. You remember Squire Gray?

COLONEL BRUCE Oh yes, I remember him well. I must call on him tomorrow and—

GENERAL NUGENT You shall not call on the Squire. No, poor soul, he met with a horrible death a few months ago.

COLONEL BRUCE You don't mean to say he is dead.

GENERAL NUGENT Yes, he was murdered—shot dead by some unknown hand, in Matt McGrath's forge.

COLONEL BRUCE Merciful heaven! The work of a rebel I presume.

(*Enter* LADY NUGENT *C., who overhears last words.*)

LADY NUGENT Why speak you of murder on a night such as this, and in the presence of our guests? When I think on that fatal night I feel so sad. But Colonel Bruce has not met as yet the Squire's daughter, Betsy. She is so pretty and so gentle that all the officers are dying about her, and even our friend Colonel Johnston. I shall introduce you to her. She is in the garden; I am sure you will be delighted to meet her.

COLONEL BRUCE Yes, it shall give me a great pleasure. Permit me. (LADY NUGENT *gives her arm and advances to C. at which* BETSY *appears.*)

LADY NUGENT Ah! She comes. Permit me to introduce you to Colonel Bruce of the Eighteenth Royal Regiment, who has recently returned home with his regiment—who is very anxious that he should know you.

(BETSY *bows to all assembled.*)

BETSY I am so highly honoured. Ladies, pardon if I seek with the Colonel alone to speak.

(LADIES *and* GENTLEMEN *bow. Exit leaving* OFFICERS, *etc.*)

COLONEL BRUCE Will you do me the honour, Miss Gray, to be my partner at the next Ballanger?

BETSY I thank you, Colonel Bruce, as a lady, but I should wish to remind you that I am not a guest to this house, but a helpless prisoner who has been dragged here from my own home by the Military, on a warrant signed by you, General Nugent.

GENERAL NUGENT As heaven is my judge, Miss Gray, you wrong me, foully wrong me. I understood from you, Lucy, that Betsy was here on your invitation.

LADY NUGENT She is held a prisoner here on the charge of a rebel.

GENERAL NUGENT By whose orders? (*Enter* COLONEL JOHNSTON C.)

JOHNSTON By my orders, General. I have had her arrested in the King's name. The country is at the present moment in a state of rebellion; only last night a murderous attack was made on my troops and I and your daughter, by a gang of the rebels led by her. We searched the cottage of Matt McGrath, and found her hiding there.

BETSY No, it is false, as heaven itself is true. I was made prisoner two days ago and held prisoner.

COLONEL BRUCE Then Colonel Johnston you lie and foully wrong this young lady.

JOHNSTON Who the devil are you that interferes, some upstart of a Militia Captain, eh?

COLONEL BRUCE By heavens, I shall teach you that you shall not insult an old soldier. . . . Come you cowardly dog, who makes war on women; here is my card, and for this insult I shall kill you here and now.

GENERAL NUGENT I demand an apology to this lady, and to one of his Majesty's best officers, Colonel Bruce.

JOHNSTON And I refuse to apologise. I shall kill this hound.

GENERAL NUGENT Gentlemen, I protest. An insult to Colonel Bruce!

(*BRUCE draws sword, places it on table and going over to COLONEL JOHNSTON strikes him with his glove.*)

JOHNSTON Yes, fight you, you cur, to the death.

(*They fight. At the second round BRUCE disarms JOHNSTON and wounds his arm, then to BETSY taking her arm.*)

COLONEL BRUCE Permit me, gentlemen, to guard this lady and lead her from the room in safety. (*Bows and exeunt both R.*)

GENERAL NUGENT Here, men, attend to his wound, which he justly deserves. Take him into the next room.

(*SERGEANT and soldiers carry him off L. At this moment a TROOPER covered with dust enters room, hands despatch to GENERAL NUGENT, then salutes and exits.*)

GENERAL NUGENT From Dublin Castle. "Arrest Munro and McGrath. Crush any attempt of rebellion in the north." Come Lucy, let's go in; our officers are to hold themselves in readiness for active service.

(*Exeunt LADY and GENERAL NUGENT R.L. At this moment MUNRO appears centre; he looks after them, then advances to C.*)

ROBERT There goes the scoundrel who holds the one I hold dearer than life itself a prisoner in this Castle. Someone comes. It is Lady Nugent returning. I shall meet her and demand her to deliver up my darling Betsy to me. Yet it would be unwise. I might ruin my chance and perhaps be made prisoner, and then she would be at the mercy of those wolves. I shall wait and see.

(*As* MUNRO *hides in recess,* LADY NUGENT *enters L. Crosses over to door R. and calls to* COLONEL JOHNSTON, *who enters.*)

LADY NUGENT Colonel Johnston, our final chance has now come; she is in the garden alone. Bruce has just left her. Come, let us have her carried away from here. You understand what I mean. A messenger has just arrived from the Castle and the country is in a state of rebellion through the cruelty of such men as you.

JOHNSTON If such is the case I have played my card and lost. But I have not lost the girl; I shall, as you say, have her carried off and placed on board some ship for America. There I shall force her to marry me, and through her marriage with me, I shall obtain all her money and estate and then let her go to the devil, and—(*At this moment* BETSY'S *voice is heard singing one verse of "Gather round the Flag." They start and listen.*)

LADY NUGENT Who can that be who dares to sing that rebel song within the walls of my father's Castle? (*Shouts heard off.*) My God! What is that! (*Goes up to C. and looks out.*) 'Tis a band of men attacking the guards at the end of the lawn, help! help!

(MUNRO *appears pistol in hand C.B. He advances to C.*)

JOHNSTON Munro! What? You here.

ROBERT Yes, here to save the girl I love from the hands of such scoundrels like—

(*Shouts and cheers heard C.B.*)

JOHNSTON Out of this you rebel dog, or I shall call the guard and have you placed under arrest.

LADY NUGENT You seek your lady love in vain, for she is not here.

(MUNRO *seizes* COLONEL JOHNSTON *by the throat; they struggle. At this moment* TWO OFFICERS *rush in and seize* MUNRO *and hold him back C. Enter* GENERAL NUGENT *L., etc.*)

GENERAL NUGENT What means this? (*Enter* COLONEL BRUCE *C.*)

LADY NUGENT It means, father, that this man, Munro, has attacked this house and attempted to murder Colonel Johnston.

ROBERT 'Tis false, I came here to save the girl I love from this scoundrel.

(MUNRO *throws off* OFFICERS *and deals him [*JOHNSTON*] a blow. He staggers and falls.* MUNRO *rushes up to B. at which* BETSY *appears. He takes her in his arms;* PEASANTS *rush in with pikes and hold back*

OFFICERS and SOLDIERS. OFFICERS withdraw swords. GENERAL NUGENT L. with LADY NUGENT.)

ROBERT Gentlemen, we shall have the pleasure of reckoning with you tomorrow at Ballinahinch.

CURTAIN

ACT IV

Scene 1

(Matt McGrath's Forge as in Act I, Scene I. Midnight. PEASANTS are discovered lying asleep here and there about the forge floor. Pikes and muskets lying against the wall at back. DERMOT seated near forge L. SHAMUS looking out through window. Enter MATT counting pike heads. Window in C. to collapse.)

SHAMUS All seems quiet outside. There is no sign of the approach of the enemy. Well, the boys can rest themselves a bit longer, for if God spares us until tomorrow, there'll be many of them sleeping their last and peaceful sleep in the grave beyond in which all men are free.

MATT Ah, true for you, Shamus, an' ye might say many a Saxon soldier too. Well, it's a true saying, that 'tis time enough to bid the devil good morrow when you meet him.

DERMOT Well Matt, at any time I'm mighty afraid of that self same gentleman, an' ye might say 'tis fear for me. Well, come along, Matt, we had better carry out the General's orders tomorrow.

MATT Aye, Dermot, avick,* talk is cheap. Was it another 100 pikes that the General said he'd be wantin' for the boys?

SHAMUS It was that, a hundred sure enough, tho' there was a big weight of woe on the poor man's heart when he set out last night with the boys to recapture the darlin' Betsy Gray, that was took by the sodgers, because they said she was a rebel a few days ago.

DERMOT And a mighty big job it was too. We had to fight every inch of the way to the Castle, and I'm tould only Sheila knew the old Sergeant that did us a good turn before. You remember the night they went to shoot Robert Munro up in

Ballinahinch gaol that he escaped. 'Tis as like as not that he would not be here tonight waiting to lead us to the attack on the town tomorrow.

MATT I'm tould that the general of the sodgers thought that she was a guest at the Ball, and I believe Colonel Johnston cleared away and can't be found ever since, for the sodgers passed this way about seven o'clock last night in search of him.

DERMOT Bedad he won't forget the lesson you, yourself, taught him, and that spawn of the devil, Lady Nugent, she's worse, though she is a purty looking girl herself.

MATT Well, she was in love with the Master and maybe ye can't blame her. Sure after all she's only a woman.

SHAMUS Look up, boys, here comes the Officers.

(*Enter* GENERAL MUNRO, *followed by* GEORGE *and other* OFFICERS *L.*)

ROBERT God speed the work, men. You are very busy, I see.

DERMOT You might say that we are, sure enough. The boys are resting themselves Sir.

ROBERT The time for action is now at hand, and every man of you must lend a willing hand. Rise up, boys, and then to your posts.

(MEN *rise up, and* EACH MAN *takes pike or musket and lines up right across stage.* MUNRO *down R.*)

ROBERT Men of County Down, I have always found you peaceful. Many of you who stand here to-night are men whom I knew from childhood and now the day has at last come that Tone and the United Irishmen have worked for. This war has been forced upon us, and as Irishmen, we are in honour bound to make one desperate effort to regain our country's Independence.

MATT And please God, General, they [not] we, shall work in vain. Let our war-cry be "Remember Orr."

ROBERT Take this party of men, Matt, and advance to within gunshot of the English out-posts, which are thrown out all around the town; there call a halt and conceal your men as to see, but not be seen by the enemy, and at daybreak open fire with your muskets, and hold your positions until we can come up with the main army which are encamped on the hill yonder. Now men, left, turn, in the name of Ireland, Quick March!

(*Exeunt all L. followed by* SHAMUS. GENERAL MUNRO *placing map on anvil.*)

GEORGE James Hope has sent the following despatch. (*Reads.*) "By the Grace of God we strike for Liberty today, and we hope to carry the town of Antrim, and drive out the enemy. If we succeed we hope to unite our army with that of General Munro and thus march to Belfast. From Henry Joy McCracken, Commander-in-Chief, of the Ulster Forces, per James Hope."

ROBERT (*gazing over Map*) It is our duty today, George, to capture and hold by force of arms, the town of Ballinahinch, and to open up as far as in our power the line of communication between here and Lough Swilly where the French are expected to land in the course of a month. George, here, you shall lead your men to the main entrance of the town which is guarded by the enemy's artillery and cavalry, to check our advances, while we shall cross the river from the hill above, capture General Nugent's Castle and drive the enemy through the wood and into the town. You at this moment open fire by musket and cannon, and by all striking together we shall succeed in driving in the artillery men and the rest is easy. Come, George, the dawn is breaking.

(*As* MUNRO *exits L. followed by all except* DERMOT, *who is on guard, the dawn slowly breaks.*)

DERMOT Long life to ye goin! an' may we soon see the Green above the Red, and ould Ireland free. Well it's mighty could comin' on to daylight, aye, I'll load this ould musket just to pass the time away.

(*Looks out of window and taking musket in his hand, begins to load, as* SHEILA *enters L.*)

SHEILA Well, is this where you are, you lazy omadhaun?* Why are you not with the boys? I suppose you are waiting 'till the fight is over and then ye'll come and tell me the brave man ye are, and how ye charged with the boys at Ballinahinch, beat the murtherin' red-coats. Here is a green sash I made for you to make you look like a real General.

(*Takes sash from basket.*)

DERMOT Ah, be the powers of Derry,* but you're a ***.

SHEILA Or do ye think I'm a fool, which I am.

DERMOT Bedad, I'd be a long time out of me money if I did.

SHEILA Here's a drop the ould Sergeant left in the bottle last night, when we wor rescuing the darlin', and I thought you'd be glad of what he left.

DERMOT No! ye may go and stay with the Sergeant, and I'll not have any man's leavin's, off ye go now.

SHEILA Well, I may tell ye, my boy, that ye are not fit to wipe the Sergeant's boots, for he's a rale gentleman, so he is, and what are you, a jealous man, that's no good to a colleen like me. Here, give me them two bags of ammunition for the boys and I'll bid ye farewell for ever.

(*DERMOT attempts to embrace her.*)

DERMOT Don't lose your temper, my darlin', sure I'd like to be after teasin' ye to show ye how much I love you.

SHEILA Now, do ye mane that, Dermot, well I'll never lave ye, and we'll fight together for poor ould Ireland to-day at Ballinahinch. (*They embrace.*)

(*At this moment GENERAL MUNRO, followed by GEORGE GRAY, enters L.*)

GEORGE Well, Sheila, I say Sheila, Dermot, I am—

ROBERT Come, come sir. What is the meaning of this? (*They turn sharply around and as they see MUNRO, they rush out.*) We are now ten thousand strong. Our army is divided into three divisions. We may now give the signal for the attack.

(*At this moment BETSY enters L.*)

GEORGE Betsy, my sister, what brings you here?

BETSY I have been in search of you, Robert, all the night. There is no use, George, or you, Robert, in trying to hide the secret from me any longer. I know that tomorrow will be the great day—the day of Glory for Ireland.

ROBERT Betsy, dearest, there is no use in you trying to persuade us, we cannot let you come with us; the work is dangerous and only fit for men.

BETSY You must let me go, I long to see the pike men charge; long to hear the roar of our muskets and cannon. Shall glory to see the setting sun go down in [and?] five hundred victorious pike-men charging thro' the streets of Ballinahinch, and we shall go side by side in the battle to lead our country's men to glory.

ROBERT This is folly, madness, on your part. Why your life would be sacrificed and to no end. No, my dear, you must leave the fighting to us. Ireland does not call upon you to do this, or sacrifice [your] blood needlessly.

BETSY Yes, it is the duty of every Irishwoman as it was the duty of the women of France to rally round the flag to strike for Liberty. It is now breaking day. I understand you are to attack the town at daybreak and now I want to warn you that I shall be ready, mounted on my pony, waiting to join your ranks as you pass along to attack the town.

(*Guns now heard firing, etc., horses, etc. galloping.*)

GEORGE That is our men attacking the enemy's outposts. General, to our posts.

(*Guns again heard, ball hits forge window. As window collapses men drag gun in through forge door L. and start to prepare.* MUSKETEERS *at window.* GENERAL MUNRO *with sword in hand. Guns heard, horses, etc.*)

ROBERT Ready Men! They are advancing. On they come. They do not see Matt's men who are hidden from view. Now lads. Open fire!!

(*All fire and spring up.* BETSY *at window with flag.* MEN *ready to charge, etc.*)

BETSY He that dares to fight for Ireland let him follow me. (*All cheer, etc.*)

BLACK OUT

Close in Quick

Scene 2

(*A street in Ballinahinch by night. As scene opens,* MATT MC GRATH, *followed by* DERMOT *and* SHAMUS *R. with pikes,* MATT *with arm in sling;* SHAMUS *with head bandaged, etc.*)

MATT I tould ye boys, that she could do it. She led us on through that fire of hell that came from the enemy's guns, an' for ten hours it was as hot as hell sure enough, an' I'm proud to say that Matt McGrath's pikes laid many a scarlet sodger low. May God forgive me if it be a sin.

DERMOT That's the truth, may God forgive us. Did any wan o' ye see Colonel Johnston today? The talk is now that he has deserted and cleared out of the country. Oh! Saint Patrick! send it is the truth, though there's no such luck. 'Tis hard to kill a serpent.

SHAMUS Well, we captured the town an' we were nigh not doin' it, and only for the way Betsy encouraged the boys with that last charge, an' I'm not so sure that we'll be able to hould it either.

DERMOT Why wouldn't we be able to hould the town, sure we have all the cannons we captured from the soldiers, and we have the men too? Why wouldn't we hold it I say?

MATT Oh, don't be mindin' him, he was always the same, always the same. He'd like to be a patriot an' makin' speeches to be sure (*looks off L.*) Who is this I see comin' down the streets. It's some poor old man; no, but 'tis the ould bell-man.

(*Enter* COLONEL JOHNSTON *L. disguised as a bell ringer of the period.*)

JOHNSTON God be with you my boys and on the work ye done today in drivin' out the hated Saxon foe from our streets. Who was your leader? What man led ye on?

DERMOT No man led us, sir. No man at all.

JOHNSTON Who then led you, my boys?

SHAMUS We were led as men were never led before by a girl.

MATT And she was only a mere bit of a girl too! She was not a big girl, but she had the courage of a lion. And she had a wonderful head of dark brown hair, and her dark eyes flashed like a lance as she led us on against the hated foe.

JOHNSTON And what was her name, did ye say?

DERMOT Her name was Betsy Gray. God's blessing be on her.

JOHNSTON Betsy Gray! My God can this be true?

MATT Oh, don't be in trouble about her, my good man. She is alright. The bullet that hit her did not do her any harm, at the time it stung her. If ye would care to see her she is inside that house down the street there, where the boys are all standing; that's the General's quarters. (*Firing heard.*)

DERMOT That's an attack. Maybe the red coats are returning. There was reinforcements expected, we wor told. Come let us get back to the boys. (*Exeunt all R.* COLONEL JOHNSTON *takes off disguise, etc.*)

JOHNSTON Betsy Gray, leading the rebels! What a valuable piece of news. Now is my time for revenge. But what can I do now? I am a deserter, an outcast, I have been absent from four roll-calls. I had better get out of this, and bid farewell to this cursed country. (*Going L. as* SHEILA *enters L., he starts back surprised.*)

SHEILA Colonel Johnston disguised as a spy.

JOHNSTON You know me then? (*Seizing her by arm.*)

SHEILA Yes, I know you, and if you dare to harm me I shall call for assistance. (*She throws him off.*)

JOHNSTON Come tell us, where is your Mistress Betsy Gray to be found; speak quickly or I shall shoot you dead upon the ground where you now stand.

SHEILA I do know where she is, and I can tell you she is where you nor your band will ever find her. That's your answer. Let me pass.

JOHNSTON No, you shall not stir from here till you answer me. Once more, I say, where is Betsy Gray? (*Pistol in hand.*)

SHEILA Where ye cannot reach her. She is well guarded.

JOHNSTON Come! On your life lead me to the spot and if you deceive me I shall kill you without another word.

SHEILA I shall not stir one foot. I defy you!

JOHNSTON Then throw your life to the winds!

(*They grapple each other, the pistol goes off. At this moment* GENERAL NUGENT *followed by* COLONEL BRUCE *enters L. with* SOLDIERS *who seize* COLONEL JOHNSTON *and* SHEILA.)

GENERAL NUGENT What is the meaning of this? What! the man we are looking for. Colonel Johnston, I arrest you in the name of the King for deserting your regiment while on active service.

JOHNSTON 'Tis false. I was with my regiment at the time the rebels attacked the town.

COLONEL BRUCE 'Tis a lie, sir. I was placed in command of your regiment after roll-call this morning, and I led them until we were forced to retreat.

GENERAL NUGENT I shall have you shot for cowardice, Colonel Johnston. But who is the girl—a rebel!

SHEILA I am no rebel, but this man tried to take my life because I wouldn't tell him where Betsy Gray is. He murdered her father last December, and now he has tried to murder me.

JOHNSTON 'Tis false! she lies. The shot was fired by General Nugent's daughter.

(*Enter* LADY NUGENT *L.*)

LADY NUGENT I did not fire the shot that killed Squire Gray, but you did.

SHEILA The plot was well arranged between you.

GENERAL NUGENT Take him away men, and at midnight he shall be shot as a deserter in time of war. Release the other girl.

LADY NUGENT Don't let her go, she is a spy.

COLONEL BRUCE No soldier shall leave a finger on her or I'll brain him.

BLACK OUT

Close in Scene 2

Scene 3

(*In a wood near the town in Ballinahinch, early morning. Full stage road leads down from C. A large bank on R. backed by a beautiful Irish landscape. As curtain rises* GEORGE GRAY *and* ROBERT MUNRO *are discovered R., outposts L.*)

ROBERT Oh! God! What a sad day for poor Ireland. The men who fought for her liberty are either dead or flying for their lives, hunted like a flock of frightened sheep; yet the men who have shed their blood have not shed it in vain. Oh, God! when shall the day ever dawn that will bring hope and freedom to our poor unhappy country again.

GEORGE Courage, Robert, the darkest hour is the hour before day. While there is a man left to shoulder a musket or handle a pike, the fight for Ireland shall still go on in spite of defeat. Oh would to God that our men but knew their duty as soldiers and men. Ballinahinch should have been in our hands for good and all.

ROBERT Such is the fortunes of war, George. In the very moment of victory our men mistook the bugle-call of the enemy for reinforcements, which was the enemy's retreat. I did my best to rally; then a few who still obeyed me perished in their noble stand to hold the town, which was so hard won a few hours before and at such a cost of the lives of our fellow countrymen. Well, there is no use in our crying over [a] dead past. We had better see how to change defeat into victory once more. How many men have answered their names at roll-call?

GEORGE There are three hundred killed and missing, and of wounded there are two hundred, mostly all of whom were cut down in our retreat from the town.

ROBERT What became of Betsy? The last I saw of her was when the men rallied round her, when she made one desperate stand to carry and recapture the enemy's guns. I saw the Green Flag go down in smoke of the battle, and then I was hit with a flying bullet, and I knew no more.

GEORGE She is not far off, my boy. Do not worry for her; I carried her off to Matt's cottage in my arms to have her wounds dressed, but we have no time to waste now in mourning over wounded sisters or dead husbands or sweethearts; our duty now is to fight and make the best stand we can until McCracken sends us some little force from Antrim, or either that, take to the hills and await the arrival of aid from France, which shall arrive in the course of a few weeks. Come, Robert, I shall help you and we shall see what's best to be done. (*Helps* MUNRO, *etc.*)

ROBERT Yes, you are quite right, for there is surely danger in delaying here long. The cottage of the Wicklow games [Widow G—?] commands full view of the enemy's position. We shall go there. (*Exeunt up L. and disappear. Enter* DERMOT *followed by* SHAMUS *R.*)

DERMOT Well, God rest poor Matt, after all his work. We laid him to rest in the ould Churchyard beyond.

SHAMUS I knew the Red coat's bayonet that he got in the hip would surely do for him.

DERMOT Well, we're not bet yet, and there's wan consolation, that the greatest enemy poor Ireland ever had was shot just an hour ago. If it be no harm to pray for his soul's peace, may God forgive him.

SHAMUS And who may he happen to be, Dermot?

DERMOT Did ye not hear the news? Why everyone knows.

SHAMUS Was it General Nugent, that's kilt?

DERMOT No, it isn't, but the ould Yeoman Captain Colonel Johnston, and more betoken, he saved us a mighty ugly job. What! Be the powers o' Derry,* but the boys are attacking the Redcoats and they are flying in all directions through the town. Come along, Shamus, and let us lend a hand.

(*Guns heard off L. as* SHAMUS *followed by* DERMOT *exits L. Enter* BETSY GRAY *R., head bandaged, etc.*)

BETSY What is that? Can it be an attack? I see our men hurrying forward, yes, and they are led on by my brother, George, and now the English are falling back. Thank God! Thank God!! The spirit of freedom hovers near. I can see the Green banner again floating in the breeze. I know our hearts were true, true to the old land, and that our arms were strong. They have carried the enemy's position.

(*Enter* LADY NUGENT *L.C. Cheering heard.* BETSY *watches off up L.*)

LADY NUGENT I have succeeded in escaping this far unnoticed by the rebels. I shall wave this signal to show that the road is clear so far. (*Waves white handkerchief off L. to English.*)

BETSY Treachery! Who are you?

LADY NUGENT Betsy Gray? What are you doing here? I shall call the guards and have you arrested and shot as a spy.

BETSY I am no spy, but you are, and once more give the enemy the signal where we are, and you shall meet the fate of a spy. (*Points pistol at* LADY NUGENT.)

LADY NUGENT I do not mean to make noise or shout or go on my knees to shriek for mercy, but I have a little wrong to settle, which must be wiped out in your blood, you wretch of the devil. You have stolen from me all that a woman treasures dearer than life itself, and that is, the man she loves. You who were the cause of Colonel Johnston's death and now I mean to revenge his death and my honour. I loved Robert Munro and he might have loved me had you never met him. You have taken him from me and now I mean to rob him of you, and—

BETSY Stop, Lady Lucy Nugent, I will hear no more. I have suffered enough at your hands all these years. You robbed me of my father. You and Colonel Johnston murdered him in cold blood. I too have an account to settle with you and only one of us leaves this wood alive. You can see how the battle goes! Look there! Can you not see your English troops flying before the victorious rebels and with this sight in your eyes I shall send you to answer, to your God, for your past life.

LADY NUGENT I fight for vengeance and the man I love. (*They fight a duel with pistols first; both miss. They whip two fallen swords and fight.* BETSY *disarms* LADY NUGENT *and runs her through. She falls dead. At this moment* MUNRO, *followed by* GEORGE, *rush in on L.* COLONEL BRUCE *and* SOLDIERS *enter on R. A duel ensues between* SOLDIERS *and* PEASANTS; *shots,* BRUCE *engages* GEORGE *and* MUNRO. GEORGE *is disarmed,* SOLDIERS *fire;* GEORGE *falls,* BRUCE *is now in the act of rushing on* MUNRO, *when* BETSY *rushes between them. Both their swords pierce her and she falls C. A cheer goes up and* SOLDIERS *retreat.* GENERAL NUGENT *is captured. Enter* SHEILA, *who lifts up* BETSY *in her arms, etc.*)

SHEILA Betsy, darlin'! Are you much hurt?

ROBERT Betsy come with me to the cabin and let me dress your wounds. General Nugent is our prisoner, and once more our arms are victorious.

BETSY Leave me to rest, Robert, where I fell. I am dying for my country. George, my brother, where are you? Let me die in peace. Good-bye to all.

(*She sinks back and dies in* ROBERT'*s arms. He removes hat, draws green flag over her; all kneel as the curtain slowly descends.*)

END

GLOSSARY

Parenthetical citations refer to works listed in the bibliography.

a cailin: oh colleen; my dear, "a young girl" (Joyce)
acushla: my darling; derived from *Acushla machree* or *cushlamochree,* "pulse of my heart" (Joyce)
agrah: my love
alanna: child; my child
arrah: oh
avic(k): my son
avourneen: my dear; my love (Joyce)

bad cess to it, bad cess to the bit: "bad luck to it" (Joyce); a vague curse, dammit
bate Banagher: references to Banagher suggest an extraordinary event (Wall)
be the powers of Derry: a literary interjection
begor, begorra: by God; indeed (Wall)
bosthoon: fool, idiot
b(o)uchal: boy
bud an' ages: see *tare an' ouns;* a rather Anglified phrase, not typical in Ireland
buneens: a derogatory phrase, possibly a version of *banveen,* which derives from the Irish for "piglet" (Sherry)

Céad Míle Fáilte go hEirinn: traditional welcome; literally, from the Irish, "A hundred thousand welcomes to Ireland"
comether, comither: come hither; to "put the comether" on someone is to charm the person
croppie, croppy: rebel

*dhrop ov the craythe*r: drink of whiskey
Dickens a ha'porth: "the devil if it's even a half-penny's worth"
doubt: fear

faix: probably "faith"
finger to nose: confidential gesture indicating that the speaker is ironic
for(e)ninst: next to, near, beside, in front of; opposite (Joyce)

gom: fool
gosso(o)n: boy, little fool

haporth: see *sorra the haporth*
hoxter: arm (rural term)

jackeen: insignificant fellow; "a nickname for a conceited Dublin citizen of the lower class" (Joyce)

mulvather, mulvatherin': blather(ing), trick(ing)
Musha: see *wisha;* "An exclamation, a disguised form of the name of Mary" (Sherry); oh, well, indeed (Wall).

na bock lish: Irish (na bac leis [Joyce]) for "don't pay any attention to it"

of the world, ov the worrld: an intensive phrase used in combination with various nouns
old harry: the devil
omadhaun: fool
on the spree: going strong

polthogues: smacks
poltroon: idiot, scoundrel
potheen: whiskey
praties: potatoes

rapporees: outlaws

scran: luck
sheebeen: pub, generally unlicensed (Joyce)
skiver: slice, put on a spit
sorra, sorra a bit: not at all, not a bit. *Sorra* is used as an intensive. A more typical phrase is *sorra the bit.*
sorra good: not a bit of good

sorra the haporth: not even a half-penny's worth

spalpeen: clown; "low rascal" (Joyce); tramp

stravagin': meandering

tare an' ouns: an interjection in the spirit of the English "'swounds"—that is, "by God's (tears and) wounds." In colloquial Irish speech, this phrase has the force of, "I declare to God."

tare and age(r)s: see *tare an' ouns*

t(h)und(h)er an' turf: an Anglified exclamation; artificial version of *tare an' ouns;* in Ireland, turf is "peat for fuel" (Joyce)

Weeskey Girsha: This phrase is difficult to read in the manuscript. Thady could be calling for whiskey in what seems to him a "frenchified" way to speak. *Girsha* means "little girl" (Joyce). *Weeskey* could also be a typographical error for "wisha," a multipurpose interjection, here vaguely suggesting "For God's sake, girl."

weisha: little

whis(h)t: be quiet, hush, silence (Joyce); "hould your whist" means "keep silent"

white boy: rural revolutionary

wirrasthrue: translation from the Irish is "O Mary of the Sorrows"; a lament; alas (Joyce)

wisha: vague term suggesting a pause in speech; well (interjection); similar in usage to *Musha*

NOTES TO PART TWO

LORD EDWARD, OR '98

1. This scene received special mention in an appreciative obituary essay in *The Irish Playgoer,* 19 April 1900. The writer applauds the lead role as played by H. Sommerfield Arnold, quoting an 1897 review to this effect: "The part of Lord Edward is taken by Mr. H. Sommerfield Arnold, who bears an astonishing likeness both in face and figure to the original. He is a refined and careful actor. He never rants; he is always consistently the gentleman of culture. The rapidity of his emotional changes shows him a genuine artiste, and like a genuine artiste he builds up his general effects with numerous little studies. We may give an instance. He is apparently absorbed in chatting playfully with his little son. Suddenly he pauses, turns to the window, and looks with a haunted look up and down the street, then resumes his badinage again. This bit of real art passes so quickly that only those who understand the value of such strokes realise its ability. We should like to add to the above that no one who has ever witnessed his powerful acting in the last act (the death scene) will fail to remember it as one of the most emotional and artistic representations ever staged" (p. 14).

2. The *Freeman's Journal* for 24 May 1798 on reports the proclamation of a curfew in Dublin from 9:00 P.M. until 5:00 A.M.

3. A deletion from the manuscript at this point demonstrates a certain amount of restraint on Whitbread's part. He crosses out the words *"Then with an effort throws it back, exclaiming."*

4. Later in this scene, Neilson and Thady plan to meet at the Dog and Duck Inn, so this scene probably takes place wholly in a nearby street.

5. Elliott notes that Pamela was "popularly believed to be the illegitimate daughter of Philippe (Egalité) Duc d'Orleans" but was actually "Anne or Nancy Syms, taken from an English foundling hospital by Egalité in 1780, and reared since the age of six with his own children" (*Partners in Revolution,* 25). That this title was indeed popular may be assumed from the fact that the *Freeman's Journal* for 22 May 1798 reported, "Early in last week, Lady *Egalite,* the natural daughter of the noted Philip of Orleans, and the *now* Consort of Lord Edward Fitzgerald, was ordered to quit this kingdom, and she has made every arrangement to retire this day" (p. 3).

WOLFE TONE

1. Although the original typescript includes only the surname "Emmett" (*sic*) in the cast list, a 1901 playbill identifies this character as "Robert Emmet." Because Thomas Addis Emmet seems to be the Emmet who appears in this play, perhaps the more well known hero found his way into the cast list through a typesetter's interpretive addition.

2. At this point in the typescript the unexplained note "Se in z" occurs.

3. In *The Queen's Royal Theatre*, de Búrca transcribes a playbill from 9 September 1901 for Kennedy Miller's *Wolfe Tone* with Tyrone Power in the leading role. Although the text in the Lord Chamberlain's Plays includes only one scene in Act IV (the encampment outside Brest), the playbill adds two other scenes, "On the Road to Embark" and "The Embarkation of the French Army for Ireland." De Búrca writes, "I can still remember the thrill of the Band playing down the Curtain to the cheers of the audience and the actors on the stage—the Band in the pit and the Band on stage playing together. The tragedy to come of Bantry Bay—and Lough Swilly—forgotten in the brief moment of excitement, ecstasy and hope!" (p. 23).

WHEN WEXFORD ROSE

1. Enhancing the background music typical of melodrama, Irish productions during the era of Whitbread and Bourke often included music-hall turns or other numbers to break up the action of the play.

FOR THE LAND SHE LOVED

1. "Remember Orr" became a United Irishmen's rallying cry after the controversial execution in October 1797 of William Orr, a Presbyterian farmer who "was capitally convicted for administering the United Irishmen's oath to two Fifeshire fencibles." As Elliott tells it, Orr's situation was widely publicized, and he became the "first real martyr of the United movement" (*Partners in Revolution*, 129).

FOR THE LAND THEY LOVED

was composed in 10 on 12 Palatino on a Mergenthaler Linotron 202
by Eastern Graphics, with display type in Palatino Semibold Outline
by Dix Type, Inc.,
and with foundry type Clearcut display initials;
printed by sheet-fed offset on 50-pound, acid-free Glatfelter Natural Hi Bulk,
and Smyth-sewn and bound over binder's boards in Holliston Roxite B,
with dust jackets printed in two colors and laminated
by Braun-Brumfield, Inc.;
designed by Sara L. Eddy;
and published by

SYRACUSE UNIVERSITY PRESS
SYRACUSE, NEW YORK 13244-5160

Richard Fallis, SERIES EDITOR

IRISH STUDIES presents a wide range of books interpreting important aspects of Irish life and culture to scholarly and general audiences. The richness and complexity of the Irish experience, past and present, deserves broad understanding and careful analysis. For this reason an important purpose of the series is to offer a forum to scholars interested in Ireland, its history and culture. Irish literature is a special concern in the series, but works from the perspectives of the fine arts, history, and the social sciences are also welcome, as are studies which take multidisciplinary approaches.

Selected titles in the series are:

An Anglo-Irish Dialect Glossary for Joyce's Works. RICHARD WALL
Beckett and Myth: An Archetypal Approach. MARY A. DOLL
Celtic Contraries. ROBIN SKELTON
Children's Lore in "Finnegans Wake." GRACE ECKLEY
Cinema and Ireland. KEVIN ROCKETT, LUKE GIBBONS, and JOHN HILL
The Drama of J. M. Synge. MARY C. KING
Dreamscheme: Narrative and Voice in "Finnegans Wake." MICHAEL BEGNAL
Fictions of the Irish Literary Revival: A Changeling Art. JOHN WILSON FOSTER
Finnegans Wake: A Plot Summary. JOHN GORDON
Fionn mac Cumhaill: Celtic Myth in English Literature. JAMES MACKILLOP
Frank O'Connor at Work. MICHAEL STEINMAN
Great Hatred, Little Room: The Irish Historical Novel. JAMES M. CAHALAN
In Minor Keys: The Uncollected Short Stories of George Moore. DAVID B. EAKIN and HELMUT E. GERBER, eds.
Irish Literature: A Reader. MAUREEN O'ROURKE MURPHY and JAMES MACKILLOP, eds.
The Irish Renaissance. RICHARD FALLIS
James Joyce: The Augmented Ninth. BERNARD BENSTOCK, ed.
Selected Plays of Padraic Colum. SANFORD STERNLICHT, ed.
Selected Poems of Padraic Colum. SANFORD STERNLICHT, ed.
Shadowy Heroes: Irish Literature of the 1890s. WAYNE E. HALL
Ulysses as a Comic Novel. ZACK BOWEN
Yeats. DOUGLAS ARCHIBALD
Yeats and the Beginning of the Irish Renaissance. PHILLIP L. MARCUS